D1342277

A HISTORY

OF

KITCHENER, ONTARIO

by

W. V. (Ben) Uttley

Reissued with an Introduction by

Gerald Noonan

With Name-and-Subject Index

Note on the Text

The major part of this re-issue of *The History of Kitchener* is a photocopy of the hard-cover, 6″ x 9″, 434-page edition written by W. V. Uttley and published by The Chronicle Press, Waterloo in 1937. The re-issue includes a new Introduction and Biography of the author written by Gerald A. Noonan, and an eighteen-page name-and-subject index compiled by Joyce Lorimer. The new cover design is taken from photographs contained in the original edition.

INTRODUCTION

The sound of Hoffman's factory bell rings a pervasive note in William V. Uttley's compiled chronicle of Berlin's building years. The factory bell, installed in 1845 at what is now the Bank of Nova Scotia corner in downtown Kitchener, "called men to labor, volunteers to quench fires, pealed for weddings, tolled for funerals, and called voters to the polls on election day" (p. 66). The multi-purpose bell suggests a centrality and clearly-defined sense of community that may be attainable only in retrospect. In the immediate present, what many city-dwellers have in common is a sense of the fragmentary artificiality of modern life, a quality generally accepted as an unavoidable consequence of our technological diversions. It is just possible, however, that the breakdown of community is something experienced in every era, a by-product of progress that was accounted as a necessary evil in the first half of the 19th century in proportionately the same way as it is in the last quarter of the 20th century. And perhaps it is only the distancing effect of time that gives the life of yester-generation its satisfying unity.

In any case, despite its own fragmentary nature, Uttley's outline of Kitchener's growth from the 1840's into this century tends, for the contemporary reader, to be shot through with a reassuring consistency and integration of purpose. Now that all in the long run has, indeed, worked out for the best, or at least for the status quo, there is little in the past that will upset us—unless the status quo is also upsetting. Certainly, there are charms associated with the sound of the factory bell, that we hear as if from memory, summoning up what Uttley elsewhere pictures as a town "in its shirtsleeves" (p. 206), or a town "of frame houses . . . with pumps at their front door, and . . . well-kept gardens" at the back, strongly-fenced to ward off cows that grazed by the right-of-way (p. 194). From this distance there is a charm too in the hardy settlers who killed rattlesnakes with a whip (p. 22), drank cider from the barrel (p. 23), and plowed the soil with a tree-top (p. 15). Next came German "mechanics" who, in "driving no nails into the air," planted trees for fruit not shade, grew vegetables not shrubs, and cultivated gardens instead of games (p. 31). Soon the frame houses were clustering within range of an increasing number of factories; a town policy adopted in 1874 gave five years' tax exemption to employers of 75 or more men, and reimbursed the company's annual building rent as well (p. 193). On that strong manufacturing base, there grew up schools and churches, railways, hotels, city halls, banks, civic fairs, clubs, sports, and sewers. For all of these, Uttley's *History* has names, locations, the leading spirits, and occasionally photographs.

For those bygone building generations, the emphasis undoubtedly was on material progress. Nothing so multi-purposed as a bell appeared on the village seal of 1854; along with the crown was a beaver, a locomotive, a cross-cut saw, and an axe (p. 97), all clear symbols of work. Local leaders were emphatically clear-sighted in working to acquire, first, the Township Hall (p. 71), and then the county seat (p. 80). In both cases, the issue was won by the prospect of prime land sites on Queen and Weber Streets offered free by Frederick Gaukel, owner of the 1835 tavern-hotel at the King and Queen intersection. When a later owner of the same hotel-site, Abel Walper of Zurich, offered the town a small triangle of land at the intersection to straighten the zig-zag of Queen Street, he asked $500 cash. The councillors in 1892 were still clear-sighted enough to accept, but the citizens objected so strongly to the price that the zig-zag remains to this day (p. 257). A consistent sense of value was still evident early in the twentieth century. "For a gift of five acres of land in Woodside Park" an American company was induced to move its Canadian plant to Berlin. And the Park Board's compensation price of $6,000 was whittled down by the local Industrial Committee to $1,000 "by appealing to their [the Park Board's] civic pride" (p. 399). Then, in 1912, when a handsome Federal Square, which might well appeal to civic pride, was proposed for a site between Frederick and Scott Streets, "property-owners defeated [the] bylaw" (p. 400), refusing to spend the money. In retrospect, therefore, the most consistent note in these civic endeavours suggests a further significance in that pervasive ringing of Hoffman's factory bell. The bell proclaimed, to all who would hear, its predominance over elections, weddings, and funerals; it proclaimed the predominance of factories.

That insight, precarious as it is, may explain a cryptic incident in Uttley's brief account of the bell: "One night the bell disappeared and could not be found. At last Andrew Borth espied it in an old well on the site of St. Jerome's College where two workmen had hidden it." Perhaps those whose morning slumbers and daily energies

iv

were rationed by the clanging symbol regularly wished its bell-like tones at the bottom of an abandoned well.

Individual response of that sort to the documented tenor of life is, as might be expected, the rarest quality in Uttley's *History*, as it is in most histories. We do get a glimpse, nonetheless, of the personal lives of store clerks in 1859 when a woman, rendered desperate by the rigors of clerking from breakfast to 10 p.m., goes so far as to write a letter to the editor. And a displeased merchant replies: "Is a transition from the legitimate sphere of women's everyday walk to that of contributing to a newspaper an action that will exalt yourself in your own estimation or that of your sex?" (p. 104). Less clearly indicated, but poignant in its way, is the plight of the "only three German girls of marriageable age in the village" in the 1840's. "Hence," reports Uttley without a tremor, "young Germans went over to Buffalo, N.Y. to seek for helpmeets" (p. 41). In what had seemed such an ideal market, it is hard to imagine that any of the three single girls left behind, looking through the frame-house window past the pump and the vegetable-garden, would watch those retreating backs of their young men and remain unmoved. It may even be, to return to Hoffman's bell as symbol, that it was the women of those good old days that approved of the factory bell, kept it ringing, and found it, in particular, reassuring. Restricted to their "legitimate sphere of women's everyday walk," and outraged worlds removed from the freedom of their own shopping trip to Buffalo, they could take comfort in the audible reminder that their menfolk too had their appointed rounds and their sanctioned roles.

In sum, the complex of life as we still know it—social freedom and social order, commerce and ecology—has its genesis here in the account compiled by William Uttley. His work comes as close to a personal anecdotal history of the city as we can hope to retrieve, a spotted chronicle of a community that can never exist again, and one in which almost every reader will find a point where past confronts present as nostalgia tugs against progress.

Gerald A. Noonan
Department of English
Wilfrid Laurier University

Waterloo, 1975

WILLIAM V. (BEN) UTTLEY

1865-1944

BIOGRAPHY OF THE AUTHOR

William Valores (Ben) Uttley was 72 years old in 1937 when he completed and published *The History of Kitchener*. It is not known how many copies of the book were printed, nor how many years Uttley had spent compiling the pieces of information he included. One story is that he was busy taking pre-publication orders for the book at the same time as he was going about interviewing and researching and recording.

His background suited him for the work. He was, in sequence, a native of Elmira, a resident of Doon, and a prominent newspaperman and civic politician in Kitchener. His own life-span, 1865-1944, linked the Victorian and modern eras, and the village of Berlin to the city of Kitchener.

He was born in Elmira on January 1, 1865, the first son of Samuel Uttley and Mary Taylor, of English and Scottish descent. He grew up there and attended Elmira Public School. Sometime after 1877, when the local directory still lists a Samuel Uttley as resident in Elmira, the family moved to Doon.

Ben Uttley attended Berlin High School, and after graduation, according to H. Lefty Weichel of Elmira, studied shorthand privately and completed study at Toronto Business College. Mr. Weichel, who was born in 1896, and whose son married Uttley's daughter, Kathleen, reports that Uttley began active newspaper work on the *St. Louis Chronicle*, Missouri.[1]

In any case, by 1888 Uttley was living in Doon and teaching at Freeport Public School (possibly known also as Limerick School[2]) just across the Grand River. The *Annual Report of the Inspector of Public Schools of the County of Waterloo* lists W. V. Uttley as the teacher at Freeport (at $400 a year) in 1888, 1889, and 1891. (The 1890 *Report* is not included in the Kitchener Public Library holdings.)

In order to shorten his walk to and from school, Uttley "constructed a cable fastened to a tree on the Doon side and a post on the opposite bank, hung a basket thereon and pulled himself quite handily over and back."[3] At age 95, Ollie A. Kummer, who was born in Doon in 1880, still remembers Uttley's crossing, near where the Pioneer Memorial Tower is today.

"I used to watch him go across," he said.[4] Mr. Kummer, who

vii

would have been between the age of eight and eleven during Uttley's school-teaching years, did not know the exact construction of the crossing device. He thought there may have been two pulleys on the cable, and he didn't recall the particular nature of the basket "except that it was strong enough."

"He would cross over with ease. It was no trouble for him to do it. He would run halfway across with the momentum of his own weight—the wire was slack, not taut. Then he'd reach up overhead and pull himself to the other shore hand over hand."

Mr. Kummer recalls that the Uttley family, Ben and his two brothers and three sisters, lived on the hill, where the Doon United Church now stands, in a house overlooking the village. "I remember him (Ben) playing football (soccer) at Doon. And I remember one time when Nelson Wildfong, who was a great hitch-and-kicker, did a hitch and kick but instead of kicking the ball, kicked Ben Uttley. Ben didn't like that very much." (A hitch-and-kick is a simultaneous jump and kick.)

As a young man, Uttley played on the Berlin Rangers soccer team, and, in later life, became a golf and lawn-bowling enthusiast.

Uttley began a quarter-century association with local newspapers on January 30, 1893 when he purchased the struggling *Berlin Daily Telegraph*. About two months later, on March 23, 1893, he changed the name to *The Berlin Daily Record*. On February 1, 1897, the name was changed again, after a merger with *The Daily News*, to *The Daily News Record*. The paper continued under Uttley's editorship until 1919 when it was sold to W. D. Euler and W. J. Motz.

Uttley then returned to Elmira and bought *The Elmira Signet* from George Klinck Sr. He sold the *Signet* to Cameron Kester of St. Mary's in either 1921 or 1923. The first date is reported in an article by W. H. Breithaupt, "Waterloo County Newspapers" in the *Waterloo Historical Society Annual Report*, volume 9, 1921. H. Lefty Weichel, however, in information supplied to the Waterloo County Hall of Fame exhibit at Doon Pioneer Village, states that Uttley worked at *The Signet* until 1923 when he retired. From then on, Mr. Weichel believes[5] that Uttley, whose hearing had become impaired, busied himself in collecting material for *The History of Kitchener*.

"I can see him yet," he said, "walking with his big fur wrap around him." The fur, apparently, was like a large scarf.

In addition to being teacher, newspaperman, and local historian, Ben Uttley had a distinguished career in municipal politics which included a brief, and rather bizarre, period in 1908 as the mayor who never was. He had been elected to the Berlin City Council in 1905, 1906, and 1907, and had served as chairman of the finance committee for all three years.

In the election of January 6, 1908, Uttley ran for mayor against Allan Huber. The next day's edition of *The Daily Telegraph* told it all on the first page—although in separate, confusing, and contradictory stories. The largest headline, in the left top corner, reported that "in the biggest surprise in the Municipal History of Berlin," ex-Reeve (i.e. chief councillor) Uttley, for three years chairman of the Finance Committee, and managing editor of *The News Record*, and "manager of the Conservative organ in town" had been defeated by Huber by six votes, 896 to 890.

At the top of the same front page, toward the right, a one-column headline appeared over a brief story noting that "town clerk Huehnergard reported a decrease of 10 votes for Huber" and that the change would mean Uttley had won the election. Sure enough, still on the same front page, about the middle, a one-column item was headed: "Mr. Uttley declared elected."

With his majority of four, Uttley assumed the mayor's duties and on January 13 presented his inaugural address to council. An editorial in the January 15th edition of *The Telegraph* (copies of Uttley's own paper are not available for 1908) noted that Uttley's inaugural stress upon the development of a good roads system, an extra fire station between Berlin and Waterloo, and an isolation hospital for smallpox cases had the effect of "materially modifying his pre-election platform."

On January 16, Judge Chisholm, who had been conducting a recount, reported so many "gross irregularities" on the part of Deputy Returning Officers that he could not complete his task. Some envelopes had not been sealed or tied, and at least one ballot box that had been sealed had been opened again "with a knife or other sharp instrument." The fault was entirely with the "sloppy" methods of the clerks, and a new election was necessary.

Meanwhile, Uttley's majority had been reduced only by two in the part of the recount completed, and he continued to preside as mayor until February 19, the "second municipal election of the year". Two additional candidates had joined the race, and Uttley finished second to Huber in the four-man contest: Huber, 690 votes; Uttley, 493; John R. Eden, 454; and John S. Anthes, 269.

Uttley returned to the fray to become an elected councillor again in 1910, 1911, 1912, and in 1917, 1918, and 1919.

In 1912, Uttley was one of the originators of the Waterloo Historical Society, and he contributed historical articles to a number of the *Annual Report* volumes which have been published every year since the Society was founded.

In 1970, he was honoured posthumously when one of the meeting rooms at a new hotel in Kitchener, The Inn of the Black Walnut (now Valhalla Inn) was named for him. And in 1972 his picture and a brief biography were included in the Waterloo County Hall of Fame inaugurated that year at Doon Pioneer Village.

Uttley was married in 1889 to Sara Matthews of Doon. He had two daughters, Vera (Mrs. B. H. Tanner of Toronto) and Kathleen (Mrs. Walter Wilken of Elmira). A grandson, John Weichel (son of Kathleen and the late Harry Weichel of Elmira) is editor of *The Stratford Beacon Herald.*

Ben Uttley died at his home on Park Avenue, Elmira, on May 26, 1944.

> — Gerald Noonan, Waterloo
> May, 1975

[1] Mr. Weichel confirmed his report, written for the Waterloo County Hall of Fame, in a telephone conversation May 7, 1975. Mrs. Vera Tanner, Uttley's daughter, is certain that her father went to Missouri after his marriage in 1889, but she is not sure of the year or the length of time spent there. She believes that her mother, in particular, did not like St. Louis, and preferred to come back to Canada.

[2] According to Ollie A. Kummer in a telephone conversation, May 7, 1975.

[3] Quoted from "Memories of the Grand" by O. A. Kummer, in the *Waterloo Historical Society Annual Report*, Vol. 61, 1973, p. 37.

[4] In telephone conversation, May 7, 1975.

[5] Confirmed in telephone conversation, May 7, 1975.

A HISTORY

of

Kitchener, Ontario

by

W. V. (Ben) Uttley

Kitchener, Ontario

- 1937 -

CONTENTS

CONTENTS—Continued

ILLUSTRATIONS

ILLUSTRATIONS—Continued

ILLUSTRATIONS—Continued

The First Settlements in Waterloo County

S AN ACORN the City of Kitchener was called the Sand
Hills and the community, Ebytown. The city was grounded
on a Pennsylvania-German settlement. The pioneers were
a branch of the Mennonite colonists who forsook their
homelands in Europe to shun military service and gain
religious freedom in Penn's Woods, Pennsylvania. There
they multiplied and prospered. Flocks of their offspring in the
seventies-eighties took up land in Virginia or Upper Canada. Later
on a group of them came to Waterloo County, Ontario, and hewed
out homes for themselves in the forested wilderness that is now
Waterloo Township.

Waterloo Township was part of a land grant made after the
American War of Independence to the Six Nations Indians by
Great Britain. The grant comprised 674,910 acres and included all
the territory lying for about six miles on each side of the Grand
River from its sources to its mouth. (I) The Indians were to keep
the lands "as long as the sun shines, rivers run and grass grows."

More white men, however, came in and coveted the Indians'
lands. In 1793 they urged the redmen to ask the Government at
Niagara to permit the leasing of tracts to them. The authorities
declined to sanction the request, but offered to sell parts of the
grant and invest the proceeds for the Indians' benefit. Chief Brant
and Hill said no and rode off in a huff to the Mohawk village at
Brant's Ford. (I)

At a council fire the Indians determined to sell 144 square miles
of their lands to Philip Stedman of Fort Erie Township. Stedman
promised to pay them $25,625 for the area sometime in the future.
Afterward the Indians pestered the Government for permission to
sell other tracts. The transfer of five more blocks, containing
352,710 acres was sanctioned in 1798. In that sale were Block No. 1,
Dumfries Township; Block No. 2 in Waterloo Township and
Block No. 3, in Woolwich Township, now parts of Waterloo County.
In the transfer of the five blocks only one mortgage was actually
executed, namely, on Block No. 2. (I)

Block No. 2 contained 92,160 acres and was purchased by

Richard Beasley, James Willson and J. B. Rosseau for £8887. The purchasers made the principal payable on April 1, 1898, a century later. Willson and Rosseau soon afterward sold their shares to Beasley. In the settlement of his Block, Beasley was fortunate. Earlier, companies of Mennonites from Pennsylvania had bought lands in the Niagara and York districts. In 1800 a group of Pennsylvanians purchased tracts of land from him.

Their Arrival

The Mennonites were not United Empire Loyalists. At the close of the American Revolution they thought that if the United States should again be entangled in a war, the Mennonites would lose their exemption from military service. Accordingly numbers of them felt that if they moved to Canada they would enjoy such exemption under British rule. (2)

Those pioneers followed the Susquehanna Trail for 100 miles through the Alleghany Mountains. The Genesee River was crossed on a flat-boat and New York State in their covered wagons, with either Lewiston or Black Rock as their goal. The frisky Niagara River was also passed in a flat-boat. From the frontier up to Block No. 2 was a serious engagement, for the primitive roads petered out into trails that lost themselves in the forest and sometimes they advanced only four or five miles a day. The distance from their old homes to Canada, according to the route followed, was either 429 or 458 miles. (3)

The settlers followed a trail along the Grand River, and used it a long time. To haul four barrels of flour through the mud from the front to the settlement took a four-horse team four weeks. (2)

Yosep Schoerg (Joseph Sherk) and his brother-in-law, Samuel Betzner, Jr., left Lancaster County, Pa., in the fall of 1799. Over winter they stayed with coreligionists at "The Twenty," in the Niagara district. Early in 1800, Richard Beasley supplied them with an Indian guide who piloted them up to Block No. 2. Joseph Sherk bought 261 acres opposite Doon; and Samuel Betzner, Jr., 200 acres on the west bank of the Grand River at Blair. Good water was the deciding factor. (3)

Joseph Sherk sold a horse to pay for his land. There was enough money over to buy a yoke of oxen and a stoneboat. On the stoneboat, he brought up his wife and wee ones from The Twenty. The family lived in a tent while the pioneer built a log house, 9 x 12 feet, with no other tools than an axe, an auger, and a handsaw. (4)

On July 18, 1800, John Biehn, forefather of the Bean families of Kitchener and Waterloo, registered the purchase of 3600 acres, which included the sites for Doon and New Aberdeen. On the same day, George Bechtel procured a deed for 3150 acres, touching the Biehn tract and running up to within a mile and a half of the City of Kitchener, and including the site for German Mills. Their deeds were registered before any others (3).

Between 1800 and 1803 further incomers included the Reichert families, John and Samuel Bricker, John and Jacob Bechtel, the Kinzie, Shupe, Clemens, Wismer, Livergood, Rosenberger, Ringler, Meyer, Sararus, Krugy, Gingrich and Stauffer households. Dilman Kinzie bought a tract of land above the old Doon mill from his father-in-law, John Biehn. (5) On it was opened the second cemetery in the township, if not in the county. Now it is known as the Kinzie-Bean Pioneer Cemetery.

The Beasley Mortgage Anxiety

The settlers were beaver-like in their labors and for a short time their economic sky was cloudless. In 1803, however, Samuel Bricker, while in York (Toronto), heard that their lands were blanketted with a mortgage. He then hurried home and told the settlers of his discovery. When seen, Beasley owned up. Two pioneers laid the matter before the Provincial officials, but did not get any redress. As a consequence a number of settlers threw up their holdings. The remaining ones did not prosecute Beasley, because non-resistance was one of their cardinal principles. Instead, they made up their minds to buy two-thirds of Block No. 2 from him. (5)

John and Samuel Bricker, among others, were sent down to Pennsylvania to get the aid of their brethren. The men whom they first saw did not respond in action. The two brothers then appealed to friends in Lancaster County. John Bricker had married the sister of John Erb, who later on founded Preston, and of Jacob, Daniel, and Abraham Erb who established Waterloo. The Erb brothers were practical men and well-to-do, and consented to become shareholders. Twenty-three other farmers joined them. The German Company was then formed and 60,000 acres purchased for £10,000.

The purchase was subdivided into 128 lots of 488 acres each, and thirty-two lots of 83 acres. No restriction was placed on the number of lots a member might buy, although lots were cast for them. Mrs. Susanna (Erb) Brubacher bought ten lots; her brother, John Erb, twenty; and Jacob Wissler, twenty-one. (3)

Daniel Erb and Samuel Bricker signed a contract at Niagara on November 28, 1803. The Pennsylvanians paid down £4692.10 in silver dollars that were brought over on horseback. Daniel and John Erb then signed a bond to pay off the balance of £5307.10, with interest at six percent on May 23, 1805. That pledge was kept. The second bulk of silver was placed in a keg on a pleasure wagon, driven by Samuel Bricker, while John Bricker, Daniel, John and Jacob Erb, mounted on horseback, acted as guards, and delivered the specie at Niagara. Afterward the wagon was presented to Samuel Bricker for his praiseworthy services. (3)

The Government saw to it that the Indians were paid in full for Block No. 2, and a clear deed issued to the German Company. Upper Canada was the gainer by the Beasley mortgage trouble, for had it not occurred it is probable that fewer Mennonites would have come in. Of all the lands sold by the Five Nations to white men, Colonel Claus, Indian Agent, said, "Block No. 2 was the only one likely to turn to any advantage to the Indians." (1)

In the fall of 1805, the owners of the 448-acre lots on which the city stands were: George Eby of Lot No. 1; John Eby, Lot 2; Jacob Herschey, Lot 3; John Erb, part of Lot 4; Abraham Erb, part of Lot 15; Henry Weaver, Lot 16; Benjamin Herschey, Lot 17; and John Eby of Lot 18.

The Abraham Weber Party

Near Blue Ball, Lancaster County, Pa., an ancestor of the Weaver kin built a home in 1762. It is of rough stones and plaster, with timbered sides and a "ziegel Dach." Henry Weaver (Weber) owned the house in 1800. After the Beasley mortgage trouble he bought eight 448-acre lots and one 83-acre lot from the German Company. From their ancient home, probably in 1806, his young son Abraham set forth on horseback for Upper Canada to select a farmsite from his father's purchases.

Abraham Weber's grandson Tilman says the youth carried only a few necessary articles, including an axe. He camped back of

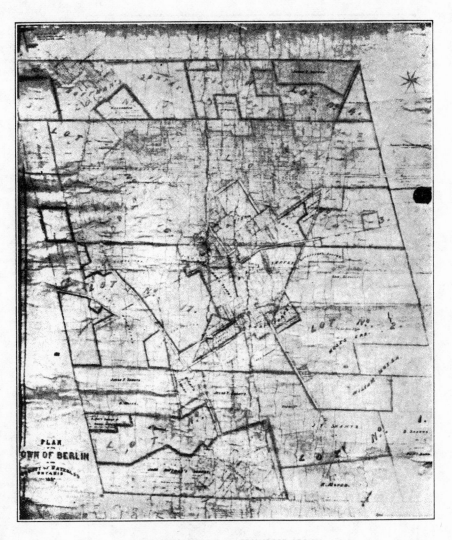

BERLIN ORIGINAL MUNICIPALITY

ABRAHAM WEBER'S 4-HORSE CONESTOGA

—Courtesy, The Waterloo Historical Society.

where the Goodrich Tire Works now stand. One account says that he slept in a hollow tree; another that it was under a fallen tree, fixed with boughs and with a blanket hung up before the opening. At night he kept a roaring fire a-going to scare away wild animals. The Indians, with whom he was soon on friendly terms, slumbered around his camp-fire. Abraham chose Lot 16 as his future home. For some unknown reason he made the long journey back to Pennsylvania on foot. (6)

In 1807, he guided a party of settlers to Beasley Township. In it were a dozen or more men, women, and children, who came over in three 4-horse and one 2-horse Conestoga. Their course ran through primeval forests in which wild animals prowled and wily Indians roamed. According to Israel Groff, the Mennonites did not carry firearms, but relied upon a Higher Power. In that party were: Joseph Schneider, his wife and four children; Benjamin Eby and wife (nee Brubacher) ; Daniel Eby, Samuel Eby, Daniel Erb, Joseph Rissor, John and Frederick Eckert, and others. (5)

By then the 60,000 acres already mentioned had been taken on. As other Mennonite families wished to buy land in Canada, the German Company bought an additional 45,195 acres in what is now Woolwich Township from Wm. Wallace of Niagara. The Abraham Weber party brought in a half-barrel of gold and silver to pay for the tract. On the fagging trail a band of robbers tried to steal the money, but were foiled. The caravan reached George Eby's home on Lot No. 1, below the location of the present First Mennonite Church, on June 21, 1807. (6) In that party were the pioneers who cleared the lands on which the city rests.

Young Abraham Weber had purchased 361 acres of Lot No. 16. (See accompanying map.) He first cleared the expanse on which the Goodrich Tire Works now stand, and built a log house. Three years later he married Elizabeth Cressman. The pioneer hired a Negro named Carroll. Once, while working in the bush, the darkey broke an arm or leg. Mr. Weber then gave the injured man a piece of land for a cabin and garden. Long afterward the pioneer's son, Abraham C. Weber, sold his holdings in the village and bought a farm at Freeport, a part of which is now the site of the Freeport Sanitorium. (6)

Joseph Schneider bought Lot 17; and Samuel Eby one-half of Lot 3. Joseph Eby purchased Lot 18 and sold part of it to Samuel

Eby, a cousin of Samuel Eby of Lot 3. Joseph Eby bought also 373 acres of Lot No. 1 from George Eby, the horse doctor. Benjamin Eby purchased Lot No. 2. In 1810, Jacob Shantz bought 136 acres, being part of Lot 1, and later on 53 acres of Lot No. 18, from Joseph Eby. (3) John Brubacher, in 1816, purchased Lot No. 57 from his mother. (5)

By now the Bowman, Cassell, Hammacher, Christian Schneider, Jacob Hallman and other households had taken up lands in Block 2. In 1825, Jacob Sauer, Samuel Bowers, John Hoffman, and William Moyer had settled in the township. In 1827, Theobald Spetz, the first Catholic settler from Europe, bought land near Erbsville. Between 1827 and 1830, numerous Catholic families from Alsace or Baden acquired lands at New Germany. Among them were Matthias Fehrenbach, Ignatius Weiler, Carl Zuber, Chrysostum Zinger, Joseph Benninger, and Joseph Wendling.

After 1825 the flow of Mennonites from Pennsylvania fell to a trickle and by 1835 had almost ceased. (5)

Pioneer Times

When the pioneers came up from Niagara there were few roads. Accordingly they drove their Conestogas in and out between the trees, which accounts for the crooked roads in Waterloo County. Trees were blazed with a single cut of the axe as guide-posts for later comers.

A home was made of rough logs, dove-tailed at the ends and the chinks stuffed with moss. The roof was of split logs. Some of their furniture was home-made.

Into the big fireplace the settler rolled a log. The mother crushed wheat on a stone with a hammer and baked the dough in an iron pot hung over the fire. Potatoes were roasted in the ashes, and barley or wheat scorched for coffee.

A mother said that her son was born in the bush and rocked in a sap-trough. Boys got one pair of cow-hide boots a year. When those were worn out, they went barefooted. In the winter men wore sheepskin coats. Families rode to church on horseback.

With the exception of corn and tobacco, the pioneers raised crops similar to those grown in Pennsylvania. But the summers were shorter and the winters colder. In cold weather more food-fats, lasting fires and warmer clothing were vital requirements.

Still, frigid February put vim in their hearts. For clothing, flax and wool were spun, woven, and sewed up in the home.

The settler at first used a wooden plow. He did not have harrows, but used a tree-top which scratched the ground a little. Jacob cut his grain with a cradle and Rebecca bound it by hand. Hay was cut with a scythe and loaded and unloaded by hand-power. Timber was burned to get rid of it. John Brubacher of the Breslau Road covered his barn with hand-made cedar shingles that lasted for seventy years.

Cattle feed was scarce. Cows ran a mile when they heard a tree fall and ate the leaves, liking them better than hay. In the fall, pigs fattened on beechnuts. Deer ran in and out among the cows; and in an hour one could catch all the fish he wanted in any of the streams. With a blunderbuss a young farmer named Shantz once shot eighty-four wild pigeons as they rose from shocks of wheat. Wild pigeons, until the middle of last century, flew over the township in tens of thousands, darkening the sky. The pigeons were shot for food or wantonly killed for sport. The species is now extinct.

Maple syrup was boiled by the hundred gallons. Anyone might tap the trees and boil the sap anywhere. Mr. Brubacher helped to cut down a bee-tree from which they got two washtubsful of honey. The pioneers gathered wild plums, wild grapes, and wild crab-apples along the creeks and in the beaver meadows. Usually the fruit was cooked in maple syrup.

When a member of a household was taken sick, the mother brewed a bitter tea of either sage or mint for him or her. When the stork alighted on a rooftree, the local midwife was sent for. When a settler broke a limb, the handyman of the neighborhood set it. The pioneers were adroit folk. Otherwise they could not have existed in the primitive country.

The settlers were musical and were taught the old-fashioned notes. There were then no newspapers. Consequently the Bible and schoolbooks were their only reading matter. Farmers went ten miles to help at a barn-raising. A big bake-oven and a smoke-house were indispensables. Numerous families had a burial plot on their farmstead. (7)

Money was rarely seen. Battered brass buttons passed as coppers and in a pinch were cut off a coat for the purpose. (8)

Sources

1. *Reserve of the Six Nations on the Grand River.* 1927. By Brigadier-General Cruikshank. Waterloo Historical Society Annual.
2. Letters written for this volume by Mr. A. R. Sherk of Victoria, B.C.
3. *History of Waterloo Township.* 1934. By Irwin C. Bricker. Phm.B., of Elora, Ont. Waterloo Historical Society Report.
4. Relations of the Rev. A. B. Sherk at the Sherk Centennial. 1900.
5. *History of Waterloo Township.* 1895. By Ezra E. Eby.
6. Information supplied us by Mr. George A. Weber, Kitchener, R.R. 2.
7. Interviews had with John Brubacher and the late Rev. Solomon Eby on Pioneer Times.
8. *Early History of Galt.* 1880. By the Hon. James Young.

JOSEPH SCHNEIDER

Founder of the City

The first stones in the city's foundation were laid in South Queen Street, in 1807, by Joseph Schneider. He was born in Lancaster County, Pa., in 1798, and married Barbara, sister of the Rev. Benjamin Eby.

On Lot No. 17, Pioneer Schneider built a log cabin. It stood on the east side of Queen Street, where John McKay's former home rests. Next he cut a roadway from the house to the Walper House corner and easterly to No. 57 East King Street, where he built a barn. South Queen Street was the first thoroughfare in the city and until the eighteen-eighties was called Schneider's Road.

Dundas was the pioneers' nearest market. One of their heaviest tasks was cutting roads to mill and store. Here, they were faced by a chain of sandhills, big and little. The hill at the foot of North Queen Street suggests what the largest ones were like. Instead of piercing the hills the settlers went around them. The main road ran from the Walper corner to Huether's brewery; skirted a swamp and "mosied" over to Weber Street, easterly along that street; verged round a big pine-clad hill that squatted on the city hall site; reached King Street, and extended down past the First Mennonite Church, to connect with the Preston-Dundas road. After they had forked out $1000, besides their labor, on their market highway, ninety-three Mennonites petitioned the government for a grant of £100 to complete it. But the legislators passed a motion to grant the sum "in the negative." (1)

In 1807 (or 1809) John Erb built a gristmill in Preston. Shortly afterward Abraham Erb erected a saw-mill in Waterloo. The roadway from Huether's corner had by then been extended to Waterloo. For years the road through the Sand Hills was called Abraham Erb's Road. Abraham Erb built also a gristmill in Waterloo in 1816. It was as welcome as money from home.

Joseph Schneider's Saw-Mill

The pioneers had then begun to replace their log-houses with frame homes. To meet a demand for lumber Joseph Schneider built a saw-mill in 1816 on Schneider's Creek. It rested on the easterly side of David Street, opposite Victoria Park. The mill dam was above the railway; and the mill-race crossed David Street between Schneider Avenue and Roland Street. The up-and-down or "muley" saw was run by an overshot waterwheel.

The City's Oldest Building

Afterward Joseph Schneider extended his roadway toward Petersburg and cut logs for the settlers in Wilmot Township. Between times he sawed timber for a larger home. It was a frame and roughcast house built in 1820, in South Queen Street, near Schneider Avenue. In the eighteen-fifties, his son, Joseph E. Schneider, removed the roughcast, weather-boarded it and added cornices to the home. The house is still in use and is the oldest building in the city. That well-preserved home is owned by J. M. Snyder, the great-grandson of Joseph Schneider, the pioneer.

A Blacksmithshop and Tavern

Shortly after the Schneiders had moved into their new home a stranger, Phineas Varnum, pulled their latchstring. He wanted to buy a parcel of land on which to run up a blacksmith shop and roadhouse. On account of the toil spent in clearing his land, Pioneer Schneider was averse to selling any part of it. Yet, after pondering the value of a smithy to the settlement, he leased Varnum a site in West King Street, near the Walper House corner. Varnum built his shop and tavern between 1820 and 1824 and, as the story goes, plied his callings there until the early eighteen-thirties. The saw-mill and the smithy were the first stirrings of urban life in the city. (2)

Four generations of Schneiders have contributed their full shares to the upbuilding of the city.

SOURCES

1. *The Reserve of the Six Nations Indians on the Grand River*. 1927. By Brigadier-General Cruikshank. Waterloo His-torical Society Annual.

2. Interviews had with David B. Schneider and descendants of the pioneer.

SAMUEL EBY OF LOT 3

Samuel Eby, who bought part of Lot No. 3, G. C. T., was a cousin of Benjamin Eby and Samuel Eby of Lot No. 18. He espoused Elizabeth Brech, and built a loghouse at the foot of the hill in Lancaster Street, where the Conger coal-office stands. First he cleared off the forest over to the House of Refuge. Later on he sold building lots to incoming villagers. He was a deacon in the Mennonite Church.

His second son, John, bought the Poor House farm. The son erected a home in Frederick Street, opposite the House of Refuge. It was made of foot-wide planks, laid one atop the other. In 1837 he married Rebecca, daughter of Samuel Bricker, who played a prominent part in the Beasley mortgage snag.

North Waterloo is indebted to the Mennonites for the intro-duction of the apple-tree and apple-butter. John Eby planted a large orchard and owned a cider-mill. Maryborough farmers drove down and bought wagon-loads of apples from him. The buyers came in one day, stayed over night, and started off the next morning.

Mr. and Mrs. John Eby were the parents of two sons and four daughters. The youngest daughter, Susanna, of 178 Frederick Street, was born in the farm house in 1858. She remembers seeing her mother spinning flax and wool, and of twisting the threads for her. The girls were taught how to bake and sew; and all the chil-dren to work and save. Miss Eby often saw the pleasure wagon

PIONEER JOSEPH SCHNEIDER'S HOME
—Courtesy, J. M. Snyder.

PIONEERS' MEMORIAL TOWER
AT DOON.
1924.

THE CAST IN "THE TRAIL OF THE CONESTOGA" — By Miss B. Mabel Dunham, B.A. Dramatized by Miss Elenore Doherty and Carl F. Klinck, M.A., of the Waterloo College.

in which Samuel Bricker brought over the mass of silver to pay for the Mennonite purchase.

Her father built a home (which is still in use), for his widowed mother, on the east side of Frederick Street, at the Five Points. In 1868 her father sold the County the Poor House farm, retaining only his home and five acres of land. His second youngest child was a daughter named Madeline (1851-1929). She was married to Martin Dunham in 1880. Eight years later her father sold Mr. Dunham the five acres mentioned and moved farther into town. Later on Mr. Dunham subdivided his purchase and sold it for building lots. The city renamed part of East Avenue and La Grange Street, Dunham Avenue, in 1933, in honor of this family.

The Ebys are of Celtic origin. *Blaikie's Modern Cyclopedia* says the Celts were the earliest Aryan settlers in Europe. That all the old Celts seem to have possessed a kind of literary order called Bards. The Canadian Ebys have produced a number of writers. Ezra E. Eby, for example, wrote a *History of Waterloo Township*; while Miss Mabel B. Dunham, B.A., great-granddaughter of Samuel Eby, is the authoress of *The Trail of the Conestoga* and other works of a historical character.

BISHOP BENJAMIN EBY

As has been seen, Benjamin Eby bought Lot 2, G.C.T., and came to Upper Canada in 1807. Before leaving Pennsylvania, he and Marie Brubacher were united in marriage. A good word is due the wives of the pioneers. Stanch as maples, they left comfortable homes in Pennsylvania, faced the difficile trail, and in a wooded wilderness bore the hardships of life without a murmur.

Benjamin Eby was of the leader type. Although just of age, he took thought of the settlers' spiritual welfare. The pioneers at first worshipped God in their home. He had them gather together at a particular clearing, one Sunday here and the next there, until all had been visited. He was appointed preacher in 1809. Besides promoting the building of a church, he interested himself in primary education. (1)

His log house stood west of the Mennonite Church. In 1814 he sold Samuel Eschelman 56 acres adjoining the church lands. So far as known he was the first settler to sell incoming townsmen plots of land. He sold his son-in-law, David Weber, 219 acres at the upper part of his big lot. His son Elias became the owner of the remaining part on the north side of King Street. The son sold his holding to John Brubacher and Menno Erb who in turn sold his land to William Moyer and Moses Betzner. As the history unfolds other activities of Ben Eby will come to light.

In 1834 a circus employee carried the Asiatic cholera to Galt. Nearly one-fifth of the inhabitants died of the scourge. Many persons from Waterloo Township attended the performance and numerous individuals, catching the disease from one another, died also, including Mrs. Ben Eby. (2)

The Rev. Eby carried on his spiritual labors until his own death in 1853. He had then been the servant of the Mennonite Society for forty-four years.

SOURCES
1. *History of Waterloo Township.* By Ezra E. Eby.
2. *History of Galt.* By the Hon. James Young.

INDIAN SAM EBY

Samuel Eby of Lot No. 18 was called "Indian Sam" because he was the Indians' minister, interpreter and lawgiver, says Ezra Eby. In a vacant log house on his clearing the first school in the settlement was opened in 1808, with John Beatty as teacher. He taught only in the winter months and parents who sent their children to school paid him for his services. The rate is unknown, but in the early eighteen-forties Benjamin Burkholder, a Waterloo teacher, charged a child two dollars for three months' instruction, with two terms during a winter. In addition every pupil had to contribute a share of the firewood to heat the schoolroom.

JOHN BRUBACHER

John Brubacher came to Canada in 1816 and was accompanied by his widowed mother, Mrs. Susanna (Erb) Brubacher. She was a plucky woman and whatever she did was done aright. On the way over Mrs. Brubacher rode on a horse and killed a rattlesnake with her whip. Her son drove a heavily-laden Conestoga. Among other articles he brought in a churn. When they reached this settlement, their first meal was eaten off a pine stump. Mother and son then threaded their way through the woods to her son-in-law, Ben Eby's place.

John Brubacher made a clearing on Lot 57 and erected a log home. His mother kept house for him until 1817, when he married Catherine, daughter of Joseph and Mary (Betzner) Sherk. Ezra Eby said that Mrs. Susanna Brubacher sold her son 896 acres for $672 and then returned to Pennsylvania. Later on John Brubacher, as has been said, bought the Elias Eby farm in the East Ward and built a home in Brubacher Street that is still in use. Eventually John is said to have acquired 3,000 acres of land and to have given each of his fifteen children a farm.

John Brubacher was a short, dark man, and could lift a barrel of cider to his shoulder and take a drink out of the bunghole. His favorite saying was: Truth lasts the longest. His great-grandfather, also named John, when urged by his neighbors in Pennsylvania to build a grist-mill declined, because he feared he might be tempted to take too heavy tolls.

Mrs. John Brubacher dressed plainly and wore a white cap. Her descendants treasure the heirlooms she handed down. There were no locks on their doors and often at night Indians entered her kitchen and slept on the floor. Once she was alarmed at breakfast time when a squaw fed a young papoose a piece of liver-sausage.

Fire was hard to make, for the settlers had no matches. A handful of dry cedar-bark was shredded and sparks struck from a flint with a piece of steel. Some families kept their fire burning the year round.

One night an Indian buck rapped on John's window and pleaded for a drink of whisky, but the pioneer did not give him any. Wild animals were all too plentiful and wolves a menace. Occasionally he heard the squeal of a pig as it was dragged from its pen by a black bear.

The Mennonites loved music. Once, while revisiting his old home in Pennsylvania, John Brubacher called on a man who owned a melodeon and had him play a hymn often sung in Ben Eby's church. As he listened tears of joy rolled down his cheeks.

The pioneer walked with his head bent. Ward Bowlby once met him in East King Street and said, "Mr. Brubacher, when walking you should keep your head up." John responded, "Mr. Bowlby, yonder is a field of wheat. Some of the stalks stand with their heads up: those are empty; the bent heads only are filled with grain." (1)

Mr. Brubacher's youngest daughter, Veronica (Mrs. Moses Betzner) died in 1936, when in her ninety-second year. She was an early riser; ate whole-wheat bread and until her fortieth year never tasted tea nor coffee—after that she drank milk or buttermilk. "Sunrise," said she, "has a virtue no other part of the day has. Work is a blessing. Without it life would not be worth living."

"This community," she added, "was based on practical Christianity. The people were honorable and in business matters no writings passed among them. It was all done by word of mouth and a man's Yes was binding." (2)

In his lecture on "The Pennsylvania-Dutchman," the late Byron Stauffer said that once Isaac borrowed a sum of money from Jacob. Isaac suggested that they do as the Englishmen did and draw up a promissory note. Jacob was willing but asked, "Who keeps the note?"

"Why, you do," said Isaac.

"No," said Jacob, "you keep it. Then you know when to pay me the money back."

SOURCES

1. Interview had with Ephraim Brubacher of Baden, Ont.
2. A conversation had with the late Mrs. Moses Betzner.

THE FIRST MENNONITE CHURCH

Soon after their arrival the Mennonite settlers bought a plot of land for a burial ground, church and school. A document owned by David B. Betzner shows that in 1810 Joseph Eby and Jacob Shontz sold 1.5 acres in East King Street to John Gressman (Cressman) and Jacob Schneider, elders of the Mennonite Society. Benjamin Eby and Samuel Eschelman too sold or gave them three-quarters of an acre above the first purchase. The deeds were not issued until 1816 and say that the plots lay in Block No. 2, on the Grand River, in the Counties of Halton and Wentworth, Upper Canada.

Benjamin Eby, the first preacher, was ordained Bishop in 1812

BISHOP C. F. DERSTINE
Pastor, The First Mennonite Church.

—Courtesy, J. M. Snyder.

THE FIRST MENNONITE CHURCH IN WATERLOO COUNTY, ONTARIO, CANADA
ERECTED IN 1813, AND KNOWN AS BENJ EBY'S

THE FIRST MENNONITE CHURCH
CHRISTIAN EBY CHURCH OF 1902
BENJAMIN EBY CHURCH OF 1834

—By Courtesy, the Rev. L. J. Burkholder.

and set about the raising of a church. In 1813 a Versamlungshaus of logs, smoothed on one side, was built. That meeting-house was the first church in Waterloo County. Bishop Eby's parish included sections of Waterloo, Wilmot and Woolwich Townships. Then Episcopal Church rectors only could legally perform the marriage service; although a magistrate might do so when there was not an Episcopal rectory within eighteen miles. Many local couples were united by a magistrate. After 1831 a minister of any recognized denomination was permitted to tie the marriage knot. (1)

On account of the society's growth, a frame annex was added to the log church in 1818. Bishop Eby opened a winter school in the annex in 1818-19. He taught in German and used the Bible as a textbook. During a teaching span of twenty-five years he was helped by roaming men, including old soldiers, and after by masons and carpenters. Later on a female teacher taught classes in the warmer months. (2) The Pennsylvania-Dutch boys were strong at arithmetic. Jacob Y. Shantz, who was one of Ben Eby's pupils, said the schoolroom "was furnished with a sort of desk on two sides of the room, with slab benches for seats. Holes were bored in the bottom of the slabs to hold the sticks or legs."

The society built a larger church of frame construction in 1834. The old annex was then moved to the lower part of the grounds and used solely as a schoolhouse. In 1841, a Sunday School was opened in the church.

The Mennonite Cemetery

For two generations the Mennonite cemetery was the chief burial ground in the village. To enlarge it, parcels of land were bought from Menno Erb, Wm. Moyer, and P. E. W. Moyer. The municipality, on becoming a town, bought an acre of land touching the Mennonite cemetery for a town cemetery. The citizens, however, recalled how kind the Mennonites had been and had the council give the acre to them. The first burial in this cemetery is said to have been an Indian. Up to 1930, there had been more than 3,500 burials made in it. There most of the local pioneers rest, and not a few non-members.

Various Changes

Until the eighteen-fifties, the church was called, "Ben Eby's"; next, "Christian Eby's"; then the "Berlin Church"; and since 1917, "The First Mennonite Church."

A division of the congregation took place in the early eighteen-seventies. A wing wished to hold regular prayer-meetings and organized a unit of the Mennonite Brethren in Christ. Since then the parent church has mothered other congregations.

The present brick church was built in 1902. A Bible Study School was started in 1907 and firmly established in 1909. Nineteen years later a handsome brick building was built for the School. Two sessions of a fortnight each are held every year, and a dozen different denominations send students to the Bible School. The attendance now exceeds 400. At present the faculty consists of the Reverends C. F. Derstine, S. F. Coffman, O. Burkholder, and J. B. Martin.

The old frame church of 1834 was purchased by D. B. Betzner and moved to Cedar Street, and turned into a woodenware factory. More recently it was utilized as a furniture factory. Fire destroyed it in 1937.

Ministers

Bishop Eby was succeeded in 1853 by Abraham C. Weber, son of the Abraham Weber who settled Lot 16, and served till his death in 1874. He was followed by Christian Eby, a son of Bishop Eby, who continued until 1879. Samuel S. Bowman was then appointed and labored till 1895. E. S. Hallman took charge in 1896 and Urias K. Weber in 1907. In addition, over the long age, the church was ministered to by Preachers who had been ordained in other Mennonite fields, including Jacob M. Oberholtzer, Moses Erb, Bishop Daniel Wismer, Moses C. Bowman, Jacob Woolner, Sr., Jacob Woolner, Jr., and David Wismer.

In the fall of 1924 the society issued a call to Bishop Derstine. The Rev. Clayton F. Derstine was born on August 17, 1891, at Souderton, Pa. On November 22, 1914, he was ordained a minister and evangelist in Altoona, Pa.; and on December 11, 1921, was appointed a Bishop of the Mennonite Church in Eureka, Ill. Three years later he accepted a call to the First Mennonite Church and is the incumbent. He is editor of the *Christian Monitor*, and author of *The Sheet Music of Heaven*.

Deacons

Samuel Eby of Lot No. 3 was the first deacon. Several years after his arrival here he was ordained and served till his death in 1844. Joseph E. Schneider, son of the city's founder, was the second one. John Brubacher of Lot 57, the next deacon, the date of whose ordination is not set down, died in 1875. when Jacob Z. Kolb, of the Breslau field succeeded him. Mr. Kolb was followed in 1890 by Benjamin Shoemaker, who died in 1919. George A. Weber was ordained deacon in 1911 and has ever since served his church.

The First Mennonite Church will in 1938 have completed 125 years of congregational life.

SOURCES

1. *History of Galt.* 1880. By the Hon. James Young.
2. *History of Waterloo Township.* 1895. By Ezra E. Eby.
3. *The First Mennonite Church.* 1930. In manuscript. By Deacon George A. Weber.

EARLY MUNICIPAL GOVERNMENT

Upper Canada was subdivided into nineteen big counties in 1792. Waterloo Township was then part of York County or the Home District. "The westerly boundary of York County ran west from Coote's Paradise (Dundas) to the westerly limit of Haldimand's grant to the Six Nations." As already noted Richard Beasley and two others bought 144 square miles on the Grand River in 1798 from the Indians. It was known as Block No. 2 or the German Block. (1)

In 1798 the legislature passed a law pertaining to the boundary lines of the townships. It was provided that divisional corners should be marked with stone or other durable monuments, and, "any person defacing or removing such stones shall be guilty of felony and will suffer death without benefit of clergy." (2)

Block No. 2 was part of York County until March 22, 1816, when it was set apart as a township. Then, "so much of the tract of land upon the Grand River in occupation of the Six Nations Indians as lies north of Dundas Street" became part of Halton County. (1)

Township affairs were managed by a bench of magistrates at Hamilton. Up to 1816 road-making and bridge-building were done at "'bees." Even after the German Block became a township, municipal government was unknown, but they groped for it by having public business transacted at "town meetings," by property owners. Certain officials were appointed and simple improvements were ordered by a show of hands. The first town meeting was held in 1822, but the name of the meeting-place is lost. George Clemens was the first clerk. David Clemens followed him. In 1830 Daniel Lutz was appointed. In 1831, David Clemens was reappointed and continued till the township became part of the Wellington District. The first assessors were Samuel Erb and Daniel Snider; and the first tax-collector, Abraham Erb. (3)

The District of Wellington was erected by the Act 7th William, on April 20, 1838. The district consisted of the Township of Nichol, certain northern Indian lands, and the Townships of Waterloo, Wilmot, and Woolwich. From today's standpoint it comprised the Counties of Waterloo, Wellington, Grey, and part of Dufferin County. Guelph was the district town. From those units nine men were elected as district councillors.

The council was organized on April 14, 1842. J. B. Bowman and James Cowan represented Waterloo Township. By 1849 the district elected twenty-one councillors. In 1850 Wellington District was organized as the "County of Waterloo." It comprised the Counties of Waterloo, Wellington, and Grey. Elias Snider of Waterloo and J. B. Bowman were the township councillors. At the end of that year Mr. Bowman gave up and was presented with a valuable snuffbox. In 1851 the representatives were Elias Snider and Henry Snider; and in 1852 Henry Snider and Dr. John Scott. In 1852 the united districts were re-erected as separate counties, when Waterloo County began housekeeping on its own account. (4)

In 1842 Division Court Office No. 2 was opened here, and Thomas Sparrow appointed clerk. Among his successors were A. J. Peterson, F. H. Rohleder, and at present, Carl E. Pequegnat.

In 1848 log houses under two stories, with one fireplace, were assessed £20, and each additional fireplace, £4. Brick and-stone houses, under two stories, were assessed £40, and for each extra fireplace, £10. The total tax receipts in the township, including the county town, Waterloo, Preston, and Hespeler, was $5,807.47. (3)

SOURCES
1. The late Dr. Alexander Fraser, Provincial Archivist.
2. Ontario Historical Society Annual. 1912.
3. Consolidated By-Laws of Waterloo Township. By courtesy of Leo Leyes, J.P.
4. Consolidated By-Laws and Records of the County of Wellington. By courtesy of Mr. James Beattie, Clerk.

THE GERMAN MECHANIC

Early in last century, thousands of Germans emigrated to America. In the new world they hoped to better themselves and escape the ever-present danger of war in Europe. Pennsylvania received many of them. There some of them tarried a while and then joined parties of Mennonites who were trekking to Upper Canada. The first Germans arrived in this settlement in 1812 and were plowboys till a Dorf was founded in the Sand Hills, when they flocked to the work-benches.

Sir Chiozza Money says that we hear much of the German soldier but little of the German spade. The Germans who came here were industrious and thrifty men—kind, yet stern, and good-mannered. Rich men did not emigrate from Germany. Instead of the heavy-pursed it was mostly men with trades. Certain hand-workers had enough means to open a shop; some a few pieces of silver left over; and others who gave the captain of the sailing ship a bond in which they agreed, after reaching an American port, to be sold at auction to a farmer for three or four years and work off the crossing charge.

An example of self-help is afforded by Christian Enslin, a bookbinder from Wuertemberg. He came here in 1834 with all his possessions in a carpet-bag. First he was a laborer; then went from house to house seeking for books to bind. Afterward he opened a bindery and bookstore, and then added conveyancing. He overcame life's hazards, and after the erection of Waterloo County was appointed Clerk of the Surrogate Court.

The hand-workers heeded their native saw: "Drive not thy nail into the air." Their every stroke was aimed at securing a good home. At first they lived in log or roughtcast dwellings, but generally ended their days in a neat brick home. Where other Canadians set out shade trees, they planted fruit trees; where others placed shrubs, they raised vegetables; and while others played games, they tilled their gardens.

Men and women alike were even-tempered and jolly. A parent in giving his son a lesson in good behaviour asked him to read I Corinthians, XIII, and for "charity" substitute "tact."

To oblige a friend they would go far out of their way, and for them the tie of blood was not to be broken. Moreover, they were loyal to their employer and said, "Wes Brod ich 'ess, des Lied ich sing." As wage-earners they preferred to discuss difficulties with their employer rather than with a foreman.

At a public meeting, the more frankly a speaker expressed his views the more highly he was esteemed. Other salient points were their love of music, of poetry, and of order.

Life in a Canadian-German Household

Work was their "open sesame" to advancement. In the spring Heinrich rose at daybreak and spaded his garden until breakfast-time; worked all day at the bench, and hummed a tune as he labored; and after supper digged till dark. Gretchen and the children planted the carrot, potato, and cabbage patches. Along the edges of the beds she grew violets, sweetpeas, and sweetwilliams; while morning-glory vines were trained up the kitchen porch. She did not cut her flowers. Whenever she had a fine bloom she invited her guests to view it in the garden. In her home the red geranium was a favorite flower.

The family raised a flock of chickens and geese. For a special dinner a goose was their choice. Besides they kept a cow and four or five pigs. The grunters were fed on peameal and kitchen offal. Butchering-day was an annual event. The porkers yielded hams, bacon, sausage-meats, and lard. After the last link of sausage was encased the family sat down to a meal called the "Metzelsuppe,"—sausage-soup. Next in importance was sauerkraut day, when cabbage was converted into Kraut. A familiar saying is: "Sauerkraut und Speck macht die alten Weiber Fett."

In Europe their ancestors invented soap. In local households, therefore, soap-making was a distinguishing custom.

The Hausfrau

To gain a competence in a primitive land was a difficult thing. A grandfather, however, was greatly assisted by his bonny wife. As she patted about her kitchen her "Kinder, spart," was heard as often as "Children, now be very good." A grandmother declared that her happiest days were when she performed her household tasks with a baby nestling in her arm, while on either side of her a little one pulled her skirt.

A century ago the Hausfrau wore a blue dress with white spots, and a headkerchief of red cloth with white spots. Before the weaver came in, she made rag mats for every room and slippers out of old garments for her husband and children. Grandmothers joined forces to make bed quilts. As they stitched up a bed-spread they exchanged news of their children, husbands, and homes; spoke of the latest newcomers; dwelt on the hat worn by the Scotch doctor's wife; the prices of store-goods; and the progress of a village courtship. At an appropriate hour the hostess, amid jokes and laughter, served Kaffee and appetizing Kaffeekuchen and Spritz-kuchen. The assisting wives then scattered to their own firesides. Subsequently gatherings of women for social purposes were called "Kaffeeklatches."

Quilts, however, were not the only things a deft grandmother made. She spun wool and flax (the latter for summerwear), and cut and sewed clothing for husband, children, and herself; made Rye-Brod, Koch-Kaese, and other kinds of cheese. In the summer she prepared a punch of vinegar, sugar, and water; and in the fall, with her husband's help, put up a cask of cider and a keg of wine. The wine was kept for christenings, weddings, and Fest days. Before a brewery was built in the Sand Hills, householders brewed their own beer.

Christmas Day and Music

In Europe their ancestors were the first to introduce gift-giving at Christmas. Here the Canadian-Germans continued the custom, including a well-laden Tannenbaum (Christmas tree). The Pennsylvania-Dutch did not give gifts at Christmas time, while their Scottish neighbors observed New Year's day, each with something new to wear.

Easter was the next German Fest, when the Haas (rabbit) brought in multi-colored eggs for the children. Both Easter Sunday and Christmas day were religious festivals. The day after Christmas and Easter Monday were set aside as holidays.

German citizens are credited with the introduction of classical music into America. Of those who settled here, a number brought in a fiddle or a flute. Vocal music, however, prevailed over instrumental until the melodeon and organ were procurable in the United States. A feature of early times, after hundreds of additional German families had come in, was the Gesangverein (singing society) of male voices. There was music too in every home, whilst lads took mouth-organs to school and played correctly the melodies their father had taught them. Music has played an important part in their life.

The city, however, mainly owes its rank to its manufacturers. In 1929 it stood fifth among Canadian cities, employed 8,374 operators, and produced wares valued at $50,315,000.

Lord Lorne, a Governor-General of 1879, said of the German colony: "Your economy and industry are worth to Canada many thousands of square miles of territory."

A VILLAGE IN THE MAKING

In the early eighteen-twenties the Sand Hills had a saw-mill, smithy, and an inn. It was the age of tools and the hand-worker; of Fettlichts and bewhiskered men in jackboots. Soon after Jacob Sauer built the first frame house; John Roat opened the first saddlery and Simon Bowman the first carpenter shop, where the Woolworth block now stands. A. R. Sherk, of Victoria, B.C., says that his father, when a boy of thirteen, was sent here with an ox-team (oxen and wagon), on Easter Monday of 1830, to get a bed-stead at big Simon Bowman's shop.

Up to now the settlers had traded at Dundas, although Yankee peddlers occasionally made the rounds. In 1830, Bishop Eby sold David and William Millar a store-site in the post-office lane. There the wives exchanged butter, eggs, etc., for dry-goods and groceries. The storekeeper, said the late William Henry, bought his stock in Montreal. On the way down he sold the produce he had taken in, for cash, in the bigger towns along the route. Millar Bros., in 1832, bought the lower corner at King and Frederick Streets (now part of the city hall site) for a larger store. Afterward they sold the store to their brother Frederick, father of the late Alexander Millar, K.C.

Jacob Hailer of Wilferdingen, Grand Duchy of Baden, bought an acre of land at the southeast corner of King and Scott Streets in 1832 from Bishop Ben Eby. A stretch of forest stood on the other side of King Street. Mr. Hailer built a home on his purchase and next a chair and spinning-wheel shop. At first he used a foot-

JACOB HAILER
Manufacturer.

FREDERICK GAUKEL
Hotelman.

RUSH BOTTOM CHAIRS, MADE BY JACOB HAILER, 100 YEARS AGO.
—Courtesy, Wm. H. Breithaupt, C.E.

JACOB Y. SHANTZ
Noted Citizen.

lathe to do his turning. Samples of his chairs and spinning-wheel may be seen in the Waterloo Historical Society's Museum. Mr. Hailer was the grandfather of a prominent city family, and actively engaged in business for more than forty years.

Shortly after the arrival of Mr. Hailer, Frederick Gaukel bought the Varnum tavern site. He was native in Wuertemberg, and first had owned a distillery and farm at Bridgeport. On November 2, 1833, he bought lots that lay from near the Walper House corner up to Ontario Street from Joseph Schneider. Mr. Gaukel bought also a block of land on the north side of King Street, between Queen and Ontario Streets, from Bishop Eby, and a small triangle on the corner of King and Ontario Streets, to complete the block, from Joseph Schneider.

Bishop Eby, accompanied by Joseph Schneider, named the Dorf, Berlin. The date is uncertain, but Mr. Hailer's deed of May, 1833, describes his acre as being in Waterloo Township; whilst Mr. Gaukel's deed of November 2, 1833, says his purchase lay in Berlin. The assumption is that the place was named Berlin in the summer of 1833.

Mr. Gaukel built a large frame hotel near the Walper House corner in 1835. It had stables in the rear and a driving-shed on the

Shantz Sawmill.

Bank of Montreal corner. At Gaukel's, a meal was sold for fifteen cents and a glass of beer for three cents. There the householders of Berlin and the township paid their taxes, and there they nominated candidates for the Wellington District Council.

Afterward Mr. Gaukel bought additional lands in West King Street, up to Gaukel Street, which was named for him. He bought also a strip in Schneider's Road, bordering the Walper corner, from Joseph E. Schneider; and lands in East Weber Street, including the courthouse site.

Jacob Shantz built a saw-mill in the mid-thirties on Shantz's Creek, a feeder of Schneider's Creek, in the South Ward. The mill and homestead passed to his son, Jacob Y. Shantz, who bought more lands for their timber and became the leading building-contractor in Berlin.

On account of their superior water-powers, both Bridgeport and Waterloo had more shops and mills than Berlin. It was fancied that Bridgeport would become the largest of the three places and that Berlin would always be the little sister.

Another School

Another school was opened in 1833 on the firehall lot in Frederick Street. There were no spring nor fall classes. A Mr. Grauel taught the "three R's" there for two winters. Alfred Hopkins was the teacher in 1836-7. In 1838 the combined attendance at the two schools was fifty-five pupils, and the value of the school properties, $400. (1)

In Upper Canada teachers were then hard to get, and the schools overcrowded. Everywhere the plea was heard that girls as well as boys should have a chance to go to school. The Government bought the textbooks for all the Common Schools in the Province. In 1832-3-4, the Assembly scattered 360 dozen New Testaments, 360 dozen Mavor's Spelling Books, 322 dozen Reading Made Easy, and 24 dozen English Readers. The average cost of the books per annum was slightly more than $600. Besides, every teacher was paid £8-4s-11½d every six months. (2)

In Berlin, four congregations joined resources in 1840 and built a frame church on the Frederick Street firehall lot. Afterward the "Free Church," as it was called, was changed into a schoolhouse.

The Wellington Institute

John Frederick Augustus Sykes Fayette, an educated mulatto, opened a secondary school here in 1840. It was housed in a building in the rear of the Royal Exchange hotel in East King Street, and named, "The Wellington Institute." Mr. Fayette was the first person to teach grammar here and to display a map. Among his students were Israel D. Bowman and Jacob Y. Shantz. Although Mr. Fayette's rates for tuition were moderate, the institute did not attract enough young folk to make ends meet. He ran into debt and after a year or two left for parts unknown. (1)

How More German Families Were Brought In

At that stage there was a further influx of German handworkers. In the main they came from Hesse, with sprinklings from Baden, Saxony, Mecklenburg, and other States. Woodworkers predominated. The Dorf however boasted a weaver, wagonmaker, hatmaker, a tailor (John Nahrgang), two shoemakers, and several carpenters, while Anselm Wagner, potter, made shilling crocks and flowerpots for the Hausfrau. A Dr. Klinkert was the first doctor.

The late Jacob Stroh of Waterloo told how one German family brought in another. John Nahrgang, for example, wrote to his friend, Yost Stroh, of Lehrbach, Hesse-Darmstadt, a small landowner and wagonmaker, urging him to come over, saying that good land could be bought at a low price. Yost Stroh reflected that his sons would soon be of age and require to serve seven years in the army; scratched his head when he thought of the seven or eight kinds of taxes he had to pay, including a head tax and a church tax; and winced when he remembered that the authorities took every tenth sheaf of grain he grew. So he resolved on emigrating.

Mr. and Mrs. Stroh and their sons John, Conrad, Henry and Yost, Jr., after a Grüsz Gott from relatives, set out on a sailing ship in 1837. The perilous seas tossed them hither and yon for twelve weeks before they reached New York. There they boarded a steamer for Albany; rode to Oswego in a train that ran on wooden rails faced with iron; at Oswego embarked in a ship they thought was bound for Hamilton but which landed them in Toronto; returned by boat to Hamilton, and hired a Negro to drive them up to Preston; then had a Mr. Guggisburg bring them up to Berlin in a wagon. When the party stepped inside John Nahrgang's door their

— 39 —

combined capital was nine cents. Work however was plentiful and the family soon became householders. Later on John bought a farm at Lexington for eight dollars an acre, and Conrad one at West Montrose for $2.50 an acre. Henry and Yost Jr. were apprenticed to shoemakers. Afterward Henry opened a shop in Schneider's Road where the Seiler and Saddler blocks now are. Henry married Frederick Gaukel's daughter Susannah, and Mr. Jacob Stroh was one of their sons.

The First Newspaper

The community was ambitious and desired to procure a newspaper and have church books printed in their mother tongue. Accordingly Jacob Erb, Joseph Schneider, Benjamin Eby, Jacob Shantz, Frederick Gaukel, Henry B. Bowman, John Brubacher, Samuel Bricker, and others advanced the necessary capital for five years, without interest, to Heinrich W. Peterson. Mr. Peterson was a printer and unordained preacher who had come here about 1832, to minister to members of the Lutheran faith. He built a printing-office on the southeast corner of King and Scott Streets, and bought a press in Philadelphia, which was hauled to Berlin with a yoke of oxen. His nephew, young Andrew Jackson Peterson, helped him to set the type and print the German weekly. It was named *The Canada Museum* and made its bow on August 27, 1835.

Other Gains and Incidents

Dr. John Scott, a Scottish surgeon, opened an office below Mr. Hailer's turnery in 1835. The doctor's house was on the library lot.

Henry B. Bowman, grandfather of the late Herbert J. Bowman, opened another store two doors below the *Museum* office, with John Hoffman as a partner. Mr. Hoffman had previously opened a carpenter shop at 206 East King Street. The hamlet then had twenty-five houses. He and his brother Jacob built fifty more. During the winter they made cabinet pieces to order. As merchants Bowman & Hoffman, among other things, exchanged merchandise for bed-feathers and rags. Rags were then as good as money. Soon afterward Mr. Hoffman contracted the "Ohio fever" and removed to that State. Mr. Bowman continued the store business. In 1839 he built a tavern, the "Golden Swan," on the cityhall site. Subsequently a temperance lecturer delivered an address, whereupon Mr. Bowman tossed his stock of liquors into the street.

As will be seen later Berlin obtained a partial postal service in 1837.

There were no butchers in the hamlet. Instead a farmer advertised that on a certain day he would bring in a carcass of beef to Gaukel's and requested those who wished to buy a piece to be at hand at six o'clock in the morning.

Volunteers cleaned and mended the streets. Villagers turned out at four o'clock in the afternoon, or sent a substitute, and repaired the roads from village pride.

Wild animals were then an evil. In September, 1837, the Berliners were bidden to arm themselves and meet at O'Lone's schoolhouse, Centreville, to engage in a general wolf-hunt. (3)

The women of Berlin dressed in the mode of the Pennsylvania-Dutch wives, and Waterloo Fraus followed the German or Holland styles. In the early eighteen-forties there were only three German girls of marriageable age in the village. Hence young Germans went over to Buffalo, N.Y., to seek for helpmeets.

The German families did not segregate themselves. By all accounts they were a friendly company and welcomed everyone who could contribute to Berlin's advancement. There was an affinity between the German and the Scot. On account of the language difficulty the Canadian-Germans looked to their English neighbors for leadership in public affairs.

Early Government

A century ago the Family Compact was in the saddle in Upper Canada. A writer thus summed it up,

> By a long succession of encroachments upon the public rights, they reduced the liberty of the people to a mere phrase; favoritism toward the chosen ones; oppression of those without the fold of personal or political kinship; the bestowal of enormous tracts of valuable land upon party henchmen . . . . distinguished and finally extinguished the party consucting the government. (4)

The German residents of Waterloo Township were less demonstrative than the Scottish settlers in Dumfries Township. Yet they contemned the government's harsh methods. Before 1830 few of them voted. When they did they supported Reform candidates. At first they voted in Dundas, where a poll was kept open for a week, and open voting was in vogue. When the officials saw that Waterloo Township electors supported Reform nominees they tried to hinder them from voting. Grey-haired Mennonites were ordered to swear that they were twenty-one years old. As they declined to make oath they were not permitted to vote. Persons from Germany could not vote until they had been naturalized after seven years' residence in Upper Canada and had become property-owners. When these appeared at the poll the officials sent them home to fetch their deeds and prove they were eligible to vote. Many did not return to the poll.

As we know the Family Compact's misrule stirred up the Rebellion in 1837, and that William Lyon Mackenzie was the leader. After the clash of arms at Montgomery's tavern, near Toronto, he fled to Buffalo, N.Y., via Bridgeport. The late Allen Huber asserted,

> A large reward was offered for his capture, alive or dead, and Dr. Scott of Berlin and J. U. Tyson of Bridgeport watched to seize Mackenzie. My grandfather, Jacob S. Shoemaker, a miller and Reformer at Bridgeport, sent out scouts to warn Mackenzie. He was taken across the Grand River and guided to the Bush Inn near Doon. From there he reached Buffalo in safety. Jacob Shoemaker often rode over to Buffalo to consult with his leader. When local sympathizers wished to send Mackenzie a message, my grandfather placed the letter under his saddlecloth. Thus when searched at Hamilton or elsewhere nothing incriminating was found on his person.

SOURCES

1. *School History of Waterloo County.* 1914. By Inspector Thomas Pearce. Historical Society Annual.

2. *Appendix to the Journal of the House of Assembly.* Printed in 1835, by William Lyon Mackenzie, and now owned by Mr. Percy Ghent, Toronto.

3. Items from the *Canada Museum.*

4. *Historical Sketch of Waterloo County.* 1881. By D. Mac-Donald, C.E., Toronto.

THE EVANGELICAL LUTHERAN ST. PAUL'S CHURCH

Within ten years Berlin obtained four more churches. One of these was founded by Pastor F. W. Bindemann of Coethan, Prussia. After serving in the army, he studied Theology and was sent to Hanover, Pa., as a Reformed Church missionary. He came here in 1834 and built a home in the Greenbush, opposite the Collegiate. While he was affable and honest, his teachings were of a rational-

REV. F. W. BINDEMANN
—Courtesy, Rev. C. S. Roberts.

THE REV. A. ORZEN
Pastor, St. Paul's Church.

THE EVANGELICAL LUTHERAN ST. PAUL'S CHURCH

ST. PAUL'S CHURCH CHOIR

Front Row—Left to Right: I. Bacher, T. Schaus, M. Popplow, R. Seibert, M. Herz, R. Weis, M. Hahn, S. Rockel, Mrs. A. Rudolph. Second Row: E. V. Merkel, Choir Leader, Mrs. E. Ruehl, O. Ronnenberg, E. Schendel, Mrs. A. Seibert, Mrs. M. Lembke, A. Merklinger, H. Lippert, M. Kennedy. Third Row: O. Bell, L. Sokolack, R. Sokolack, C. Albrecht, A. Rudolph, J. Ruehl, H. Lembke, M. Glossop, a. W. Stamm

istic order. He organized a half-dozen congregations, including Berlin (1835), Waterloo (1837), and Preston, and ruled them like a bishopric. The Berlin body was called, "The German Protestant Evangelical Church."

Pastor Bindemann kept his cluster of churches together until a further freshet of immigration set in. More Lutherans came in and wanted Lutheran ministers. Preston broke off in 1838 and Waterloo in 1841. Berlin, however, was his citadel until his death. The local congregation erected a frame church in South Queen Street in 1835 and replaced it with a fair-sized brick church in 1864. During his pastorate, the Rev. Bindemann is said to have united 2,000 couples in marriage, numbers of whom were young Mennonites, who were not yet church members.

He rode from place to place on a white horse and often cantered over to Bridgeport. At Bridgeport there was a merchant named Tagge who had just been made a magistrate and who was puffed up. One afternoon, on seeing Mr. Bindemann riding in, he said to several customers at his store-door, "Stay, and we'll have some fun with the preacher." When the rider reached the store, Tagge droned, "How is it, Pastor, that you must have a grand white horse when our Saviour was content to ride about on a humble ass?" The riposte came forth, "We can't do that any more, for all the asses have been made magistrates."

Pastor Bindemann died in 1865 and was buried in the First Mennonite Church cemetery. Of him the Rev. John Schmieder wrote in 1929,

> Though his body has long since become dust and ashes, Bindemann is still a name to conjure with. and his romantic figure is remembered today even by those who never saw him face to face. The legendary white horse and its rider, wrapped round with a great shawl against the elements, still haunts the memory of Berlin's aged citizens; and his words are even now repeated by their children; while his influence is still potent in all the territory he traversed.

The Course Since Followed

After Mr. Bindemann's death the congregation engaged the Rev. Wm. Helfer. He proved unfaithful to his trust, both in connection with his teachings and mode of living. The congregation then advertised in a Buffalo newspaper for a Lutheran minister, and as a result the Rev. P. H. Leutsinger was appointed pastor.

He preached repentance and urged his hearers to live the good life, but rejected the Lutheran tenet of confirmation and other doctrines. His course convinced the congregation that he wished to lead them into the Presbyterian fold. Hence, in 1867, they relieved him of the charge, and determined to secure a bona-fide Lutheran minister.

At Elmira, Ontario, there was then stationed a member of the Missouri Synod, the Rev. A. Ernst. A delegation was sent up to interview him and obtain his advice. Pastor Ernst told them that the Missouri Synod was experiencing difficulty in supplying the existing charges in Canada. The delegates stayed over for the succeeding Sunday services and heard him preach a sermon. Edified by his discourse, they invited him to come to Berlin and deliver a scriptural lesson. Pastor Ernst answered that he could not accept with a clear conscience, but would consult his congregation and if they raised no objection he would accede to the request. He came to the Berlin church on October 13, 1867, and after the sermon gave the congregation a synopsis of the principles adopted by the Missouri Synod. Forthwith the congregation decided to subscribe to the Lutheran confession of faith, and pressed him to become their pastor.

Pastor Ernst obtained the assent of his Elmira congregation and accepted the call to Berlin on November 3, 1867. He drew up a constitution in 1869 and it was adopted by the members. On Whitsunday in the year following the Missouri Synodical hymnbook was introduced into the church for the first time. Pastor Ernst's labors in the vineyard were fruitful. In August, 1871, the congregation sent a delegation to the Eastern Conference which convened in Buffalo, N.Y., and applied for admission to the Missouri Synod as a member church. The application was accepted. Soon afterward the congregation cast off the old church name and chose the present appellation: "The Evangelical Lutheran St. Paul's Church."

The Rev. Mr. Ernst served St. Paul's Church for thirteen years. During his pastorate the church witnessed a steady increase of members. He was succeeded by the Rev. Mr. Andres of Haverstraw, N.Y., in 1880, and accepted a call to a church in South Euclid, Ohio. The Rev. Andres was inducted on the thirteenth Sunday after Trinity by the Rev. Mr. Froesch of Elmira. Under Pastor Andres

ZION EVANGELICAL CHURCH

THE. REV. C. A. HIRSCHMAN
Pastor.

SECOND
ZION EVANGELICAL
CHURCH

FIRST
ZION EVANGELICAL
CHURCH

THE REV. S. R. KNECHTEL
A Former Pastor.

THE REV. J. P. HAUCH
A Former Pastor.

the congregation built a Sunday School and in 1889 erected the present church. He ministered to the congregation until 1894, when he removed from Berlin to a town in Michigan.

After an interval of two years the Rev. W. Boese of Lake Road, N.Y., was appointed pastor of the church. He faithfully discharged both his ministerial and civic duties. For years he was active in behalf of the Children's Aid Society and its chairman; and for a period was president of the Ontario Division of the Missouri Synod. Meanwhile his own church flourished under its leadership, but on January 1, 1922, while driving to Linwood to conduct a service, he suddenly deceased.

Pastor Boese was succeeded by the Rev. A. Orzen of Ottawa, Canada, in May, 1922. Under this earnest clergyman St. Paul's Church has increased its membership and influence.

For a century it has been well served by its successive church choirs. The Sunday-School teachers and various congregational societies have likewise contributed materially to church growth. Among the organizations are the Ladies' Aid Society and the Men's Club.

SOURCE

Extracts from the church records supplied by the Rev. Mr. Orzen.

ZION EVANGELICAL CHURCH

Zion Evangelical Church is a member of the international body known as "The Evangelical Church." The denomination was founded in 1800 in Pennsylvania by Jacob Albright. Someone in Waterloo Township heard of his work among the Germans and wrote to him in 1816, saying, "Our Germans are like sheep without a shepherd." The Rev. J. Driesbach came over and afterward recommended that a missionary be sent here. But the Association was not then able to open a mission in Canada.

Time passed, and a Berlin family removed to Ohio. There they attended an Evangelical camp-meeting. Later on they wrote to friends in Berlin about it, and sent them copies of the *Christliche Botschafter*. John Hoffman and Henry Hiestand then went over to learn more. After their return, an appeal was made for a missionary. The Rev. Carl Hammer came here in 1836 and preached to appreciative gatherings. He came over again in 1837 and brought the Rev. Mr. Dellinger with him. In May, 1837, the Rev. Joseph Harlacher reached the Dorf and preached nine times. The Rev. Joseph Riegel followed him, but the Rebellion of 1837 in Upper Canada halted their labors.

Nevertheless the seed sown by them sprouted. A Sunday School was started in Jacob Hailer's spinning-wheel shop in 1837 and fully organized in 1839. The leaders were: Jacob Hailer, John Hoffman, Jacob Sauer, Henry Hiestand and H. W. Peterson.

A Significant Camp-Meeting

Meantime the Rev. Christian Holl had held services in 1838. He came again in 1839 and opened missions at Black Rock, Chippawa, and Berlin. The local field was called the Waterloo Mission. In 1839 a camp-meeting was held in David Eby's grove, near Waterloo village, and was attended by between 600 and 800 persons. Six ministers, including Bishop Seybert, were present. The bishop's salary was forty-three dollars a year, and he rode 390 miles on horseback to preside at the services. There were 26 converts.

The converts were formed into two classes—the Waterloo and Lexington Class and the Berlin Class. John Hoffman was appointed leader of the Berlin Class, and Adam Ruby, exhorter. At first services were held in the Common School on the firehall lot, but objections were made and the school closed against them. Then they met in John Hoffman's carpenter shop.

The Rev. Joseph Harlacher of Buffalo, N.Y., came over in 1840 and headed the Mission. He founded also missions in Wilmot Township and Puslinch Township. During his term the Berlin Class built a frame chapel in South Queen Street, at the foot of Church Street, which was dedicated on September 25, 1841, by the Rev. Carl Hummel of Buffalo, N.Y. Within a month after the dedication, a band of rowdies burned the Rev. Harlacher's effigy in King Street for preaching down intemperance. Afterward a number of them were converted and two of them entered the ministry.

The Berlin Church thrived on opposition. Before the end of 1841, appointments were opened at New Hamburg, Sebringville, Tavistock, Morriston, Blenheim, Hespeler, St. Jacobs, Upper Woolwich, and Koenigsbusch. Thus Berlin became the heart of the Evangelical Church. To circulate the Gospel, the leaders held services in homes, barns, groves, schools, and even on the roadside.

The first Quarterly Conference was held in Berlin on November 13, 1841. William Schmidt was then appointed preacher. His was the first license issued by the Association in Canada.

In 1842 the Waterloo Mission was made a Circuit, with the Rev. M. Eis in charge of it. The circuit was attached to the East Pennsylvania Conference until 1848, when it became a member of the New York Conference. In 1852 the New York Conference convened in Berlin. The Rev. J. Wagner was appointed Preacher-in-Charge and the Rev. J. G. Staebler assistant Pastor; while the Rev. William Schmidt became Presiding Elder.

The Second Church

Members in Waterloo attended the Berlin Church until 1850, when they built a church of their own. In 1865 the newly-formed Canada Conference met in the Berlin Church. The congregation sold their first church building in 1866. It was moved to Elgin Street and is still in use as a dwelling. On the Queen Street site, a spacious brick church was built and dedicated by Bishop J. J. Escher. The Church then had eighty-three communicants and the Sunday School, eighty-two scholars. In 1867, the Circuit was raised to a Station.

The Rev. J. J. Kliphardt formed a Ladies' Aid Society in 1879; the Rev. J. P. Hauch organized a Young People's Alliance in 1890; and the Rev. J. G. Litt a Junior Alliance in 1892.

Zion Evangelical Church

In the interim, the second church had become too small. During Mr. Litt's term of office, the trustees bought a site (1893) in West Weber Street for a larger edifice. The second church property was purchased by John S. Anthes and Jacob Kaufman. In building the new church, the carpenter-contract was awarded to Jacob Kaufman and the mason-contract to George Schlee by the Building Committee. Chairs for the altar, choir-loft and Sunday School were made by Daniel Hibner, and the altar and pulpit furniture by John S. Anthes.

The ground plan of the present church is in the form of a Maltese cross, with dimensions of 82 x 94 feet. It is of Gothic style and has two towers facing Weber Street. The left one ends just above the roof, while the right tower rises 104 feet, forming a landmark. Auditorium and gallery comfortably seat 800 people. Behind the pulpit is a second gallery that seats fifty choristers. The large basement was used as a Sunday School. Five stained-glass windows commemorate early pillars of the church. The big bell was the gifts of Mrs. A. B. Augustine, then of Racine, Wisc.

As the new church neared completion, the Rev. J. P. Hauch succeeded Rev. Mr. Litt. The dedicatory services were held on June 15, 16 and 17, 1894, when Bishop Escher, who dedicated the second church, and Bishop Thomas Bowman shared in the direction of the ceremonies. The new edifice was named, "Zion Evangelical Church." The Rev. J. G. Litt preached the first sermon in the church.

Advancements Since 1894

The Rev. S. R. Knechtel was appointed Pastor in 1895. In that year L. J. Breithaupt was the lay delegate to the General Conference in Elgin, Ill. During the Rev. Mr. Knechtel's pastorate, Mrs. Catharine Breithaupt presented the church with a fine pipe-organ in memory of her son, E. Carl Breithaupt.

The Rev. A. Y. Haist followed Mr. Knechtel. In 1899 the congregation celebrated the sixtieth anniversary of the Sunday School. Three scholars who had attended the school in 1839 were present: Mrs. C. Breithaupt, Mrs. M. Bean, and A. J. Peterson.

In 1903, while the Rev. L. H. Wagner was Pastor, the first General Conference of the Evangelical Church, in Canada, was held in Zion Church. Exotic delegates came from the United States, Europe and Japan. The delegates were welcomed by the Hon. G. W. Ross, Premier of Ontario.

A "Men's New Movement" was founded in 1906, while the Rev. G. D. Domm was the minister. In 1907, L. J. Breithaupt was lay delegate to a General Conference in Milwaukee, Wisc. The Rev. S. M. Hauch succeeded Mr. Domm in 1911. In that year John C. Breithaupt was lay delegate at a General Conference held in Cleveland, O. The Rev. Mr. Hauch, on account of sickness, resigned in 1912 and was succeeded by the Rev. M. L. Wing. In 1913 a group of members bought the John Moffatt property near the church for $7,500 as a future parsonage. J. E. Bilger, superintendent of the Sunday School, petitioned the Quarterly Conference here for a separate Sunday School building, while A. A. Voelker recommended

ZION CHURCH CHOIR

Reading left to right.—Front row: Mrs. A. Koehler, Miss M. Hagedorn, Miss K. Hessenaur, Mrs. L. Shantz, Mrs. I. Ernst, Miss H. Christner, Miss R. Myers, Miss M. Roehr. Second row: Miss H. Snyder, Mrs. A. Bender, Miss F. Capling, Mrs. G. Capling, Miss H. Schmidt, Miss R. Sitler, Miss D. Reiber, Miss F. Pfeffer, Miss M. Werner. Third row: Miss M. Wettlaufer, Miss G. Wendt, Mrs. E. Fahrner, Mrs. E. Hamel, Miss R. Sweitzer, Miss K. Kruspe, Mr. R. Hahn, Mr. D. Vetter, Mr. L. Pflug, Mr. F. Dancey. Fourth row: Mr. L. Shiry, Mr. G. Capling, Mr. F. Capling, Mr. L. Wambold, Mr. P. Ricketts, Mr. O. Hagedorn, Mr. A. Bender, Mr. P. Bender, Mr. G. Kruspe.

TRINITY UNITED CHURCH

THE REV. CLARKE LOGAN
Pastor, Trinity United Church.

THE REV. W. J. ZIMMERMAN
Pastor, Olivet Evangelical Church.

THE REV. G. F. BARTHEL
Pastor, Calvary Memorial Church.

more English preaching, which was provided for. The Rev. W. O. Ruby was chosen assistant pastor in 1914. By then the church membership had mounted to 740 and that of the Sunday School to 530.

The Rev. J. P. Hauch returned from Japan in 1913, where for fourteen years he had labored as a missionary. Sickness obliged him to retire from the field. Throughout his sojourn in the Land of the Rising Sun, Mrs. Hauch stood at his side and proved to be a true helpmate. Mr. Hauch was reappointed pastor of Zion Church in 1915 and served them till 1923. During those years, an Intermediate Young People's Alliance was formed and a model Sunday School built in the rear of and attached to the church. Like the main edifice, it conforms to the Gothic style, and has twenty-three separate class rooms. The capacity of this new addition is about 1,200 persons. This building was dedicated April 2nd, 1916, by Bishop S. C. Breyfogel and cost complete $24,000.

In 1915, Jacob Kaufman was a lay delegate to the General Conference in Los Angeles, Cal. John C. Breithaupt was appointed lay delegate to the General Conference in Cedar Falls, Iowa, in 1919; to the one held in Detroit, Mich., in 1922; to Williamsport, Pa., in 1926; to Milwaukee, Wisc., in 1930; and to the General Conference in Akron, Ohio, in 1934.

Prior to his death, Jacob Kaufman had intimated his willingness to subscribe and pay for one-half of the first mission church to be erected in Kitchener. This promise his family carried out. Thus was formed the nucleus of the Calvary Evangelical Memorial Church in Park Street. Shortly afterwards his wife, Mrs. Mary Kaufman, donated the fine pipe organ in memory of her husband. Since that time a second mission church has been erected, "The Olivet Evangelical Church, in Onward Avenue. The Rev. S. R. Knechtel had charge of the Olivet congregation when they were a Mission. In 1937, the Rev. W. J. Zimmerman was pastor of the Olivet Church; the Rev. George Barthel of Calvary Church; and the Reverends C. A. Hirschman and E. E. Hallman of Zion Church.

A fitting service marking the 100th Anniversary of the beginning of Sunday School work in the Evangelical Church in Canada was held in Zion Evangelical Church Sunday School Auditorium, Sunday, September 26th, 1937.

Mr. J. E. Bilger, General Superintendent of the School for a period of twenty-five years, was in charge. The guest speaker for the occasion was Bishop G. E. Epp, D.D., Bishop of the Central Area of the Church and of the Canada Conference. Other speakers were Mrs. Mary Kaufman, one of the oldest members of the School, who gave reminiscences from her experiences of 80 years as a member of the Sunday School, and Mr. A. L. Breithaupt, one of the past Superintendents of the School, who gave a brief sketch of the history and development of the Sunday School in Zion Church.

Suitable recognition was given the oldest and youngest scholars of the school, they being respectively Mrs. George Steinmetz and Robert W. Breithaupt. Note was also taken of the fact that a number of descendants of Jacob Hailer, in whose shop the Sunday School had originally started, were still active in Zion Sunday School. Among them was Mr. A. L. Breithaupt, a grandson, and one of the speakers of the day, Mrs. A. F. Bauman, a grand-daughter who was honored for her long years of service as a teacher, and Robert W. Breithaupt, a great, great grandson, the youngest member of the school.

Source

The Zion Evangelical Church. 1925. In manuscript. By the Rev. J. P. Hauch.

TRINITY UNITED CHURCH

A Wesleyan Methodist Mission was opened in Berlin in 1841 as a charge of the Guelph Circuit. There was then no highway between the two villages. The missionaries, mounted on horseback, followed trails through the forests. On the journey they may have glimpsed wild animals and seen Indians hunting game. The preachers were called circuit riders.

The Berlin Mission was served by the superintendents of the Guelph Circuit. Among the Gospel riders were: the Reverends Stephen Brownell, Thomas Cosford, John Braddin, Charles Fish, James Spencer, George Goodson, and Lewis Werner—men renowned in early Methodism in Upper Canada. In turn they came over every fortnight and held services in homes and other buildings. Since there were few English-speaking people here, at first progress was slow-paced.

Later on the Berlin group bought a plot of land at the corner of Church and Benton Streets—amply large for a chapel and cemetery. The knot then drew on their slender resources and built a frame church capable of seating 120 persons, which allowed for growth. Some of the supporters objected against the undertaking and stayed away from church. Yet at the darkest hour there was a cluster who remained steadfast. These were obliged to go to the money-lenders, who salted them eight and ten percent for the sums borrowed. When a stand is taken for principle's sake, it is a peculiarity in human affairs that if one drops out one or two others take his place. So it was with the newfledged Methodist Church. Soon the seats were more nearly all filled.

In 1854 Berlin was made the focus of a circuit. The appointments included Berlin, Waterloo (whose members worshipped in Berlin), Breslau, Linwood, Elmira, and Winterbourne. The itinerant preachers were: the Reverends John Williams and Richard Pinch, with Andrew Smith as their assistant. By then the saddle-horse had been superceded by the stage-coach and next by the railway train. In 1856 the Berlin and Galt Circuits were amalgamated, but in 1857 were again separated. The Rev. L. O. Rice was head of the Berlin Circuit and had the Rev. Alexander Sutherland as assistant.

The Berlin church then had 114 members. Up to the eighteen-seventies the pastors were: the Reverends C. S. Philip, Sr., C. S. Philip, Jr., David Kennedy, David Chalmers, R. L. Tucker, Elias Frazee, J. Hyndman, J. H. Keppel, Wm. Savage, John Armstrong, G. M. Brown, J. A. Shepley, Thomas Ferguson, John Scott, Isaac Tovell, J. F. Metcalfe, Thomas Stubbs, Wm. Mills, and Jabez Edmunds.

The congregation purchased their first parsonage in 1873—Mr. Burkholder's house in North Water Street—for $1,150. Largely the sum was raised by subscriptions and the balance by selling the old Cornell church in the Preston Road, which had come into their possession. The Church Board then consisted of Thomas Hilliard, Edgar Chrysler, Jacob Stupe, H. Durrant, Matthew Durrant, David Elsley, and John F. McKay.

Until then the Berlin Circuit was a unit of the Canadian Wesleyan Church. The denomination was founded in 1829 by Henry Ryan and James Jackson, formerly of the Canadian Methodist

Episcopal Church. For years groups within the two bodies had labored to bring about a union. That was achieved in 1874, when Berlin became a branch of the fusion. When the union occurred the Rev. C. Cookman was pastor.

The Waterloo members gracefully withdrew in 1875 and formed a congregation of their own. The Berlin church then elected a board of local members: C. L. Peterson, J. B. Fellman, and Dr. G. W. Wright.

The Church Buys the Township Hall

The Methodists were a progresive community and benefitted by a windfall. Sheriff Moses Springer then had the Township Hall in North Queen Street up for sale. The hall was owned by the Ontario Department of Crown Lands, who wished to get rid of it. On meeting Trustee Chrysler the sheriff offered to accept $200 for it if the deal was closed within forty-eight hours. Mr. Chrysler was a clerk in John Fennell's hardware store. He laid the proposal before Mr. Fennell who advised him to buy the property and endorsed a note for the sum. Mr. Chrysler then turned it over to his church. The Church Board expended about $5,000 in alterations and improvements. A basement was constructed and the building veneered with brick. The rehabilitated building was dedicated as a church in 1879.

The pastors during those fruitful years were the Reverends John Scott and R. W. Williams. In 1879, E. P. Clement, a young barrister who helped to make church history, was appointed Secretary-Treasurer, a post which he filled until his elevation to the bench as Judge of Essex County.

In the meantime the Board had sold the original chapel to the United Brethren. The cemetery however was retained until 1876, when it was sold to William Moyer, father of P. E. W. Moyer. In the cemetery were fifteen beech trees. Wm. DeKay removed the dust and ashes to Mount Hope Cemetery, after which the land was sold for building lots.

At Trinity the Rev. Williams was followed by the Rev. W. J. Ford. In 1889 Mr. Ford was succeeded by the Rev. J. W. German. In the preceding decade the membership had doubled. The Rev. German's successor was the Rev. J. E. Howell. In 1891, while he was pastor, a wing on the west side was built on the church at a cost of $5,000.

The next pastor was the Rev. John Scott who served for two years and then went to Japan as a missionary. He was followed here by the Rev. W. C. Henderson. In 1889 the Rev. J. S. Williamson was in charge. During his pastorate a mortgage of $6,000 was lifted and a pipe-organ purchased for $1500. By then the capacity of the church had been exceeded. The Board proposed to exchange properties with St. Peter's Lutheran Church. The Methodists realized that they would have to give something to boot. However the plan was never realized. Yet expansion at Trinity Church soon forced action.

The Rev. D. W. Snider was appointed pastor in 1902. In 1904 the church property was sold to the newly-organized St. Matthew's Church for $7,000 and the Springer properties in Frederick Street acquired for $3,100. Two ancient houses were razed and a handsome red-brick edifice erected on the site. The cornerstone was laid on August 14, 1905, by the Rev. A. Sutherland, with the assistance of Mrs. (Rev.) German and the Rev. Mr. Snider. Aaron Bricker acted as building superintendent. While the church was under construction the congregation held services in the opera house and the Salvation Army barrack. The church was dedicated on June 10, 1906, by the Rev. R. J. Elliott, President of the Hamilton Conference, assisted by the Revs. Antcliff of Galt and Mr. Snider. The completed structure represented an investment of $31,227.

The Rev. Mr. Snider's immediate successors were: the Reverends S. E. Marshall, H. W. Crews, C. L. McIntyre, C. A. Sykes, J. H. McBain, and W. E. Pescott.

A Major Union

While Mr. Pescott was the incumbent a union of the Methodist, Congregational, and Presbyterian denominations of Canada was brought about. In this city, St. Andrew's Presbyterian congregation voted three to two to continue their old connection. However, on June 14, 1925, the pastor, the Rev. G. D. McLellan, and 140 Presbyterians united with Trinity Church.

The pastors at Trinity United Church after the union included the Reverends W. H. Barraclough, G. D. McLellan, and H. F. Dellar. Next the Rev. D. Spence accepted a call. During his pastorate the church and Sunday School were enlarged, at an outlay of $40,000.

The Rev. Clarke Logan became pastor in 1932. In 1936 the Rev. R. C. Nunn was assistant pastor.

The church has a large membership. In its upbuilding, the Sunday School, the Ladies' Aid, the Christian Endeavor Society, and other organizations have been important factors. Trinity Church has an excellent choir. For a number of years it was led by Mrs. A. B. Pollock, and of late years by Professor George Ziegler.

At the General Council of the United Church in Ottawa (1936) the Rev. J. P. Hauch predicted that the Evangelical Church of Canada will eventually be incorporated with the United Church.

Knox United Church

A Joint Committee of Trinity Church and St. Andrew's Church founded Knox United Church in 1925. It was begun as a Sunday School with J. F. Reeve as superintendent, two teachers, and twenty scholars. In the same year the young congregation built their present church at No. 180 South Albert Street. Their first minister was the Rev. C. B. McLennon.

The installation of the present pastor, the Rev. G. H. Thomas, took place on July 1, 1934. Knox United Church has an enrolment of sixty-five members, and is steadily advancing. The Church Board consists of the members that follow: Session, Mrs. M. Brown, Wm. Charlton, V. Cressman, Mrs. C. Davis, E. D. Heist, A. Gottesleben, and Wm. McGeagh. Stewards: N. Brenner, J. F. Reeve, Mrs. J. F. Reeve, R. Thoman, and Mrs. R. Thoman.

The Sunday School has now 150 scholars. Dr. E. D. Heist is superintendent and is assisted by twenty teachers.

(Reviewed by the late Mr. Thomas Hilliard of Waterloo.)

THE CHURCH OF THE GOOD SHEPHERD

Nearly a century ago a group of Swedenborgians assembled in Berlin for services. Among the earliest adherents were: Adam Ruby Sr. and wife; John Jacob Lehnen; Charles A. Ahrens and wife; Henry Rothaermal and wife; John S. Roat and wife; William Benton; and John Walmsley. Included among the non-resident members were: Adam J. Ruby and Peter Knechtel and wife of Mannheim; August Rieby of Wellesley Township; William Knech-

THE CHURCH OF THE GOOD SHEPHERD

Church Council when built: C. W. Hagen, Stanley Shupe, F. H. Schneider, H. Halliwell, R. J. Wright, late Charles A. Ahrens, and the Rev. John W. Spiers.

THE REV. JOHN W. SPIERS
Pastor,
The Church of the Good Shepherd.

THE REV. OTTO C. SCHUETZE
Pastor,
The Evangelical Lutheran Church
of the Holy Trinity.

THE CARMEL CHURCH
Pastor, The Rev. A. Gill.

tel of Hamilton; George Hachborn and wife of Waterloo; Christoph Doering and wife of Philipsburg; Charles Hendry and wife of Conestoga, and others.

Christian Enslin was their leader. He came from Germany to the American continent in 1830 and in 1833 arrived in Berlin. In the summer they held services in Mr. Enslin's orchard in the rear of his bookbindery, which stood near where Dr. J. E. Hett's office now rests. In the winter they met in the bookbindery. That routine was followed for several years.

In 1842 a unique step was taken by four budding congregations. After pooling their resources they built a frame, "Free Church" on the firehall lot in Frederick Street. The only body now remembered as having used the church is the Swedenborgians. However the four denominations utilized it until severally able to build a church for themselves. When the building was finally vacated, the Berliners, who wasted nothing, converted it into a school.

The Swedenborgians received the Rev. John Harbin, a New Church missionary, in 1843. In his early manhood he had been a surgeon in the British army. While practising his profession in Salisbury, England, he joined the Swedenborgian Church and resolved to devote his life to the dissemination of its doctrines. He emigrated to Canada in 1830 and labored as a missionary at Markham, Upper Canada, and in the district lying west and north of Toronto. The Berlin congregation then invited him to become their pastor. He accepted the call in 1844 and held services in the Free Church.

The Rev. Mr. Harbin was the grandfather of the late Charles A. Ruby, a former manager of the Mutual Life Assurance Company of Canada. Mr. Harbin often assisted Dr. John Scott at performing a surgical operation. A friendship ensued and Dr. Scott and wife joined the Swendenborgian Church. Three other prominent men, Henry S. Huber, John Hoffman and William Hendry, (the first manager of the Mutual Life Assurance Company) and their families likewise became members.

By 1847 the seating space afforded by the Free Church had been outgrown. On that account a site for a church, on the northwest corner of Benton and Church Streets, was purchased from Joseph E. Schneider. On it a frame church, capable of seating one hundred and fifty persons, was erected at a cost of $400. It was called the "New Church" to connect it with the prophecy that the Lord on his Second Coming would build a New Church. A Sunday School was also opened. Thereafter the congregation affiliated with the General Convention of the New Church of America.

Greater growth followed in the new church. But in 1851 their esteemed pastor died. After his death the church was served for several years by Adam Ruby, a lay preacher, and by missionaries. The Rev. Thomas Wilks had charge in 1855; the Rev. Thomas Whittaker for part of 1856; and for a short time, the Rev. A. O. Brickman of Baltimore, Md. In June, 1857, the Rev. F. W. Tuerk was engaged as their regular pastor.

Mr. Tuerk was native in Elberfeld, Prussia. As a youth he was prepared for the missionary field in India. After his graduation his parents heard that several missionaries had been put to death by the natives and forbid him to go. Instead he was taught the mechanic's trade in his uncle's foundry. While there his desire to become a missionary was born again. He came to Canada in 1830 and served an office at Sebringville, Upper Canada, until called to Berlin. Here he lived in a neat, white frame house on the site of the York Apartments in South Queen Street.

CHURCH OF NEW JERUSALEM
NOW THE EVANGELICAL LUTHERAN CHURCH OF THE HOLY TRINITY

Under his leadership the membership was enlarged by a growth that caused a need for a bigger church. The building was sold and a lot on the southeast corner of King and Water Streets purchased from the Lawrason estate. There an attractive stone church, with a seating capacity of 250, was erected in 1870—one of the few stone structures in the town. It cost between $8,000 and $10,000. The congregation installed the first pipe-organ ever brought into the city. The temple was named, "The Church of the New Jerusalem."

The Carmel Church

In September, 1888, a day-school was instituted by the society with the Rev. F. E. Waelchli as head-master. This was continued until 1891, at which time the congregation divided, a portion of which moved to West King Street, erecting a building nearly opposite the High School, being under the pastoral charge of the Rev. Waelchli, and known as "The Academy Church." The day-school previously mentioned was continued under the auspices of this body. Subsequently, during the pastorate (1897-98) of the Rev. J. E. Rosenqvist, the name of this congregation was changed to "The Carmel Church."

The Rev. E. J. Stebbing ministered to the society for two years, commencing in October, 1898, and in 1900 the Rev. Mr. Waelchli returned to assume the pastorate for the second time. The Rev. H. L. Odhner succeeded him in 1916, and the Rev. L. W. T. David assumed charge in 1920. The incumbent of the office, the Rev. Alan Gill, has acted since September, 1928.

The Water Street Church

The other part of the congregation continued in the Water Street Church under their veteran pastor. The Rev. Mr. Tuerk served them until his death on July 3, 1901, when in his eighty-first year. He had then been their pastor for forty-four years. (1)

After his death the church engaged the Rev. A. B. Francisco, who served three years. He was followed by the Rev. James Taylor, who was their pastor till April, 1905. The Rev. W. E. Brickman succeeded him in July, 1905, and remained until May, 1908. In February, 1909, the Rev. E. D. Daniels was installed and continued until August, 1916. The Rev. Eric Wethey came in October, 1916, and stayed till May, 1919. From December, 1919, until May, 1920, the Rev. L. Slight was pastor. The Rev. A. Diephius was inducted in May, 1920, and ministered to the growing congregation till September, 1928. Beginning in October, 1928, the Rev. R. Eaton served until 1935. The Rev. R. J. Spiers was appointed pastor in 1935 and is the incumbent. (2)

In 1929 the congregation sold their church property to the T. Eaton Company for a sum said to exceed $100,000. In 1935 they purchased the Wm. Roos residential property, including grounds of 200 x 190 feet, at the corner of Queen Street and Margaret Avenue. On the property a stately, grey-stone edifice has been built, with a parish hall in conjunction, at a cost of $73,000. The edifice was renamed, "The Church of the Good Shepherd."

The Water Street church is now made use of by the Evangelical Lutheran Church of the Holy Trinity, with the Rev. Otto C. Schuetze as pastor.

SOURCES
1. Information supplied by the late Mr. Jacob Stroh.
2. List of clergymen by Secretary R. J. Wright.

GLIMPSES OF THE EIGHTEEN-FORTIES

In the eighteen-forties, Berlin gained divers factories. John Hoffman, for example, returned to the village from Ohio and built a furniture factory on the Bank of Nova Scotia corner. He made also tombstones, and opened a general store east of the factory. At various times, Jacob Sauer, J. G. Wegenast, Mr. Hoffman's son-in-law, Isaac Weaver, and his brother, Jacob Hoffman, were his partners.

In the mid-forties, Mr. Hoffman bought a steam-engine and boiler in Buffalo, N.Y. Those units were hauled over clay roads to Berlin by Isaac Shantz with three span of horses. The steam-engine introduced a new era into the village.

John Hoffman bought also a factory bell in 1845. It called men to labor, volunteers to quench fires, pealed for weddings, tolled for funerals, and called voters to the polls on election day. One night the bell disappeared and could not be found. At last Andrew Borth espied it in an old well on the site of St. Jerome's College, where two workmen had hidden it. Men replaced the bell, and until

JOHN HOFFMAN
Furniture Manufacturer.

VIEW OF FOURTH POST-OFFICE
61 - 63 South Queen Street.

REINHOLD LANG
Founder, R. Lang & Son.

LOUIS BREITHAUPT I.
Founder, The Eagle Tannery.

WILLIAM SIMPSON
Furniture Manufacturer.

EMIL VOGELSANG
First Button Manufacturer.

the 1860's it filled the role of town bell. As a wedding was seen coming along King Street, workmen stretched a rope across the road and halted the party till the bridegroom paid tribute. With the largess, the Robin Hoods made merry in the evening at Gaukel's. William Simpson, furniture manufacturer, gave the ancient bell to the Park Board in 1909.

It will be recalled that John Hoffman and Henry B. Bowman were once joint owners of a general store. When Mr. Hoffman opened another store in opposition to Mr. Bowman, things happened. Mr. Bowman and a Mr. Correll grounded a second furniture factory in East King Street. Since there was only a neighborhood market for furniture, the competition between the two firms was keen.

Henry Bowman helped to establish several other industries. He and a Mr. Frick, for example, built a foundry in South Ontario Street and made sugar-kettles, wagon-bushings, and cast-iron stoves. A number of their stoves were in use here until the end of last century.

Previously John Winger had started a pumpshop in South Ontario Street. His son John succeeded him and built a factory west of the King and Frederick Street corner. One cold winter it was utilized for a school.

George Rebscher built a brewery in Frederick Street in 1840. It was the first lager-beer brewery in Canada. Beer was sold for sixpence a quart, two shillings a gallon, and £1 (four dollars) a barrel. He made vinegar also and sold it at beer prices. Village boys were sent to the brewery for Bierhafe.

In the forties Noah Ziegler built a steam-driven Mobel Schreineri on the southwest corner of King and Albert Streets. He built houses in the summer and made furniture in the winter. Enoch Ziegler came to Berlin in 1847 and manufactured furniture in those premises. A few carpenters likewise made cabinet pieces in the wintertime. Woodworking thus became the principal industry in the village.

The Lang Tanning Company was founded in 1849. Reinhold Lang, the founder, was native in Baden, Germany, like Adam Beck's father. Mr. Lang built a tannery on the northeast corner of King and Ontario Streets, where now H. W. Shoemaker's drugstore stands. He made all classes of leather required by saddlers and shoemakers. His sons George, William, John and August followed in their father's footsteps, and his grandsons, Louis L., Reinhold, Jerome and George W., direct the large industry.

General Advances

H. W. Peterson was appointed Registrar of the Wellington District in 1840. He sold the *Canada Museum* to Henry Eby, son of Bishop Eby. The new proprietor renamed the weekly the *Deutsches Canadier* and built a printing-office near the corner of King and South Eby Streets. In 1841 he bought the subscription list of the *Waterloo Morgenstern*, a German weekly that had been founded by Benjamin Burkholder a few months before the *Canada Museum*.

Berlin boys hunted in the woods and fished the streams. Samuel Moxley warned them against trespassing on his lands, especially on Sunday. Their Sabbath roaming possibly led to a Sunday School being opened in Ben Eby's church in 1841. Boys of sixteen and upward, unless exempted by law, were compelled to meet every year at Centreville for military drill. If a lad failed to report he was hailed before a magistrate and fined.

A branch of the Upper Canada Bible Society was opened in 1841.

The Climate

Men of the forties said, "A right winter makes a right summer." A certain householder as he stood in his doorway in the morning, whether wet or dry, hot or cold, always remarked, "This just suits me." One late season a storekeeper asked a farmer whether he thought spring would ever come. The farmer answered, "'It alvays hes."

The End of the World

The *Deutsches Canadier* said early in 1844: "Inasmuch as the end of the world is to come on the 22nd of March, according to Miller's prophecy, we respectfully request all our readers who are in arrears with their subscriptions to call and settle at once, otherwise it will go hard with them on Judgment Day."

The First Village Band

An item about a band appeared in the *Canadier* on March 27, 1845. On the previous Saturday evening the Bridgeport and Berlin Band had given the Berlin citizens proof of their musical skill. (2)

The Berlin of 1846

Said Smith's *Canadian Gazeteer* of 1846; BERLIN: a village in the Township of Waterloo, nine miles from Galt, contains about 400 inhabitants, who are principally Germans. A newspaper is printed here, called the German Canadian, and there is a Lutheran meeting-house. Post-office twice a week. Professions and trades: one physician and surgeon, one lawyer, three stores, one brewery, one printing-office, two taverns, one pumpmaker, two blacksmith shops.

The Township Hall

For several years in the eighteen-forties the Waterloo Township Hall was located in Berlin. Before it was secured a warm contest ensued between Preston and Berlin. At a decisive point Frederick Gaukel gave the township a free site in North Queen Street, where the First English Lutheran Church now is, and turned the scale in Berlin's favor.

STORY OF THE POST-OFFICE

Now, at his door, the householder receives his mail twice a day from a man in uniform. When the villagers first obtained a postal service they were content to get their letters once in two weeks and call at the office for them.

Until 1851 the Canadian postal service was a branch of the English Post-Office. In 1821 there were only thirty-five post-offices in Canada, and the mails were borne from place to place by post-riders. The charge for carrying a letter from Toronto to Niagara was twenty cents; and to London, England, one dollar.

For Waterloo Township the nearest post-office at first seems to have been at Dundas. Galt obtained a post-office in 1827, and Waterloo one in 1831. Daniel Snyder was the first Waterloo post-master. The Berliners trudged to Waterloo for their mail. In 1837 an office was assigned to Preston. (1). Letters for Berlin were addressed to Preston. Before the close of 1837 Bishop Ben Eby, Henry Bowman, and H. W. Peterson were sent to Toronto to petition the Deputy Postmaster-General for a post-office. However they had to be satisfied with a half-loaf. The stage-driver was instructed to drop a mail-pouch bi-weekly at Peterson's printing-office. For five years the citizens called at the *Museum* office for their correspondence.

An increase of population led the authorities to open a post-office in Berlin on October 6, 1842. George Davidson, merchant, was the first postmaster, and kept the post-office in his story-and-a-half, frame store on the American block corner. Soon afterward the village obtained a weekly service; and in 1845 a daily mail from Preston. All post-offices were opened on Sunday.

Letters were written on paper made in England. With a sharp knife the writer made a pen out of a goose-quill; the ink by boiling the inner bark of the oak tree with a small quantity of copperas. He wrote only on one side of the sheet; folded it; then scribbled the address on the other side. The missive was sealed with wax. Envelopes were not used until the eighteen-fifties. Letter carriage was paid in cash, but a letter might be either paid in advance or sent collect. Needless to say the most of them were sent collect. In 1849 the letter rate was six cents for a half-ounce. In 1850 post-offices were closed on Sunday; and a year later the postage-stamp was ushered in. (2)

The local postoffice remained at the corner of King and Queen Streets until 1845. Postmaster Davidson then built a three-story, frame store and post-office at No. 32 East King Street, parallel to and standing back several feet from the street line. The post-office was located in the eastern end. In 1847 George Davidson admitted his brother William to partnership and removed to New Aberdeen, six miles below Berlin. Nominally he continued to be the post-master until 1851, when his brother William was appointed in his stead.

William Davidson built the third post-office building in 1855, on a lot between Boedecker & Stuebing's bookstore and the American corner. It was a one-story frame building, with a gable and verandah facing King Street. He lived in a house nearby that until 1853 had been the home of Carl H. Ahrens, the first county treasurer. At the back end of the kitchen Mr. Ahrens built a brick vault that was said to be fireproof, and contained an iron chest for storing cash and documents.

When that post-office was ready for use Mr. Davidson sold the building at No. 32 East King Street to Carl W. C. Kranz and Henry Stroh, general merchants. Later on C. Kranz & Son built a frame annex in front of the store and brought it up flush with the street.

Carl Kranz I's son-in-law, Henry Knell, then leased the former post-office for a jewelery store. (2)

William Davidson, the postmaster, bought a home in Schneider's Road (S. Queen Street) in 1858 from George Seip, the brewer. When he quitted his King Street home, Dr. R. Mylius leased it. After moving to Schneider's Road, Mr. Davidson built a frame post-office in front of his house. To-day the building is numbered 61-63 S. Queen Street and is used as a store. When Mr. Davidson announced his intention of building an office in Queen Street, merchants in King Street objected, fearing they might lose custom. Postmaster Davidson conducted also an express and telegraph office in the little building. He continued till 1862, when he left for the United States. (3)

William Jaffray succeeded William Davidson in 1862 and carried on the three services in Schneider's Road until 1865. The expansion of the village then obliged him to procure larger premises. He removed the postoffice, express, and ticket-office to No. 52 East King Street, where the Misses Glick had erected a block for him. In 1869 a further increase of population motivated him to lease the western end of the town hall, just nearing completion. Sixteen years later, the Dominion Government built a federal building on the northwest corner of King and Benton Streets. Before the site was actually purchased the storekeepers west of Queen Street in King Street petitioned the town council to prevent the office from being put up there. They claimed that it was too far from the centre of the town and from the G.T.R., and requested that the question be submitted to a popular vote. The council, however, were helpless. The Government purchased the land from Casper Heller, proprietor of the Market Hotel. Earlier it had been the site of Meinke & Stroh's marble works. Mr. Jaffray was the first postmaster in the new building (1886) and continued until his death in 1896.

Since then the postmasters have been: Charles F. Niehaus (1897); Fred H. Boehmer (1915) E. H. Lindner (1919); Harvey M. Schaub (1929); Fred C. P. Davey (1932-35); T. H. Hachborn, Acting Postmaster, (1935); and Mr. Hachborn postmaster since 1936.

A mail-delivery service was begun in the town on August 27, 1907. The first carriers were: Ray Kaufman, Ira Underwood, W. H.

Halliwell, A. G. Kaufman, A. L. Fraser, Wm. Witzel. By 1930 the number of carriers had increased to twenty-five. Before that service was ushered in, Miss Agnes Ward and Miss A. Rathman were popular office clerks.

There were six clerks employed in the inside service in 1900. In 1930 there were twenty-five. No record is available of the postal receipts between 1850 and 1860. In 1870 the receipts totalled $2,212; in 1929 they had mounted to $120,499. (3)

Since the present building has been in use, the caretakers that follow have been in charge: August Meinke, who was appointed in 1885; Edward Lyons, who succeeded him in 1891; Jacob Clemens, appointed in 1896; and James Carse, who followed Mr. Clemens in 1921.

Kitchener is to obtain a new federal building that is to occupy lands which face Duke Street and extend from Queen to Frederick Street. The Hon. W. D. Euler, Minister of Trade and Commerce, influenced the Dominion Government to erect in his home city a befitting structure to accommodate the Post-Office, the Customs and Excise, the Income Tax division, and the Radio Corporation service. The contract has been let and the building is expected to be completed in 1938, at an outlay of $300,000. Ball Bros. Ltd. will construct it.

SOURCES
1. Public Archives of Canada. 1931. Ottawa.
2. The late Mr. Jacob Stroh. Waterloo.
3. The Post-Office Department. Ottawa.

THE STAGE COACH

In grandsire's day trade flowed southward to Preston and Dundas. Over muddy corduroy roads or through pitch-holes he rode to the poll or to court. For such errands there was not a public conveyance available until 1835. A Vermonter, Captain Thomas Smith of Winterbourne, then began a service to Preston, via Waterloo and Berlin. Other men followed his lead. The arrival of the stage-coach hastened the construction of a better highway. In 1837 the Dundas road was macadamized up to Preston, or possibly to Berlin. It was said of the coachman, "his only point of interest on the road is to save time and see whether the coach keeps the hour."

WATERLOO COUNTY COURT HOUSE AND JUDGE'S CHAMBERS
—Courtesy, The Waterloo Chronicle

JUDGE E. W. CLEMENT

REGISTRAR G. V. HILBORN

WATERLOO COUNTY'S OLD FOLKS' HOME

One of the most modern in Canada.

In 1848 the *Deutsches Canadier* carried Mr. Smith's advertisement, which reads,

> Will go down every Monday, Wednesday, and Friday, and will return the day after: viz., every Tuesday, Thursday, and Saturday. Leaves home, Woolwich Post-Office (Winterbourne) always at 12 o'clock noon, the village of Waterloo at 2, and Berlin at 2½ o'clock; and again, on the return, leaves Preston at 7 o'clock in the morning, Berlin at 9, and Waterloo at 9½. The prices for carrying passengers, down or up, from Waterloo to Preston, 2 shillings and sixpence, and from Berlin 2 shillings York, and vice versa. He will arrive in Preston in time for the night coach to Hamilton, where travellers will find ample accommodation early in the morning for all parts of the world, and likewise find a coach ready to convey them farther westward.
>
> Thomas Smith.

In 1845, as the appended notice shows, Captain Smith had met with opposition,

> *Mail Coach.* A daily mail coach leaves the hotel of the undersigned (Preston) at 3 o'clock, p.m., for Berlin and Waterloo. Travellers are taken up and left off at suitable places. At five o'clock in the morning it leaves the hotel of W. Rebscher, Waterloo, calls at the hotels along the route and reaches Preston in time for the south-going mails. The coach is covered and rests on springs for the comfort of the passengers.
>
> George Roos, Proprietor.

At cockcrow Waterloo passengers seated themselves in the coach, while the whip stored the mail-pouch and carpetbags in the boot. With a blare of his horn he was then off for Berlin, where he picked up additional mail and passengers. His next stop was at Jost Stengel's tavern, between Centreville and Freeport. The stage crossed over the Grand River at Freeport on a toll-bridge. The coach was taxed sixpence and every passenger a half-penny. Then it wheeled directly to Preston.

In 1850 Emmanuel Ziegler operated a stage between Waterloo and Preston. The fare was three York shillings (37½ cts.). Soon after John Blevins of Guelph conducted a coach between Guelph and New Hamburg, coming by way of New Germany and Bridgeport. He changed horses at the Queen's Arms, on the cityhall site, Berlin, and then rolled on westward. A year later S. Cornell ran a stage from St. Jacobs to connect with the Great Western Railway service at Galt. He announced, "a new coach and fast horses;"

and made capital of an incident where two countrymen had been fleeced at cards by sharpers on a train, warning, "Huetet Euch vor Schwindlern and fahrt in Cornell's Postkutsche."

In the early fifties Henry Stuernagel of Elmira ran a stage between Glenallen and Berlin. He was known as "Unser Fritz" and in forty years seldom missed a day. In 1857 William Ross had a coach plying between Berlin and Millbank, coursing through Waterloo, Heidelberg, St. Clements, and Crosshill. Later on a stage plied from Crosshill to Berlin. The last owner of a stage-coach running between Preston and Waterloo was Christopher Kress of the Kress House, Preston. For twenty years he had a trustworthy driver named Charley Feick, whose duties began at four o'clock in the morning and ended at eleven at night.

THE CONTEST FOR THE COUNTY SEAT

By now this region had been more densely settled. To obtain more judicial centres it was proposed to subdivide the Gore and the Wellington Districts. Early in 1848 Galt petitioned the Canadian Parliament to erect the Townships of Dumfries, Waterloo, Wilmot, Wellesley, and parts of Woolwich, Puslinch, and Blenheim as the Bruce District, with Galt as the District Centre. The proposal found favor in Berlin and Waterloo Township.

In March, 1848, however, the *Canada Gazette* announced that the lower half of Dumfries Township was to be attached to a Brant District. That decision disturbed the Galtonians. Moreover Guelph, as the centre of the Wellington District, objected against the loss of their western townships. Nevertheless Berlin supported Galt's aspirations. In commenting on a meeting about to be held in Preston to promote the Brant District the *Deutsches Canadier* said,

> The only argument we ever heard against the new formation is the matter of costs—the fear being that the people would have to pay double taxes: for new buildings at Hamilton and new buildings at Galt. Yet the main advocates of the Wellington District were English of the aristocratic class. Therefore every building was put up according to magnificent style, which could be done with foreign money, since it is well known that John Bull is liberal and Pat a spendthrift. On the other hand it is known that the Scotch can be as close-fisted as the Germans and that neither of them like to be pompous in public works.

Now everybody knows that Galt and Dumfries are populated by Scotch, who are practical business men. So that there is not the least danger that too much money will be spent on public buildings. If Waterloo Township elects a few real close-fisted councillors, as Wilmot is already doing, we will have no complaint about high taxes. Besides Galt has raised or promised $6000 toward the district buildings.

At Preston the delegates approved of a Bruce District with Galt as the district town. Galt citizens then made up a purse of $600 and sent James Cowan and Absalom Shade to Montreal to interview the Government. There they learned that a Bill had been introduced to subdivide the region into four districts, which were to function for three years and then become counties. For Galt the wormwood in the Bill lay in a clause that said the reeves of the Bruce District would determine whether Berlin or Galt should be the district centre.

The Galtonians nevertheless bestirred themselves to capture the prize. While busying themselves the Government dropped the plan to form four new districts and decided to organize eight new counties. A Territories Bill was framed for this purpose in 1850 and provided that Waterloo County should comprise the Townships of Waterloo, Wilmot, Wellesley, Woolwich, North Dumfries, and the incorporated Village of Galt. In passing Galt then had 2,000 inhabitants and Berlin, 652.

After the Bruce District had been ditched Berlin and Waterloo Township felt they were no longer honor bound to support Galt. Moreover the upper townships argued that on account of Galt's southerly position in Waterloo County it could not properly serve more than a quarter of its 26,000 people.

Meanwhile the legislative seat had been shifted to Toronto and Galt sent down a deputation to interview the cabinet. On their heels a group of friendly reeves followed and presented Berlin's claims. As a consequence of this the Territories Bill was held over till 1851. *The Galt Reporter* then savagely attacked the Germans of Berlin and the townships. The onslaught only spurred the northerners on. Mr. Ferguson, the local member of Wellington District, was invited to Berlin and banquetted on September 12, 1850.

Citizens in carriages and on horseback met him and his father, the Hon. Adam Ferguson, two miles beyond Bridgeport. There the

Elora band and a special carriage drawn by four horses awaited them. The horses were decorated with gay ribbons and Union Jacks, while two postilions in scarlet jackets bestrode them. John B. Bowman, Reeve of Waterloo Township, and George Davidson, councillor, seated themselves with the guests. At Bridgeport the carriages were drawn over a gaily-decorated bridge and under festive arches to the village inn, where a cold collation was served. Guests, officials and citizens then formed a procession and rode up to Berlin. Here they passed under a series of arches in the main road. Flags fluttered, the band played, guns popped, and the citizens cheered.

At Gaukel's Wirtshaus Mr. Ferguson thanked the big crowd for their warm reception and congratulated them on Berlin's progress. In the Township Hall in North Queen Street a banquet was spread for 100 persons. After a bountiful German dinner Mr. Ferguson sent the diners away happy by declaring that Berlin would not long remain only a village.

The member and the local leaders then put their heads together and planned how the county seat should be won. It was believed that the township reeves would make the choice. The first move was to steer the return of reeves friendly to Berlin's purpose and to avoid dissension it was decided to have the electors determine whther they preferred some unnamed village in Waterloo Township to Galt. Almost every voter was canvassed by both contestants. As the issue hung in the balance Frederick Gaukel offered to give the county two and a half acres of land, at the corner of Queen and Weber Streets, if Berlin were chcsen. At the elections of 1851 the property-owners of the county cast a majority of 140 votes for some village in Waterloo Township.

After the elections a poll of the reeves was taken. Eight favored Berlin, two for Galt, and one from Preston, while the Reeve of North Dumfries refrained from voting. In May, 1851, Premier Hincks introduced a revised Counties' Bill into the legislature, but none of the county towns were named. A monster petition was then sent down praying the Government to name Berlin as the county-town. On March 25, 1852, the authorities announced that Berlin had been selected.

WATERLOO COUNTY COUNCIL, 1937

Reading left to right.—Back row: Edwin Huehn, Heidelberg; Fred Toletzki, Waterloo; Milton Weber, West Montrose; Ford L. Wilson, Preston; A. W. Hoffer, Elmira; Ed. Amos, Supt House of Refuge. Middle row: Bernard Flynn, Hespeler; Wm. J. Pelz, Preston; Albert Heer, Waterloo; Lorne B. Weber, Waterloo; Simon Ditner, Petersburg; Wesley Howlett, West Montrose; W. H. Shaw, Ayr; Gordon Cook; Front row: Walter Hostettler, New Hamburg; N. G. McLeod, Galt; P. A. Wagner, Wellesley; Simon Kinsie, Warden, Breslau; Samuel Cassel, County Clerk, Kitchener; Milton H. Schmidt, Wilmot; A. Fellows, Government Road Engineer; D. G. Emery, Road Superintendent, Kitchener.

Mr FOLEY'S RECEPTION IN BERLIN APRIL 4TH 1864.

1. *The Postmaster General blushing through his specs at the Grand demonstration.*
2. *Barman. The Grand is not very large. Mcfoley but its respectability will make up for that effect.*
3. *Dr F. Is that all? I must confess that is rather a hard looking squad. caliar off my exertions.*
4. *McGroil. This is a black looked out for our Side W. and all the PILLS in your box went stav'm.*

5. *Col Lady Golly. Waira Groff how you do march to the Music.*
6. *Pat. Holney. Y are the very Ye darby blackguard in a Sin are a culd. Vaggur till I get a sqaint at McKeg.*
7. *Barney Finnigan a GTR Employee. Ase boys three Cheers for Wiskey and the Grand Trunk.*

Waterloo County Organized

The Provisional Council of Waterloo County met here on May 3, 1852. The members were: Dr. John Scott, Berlin, Reeve, and Henry Snider, Deputy-Reeve of Waterloo Township; John Ernst, Reeve, and Anthony Kaiser, Deputy-Reeve of Wilmot Township; Charles McGeorge, Reeve, and Duncan Ferguson, Deputy-Reeve of North Dumfries Township; Absalom Shade, Reeve of Galt; John Hawke, Reeve, and Gabriel Hawke, Deputy-Reeve of Wellesley Township; Jacob Hespeler, Reeve of Preston; and John Meyer, Reeve, and Peter Wenger, Deputy-Reeve of Woolwich Township. Dr. Scott was chosen warden.

One of the council's first actions was to approve the principle of having the people manage their own local affairs. The first by-law provided for a county seal with the figures of a lion lying down with a lamb.

Since the county purse was empty, the councillors jointly signed two notes for £200 each and discounted them at the Gore Bank in Hamilton. Next, they awarded the contract for building a court house and jail, amounting to £4875, to a Brantford firm. The county used the land that Frederick Gaukel had presented. The buildings were completed in 1852 and the court house set apart for judicial purposes on January 21, 1853. A big celebration followed the opening.

William Davidson, a Berlin merchant, was the first county clerk. In 1861 he was succeeded by Israel D. Bowman.

Charles H. Ahrens was the first treasurer. His office was only opened on Saturday; and his salary, £50 a year. When men from the upper part of the county came to do business, he often took them home for dinner. In time, they brought in their friends with them. Thus a deal of his salary went for free dinners. As a consequence, he gave up in 1855. Christian Enslin was appointed treasurer in 1855, but died in 1856. Charles Stanton was the next treasurer and continued until 1879. The positions of Clerk and treasurer were then joined, with Israel D. Bowman filling the dual role. After Mr. Bowman's death in 1896, his son, Herbert J. Bowman, C.E., succeeded him and continued until his death in 1916. Samuel Cassel followed him. Before Mr. Cassel's appointment, he had served in every position in the Wilmot Township Council, been

Warden of the County, and a successful farmer and stock raiser. He is well posted in Municipal Law.

County Judges

SENIOR JUDGES

William Miller—1853-1887.
Anthony LaCourse—1887-1895.
Duncan Chisholm—1895-1913.
C. R. Hanning—1913-1920.
E. J. Hearn—1920-1929.
E. W. Clement—1929, to the present day.

JUNIOR JUDGES

Anthony LaCourse—1873-1887.
Duncan Chisholm—1894-1895.
William Reade—1912-1917.
E. J. Hearn—1917-1920.

Sheriffs

George Davidson—1853-1881.
Moses Springer—1881-1898.
John Motz—1901-1912.

Dr. H. G. Lackner—1912-1925.
W. A. Kribs—1925-1934.

Registrars

D. S. Shoemaker—1853-1866.
Dougall McDougall—1866-1891.
Isaac Master—1891-1898.

J. D. Moore—1898-1917.
Oscar S. Eby—1917-1934.
G. V. Hilborn—1934.

County Crown Attorneys

Aemilius Irving—1853-1859.
Thomas Miller—1859-1867.
W. H. Bowlby—1867-1917.

D. Shannon Bowlby—1917-1934.
W. P. Clement—1934 to present.

Surrogate Court Clerks

Christian Enslin—1853-1855
A. J. Peterson—1855-1900.
John McDougall—1900-1906.

J. M. Scully—1906-1925.
E. H. Scully—1925 to present.

Clerks of the County Court

James Colquhoun—1853-1877.
John McDougall—1877-1908.
E. J. Beaumont—1908-1924.

Charles H. Mills—1924-27.
Charles H. Hahn—1927-1934.

Gaolers

William Walden—1853-1873.
John Pearson—1873-1887.
Jonathan Cook—1887-1929.

Leslie Bullock—1929-32.
E. H. Landridge—1932 to present.

In 1934, the offices of Clerk of the Surrogate Court, Sheriff, and County Court were united, with Mr. Scully at its head.

After Dr. Scott, the Berlin Reeves who were elected Warden were: H. S. Huber (1862-3); Abram Tyson (1874); J. M. Scully (1886); Louis J. Breithaupt (1898); and George M. DeBus (1905) The city separated from the county in 1912.

THE CLIMB

Waterloo Township, in 1850, had 6,500 residents of German lineage, of whom 1,955 were native in Germany. In the eighteen-fifties there was further inflow of German families into Berlin. The men were mostly hand-workers who had served a seven-year apprenticeship and thereafter journeyed from town to town to learn trade secrets. On their return they made a masterpiece and were then regarded as full-fledged mechanics.

Berlin then had four wood-working shops, a tannery, a foundry, two wagon-shops, a brewery, a soap-chandlery, a pottery, two brick-yards, two smithies, two saddleries, five weavers' handlooms, and a hat-maker's stand. The hat-maker, John Kidder of Kentucky, made beaver hats for the "swells", at twelve dollars apiece.

In 1852 a general census credited Waterloo with 300 heads, New Hamburg, 508, Berlin, 782, Preston, 1150, Guelph, 1850, and Galt with 2200. Berlin then had 123 houses, three schools, four stores, four taverns, and five churches. The religious denominations were represented by 4 Universalists, 8 Zwinglians, 13 Baptists, 19 Anglicans, 20 Primitive Methodists, 22 Disciples, 37 Presbyterians, 43 Wesleyan Methodists, 44 Swedenborgians, 50 Evangelicals, 122 Catholics, and 285 Protestants.

Of the 123 houses only six were of brick and only one of two stories. The residential streets were like the Short Street of today. Newcomers lived in two or three-roomed dwellings, but every home had a spinning-wheel. A householder bought a web of cloth and hired a tailor to stitch up his own and his boys' suits. The tailor received seventy cents a day and his board. Similarly the householder bought a roll of leather and had a shoemaker come in and sew the family's footwear.

Ahrens & Huber

Carl von Ahrens, a nobleman's son, came to Berlin in 1835 and followed the millwright's trade. Since there was another Carl Ahrens in the village he dropped the "von" and called himself Carl H. Ahrens. He married Frederick Gaukel's daughter Elizabeth. Their own daughter became Mrs. Richard Roschman, while their son, Dr. A. E. Ahrens, practised in Stratford and was elected a member of Parliament. Another son, Herman, was a noted athlete and the father of the late Carl Ahrens, the distinguished landscape painter.

Grandfather Ahrens, in the late Forties, remodelled Jacob Shoemaker's mill at Bridgeport. There he formed a friendship with a young merchant, Henry S. Huber. In 1851 they opened a general store on the American House corner and a foundry in South Ontario Street, to make stoves and threshing machines. Before the official opening of the court-house they cast a cannon for the celebration.

Shortly after the foundry was grounded a Hollander named Claus Maas, a piano-maker, came in. Mr. Huber imported a batch of piano wires from Germany and the firm gave him a workroom in the foundry. Mr. Maas made six pianos and sold them to as many leading families. The demand having been filled he then removed to Preston.

After Mr. Ahrens' death Sheriff Davidson bought the foundry and dismantled it. John J. Woelfle, who had been foundry foreman, then began manufacturing plows on the southwest corner of King and Gaukel Streets. He made good plows. From as far distant points as Walkerton farmers drove down with loads of wheat and exchanged the grain for his plows.

At that period the first runaway slaves from the Southern States reached Berlin on "the underground railway." That is, travelled at night, with the polar star as their only guide, and hid themselves in the daytime. The refugees called Canada, "God's country."

Mr. Huber and other sympathizers aided the escaped slaves to found a colony in Peel Township. One fugitive, P. E. Susand, opened a barber-shop and coffee-stall in Berlin; another, R. Sutherland, hung out his shingle as a lawyer. When Dan Rice's circus visited the village, Sutherland bought a seat. The clown spotted him and yelled out repeatedly, "I smell a nigger!" His cries displeased the Berliners. A half-dozen of them sprang up out of their seats and dashed after the clown, who fled into the woods nearby —lucky to escape without a broken crown.

New Services

The new county-town attracted the attention of several corporations. In 1853, for example, the Grand Trunk Telegraph Co. sold the business men $800 of stock and appointed Henry B. Bowman a director of the company. Poles were then erected and wires strung to Berlin. The first instrument was placed in Mr. Bowman's store and his son Israel given charge of the key.

Several months later the Huron & Toronto Railway Co. surveyed a line through the East and South Wards. The company was afterward induced to run a survey through the western part of the village, when they proposed to build a station in the West Ward. Henry Bowman and other leaders then gave them eight acres of land to build it in West Weber Street. After the gift was made a number of men purchased lots between Ahrens Street and Margaret Avenue, (not far from the railway tracks) in the expectation that the locality would become the centre of a new business district.

The Huron & Toronto Railway Co. and the Grand Trunk Railway were amalgamated in 1853. To Sir Casimir Gzowski was awarded the contract of constructing a line from Toronto to Sarnia. He sub-let the building of bridges, stations, and freight-sheds to Michael Farr of Vermont. Mr. Farr was killed in the Das Jardins Canal accident in 1855. His nephews, George and Shuball Randall, thereafter completed the Breslau bridge.

Jackson & Flowers built the railway itself from the Breslau bridge to New Hamburg. Henry F. J. Jackson and his accountant, J. S. McDonald, set out from Montreal in a steamboat bound for Hamilton and from there rode to Berlin in stage-coaches. Mr. Jackson transacted his banking in Hamilton, driving down and back in a buckboard. The partners completed their contract in 1855, but the Grand Trunk ran out of money, which delayed the opening of the line till the following year.

Mr. Jackson liked Berlin and decided to make it his abode. He bought the Moxom farm, touching Margaret Avenue, and the triangle bounded by King, Water, and Francis Streets. On the triangle he built a handsome residence and named it "Geneva Lodge," in honor of his daughter, Miss Geneva Jackson.

George and Shuball Randall likewise became residents. George Randall played a leading part in both Berlin and Waterloo. Moreover a number of Irish workmen who had helped to lay the rails became householders.

Before the end of 1853 Berlin obtained its first bank. A branch of the Bank of Upper Canada was opened in North Queen Street, near where St. Peter's Church now stands, and proved a convenience for business men.

Other Changes

Fire broke out in Reinhold Lang's tannery in 1853. The volunteers with their buckets were unable to quench it. The fire destroyed the tannery and a number of frame houses nearby. Afterward he purchased a large area of land at the corner of King and Francis Streets. On the site were several springs, while a small creek that rose in Breithaupt Woods flowed through it. Men and boys fished the stream for trout and in the winter village lads skated on its surface. Mr. Lang built a new frame tannery on the corner of Francis and Charles Streets.

In the same year John Hoffman and Isaac Weaver sold their furniture factory and store to Jacob Hoffman and removed to Waterloo. Jacob built a saw-mill close to his factory. It was afterward converted into tenements, which are still in use. His son Isaac inherited the factory and store and had as his accountant the late John S. Anthes.

Frederick Gaukel died in 1853. In an advertisement his executors said, "It is the universal testimony of all strangers who ever visited Berlin that they never found anywhere a county-town more prosperous nor more agreeable." Levi Gaukel bought his father's hotel, but soon sold it to James Potter, who renamed it "The Western Hotel." At the executors' sale choice lots in King Street fetched from $250 to $500, while the Bank of Montreal corner was sold for $1600.

The First Land Speculator

Before G.T.R. trains steamed through Berlin, Sheriff Grange of Guelph speculated in Berlin real estate. He bought from Samuel Moxley forty acres on the south side of West King Street and sold Ward Bowlby eight acres situated at the corner of King and Wilmot Streets. Mr. Bowlby built a residence and named it "Bow Hill." Bow Hill, Geneva Lodge, and Sheriff Davidson's "Forest Hill" were then the three most imposing homes in Berlin. Sheriff Grange bought also lands in the North Ward and subdivided them into building lots. In November, 1853, at an auction sale, he sold £6000 worth of lands. He was the first land speculator in Berlin.

Gravel Roads

Up to then clay and corduroy roads were the model. *The Hamburg Beobachter* suggested that the county council build a gravel road from Hamburg to Berlin and from Berlin to Preston. The council moved to construct the road. A southern reeve, however, objected against the proposal, saying that if they were built the people would be too poor to pay for them and as a consequence they would have to be toll roads. In the end it was found that the county council could not legally build the road, since road-building rested with the townships.

Wellesley and Woolwich Townships agitated gravel roads to Berlin, so as to benefit from the prospective railway service. The first gravel road was laid between Elmira and Berlin, and followed by a tri-weekly stage.

The Preston stage brought in copies of a Toronto daily newspaper for hotelmen, that cost seventeen cents per copy. Inns were then the men's clubs. Grandfathers, in short black coats with horn buttons and round peaked caps, each bought their own Schuppe Bier—the "Dutch treat"—and greeted his neighbor with a friendly "Prost". Then they chatted of many things: the G.T.R., the incorporation of the village, the need for a Grammar School, of the stranger who extracted aching teeth, and who made dauguerreotypes at one dollar each, the appearance of "Uncle Tom's Cabin" in Enslin's bookstore, of John Wissler's two-foot wire foot-bridge across the Grand River at Lexington, the introduction of the decimal system of currency in Canada, and the widening of the parliamentary franchise to men who were assessed in at least $300 on real property.

Among the citizens who arrived in the village in the forties and fifties were: Johann Heller, watchmaker; Gottlieb J. Rathmann, tailor; Dr. Delion, father of F. H. Delion; Otto Fleischhauer, merchant; G. M. DeBus, hair-dresser and dentist; Balthazar Schmalz, an artistic weaver; John Klein, teacher; Dr. D. S. Bowlby, physician; W. H. Bowlby, barrister; Jacob Kraemer, owner of the Black Horse Inn; Herman Rathman, finisher; Adam Wagner, butcher and hotelman; John B. Hett and Henry Hett.

Henry Eby sold the *Canadier* to his brother Peter, who founded the first English newspaper, *The Berlin Telegraph*, in 1853. The editor commented on education: "The free school question is gaining ground in this township. Four years ago there were no free schools. Now the majority favor them."

The village was about to buy more fire-fighting apparatus. *The Galt Reporter* jeered: "The inhabitants of Berlin, at the suggestion of the Telegraph, have decided on buying a squirt from Mr. Strong, druggist, Galt, at a cost of one shilling and sixpence, for the extinguishment of fires in the county town."

Music in the Eighteen-Fifties

The settlers held singing classes in the schoolhouses. In 1853, the United Male Singing Society of Berlin, Bridgeport, and Waterloo" was organized. Of it the Canadier said in part,

> "Wo man singt da lass dich ruhig nieder:
> Boese Menschen haben keine Lieder."

We had recently the pleasure of attending a rehearsal of the United Male Singing Society of Berlin, Waterloo, and Bridgeport, at Bridgeport. And we wish to make some comments about it. The goal is far off, but the commencement has been made. Therefore singers of Berlin, Waterloo and Bridgeport do not lose courage, but strive to follow the directions of Mr. J. Biedermann, who spares neither pains nor expense to support the noble undertaking. Then your efforts will be crowned with success.

Although you have to bear the heat and burden of the day, and though you have to walk two miles, just remember you do it for education, amusement, and recreation. Then, after you have sung the gladsome songs, you will return home with happy hearts, and will not soon forget the hours spent there in song.

> "Only song can cheer up life;
> It drives out the pain one feels,
> And whilst it brings joy to all,
> Many a sore heart it heals."

It is not known how long that Maennerchor continued. Afterward the Liedertafel was organized in Waterloo, and in 1859, a Male Glee Club was organized in Berlin.

Then practically everyone sang and the majority of citizens were able to play some kind of musical instrument. At first folk songs were sung; next, advanced musicians interpreted Bach, Beethoven, Mendelssohn, and other great German composers. In the churches, homes, Gesangvereins, and Musikchors music played a shining role in the refinement of the citizens.

THE REV.
CLARENCE M. KEEN

THE BENTON STREET
BAPTIST CHURCH

BERLIN IN 1856

THE BENTON STREET BAPTIST CHURCH

The Benton Street Baptist Church was originated at Bridgeport, Ontario, eighty-six years ago. It was the first German Baptist Church in Canada. Previously, Henry Schneider had been sent to this district as colporteur by the American Tract Society. Mr. Schneider organized the congregation on September 10, 1851, at Bridgeport, with sixteen charter members. Of them, three had come here from New York City, while thirteen had been recently baptized by Professor A. Rausenbusch of New York City, who had come over to help them effect an organization. Before October 15, 1851, they had enrolled fifteen more members, some of them from Wilmot and Woolwich Townships. The group adopted the creed of the Grand River Baptist Association after Professor Rausenbusch had translated it into the German language for them.

The first deacons of the church were Daniel Weber and J. O. Fleischauer. In 1852, Ad. Schmidt was also elected deacon. Julius Boedecker was church clerk.

Henry Schneider, whom they themselves licensed to preach, was their first pastor. He gave one-half of his time to the church and the other half to the American Tract Society. Each party paid him $130 a year. His itinerary included four stations: Bridgeport, Woolwich, Unterstrasse, and Gedeckte Bruecke. In November, 1852, the Council of Baptist Churches ordained him a minister of the Gospel; and in 1853 he gave his whole time to his church duties. Part of his support thereafter came from the American Baptist Home Mission Society.

A chapel was built in Wilmot and another in Woolwich in 1852. Then, before the end of 1852, it was decided that the Wilmot and Woolwich bodies were each to have their own organization. As a consequence of that agreement, the meeting-place of the Bridgeport group was transferred to Berlin, and a building erected on the site of the present parsonage. Otto Fleischauer was named to go to Simcoe and solicit help for the building, while Mr. Boedecker, Mr. Hendrich and Mr. Oberholtzer were appointed a Building Committee. (I)

About 1846 or 1847, a German Baptist lady started a sewing-class for little girls. It was held in a small hall in Frederick Street, near King Street. Soon afterward she asked the girls to meet there on Sunday and form a Sunday School. That was done and attracted many children. When the church was completed, the Sunday School class was moved to the church. (2)

The German Baptist Church became a member of the Eastern Conference of German Baptist Churches, partly located in the United States. In 1855 the Eastern Conference convened in the Berlin Church.

The Rev. H. Schneider was pastor of the church till 1863. The Rev. Mr. Austermuehl then succeeded him and remained until 1864. The next pastor was the Rev. C. Bodenbender, who began his ministry in 1865. From 1871 to 1873 the church was without a regular pastor. A call was then extended to the Rev. J. Albert, a student at the Rochester Theological Seminary. During his pastorate a parsonage was bought in Church Street for $1070.

The Rev. Mr. Albert resigned in 1875 and went to Cincinnati, Ohio. He was followed by the Rev. W. Argow of Albany, N.Y., in October, 1875, who on account of poor health retired in July, 1876.

The German Baptist Churches in this part of Ontario organized the Canadian German Baptist Mission in 1876. Home Mission money thereafter remained in Canada, and the local church actively supported the enterprise. J. O. Fleischauer was responsible for collecting offerings for that purpose. That diversion of offerings from the Eastern Conference, however, did not continue any great length of time. At that period the church burial ground was removed to Mount Hope Cemetery.

The Rev. J. Fellman of Baltimore, Md., was appointed pastor on August 23, 1876. A year later, after a revival service, forty-one persons were baptized at one time. While he was pastor, a Prudential Committee was chosen and comprised Carl Boehmer, H. S. Boehmer, A. Doering, Karl Zuelsdorf, A. Huff, Deacon Fleischauer and Deacon Henry Lang. For the growth of the congregation necessitated a larger church. In 1881, a nest-egg of $2,000 was contributed by the members and the Building Committee that follows appointed: J. O. Fleischauer, C. Bauers, P. S. Lautenschlager, A. Doering, H. S. Boehmer, C. Boehmer, and Henry Dunke. The new church was built on the corner of Benton and St. George Streets, and dedicated on the first Sunday in December, 1883. The Eastern Conference met in the new church in 1889.

The Rev. Mr. Fellman resigned in 1890 and removed to Chicago. His successor was the Rev. G. Fetzer, of Cleveland, who entered upon his duties on July 21, 1890. Soon after his arrival it was decided to have English preaching on Sunday evenings. During the Rev. Fetzer's pastorate and also the Rev. Fellman's, there were numerous accessions of members. Mr. Fetzer withdrew in July, 1897, going to the Harlem Church in New York City. He was followed here by the Rev. F. Friedrich of Cleveland, Ohio.

Then as now, the church had an excellent choir. In 1900-01, the congregation remodelled the church, erecting a large and well-appointed Sunday School building and attaching it to the auditorium. The auditorium was also improved, obtaining new windows, pews, and a new pipe-organ. The entire outlay was $7500. On September 15, 1901, Professor Kaiser of Rochester, N.Y., preached the dedicatory sermon. The Building Committee consisted of: Arthur Pequegnat, R. Boehmer, C. S. Boehmer, August Boehmer, P. S. Lautenschlager, R. Dunke, and the Pastor.

September 25, 1901, was a red-letter day. The Thirteenth Triennial Conference of the German Baptist Churches of Canada and the United States then met in the remodelled church. It was said that it was the largest gathering of German Baptists till then ever held on the continent.

The Rev. Mr. Friedrich accepted a call to Buffalo, N.Y., in 1904. On August 4, 1905, he was followed by the Rev. Frank Kaiser of New York. English preaching was the order every Sunday evening and the Torrey-Alexander Hymnal used at the services. Mr. Kaiser was called to Rochester, N.Y., in October, 1908.

The Rev. A. P. Miehm of Brooklyn, N.Y., became pastor of the church in February, 1909. During his pastorate a weekly offering envelope system was introduced to provide for bi-monthly missionary contributions; and the Ladies' Aid Society presented the church with an individual communion service. On July 13, 1913, the Rev. Mr. Miehm accepted a call to the First German Baptist Church in Pittsburgh.

Numerous members gave the church outstanding assistance. J. O. Fleischauer, for example, was appointed Deacon in 1851 and continued till his death in 1902; and Henry Lang, who was appointed Deacon in 1866, served until the end of his life, in 1915.

P. S. Lautenschlager served as trustee and Superintendent of the Sunday School for a number of years; while Arthur Pequegnat acted as Superintendent of the School from 1887 to 1912—a period of twenty-five years. After his retirement the Sunday School workers elected his son Edmond in his stead. The latter was Superintendent of the Sunday School until 1924, and since then his brother Marcel. (1)

The Rev. F. Schade of Nottingham, Ohio, succeeded Mr. Miehm in March, 1914. Notwithstanding the world war, the church membership increased and the Sunday School attendance was doubled. In 1915, the church gallery was remodelled to accommodate the Primary Department of the Sunday School. Bible conferences were held under such men as Dr. Neighbor, Dr. Conant, Evangelist Compton, and others. In March, 1918, the congregation discontinued the use of the German language and renamed the church the Benton Street Baptist Church. In 1920, they separated from the Eastern Conference and united with the Ontario and Quebec Conference. During his ministry the Rev. Mr. Schade baptized 121 converts; and saw a number of young women enter Toronto Bible College to prepare themselves for the missionary field. In his term, the Rev. Mr. and Mrs. Percy Buck entered the missionary field in Bolivia; Albert Eikenaar, Summer Pastor, and the Reverends August Staubitz, Ian Macdonald, Herman Lang, E. H. Thamer, Miss Lydia Dankert and others entered upon definite Christian work. A Mission was started at Waterloo by the Church in 1921, when Mr. Arthur Schulte performed the pioneer work. Afterward it was continued by the Rev. Stewart Boehmer. A place of worship was there dedicated on August 5, 1934—Waterloo's first Baptist Church.

The Rev. S. Imrie, B.A., was appointed pastor in 1923 and served the congregation until July, 1930. While incumbent, a second story was added to the Sunday School and dedicated on September 25, 1927.

The congregation became an Independent Baptist Church on January 25, 1928. All ties were then severed with the Convention of Baptist Churches in Ontario and Quebec. The Radio Broadcasting of Sunday evening services was also introduced and subsequently the broadcasting of Wednesday evening Bible Studies. The Church Officers of that decade were: E. B. Dunke, Treasurer; R. W. Lautenschlager, Mission Treasurer; B. C. Schulte, Clerk, Board of Deacons; Arthur Pequegnat, Henry Grube, Thomas Klippert, George Boehmer, and Edmond Pequegnat. Trustees: C. B. Dunke, H. F. Boehmer, and William Thoman.

Pastor A. J. Lewis, a returned missionary from Nigeria, assumed charge of the church on December 1, 1930. The Rev. Mr. Lewis and Mrs. Lewis labored with zeal. His was a teaching and evangelistic ministry. Mr. Lewis resigned his office in September, 1936, and removed to Cleveland.

This church supports missionaries in Nigeria and, until the civil war broke out, others in Spain. On account of the war, these have left Spain and located in Southern France, where they minister to Spanish refugees.

Their present pastor is the Rev. Clarence M. Keen, formerly of Williamsville, N.Y. He was inducted on May 9, 1937. Under his leadership the church continues to march forward.

SOURCES

1. A Historical Sketch of the Church prepared by the Rev. H. F. Schade. 1923.

2. An item sent to the writer for this history by Mr. A. R. Sherk of Victoria, B.C. 1937.

3. The Historical Sketch of the Church continued from 1923 to the present by Mr. B. C. Schulte, Church Clerk.

INCORPORATION OF THE VILLAGE

Late in 1853 a local census indicated that Berlin had 1,000 inhabitants. Straightway they procured a village charter. The first council was elected in the following year and met on January 7, 1854, in the court house. That practice was continued for some time. The council consisted of Dr. John Scott, Reeve; and Henry Stroh, Gabriel Bowman, Enoch Ziegler, and George Jantz, Councillors. William Davidson was appointed clerk; Henry B. Bowman, treasurer; Wm. Gywnne, solicitor; John Klein and Thomas Sparrow, auditors; W. K. Moore, assessor; and Wm. Benton, constable, who named Benton Street.

The council bought a village seal, in the form of a shield with four quarterings. On it were a crown, a beaver, a locomotive, a cross-cut saw and axe, and the words: "Municipality of Berlin, 1854."

When the village separated from the township it did not have a single sidewalk. A £300 contract was awarded to Jacob Y. Shantz to lay down walks on one side of the roadways in the central parts of King, North Queen, Weber, Frederick, Benton Street, and Schneider's Road.

Before incorporation the hamlet had depended for fire protection on two hand-engines, purchased with public subscriptions. The reason for two engines was the rivalry that existed between Upper Town (Berlin) and Lower Town (Ebytown). After incorporation the two engines were placed in Emmanuel Ziegler's blacksmith shop (the Spritzhaus) in King Street. The council then bought hooks and ladders and formed a volunteer brigade. In 1855 they passed the resolution that follows:

> That we sink two wells, eight feet in diameter and as deep as practicable so as if possible never to contain less than four feet of water; and each fitted with two wooden pumps; one well to be at the corner of King and Cedar Streets, and the other in a line with Emmanuel Ziegler's blacksmith shop.

The old Free Church was also fitted up as a school. Adam Ruby was one of the teachers in the Frederick Street Schools and John Klein in the Red Schoolhouse. The village council persuaded the county to buy a large plot in mid-Frederick Street for a Common and Grammar School. At a cost of $7,896 a charming building was erected in 1856 and put in use in January, 1857. The first principal of the new Common School was Alexander Young. His assistants were John Strang and Elizabeth Shoemaker. (1)

The Mechanics Institute

A Mechanics Institute was opened in Henry Eby's former printing-office in 1854. Chiefly the institute was supported with dollar membership fees and private subscriptions. Books were only exchanged on Saturday night. Within a decade the library boasted not fewer than 1,000 German and English volumes. The institute and contents were destroyed by fire in the late sixties. After the town hall was erected the institute was lodged on the first floor. In 1871 the library had 600 volumes. George Howard and Henry Gauntley successively acted as librarians, without remuneration. Later on the subscriptions dried up and for a time the institute was closed.

Bands of the Eighteen-Fifties

In 1856 instruments were purchased with private subscriptions and the Berlin Band re-organized. Mr. Kelk, a music dealer, was the leader. The spark was soon snuffed out, when the instruments became village property. Two years after a 24th of May celebration was described as follows,

> Some of the hotels in Berlin were plentifully decorated with evergreens and flags flying in every direction. In the morning and afternoon the cannon belched forth its thunders and the fire-brigade turned out in strength and walked through the town headed by— an accordion—the band being scattered some time ago to the four winds.

The Berlin Music Band was organized in 1859, with George Hess as secretary and Henry Glebe, bandmaster. Mr. Glebe was a hat-maker and subsequently lessee of Weaver's hotel.

New Industries

William Simpson, cabinet-maker of Hamilton, came here in 1856 to manage Enoch Ziegler's east-end furniture factory. Within a few months he and Menno Eby bought the factory. Afterward Mr. Eby withdrew, when James Potter and D. S. Shoemaker entered into partnership with Mr. Simpson. Some of their furniture was in use for fifty years. Time elapsed. Mr. Simpson and John Aldous then purchased Mr. Potter's and Mr. Shoemaker's interest and traded as Simpson & Co.

Through two marriages Berlin obtained another industry. First, the Rev. Jacob Wagner, an Evangelical minister, married Margaret, daughter of Mr. and Mrs. Jacob Hailer. Pastor Wagner was later stationed in Buffalo, N.Y., where he formed a friendship with Louis Breithaupt, who was associated with his father, Liborius Breithaupt, in a tannery. Periodically the son came to Upper Canada to buy hides. Secondly, through the Rev. Wagner he was introduced to the Hailer family and in 1853 espoused Miss Catharine Hailer. After their marriage the young couple resided in Buffalo.

Mr. Breithaupt was energetic and desired a business of his own. In 1857 he founded a tannery in Berlin, at the head of Margaret Avenue, but continued to live in Buffalo. After the outbreak of the American Civil War, Mr. and Mrs. Breithaupt and their sons Louis J., William H., and John C., removed to Berlin. Until the founder's death in 1880 his life was one of unremitting activity. He built up a large industry, shared in public life, became an extensive land-owner, and when he deceased was Mayor of Berlin.

By his example Mr. Breithaupt increased the Berliners' faith in their town. Soon after his arrival he purchased the southeast corner of King and Queen Streets, then covered with frame shacks, and in 1862 built the American block. *The Berliner Journal* said of the structure,

"American House"—Das neue dreistöckige Backstein Gebäude des Herrn L. Breithaupt an der Ecke von King- und Queen- Strasze ist seiner Vollendung nahe und wurde am Freitag die Taufe desselben auf dem platten Dache vollzogen, wobei die Musik Band aufspielte, Reden gehalten und einige Fäszchen Bier vertilgt wurden und es den Namen "American House" erhielt. Es ist eines der schönsten und bis jetzt das gröszte Gebäude der Stadt. Seine Länge beträgt 114, die Breite 40 und die Höhe 40 Fusz. Die Front an King-Strasze ist zu zwei Kaufläden eingerichtet, welche eine Tiefe von 55 Fusz haben, und in dem Theil hinter diesen kommt ein Hotel and ein Leder-store. Der ganze Raum im zweiten und dritten Stock, mit Ausnahme des Theiles über dem Leder-store. wird zum Hotel gehören, welches über 30 Zimmer enthalten und daher keinen Mangel an Räumlichkeit haben wird. Das Innere ist sehr zweckmäszig eingetheilt und beweist dasz der Architekt des Baues Hr. C. Krull seine Sache gründlich versteht. Die Baukosten belaufen sich auf $9,000. Das Haus ist eine Zierde der Stadt und bildet mit seinen langen Reihen Bogenfenstern an den zwei Straszen einen angenehmen Kontrast zu den alten Baracken, welche diese Ecke früher verunstalteten. Hr. John Kimmel hat den Kontrakt für die Maurerarbeit und Hr. Krull für die Schreinerarbeit, and sie haben beide ihre Aufgabe befriedigend erfüllt. Möge das Beispiel des Herrn Breithaupt noch recht viele Nachahmer finden.

The Berlin Chronicle

William Jaffray of Galt and Casper Hett established the *Berlin Chronicle* in 1856. The English weekly was sold in 1860 to Christian Kumpf and Mr. Bowman and removed to Waterloo. Shortly after Mr. Jaffray was appointed postmaster of Berlin. Mr. Hett volunteered for service in the American Civil War with the Northern forces. Afterward he returned to Berlin and was one of the *Freie Presse's* founders.

Willie Spiers

Spiers & Osborne of Galt opened a general store in Berlin in 1856. David Spiers' brother William, newly arrived from Ayrshire,

Scotland, applied for the post of manager and offered to show a profit at the end of the year or forfeit his wages. His bid was accepted. He came to Berlin with a key and a cashbook. Six years later he bought the store and built a brick block where the Waterloo Trust & Savings Co.'s office now stands.

The G.T.R. Begins Its Service

Everyone rejoiced on May 14, 1856, when a Grand Trunk locomotive steamed into Berlin. It brought in the contractors and certain officials, whom the council banquetted at the Queen's Arms. A daily passenger service of two trains each way was begun on July 1, 1856, while a three-day-a-week freight service soon followed. The first station agent was A. D. Moody. Up to 1894 the agents were: R. Hunt, J. Cossey, T. Savage, and J. Strickland. From 1904 to 1909, D. B. Dover; and from 1909 to the present day, John Milhausen.

The Preston & Berlin Railway

From the day of the ox-cart Waterloo Township had traded at Dundas and Hamilton. When the G.T.R. started building its line to Sarnia, Hamilton bought $200,000 of stock in the Galt & Guelph Railway (later part of the Great Western) and urged the construction of a branch railway from Preston to Berlin. In 1855 Berlin was asked to buy $20,000 of the P. & B. stock. The railway agents gave a verbal promise that the debentures would only be used as collateral security. Hence in drawing up the bylaw no provision was made for their redemption. The property-owners sanctioned the by-law and from November, 1857, to February, 1858, the village was served by two railways.

The debentures, however, were handed to the contractors as part payment of their work. Before they discovered the omission the company reappeared with another proposal: to extend their line to Waterloo unless Berlin agreed to buy a second $20,000 of stock. The electors approved of the purchase, but before the debentures were handed over the first issue caused a peck of trouble.

The contractors had discovered that the first batch of debentures were toothless. Accordingly they demanded that the issue be amended by a clause pledging their redemption in twenty years. When a new bylaw was submitted to the electorate they recalled that the issue was only to be used as collateral security; that on account of the short curves trains could not be operated at more than ten miles an hour; and that the company had broken a promise when they placed their station in West King Street, near the G.T.R. tracks, instead of near the G.T.R. station in Weber Street. The bylaw was defeated. The company then sued the village, when the court ordered the sheriff to replevin the debentures.

In the ferment a flood of February 3, 1858, swept away the P. & B. bridge, spanning the Grand River below Doon. That disaster stirred up the company to force the village to redeem the first lot of debentures and to complete the purchase of the second. A private Bill was introduced into the Canadian Legislature to that end and the legislature, although the trainless railway was buried in weeds, ordered Berlin to redeem the first issue and to pay six per cent. interest until their maturity. With regard to the second block the legislature advised the company to sue the village in the Court of Chancery. "Im Schmerz sind Wuerm und Loewe gleich."

Berlin's total assessment then was only $37,785; while its tax-rate of twenty cents in the dollar only yielded $7,157 a year. The addition of $1200 staggered the ratepayers. To make matters the worse a majority of the council was willing to buy the second $20,000 of stock to avoid a law suit. Such subserviency displeased the electors. A largely-signed petition was circulated praying Henry S. Huber, Reinhold Lang, Henry Stroh, Dr. D. S. Bowlby, and Dr. T. H. Legler to stand at the municipal election of 1859, which they did. Two-day elections were then in vogue. At the end of the first day's polling the "Pro-Railway" group were in the lead, but at the close of the poll on the second day the five "Anti-Railway" men were declared winners. Flocks of rejoicing citizens staged a celebration. Sleighs were volunteered, the Waterloo band engaged, and a tour of both villages made by the victors and their supporters.

When the law-suit in connection with the second $20,000 of stock was tried Berlin won its case. The court ruled that the company had no grounds either in law or equity for entering the action.

That verdict did not affect the first block of debentures. For years Berlin continued to pay interest on them. A release came in 1873. The Mowat Government then distributed a provincial surplus among the municipalities of Ontario. On general account Berlin was awarded $27,000 and for having aided the Preston & Berlin Railway the sum of $23,125. Moses Springer, M.P.P., obtained the grants. At a public dinner the grateful Berliners presented him with a gold watch and chain. Other municipalities who had helped the railway company did not fare so well. It was said, "In Berlin only did the man not fall on his head."

THE STADTHALLE AND OTHER MATTERS

THE FIRST STADTHALLE

After the Crimean War there was a period of hard times in Canada. The Berlin council petitioned the Government to exclude from Canada all office-clerks, literary persons without capital, and office-seekers. When the council attempted to sell a £2000 debenture no-one would buy it. A smaller sum was then borrowed at twelve per cent. interest.

That financial stringency accounts for the manner in which they procured a Stadthalle. The council converted the old Free Church into a council chamber and firehall. The council met upstairs on April 6, 1858, illuminating the chamber with tallow candles. A year later they decided to forego payment of their services as councillors.

The ground floor was used as a firehall and a "pumper" fire-engine bought for £200. Water tanks were placed at the principal street corners. The one in front of St. Paul's Church was filled from Schneider's creek by hand-power. When it was filled up the contents were repumped to the next nearest tank and the chore repeated until all were filled. Among the earliest chiefs of the volunteer brigade were John Winger, Enoch Ziegler, and August Meinke.

The Commercial Bank

At that stage the local agent of the Bank of Upper Canada loaned a citizen private funds in the sum of $400 for six months and exacted $188 in interest. A group of resolute men prosecuted him for usury. Seven members of the grand jury recommended a true bill, but the agent's clerk was on the jury and prevented them from reaching an accord. The group then had the Commercial (later the Merchants) Bank build an office on the corner of Queen and Duke Streets, which Dr. H. G. Lackner subsequently purchased. The Bank of Upper Canada then closed its doors.

A Seed Fair and First Sewer

In 1859 the council made a grant to a seed fair. It was well attended and led to the holding of monthly cattle and butter fairs. The council in that year laid down the first sewer, between Queen and Ontario Streets, with an outfall in Schneider's pond.

The brickmakers of the period were John Bramm, Henry Schwenn, and Joseph Dauberger. Henry B. Bowman built a three-storied brick block in 1858, on the Bank of Montreal corner, which was probably the first of its kind in Berlin. Other merchants followed his example and lived in quarters above their store.

Store clerks took down the wooden shutters and swept the floor before breakfast. At night they stayed till ten o'clock or later. Grave seniors sat around a hot stove on a winter evening and settled the destiny of their neighbors, the village, and the nation. An open cracker barrel invited sampling and the storekeeper gave them something fluid to wash down the dry morsels.

The clerks finally made a plea for shorter hours. In support of the request a woman who signed herself "Fanny" wrote a letter to one of the papers. That displeased one merchant and he replied, asking,

> Is a transition from the legitimate sphere of women's everyday walk to that of contributing to a newspaper an action that will exalt yourself in your own estimation or that of your sex?

THE REV.
WM. KLOEPFER, C.R.
A Late Pastor.

THE VERY REV. C. B. MEYER, C.R.
The Present Pastor.

ST. MARY'S CATHOLIC CHURCH

ST. MARY'S CHURCH CHOIR, 1933 — *B. J. Zollner, Director; J. A. Bauer, Assistant.*

Reading left to right.—*First row: B. Scanlon, Wm. Bear, J. Tilger, D. Riedel, J. Bauer, Wm. Miller, A. Kraemer, D. Hinsperger, A. Kroetsch. Second row: L. McCarthy, E. Carey, J. Tilger, S. Horton, B. J. Zollner, A. Schell, H. Schnitzler, I. Nagle, C. Boegel, T. Mackin, Rev. C. B. Meyer. Third row: E. LaVaigne, D. Shoemaker, Ida Roth, E. Miller, B. Roth, L. Huber, B. Kreiner, A. Schmidt, M. Spencer, F. Schmidt, Mrs. W. Miehm, C. Schmidt, M. Cushing, I. Hinsperger. Fourth row: E. Kiffman, K. Kampman, H. McKelvie, T. Anstett, I. and M. Zollner, C. Malleck, F. Malleck, E. Didena, M. Lauber, A. Kroetsch.*

Sports and Recreations

In the Fifties there were no golf clubs. Generally German mechanics putted with a hoe in their garden. In 1856 Henry F. J. Jackson, owner of a farm off Margaret Avenue, gave a group of English cricketers the free use of four acres of land. Other sportsmen introduced horse-racing and held meets off Joseph Street. Yet others hunted wild turkeys in Dumfries Township. English citizens had a Debating Club in 1858 and once debated, "Should slavery be abolished immediately?" The negative side won.

It was said that wherever two Germans settled they straightway formed a Verein. Here there were several singing societies and in 1859 they organized a Turnverein. In a description of them Dr. Otto Klotz of Ottawa said the essential feature was physical development and the motto, "Gut Heil." The members met weekly or oftener at the Turnplatz and, under the direction of the Turnwart, exercised on the Reck, on the Barren, and on the Pferd. The Turners had also climbing poles and a swing with two covered rings. Sometimes the exercises were closed with a Dauerlauf. The Turners arranged social gatherings, theatricals, and dances. Every year a Turnfest was held and every second year a two-day Fest at some point in the county that had a Turnverein.

Additional Newspapers

In 1859, John Motz and Frederick Rittinger founded the *Berliner Journal*. It became the principal German newspaper in Canada. In the same year, Robert Logan launched the *Sporting Chronicle*, the first of its class in Canada, but the fig-tree soon withered. Previously Dougall McDougall had purchased the *Berlin Telegraph* and the *Deutsches Canadier*. After the establishment of the *Journal*, Mr. McDougall ceased publishing the *Canadier*. Mr. Motz, who served as Mayor and who was later on appointed Sheriff of Waterloo County, was the father of W. J. Motz, Managing Director of the *Kitchener Daily Record*.

ST. MARY'S CATHOLIC CHURCH

In the mid eighteen-thirties there were only four Catholic families in Berlin. The region between Puslinch and Goderich, in which there was not then a single Catholic Church, was served by an Alsatian missionary, the Rev. John Wiriath. After him, the Rev. Peter Schneider traversed the same territory until 1844, when the Rev. Simon Sanderl ministered to the scattered flocks for about two years. Mass was celebrated in log schools or, where there were only a few families, in homes. The Jesuits opened a mission at St. Agatha in 1847, after which the Berlin families worshipped at St. Agatha.

In the early eighteen-fifties the Catholic families of Strassburg and Williamsburg planned a church. As numerous young farmers of the township had removed to Grey and Bruce Counties, allured by cheap land, the Rev. Rupert Ebener, S. J., suggested that if they united with local households and built a church in Berlin they might in time be able to obtain a resident priest. His advice was taken.

A site on the southwest corner of Weber and Young Streets was purchased in 1854, from David Weber for $200. In that year a red-brick structure was begun, completed in 1855, and designated St. Mary's Church. Although it had neither Sanctuary nor tower, it was probably the finest church west of Toronto. The Rt. Rev. John Farrell, first Bishop of Hamilton, dedicated the church in 1856. Mass was celebrated monthly or at longer intervals by priests from New Germany.

In the fall of 1857 the Rev. George Laufhuber, S.J., arrived here and made Berlin his quasi home while performing his missionary duties. He made a house canvass and collected enough money to build a Sacristy and rectory and in 1859 organized a Separate School.

When the church was erected the congregation was almost wholly German. After the completion of the Grand Trunk Railway, however, numerous Irish railway workers became residents of Berlin and members

Father Laufhuber was transferred to another field in 1859. The Rev. Edward Glowacki, C.R., of St. Agatha, followed him in 1860 and remained till 1861, when the Rev. Francis Breitkopf, C.R., was inducted. In 1863 a frame tower was built on the church and two large bells and a four-dialed clock installed in it. Years afterward the clock was presented to the parish of St. Clement's. About then the first Poles came to Berlin, probably because Father Breitkopf could speak their language. He often preached to them and had them sing Polish hymns after High Mass. The colony increased and took root. Father Breitkopf left Berlin in 1865. He said of the congregation that they distinguished themselves beyond all others by their liberality in building, equipping, and decorating the parish buildings, etc.

Present Choir

Present Choir, 1937: B. J. Zollner, Director, J. A. Baur, Assistant. Sopranos — Mrs. Winifred Miehm, Beatrice Kreiner, Mary Zollner, Ida Zollner, Alfreda Schmidt, Fridolyn Schmidt, Pauline Stalzer, Kathleen Miller, Irene Hinsperger, Helen McKelvie, Kathryn Kampman, Olive Lang, Emma Kiffman, Loretta Daub, Camille Malleck. Altos—Mrs. Herb. Oleheiser, Dolly Roth, Theresa Anstett, Eleanor Miller, Dolly O'Neil, Ida Roth, Rita Weber, Bernice Roth, Frances Wey, Olga Kiffman, Bernice Anstett. Tenors— Alf. Heintzman, Len Dooley, Cyril Boegel, Victor Smith, George McCarthy, Stephen Meinzinger, Dan Hinsperger, Carl Schell, Robert Sobisch, Bert Scanlon. Basses—Sid. Horton, J. A. Baur, Pat Hannon, Francis Montel, Eddie Schmidt, Herb. Schnitzler, John Nagle, Ed. Carey, Wm. Bear, Len Collins, Carl Reinhardt, Jerome Burbach.

The Rev. Louis Funcken

St. Jerome's College was removed from St. Agatha to Berlin in 1866 by its founder, the Rev. Dr. Louis Funcken, C.R. He was appointed rector of St. Mary's and, with the assistance of priests from the College, introduced regular Sunday services. The prospect however was dark. The farmers formed the backbone of the congregation but the introduction of machinery caused a further exodus of farm-hands to the "Saugeen" and the United States. Moreover a succession of poor crops crippled the storekeepers and nearly all towns were at a standstill. Nevertheless Father Funcken was undaunted by adverse conditions.

Soon after his arrival the Board of Health forbid further interments in any churchyard. The congregation then bought two acres of land in the North Ward for a cemetery and subsequently an additional 4.5 acres.

Father Funcken had a new Sanctuary erected in 1871 and embellished it with stained-glass windows imported from Holland. Six years later the church interior was redecorated and refurnished.

A larger Sacristy was built in Weber Street in 1881 and two years after a large pipe-organ installed at a cost of $1,750.

"Father Louis," as he was affectionately called, suffered a physical breakdown in 1889, due to over-exertion. He went to Roremond, Holland, to recuperate, but death intervened on January 30, 1890.

The Rev. William Kloepfer

Dr. Funcken's successor at St. Mary's was the Rev. Dr. William Kloepfer, C.R. He was native in New Germany and the first Canadian to enter the Congregation of the Resurrection. Berlin was then experiencing its first development as an industrial centre and the congregation had increased to such an extent that the number of services had to be doubled. In 1891 the Waterloo members, who had attended public worship in Berlin, built St. Louis' Church in Waterloo. That movement only gave temporary relief. Father Kloepfer started a monthly collection in 1892 for a larger church. Seven years later a site fronting in Young Street, south of the first church, and extending to Duke Street, was purchased for $7,500.

The first sods for the new church were turned by the congregation on Sunday, May 27, 1900, and the cornerstone laid by the Rt. Rev. T. J. Dowling on September 30, 1900. The massive structure is of Gothic style and in the form of a Latin cross. Length over all, 186 feet; width of nave, 61 feet; width of face, 100 feet. A large tower on the right and a smaller on the left give dignity to the edifice, while four doors, receding deeply, and a spreading rose window over the central ones, give it grace. Without the gallery the church seats 1,000 persons. The magnificent altar was the gift of the ladies and the fine stations presented by Mrs. (Dr.) A. Kaiser of Berlin, Germany.

Three years were required to complete the structure. On December 13, 1903, it was dedicated in the presence of the Most Rev. Donata Sbaretti, Papal Delegate to Canada. Several prelates, many priests, and a great throng from near and far witnessed the function. As Father Kloepfer left it the church represented an outlay of $90,000. Mr. August R. Lang supervised its construction, and that of St. Mary's Hospital.

THE REV. JOSEPH SAMBORSKI, C.R.
Pastor of Sacred Heart Church.

ST. MARY'S HIGH SCHOOL, ROSARY HALL AND ST. MARY'S HALL

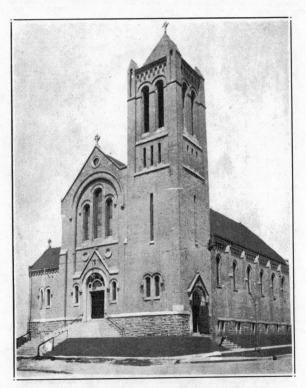

THE SACRED HEART CHURCH

DIRECTORS OF ST. MARY'S HOSPITAL
First row: Rev. C. B. Meyer, C.R., W. M. O. Lochead, W. J. Motz, M.A.,
 Chairman; E. R. Purtle, A. Heer.
Top row: E. Bauer, R. Krug, I. A. Shantz, A. Lockhart, F. M. Hearn.

The Polish Church of the Sacred Heart

Polish settlers from Posen and West Prussia arrived here as early as 1872. Brother Idzi Tarasiewicz, stationed at St. Jerome's College, organized the Polish people and founded the St. Joseph Fraternal Society in the eighteen-eighties. The Rev. Stanislaus Rogalski, C.R., took charge of the group in 1895. He used an old school as a Polish chapel. When it was removed in 1899 the congregation met in the upper story of St. Mary's School.

Father Pieczynski succeeded Father Rogalski in 1901 and continued until 1904. He was followed by the Rev. Paul Sobczak, C.R. In 1912, the Poles formed a separate parish. Four years after, a site for a church, at the corner of Charon and Shanley Streets, was purchased; in 1918, an attractive church was built at a cost of $52,000. The present pastor of the Sacred Heart Church, as it was designated, is the Rev. Joseph Samborski, C.R.

St. Mary's Church Since 1909

Among the Rev. William Kloepfer's assistants were the Rev. Joseph Halter, the Rev. W. Vincent Kloepfer, and the Rev. A. J. Fischer. Father Kloepfer died on December 3, 1909. St. Mary's congregation then consisted of more than 600 families. Included were a number of French, Italian, and Syrian households.

The Rev. A. J. Fischer, C.R., was the next pastor of St. Mary's, and served the church for two years. During his pastorate, a school was built in the North Ward.

From 1911 to 1915, the Rev. Theobald Spetz, C.R., the first Berlin youth to enter the priesthood, was pastor of St. Mary's. Under his direction the church was redecorated by a Roman artist, Ilario Panzironi, at an outlay of $10,000. Father Fischer was recalled from Waterloo in 1915 and labored here until 1919. The next pastor was the Very Rev. A. L. Zinger, C.R., a former President of St. Jerome's College.

Under his leadership, St. Mary's Rectory in Duke Street and St. Joseph's School in the South Ward were built. Operations were also begun in 1924 on the $600,000 St. Mary's Hospital for the Sisters of St. Joseph. In 1925, the Sacred Heart School was enlarged; in 1927, the Sacred Heart Convent and St. Mary's Parish Hall were built.

Father Zinger was transferred to Chicago in 1928. His successor at St. Mary's was the Rev. M. Hinsberger, C.R. In the latter's term of office, among other improvements, St. John's School was built in the West Ward, St. Mary's School remodelled, and a Novitiate for the College built in Young Street.

St. Joseph's Church

By then St. Mary's congregation had grown too large for proper spiritual direction. Father Hinsberger informed the Rt. Rev. Bishop McNally of the situation, when the Bishop formed another parish in the South Ward. The Rev. Rueben Haller, C.R., of Hanover, was requested to organize the new congregation, to be known as St. Joseph's Church. A site was purchased at the corner of Albert Street and Courtland Avenue in 1930 and a large basement built. While the members worship in the basement, they plan to erect a $100,000 church.

St. John's Church

Early in April, 1937, the church authorities resolved on the erection of a fourth Catholic Church for the benefit of 200 families in the West Ward. The Rev. W. S. Gleason of Guelph was chosen to form the new parish, and make the necessary preparations for building a church and parish hall. The cornerstone of St. John's Church was laid on August 15, 1937, by the Very Rev. W. Beninger, C.R.

Church Societies

At St. Mary's Church, much of the development was owed to various societies. An Altar Society was formed in 1858 to provide supplies for the altar, flowers, and other decorations. Later on the Frauenverein—Ladies' Aid Society—attended to some of that work and the needs of poor people. This society is still active but confine themselves to charitable deeds. A Young Ladies' Society was organized many years ago, and chiefly occupy themselves with Literary and Dramatic entertainments.

The Catholic Women's League is of more recent birth and they devote themselves to the promotion of church work of all kinds. By means of bazaars, card-parties, and teas they raised large sums for the payment of church debts, for the erection of a Parish Hall, and the Novitiate.

There are also a number of men's societies. The Catholic

ST. MARY'S R.C. HOSPITAL
One of the Dominion's Best.

ALMA STREET UNITED BRETHREN CHURCH
The Rev. G. R. Shepherdson, Pastor.

ST. ANDREW'S PRESBYTERIAN CHURCH

Mutual Benefit Society, numbered 12, is one of the oldest in Canada. The St. Boniface Sick Benefit Society is a purely local organization with a good record. For many years a branch of the Catholic Order of Foresters has also been established. The Holy Name Society, whose functions are mainly devotional, was formed in 1913. At present the most flourishing society is the Knights of Columbus, with a membership of 700 Knights in Waterloo County.

The pastor of St. Mary's Church now is the Very Rev. C. B. Meyer, C.R.

BIBLIOGRAPHY

The Catholic Church in Waterloo County. 1916. By the Rev. Theobald Spetz, C.R., D.D., Toronto.

ST. ANDREW'S PRESBYTERIAN CHURCH

The cornerstone of today's Presbyterian Church was laid on October 10, 1906. The Rev. W. A. Bradley was then pastor of the church. At the ceremony two former ministers, the Rev. A. B. Winchester of Toronto and the Rev. Robert Atkinson of Chesley, assisted him, and the Rev. S. M. Hauch, pastor of the Evangelical Church, Waterloo, delivered an inspirational address. Mrs. James Potter, the oldest member of the congregation, laid the cornerstone. As a memento she was presented with the silver trowel she had used. The new structure represented an outlay of $30,000.

St. Andrew's is one of the oldest congregations in the city. For it was engendered in 1854. At the commencement religious services were periodically held in private homes. Toward the end of that year, more frequent meetings were held in an old schoolhouse on the firehall lot in Frederick Street. The members then sent a petition to the Hamilton Presbytery, affiliated with the Free Church of Scotland, praying connection with the Presbyterian Congregation of Woolwich Township. The Rev. Dr. Smellie of Fergus, the Rev. James Young of Guelph, and Sheriff George Davidson of Berlin, presented the application. Their petition was granted and on January 23, 1855, the members were organized as St. Andrew's Presbyterian Church. For the infant congregation the Rev. W. Pirie of Doon conducted the first service. Subsequently, whenever he was unable to come up, the Presbytery sent a substitute.

Included in the membership of 1855 were: Mr. and Mrs. George Davidson, Mrs. Fischer, Mrs. Tagge, Mr. William Smith, Miss Ellen Smith, Mr. and Mrs. McWilliams, Mr. and Mrs. James Taylor, Mrs. Alexander Mackie, Mr. James Merrilees, Mrs. James Colquhoun, Miss Dobbin, Mrs. Jackson, Mrs. Hale, Mrs. Kidder, and John Smith, M.D.

In the year of organization a call was extended to the Rev H. McMeekin. A delay ensued in the call being ratified by the Presbytery. In the interval he was appointed principal of the Berlin Grammar School. He served as pastor until November, 1855. For a considerable time young divinity students filled the pulpit, including James Tait. In 1856 the congregation undertook to erect a church. In that work Sheriff Davidson was especially active. For a nominal sum he sold the elders a site on the northeast corner of Queen and Weber Streets. He canvassed the members and his friends for subscriptions, which with his own sufficed to erect a church. Their house of prayer was dedicated in 1857. The first managers were: Colin Groff, William Davidson, John Lake, and W. Moodie.

The Rev. A. Constable Geikie was installed as pastor on June 28, 1857. About the same time the congregation separated from the Winterbourne Church. Mr. Geikie's stipend was £125 a year. One year the board spent £4-12-6 on candles and firewood. Two years later the Rev. Geikie was transferred to Galt as the assistant of Dr. Boyne. Subsequently he was called to a Presbyterian Church in New South Wales.

At St. Andrew's he was succeeded on December 15, 1859, by the Rev John MacMechan. The first election of congregation leaders was held in 1863, when Joseph Hobson, C.E., Alexander Mowat, George Davidson, and George Underwood of Berlin; Alexander Murray of Bridgeport and Robert Lake of Waterloo were chosen. With the exception of Mr. Mowat and Mr. Murray, all declined the honor, necessitating the election of others. While the Anglicans were building a church they held services in St. Andrew's. While they lived in Berlin a son was born to Mr. and Mrs. MacMechan, whom they named Archibald. In Nova Scotia he rose to prominence as a poet and historian. Among his works were: "Sagas of the Sea;" Old Province Tales;" and "Red Snow on the Grand Pere." His father ministered to St. Andrew's until 1866.

Meanwhile, in Upper Canada, a union had been formed in 1860 between the Presbyterian Church of Canada and the United Church of Canada. As a consequence St. Andrew's came under the jurisdiction of the Guelph Presbytery.

After the Rev. Mr. MacMechan's withdrawal the pulpit was vacant for several months. The Rev. Thomas Cummings was inducted as pastor on December 13, 1866. The Presbytery discovered a small defect in his certificate and although Sheriff Davidson pleaded for him, on the ground that the irregularity was a trivial one, the Presbytery declined to sanction the appointment. The minister was offended and returned to his home in Nova Scotia. From March, 1867, until August, 1870, the Rev. A. J. Traver was the presbyter. After his departure there was a hiatus of about two years, during which time the Rev. Thomas Wardrobe of Guelph was moderator.

The Rev. J. F. Dickie

A young divinity student, the Rev. James F. Dickie, fresh from a Scottish College, was inducted on February 13, 1872. Subsequently he married the late Sir Adam Beck's only sister. Mr. Dickie continued at St. Andrew's until the late eighteen-seventies. In 1875 the session was increased by the appointment of the elders whose names follow: Alexander Young, William Cowan, J. Muir, Charles Bedford, John Moffat, William Cowan, and Alexander Roy.

The Rev. Mr. Dickie demitted his charge in Berlin and accepted a call to the Central Presbyterian Church in Detroit. Later on he was appointed minister to the American and British Church in Nollendorf Platz, Berlin, Germany. In December, 1913, he revisited Berlin, Canada, and in part said,

I knew Berlin better in 1871 than I do now. I note how wonderfully it has grown and how it has become a hive of industry. But whether or not it is a more agreeable place in which to live, I cannot say. When I first knew it, it was a delightful place. It hadn't many manufacturies, but it had a number of scholarly, cultivated gentlemen, and very genial and hospitable ladies.

Then, you heard scarcely anything spoken in the streets but German. It was necessary for anyone living here to speak both languages. I had for my instructor Adolph Mueller, who was one of the best teachers I have ever met. He did much to draw the German and English speaking people together.

What impressed me most on coming to Berlin, Ontario, was the fact that a little town of 2,500 inhabitants had fourteen churches. The Lutherans were the largest group, while all the churches drew from the country. I recall that the first street-light, burning coal-oil, was placed in 1874.

Had I not been in little Berlin, I should never have been in Berlin, Germany. For it was here that I acquired an interest in German life and language.

After Dr. Dickie removed to Detroit he was succeeded by the Rev. Donald Tait (1879-1889). In his time the Presbyterians of Waterloo who attended St. Andrew's organized a church of their own. The Rev. Mr. Tait was followed by the Rev. A. B. Winchester, who had been a missionary in China. In 1891 Mr. Winchester was appointed minister to a Chinese colony in British Columbia. The Rev. Robert Atkinson accepted a call to St. Andrew's in 1893. The church then had a membership of three hundred. Mr. Atkinson continued until 1899, when he was succeeded by the Rev. W. A. Bradley. Under his leadership the congregations added several hundred members and erected the present church, which was dedicated on September 8, 1907. The Building Committee consisted of: W. M. Cram (Chairman), C. K. Hagedorn, H. J. Sims, George M. DeBus, R. Reid, R. Smyth, and Wm. Metcalfe.

The congregation installed a new organ and several members donated a beautiful stained-glass window. Mrs. Wm. Roos erected one, the "Easter Morn," in memory of her father and mother—Sheriff and Mrs. George Davidson; Dr. G. W. Wright one portraying "Christ at the Door;" Mrs. James Potter donated two windows, picturing "Christ and the Woman at the Well;" Mr. John Moffatt bestowed another, in memory of his wife, entitled "The Good Shepherd;" and Dr. H. A. Pirie presented a window styled "Christ in Gethsemane."

St. Andrews has continued to progress in the new church. When in 1912 the Rev. Mr. Bradley was called to Teeswater, he was succeeded by the Rev. Marcus Scott of Detroit. Since then the church has been ministered to by two other clergymen: the Rev. B. McLennan, up to 1925, and the Rev. George Taylor Munro, from October 1, 1925, to July, 1937.

THE BERLIN HIGH SCHOOL

Analogous with other great institutions, the K.-W. Collegiate and Vocational School sprang from a seed. Directly the village was incorporated its leaders petitioned the County Council for a Grammar School site. The county fathers acceded to the request and on January 1, 1855, conveyed three and a half acres in Frederick Street, where the Suddaby School rests, to the village for a joint Grammar and Common School. The land cost £160 ($640). The secondary school was named, "The Berlin Senior Grammar School of Waterloo County." The first trustees were: Henry S. Huber (Chairman), Dr. John Scott, David S. Shoemaker, David Chalmers, Isaac Clemens, and Wm. Davidson (Secretary-Treasurer).

Before the school was built a Grammar School was opened in 1855 in Henry Eby's former printing-office, at 163 East King Street. It opened with thirty pupils, who paid fifteen shillings each per quarter for tuition. The Rev. Henry McMeekin was employed as master at a salary of £150. Near the end of that year the provincial authorities discovered that he had not procured a teacher's certificate. He withdrew, when Donald McLellan completed the term. In 1856 the duties devolved on Francis Evans.

In 1856 a Grammar and Common School building was erected in Frederick Street and opened in January, 1857. The Grammer School occupied two rooms on the second floor. For the spring term the trustees engaged Patrick Clerihew, M.A., a local editor, and for the fall period, an experienced teacher named Robert Mathieson, who instructed forty pupils. Mr. Mathieson was followed in 1859 by Charles Camidge.

Among the new trustees were Moses Springer, James Colquhoun, and the Rev. E. R. Stimson. Wm. Davidson, the secretary, left Berlin in 1861 and was succeeded by Mr. Stimson. In the following year the secretary and the teacher were at variance. The secretary reported to the Board that he had been discourteously treated by the master while on an official visit. On his part the teacher averred that the secretary had acted in an overbearing manner. The Board re-engaged Mr. Camidge, but requested him to be tactful in his relations to the secretary. Because of the teacher's re-engagement the secretary resigned his office. The resignation set tongues wagging and the secretary's friends clamored for the teacher's dismissal. To pacify them the Board devised a set of rules for the master's guidance and asked him to hang them up in the schoolroom. Instead he pinned a notice on the door announcing that he was about to quit the school. In an advertisement for a teacher the Board said, "unmarried men and clerical candidates are considered unsuitable." Hugh Strang, B.A., filled in until midsummer of 1863, when David Ormiston, B.A., was engaged.

Under Mr. Ormiston the school was advertised in the local, Hamilton and Toronto newspapers. Fifteen dollars in prizes were awarded to those primary-school pupils who stood highest at the Christmas examinations and scholarships to the three who headed the list. The Rev. F. W. Tuerk was also engaged as German teacher, at eighty dollars a year. That year Rev. Mr. McMeekin was appointed secretary and Dougall McDougall elected trustee. In 1866 the Board resolved, "That female pupils wishing to study French and the Higher Mathematics be admitted to the school on the same terms as other pupils." The Rev. A. Caesmann and Dr. D. S. Bowlby became members of the Board in 1866 and a year later P. E. W. Moyer, M.A., joined them. Mr. Ormiston resigned in 1867 and was followed by C. A. Neville.

The Common School's Request

Meanwhile the number of pupils at the Common School had mounted. In 1868 the Common School Board asked the Grammar School Board to permit the lower school to use part of the second floor. The appeal was granted, but it was another case of the camel getting its nose into the tent.

Mr. Neville gave up his position early in 1869, when the Rev. Mr. Traver completed the term. J. H. Thom, M.A., was engaged for the fall term and taught until the end of 1870. In that year Wm. Oelschlager, W. H. Bowlby, and Hugo Kranz joined the Board. Mr. Kranz was chosen Secretary-Treasurer in 1871. After Mr. Thom's withdrawal the trustees engaged James W. Connor, B.A., of Renfrew, Ont., as master. He commenced his labors on January 5, 1871, and for several months taught upward of sixty pupils in the Frederick Street school. Then, through the Town Council, the Common School invited the Grammar School to remove to the vacant Swedenborgian Church on the corner of Benton and Church Streets. The Grammar School assented but first resolved,

Provided it (the old church) be furnished by the Town free of rent and be properly fitted up to the satisfaction of the chairman by the town council; but this Board do not abandon their right to the Public School building, and hereby reserve their right to two rooms in the Public School building hitherto occupied by the Grammar School, according to the deed of January 1, 1855, conveying the school premises to the joint use of the Grammar and Common School.

The old church was then owned by Peter Good, who leased it to the town for $5.30 a month. In the first three years in the former church the number of pupils decreased on account of scanty accommodation. The town was then bearing the whole cost of maintenance. To get some support from other municipalities the Board solicited the County Council to divide the county into two High School Districts. The county however put its telescope on its blind eye. The Board then petitioned the Legislature to press the county to act, saying,

The County Council have evaded their duty by refusing to include in our district any other municipality than the town in which the High School is situated, although the inhabitants of all parts of the county are admitted to the school on the same terms as residents of the said town; and thereby an undue and excessive share of the cost of supporting the said High School is thrown on the heavily-taxed inhabitants.

While the Legislature had that petition under consideration the Department of Education put on the screws. The trustees were ordered to build a new school and employ another teacher on pain of forfeiting the Provincial grants. An application was made to the county for a grant of $2,000 toward a new school. The Chairman of the Education and Printing Committee however had the request shelved. Afterward Secretary Kranz wrote down in his minute book,

That honorable body seemed to labor under the impression that High Schools interfere with the good working of the Common Schools, and that the Common Schools teach everything that is necessary to be known by the ratepayers of Waterloo County.

A change for the better took place in 1875. The County Council divided the county into the Berlin High School District and the Galt High School District and agreed to help Berlin to build a new school—thanks to Moses Springer. Berlin then approached Waterloo, who consented to assist if a site were purchased in the Greenbush, if the cost of the school and its maintenance were borne according to the towns' respective assessments, and if Waterloo elected one-half of the trustees. That offer was accepted and the new Board bought three acres of land on the sand ridge in West King Street, from G. M. Bellinger of Wellesley for $650. The site was a potato patch and beside it were the Bachmann and Carroll places,—the latter the log cabin that once had been Waterloo's first school-house.

To John B. Hett and Henry Jaeger was awarded the contract of building the school, for $5,804. It was opened to use in January, 1876, with an attendance of ninety-one pupils. The staff comprised Mr. Connor, the Rev. Mr. Tuerk, and G. E. Shaw, M.A., Mathematical Master.

David Forsyth and Adolph Mueller

Mr. Shaw resigned from the teaching staff in March, 1876. The Board then engaged David Forsyth, B.A., of Galt. Mr. Forsyth was a man of original perceptions and wrapped up in Science. He was a pioneer in the introduction of practical work in the laboratory for pupils pursuing science courses in Ontario High Schools. Subsequently the Department of Education changed the textbooks so as to require practical experiments in chemistry, for example, instead of committing dry facts to memory.

At the B. H. S., athletic games were the handmaidens of study. Principal Connor encouraged cricket and Mr. Forsyth ushered in Association Football. Mr. Forsyth interested other High Schools and towns in "Soccer" and organized the Western Football Association. He was, too, a curler, played lacrosse, and bowled on the green.

His friend, Adolph Mueller, joined the teaching staff in 1876 and in succession of Mr. Tuerk taught Modern Languages. Mr. Mueller played football and gave good service to the Public Library, the Musical Society, and the B.-W. Hospital.

Meanwhile the attendance had increased. In 1881 the school had 105 tyros. Inspectors McLellan and Marling complimented the Board on the school's organization, equipment, and instruction. At that stage J. B. Dalzell and W. Mulloy were assistant teachers. Professor Cresswell Shaw was engaged to teach Music and Mr. Powell to teach the Commercial subjects in 1884. W. F. Chapman succeeded Mr. Powell and stayed until 1888. F. W. Sheppard followed Mr. Chapman and continued until 1904, when he was appointed an inspector of Public Schools.

Many boys who are now sucessful business or professional men were at that period graduated in the B. H. S. A group of youths have since risen to prominence in the Provincial and Dominion political fields and scores of graduates have gained enviable positions in commercial or professional life in the United States. Moreover there was a long train of boys and girls who entered the teaching profession and many who followed the light for culture's sake.

So far as school policies were concerned much of the school's progress was owed to long-time service by certain trustees. Among out-of-town members were: John B. Snyder, Christian Kumpf, Benjamin Devitt, George Moore, George Randall, and John Killer of Waterloo; Charles Hendry of Conestoga; A. Peterson and Dr. Vardon of Hawkesville; R. Y. Fish of Linwood and Dr. Morton of Wellesley. Here, John Motz and August R. Lang alternated as trustees. Dr. Bowlby was a member for thirty-five years and chairman for twenty-seven; Peter Shirk of Bridgeport served also for thirty-five years; whilst Hugo Kranz sat thirty-one years and for twenty-eight years was secretary.

In 1891 the Board bought the Carroll lots for $400 and expanded the playground. Captain Clark was then engaged to teach Gymnastics. Later on Miss Elizabeth Fennell was engaged to teach the girls Calisthenics and Captain Martin to drill the boys.

Changes

New trustees in the nineties were L. J. Breithaupt, Conrad Bitzer, P. S. Lautenschlager, and Dr. L. B. Clemens. From Elmira, Dr. Ulyott and A. W. Werner served in rotation.

The High School suffered a distinct loss on January 8, 1898, when Adolph Mueller suddenly expired. For nearly twenty-two years Mr. Connor,, Mr. Forsyth, and Mr. Mueller had labored side by side in behalf of the institution. As a mark of esteem his classes erected a tablet to his memory in his old class room.

A year previously Hugo Kranz had resigned the office of treasurer and been succeeded by his son Carl Kranz. Mr. Kranz, Sr., retained the secretaryship until 1899, when his son succeeded him, but remained on the Board till his death in 1901.

The Board expended $6,000 in remodelling the school in 1899. Shortly after W. A. Greene, of the W. G. & R. Co., while in New

York sent an account of the Manual Training work introduced by the city. It created interest here and the High School appointed Edward Smyth, Conrad Bitzer, A. R. Lang, and August Werner to investigate the merits of Manual Training.

Mr. Connor resigned the principalship in 1901, because of his impaired hearing. During his thirty years of service he never spared himself wherever the pupils or the school was concerned. In his teaching he strove to develop character and interested himself in the pupils' individual advancement. He once walked down to Doon, a distance of seven miles, to tell a youth he had passed a departmental examination. Mr. Connor assisted at the compilation of a High School Grammar, was the author of a work on Philology, and edited several English texts. For about two years the Board retained his services as Classical Master. Former pupils then presented him with a testimonial and a purse of $1,000. In 1925 the Old Boys' Association supplemented the gift with his portrait in oils, by Percy Ives of Detroit. Mr. Connor gave the portrait to the school. He was born in Wicklow, Ireland, on January 30, 1843. After his retirement he spent his closing years in Hamilton, where he deceased on November 3, 1929. His body was interred in Mount Hope cemetery, within hailing distance of his old school. (1)

Mr. Forsyth as Principal

Mr. Forsyth succeeded Mr. Connor as principal of the school. On his new duties he brought energy and a deal of executive ability to bear. Industries were then multiplying and the need for technical education arising. A wing was added to the school in 1903 for Manual Training and Domestic Science and a modern Commercial Course introduced. In 1904 the Department of Education raised the school to the status of a collegiate institute—The Berlin Collegiate and Technical Institute. The Board was then comprised of Edward Smyth (Chairman), Carl Kranz (Secretary), D. B. Detweiler, W. J. Motz, and A. L. Breithaupt of Berlin; W. A. Greene of Waterloo, Peter Shirk of Bridgeport, and A. W. Werner of Elmira.

The staff consisted of David Forsyth, Principal and Mathematics; D. S. Jackman, Science; H. G. Martyn, English; H. W. Brown, Art and Mathematics; W. H. Williams, Moderns; G. R. Dolan, Classics; L. Norman, Commerce; E. Detweiler, P.T. and English; Miss M. Zoellner, P.T.; D. W. Houston, Manual Training;

THE LATE PRINCIPAL DAVID FORSYTH, B.A.

THE LATE PRINCIPAL J. W. CONNOR, B.A.

H. W. BROWN, B.A.
Secretary-Treasurer.

PRINCIPAL R. N. MERRITT, B.A.

and Miss K. A. Fisher, Household Science. Miss Fisher is now on the staff of *Good Housekeeping* Magazine in New York City.

The Royal Commission on Technical Education

The Dominion Government appointed a Royal Commission in 1910 to investigate Technical Education. The commissioners, of whom Mr. Forsyth was one, spent eighteen months on a tour of America and Europe. Afterward their digest was made the basis of national legislation. During Mr. Forsyth's absence, W. H. Williams, M.A., acted as principal. Mr. Williams later joined the staff of University Schools, Toronto, with which institution he was connected up to the time of his death in the spring of 1937. Mr. Forsyth resumed his duties at the Collegiate in 1912.

At the Collegiate the attendance continued to increase. The Collegiate District was enlarged in 1914 to include the Town of Waterloo and the name of the institution changed to, "The Berlin and Waterloo Collegiate and Technical Institute." More accommodation was needed. Plans for a larger school were under consideration when the World War put a period to the project.

The Kitchener and Waterloo Collegiate

After the Great War the Dominion Government implemented the recommendations of the Royal Commission on Technical Education. Grants were made to every Province that was ready to supplement them. Ontario availed itself of the subsidy and extended assistance to every municipality willing to make provisions for a suitable site, erect adequate buildings, employ qualified teachers, and install the necessary equipment. That offer appealed to the local collegiate. A plan was evolved to demolish the old school, remodel the newer wing, and to erect a special building for technical education.

In 1921, while the plan was under consideration, Mr. Forsyth gave up the principalship. The Board conferred on him the title of Principal Emeritus, and for one year he acted as Mathematical Master. When he retired, it ended a teaching career of forty-six years, of which forty-five were spent in the one school. Afterward he bought a fruit farm near Beamsville, Ontario. where he indulged in his love for growing things. At the Old Boys' Reunion on August 5, 1925, Ora Walper of Detroit, a former student and admirer of Mr. Forsyth, presented his old principal with a portrait of himself, from the brush of Mr. Ives, which Mr. Forsyth gave to the school. He died on September 13, 1936, in his eighty-fourth year, and was laid to rest in Mount Hope.

Principal R. N. Merritt

After Mr. Forsyth's retirement, the Board was obliged to seek for a principal of unusual qualifications. For, says the school historian, "They were about to launch on a somewhat crowded sea of education a type of school quite new in the Province." The trustees selected Principal R. N. Merritt, B.A., of Owen Sound, in June, 1921. Mr. Merritt shouldered the task of building on a large scale, organized the combined school, and chose the teachers for the technical departments.

While the new collegiate was in course of construction, those that follow were members of the Board: E. O. Weber (Chairman), John A. Lang, Dr. J. F. Honsberger, C. W. Schiedel, M. S. Hallman, C. Reitzel, W. T. Sass, and Norman Schneider. The Advisory Committee consisted of: J. H. Baetz, H. F. Wilson, A. H. Welker, R. J. Wright, Arthur Foster, and O. H. Hughes, with Harry W. Brown as secretary of both bodies.

The K.-W. Collegiate and Technical School

The institute was opened for class-work on September 4, 1923. It was named, "The Kitchener and Waterloo Collegiate and Vocational School," and was formally set apart on April 4, 1924, by the Hon. H. J. Cody, Minister of Education.

The Departments

That youth prizes the educational advantages that the Collegiate offers them is evinced by the Attendance. In 1932 there were 1,418 names on the roll. As the number seemed likely to increase, and to avoid building while trade was in a decline, the Collegiate Board induced the Public and Separate School Boards of the Twin-City to open Fifth Form Classes, which gave some relief. Even so, there were 1,240 students on the Collegiate register in 1933. Of the number 571 were in the Academic Department, 452 in the Commercial Division, and 217 in the Technical School.

As the figures disclose, nearly fifty per cent. of the students followed academic courses. Of those who were graduated, fifty-eight gained Honors; twenty-five attended college or university;

THE KITCHENER AND WATERLOO COLLEGIATE AND VOCATIONAL SCHOOL BOARD

From left to right.—Standing: H. W. Brown, Sec'y-Treasurer, Rev. R. M. Haller, J. C. Klaehn, C. M. Reizel, R. N. Merritt, Principal, Dr. J. F. Honsberger, C. H. Harding, T. H. Kay, H. A. Gerbracht, Attendance Officer, W. H. Sage. Seated: C. W. Cressman, Mrs. O. W. Thompson, R. A. MacGillivray, Chairman, A. M. Snider, Vice Chairman, Mrs. P. J. McGarry, A. H. Welker. Absent: H. G. Mistele.

THE TEACHING STAFF

From left to right.—Rear row: A. W. Thomson, C. R. Philp, M. R. Smith, H. M. Sperling, C. T. Laing, R. C. Harding, W. MacMillan, H. D. Wallace, H. W. Casselman, F. H. Pugh, W. M. Prudham, C. B. Price. *Middle row:* W. J. Unwin, E. H. Devitt, H. E. Class, H. G. Crozier, F. H. Montgomery, E. M. Black, Miss M. L. Brill, Miss C. C. Coumans, Miss H. M. Tangney, B. N. Thompson, R. J. Hodd, A. F. Duncan, F. W. R. Dickson, M. F. Dickson. *Front row:* S. W. Hann, Miss M. B. Oaks, Miss E. J. Roberts, Miss S. R. Puncher, Miss P. Detenbeck, Miss H. C. Toll, H. W. Brown, Mr. R. N. Merritt, Principal, Miss L. C. Augustine, Miss M. M. Douglas, Miss M. A. Hayes, Miss E. Spohn, Miss M. E. Smith. *Absent:* Miss G. Logan.

while others either obtained positions or continued their studies at the Collegiate. In 1933, Betty Clement won the Bishop Strachan Scholarship and the University Women's Club Scholarship, and then enrolled herself at Toronto University. Margaret Sturm achieved the Toronto University Bursary and also studied there. The Second Carter Scholarship was won by Grace Schmidt, who afterward attended the Waterloo College. Doris Reuel was the winner of the Middle School Proficiency Medal, while Wilson Martin, by his gift of oratory, carried off the Principal's Prize for Citizenship. First Citizenship pins were won by Wilson Martin, Clay Hall, and William Wight. Annually a Poetry Contest, sponsored by the Western Ontario Branch of the Canadian Authors Association, is held among secondary schools. Recently, William Wight was awarded a gold medal for his poems and Grace Budd, the third prize.

Of the Commercial Course graduates, twenty-six obtained Honors in the Special Commercial; twenty-three in the Three-Years' Accountancy Course; and thirty-six in the Three-Years' Secretarial Course.

The Technical and Vocational School

Students of the Technical and Vocational School may take a three-year course in Electricity, Automobile, Machine Shop Practice, or Drafting. The departmental shops are equipped with modern machinery and apparatus, and the instruction imparted is highly practical; for the purpose is to graduate boys who will be of real use to their employers.

In the Drafting Room, for example, the student is taught how to draw a machine-part or piece of furniture to scale and therefrom to make a blue-print. If it be a tool or machine part the blue print goes to the Machine Shop, where it is implemented in steel. Should it be a piece of furniture it is handed to the Woodworking Department, where first a pattern is made and then the desk, table, or other article cabinetted as a factory mechanic does it. This division is provided with sawing, planing, dove-tailing, sanding, and other electrically-driven machinery, all of which was manufactured in the city by the Jackson & Cochrane Company.

In a community famous for its furniture, one might expect to find the largest number of students thronging at the woodworking benches. That division does attract many boys, but, owing to the demands of furniture and other manufacturers for young men capable of erecting and caring for machinery, slightly more boys go to the Machine Shop. Moreover, because of the openings for skilled mechanics in the motor-car trade, the Automobile Departments draws a shade more students than the other two divisions. On its floors may be seen several different makes of cars. Yonder one is minus its engine; this its speeding mechanism; and that its ignition device. Around each appliance stands a knot of young Henry Fords with tools in their hands and the trade-mark of their calling imprinted on their faces and on their overalls. Yet another groups are trying to locate motor troubles with the aid of meters.

The tuition in the Electrical Department likewise combines theory and practice. There the student learns how to bridle the mysterious force and set it to work to drive machinery, heat plates on an electric range, and illuminate homes and offices. While one group explores the "innards" of a motor, another and larger cluster may be seen wiring a house. As the young Knights of the Kilowatt study and experiment, they may perchance dream of the wireless transmission of power. Thirty-eight students were graduated from the Vocational School in 1933.

In the Domestic Science and Household Science Departments, the girls are given instruction in Foods, Cooking, and Clothing. To illustrate how the influence of the department has spread into all parts of the community, take the case of a man who called upon a city friend and found him making soap. "What are you busying yourself with?" the visitor inquired. The householder responded "Domestic Science."

Collegiate Clubs

The Collegiate has many clubs. Among them, the Poster Club, the Interform Debating Club, the Glee Club, the Orchestra, and the Dramatic Club.

Public Speaking Contests are a feature. Not long since, in the Junior Girls' Contest, Edith Gailer spoke on "Soviet Russia." She had once lived there and had witnessed the scenes she described. Her effort won the silver medal. At the same time, Mabel Kilian won the bronze medal for her, "Walking from Cape Town to Cairo." The Collegiate sends a team to represent the school in intercollegiate contests.

THE KITCHENER AND WATERLOO COLLEGIATE AND VOCATIONAL SCHOOL

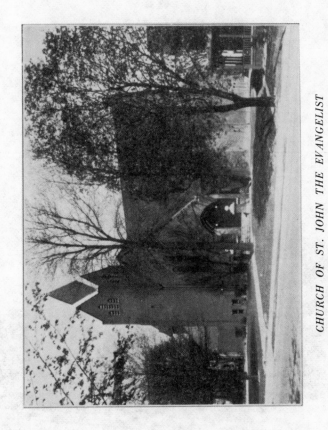

CHURCH OF ST. JOHN THE EVANGELIST

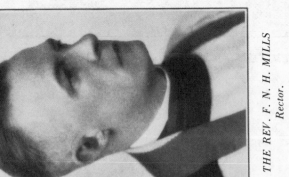

THE REV. F. N. H. MILLS
Rector.

Principal Merritt, who is an ardent curler, forwards athletic sports. Baseball, rugby, basketball, and field games are popular among the boys; while the girls enjoy baseball, basketball, and other pastimes.

The students issue a periodical called *The Grumbler*. It is a creditable production and has twice won the highest award in the Province, namely the Toronto Star Shield. In 1934, the Sports Editor said, "Today we realize the necessity of sport in the school; it is recognized as a foundation for success. It teaches us to be good losers, and assume a proper attitude toward our opponents. It builds us physically and mentally, and the 'knocks' received during the game prepare us for the struggle of life."

A component part of collegiate government is the Students' Council. It forms a link between the management and the student body, and makes for greater interest in studies and the school's welfare. As *The Grumbler* puts it, theirs "To strive, to seek, to find, and not to yield."

SOURCES

The first Minute Book—1855.
The Kitchener and Waterloo Collegiate and Vocational School.
1927. By H. W. Brown, B.A. Waterloo Historical Society's Annual.

CHURCH OF ST. JOHN THE EVANGELIST

From a modest commencement the Church of St. John the Evangelist (Anglican) has risen to prominence among city congregations. In 1835 a Church of England missionary visited Berlin. The *Canada Museum* announced: "On Saturday evening next, at candle light, there will be preaching in the English language in the church in this village."

Other Anglican missionaries may have come in later, but unfortunately the early records have been lost. The facts herewith presented were furnished from memory by Mr. Jonathan Cook.

The organization of Waterloo County and the construction of the Grand Trunk Railway brought in a number of Episcopalian families. For several years they had neither a place of worship nor a rector. In 1856 William Jaffray of Galt came here and founded a weekly newspaper. As an Anglican he missed the opportunity of attending the church's services. On inquiry he learned that there were a dozen or more Episcopalians in Berlin. To them he suggested that they lease a small building that rested east of the former Hagedorn Suspender block. Among the Anglicans who approved of the suggestion were: Dr. and Mrs. D. S. Bowlby; Mr. and Mrs. Abram Tyson; Mr. and Mrs. Ward H. Bowlby; Mr. and Mrs. Charles Stanton; Mr. and Mrs. James Colquhoun; and Mr. and Mrs. Henry F. J. Jackson.

The cluster were not numerically strong enough to engage a rector. Instead Mr. Jaffray acted as lay reader. The village continued to expand and the young congregation with it. In the late eighteen-fifties they appointed the Rev. Thomas Swaniston Campbell their rector and he ministered to them until 1859. The Rev. Campbell was succeeded by the Rev. Mr. Stimson. The erection of a church was undertaken in 1862, when the congregation purchased a lot in North Water Street, now the site of a later edifice.

With the passage of time the membership increased. In the early nineties the accommodation afforded by their first church had been overstepped. Accordingly, early in 1893, the construction of the present church was begun. The Building Committee consisted of Dr. D. S. Bowlby, John Fennell, and Jonathan Cook. Ere the end of that year the church was dedicated by the bishop of the diocese.

After the removal of the Rev. Mr. Stimson to another parish he was followed by the Rev. Mr. Baldwin, later Bishop Baldwin. After him came the rectors whose names follow: the Reverends Mr. Schulte, Mr. Murray, Mr. Beaumont, Mr. Falls, Mr. Sylvester Smith, Mr. Downie, Mr. Steen, Mr. Carl Smith, Mr. J. W. J. Andrews, Mr. H. M. Lang-Ford, and the Rev. J. N. H. Mills, the incumbent since 1935.

Numbered among the choirmasters have been: Messrs. Cline, Wm. Jaffray, Heinike, Tremble, Lamont, Wedd, Stairs, Zoellner, Herrickson, and W. R. Mason.

A number of years ago the congregation erected a handsome parish hall in Short Street.

William Wilfred Campbell

While the Rev. Mr. and Mrs. Campbell were residents of Berlin a son was born to them whom they christened William Wilfred Campbell. The date of his birth was probably June 1, 1858. The

Rev. Campbell was a relative of the Scottish poet, Thomas Campbell, and of Henry Fielding, the English novelist. His own son became a poet and man of letters. In 1889 he published a volume of poems entitled, *Lake Lyrics,* which gained him the title of the "Poet of the Lakes." His greatest achievements, however, were in the field of drama. The dramas *Mordred* and *Hildebrand* are said to be the best yet produced in Canada.

ALMA STREET CHURCH OF THE UNITED BRETHREN IN CHRIST

Bishop Jacob Erb was the first United Brethren preacher to come into this settlement. His home was in Pennsylvania, but he had relatives and friends in Waterloo Township, including a brother at Bridgeport. Yearly, at least, he preached to the settlers. On one occasion, in the eighteen-thirties, he conducted a revival at Waterloo, when a hundred conversions were registered. Later on, an Evangelical minister visited the community and opened an appointment. He found the way paved for his labors, since the Evangelical Association and the United Brethren faiths were similar and the people of German tongue and origin. Thus, the whole United Brethren class joined the Evangelical Association.

The United Brethren missionaries did not wholly cease activities. Subsequently, Israel Sloan, under the direction of Bishop Erb, opened a mission in the "Uncle Johnny Cornell's Church" in Sheffield, which was built by Mr. Cornell after his conversion. The Rev. Mr. Sloan remained for a number of years and organized the first class in Berlin in 1855. He was the earliest Presiding Elder for the district. After years of successful labors, he was drawn by reports of the gold rush to California.

While in the bud, the Berlin congregation purchased a small frame building, on the site of Grace Tabernacle, from the Wesleyan Methodists. From 1880 to 1889, it was turned to profitable account by the United Brethren. In 1889, a division which affected several American States and the Province of Ontario, occurred at a General Conference, when it was proposed to amend the Constitution of the Church. Those who favored the amendment were called Liberals.

They argued their case on four points: (a) an amended constitution; (b) a revised confession of faith; (c) lay delegations; (d) and secret societies. When the amendments were introduced into the conference, those who stood for the original constitution held that there could not rightly be any basic change made by the General Conference before a request had been received from two-thirds of the entire church body. The Liberals, however, contended that if they should be supported by a two-thirds vote of the conference, they had the power to amend the constitution. The cause was finally carried to the courts of Ontario and several States. The Supreme Court of Michigan ruled that the parties upholding the original articles of the constitution should obtain and retain the church properties. The Ontario courts decided that a General Conference, after the parliamentary method, had the power to amend the constitution. Accordingly, the Berlin Church was awarded to the Liberals. Eventually, the Liberals united with the Congregationalists.

After the courts had awarded the church property to the Liberals, the steadfasts determined to carry on. One of their members, Moses Eschleman, bought the Jerry Strome property in Church Street. The lot had a frontage of sixty feet in Church Street and extended to newly-opened Alma Street. Mr. Eschelman donated the upper part of the lot to the congregation, including a frame house facing Church Street. The congregation worshipped in that house until 1893, when the present Church Home in Alma Street was built and dedicated. This denomination has since flourished under the name of "The Alma Street Church of the United Brethren in Christ." Their parsonage is situated at No. 67 Alma Street.

Church Activities

The United Brethren Church founded the Freeport Academy in 1867-8 and conducted it until 1874. The academy was a select school where youths might procure a higher education under religious leadership and become grounded in the tenets of the United Brethren Church. The first principal was Isaac L. Bowman, father of the late Dr. Hervey Bowman. Isaac Bowman was followed by George Scott. Another instructor was the Rev. John B. Schlichter. In the class of 1869, there were twenty-one students. After seven years, the academy was closed owing to a lack of funds.

PARISH HALL OF ST. JOHN THE EVANGELIST CHURCH

ST. JOHN THE EVANGELIST'S CHURCH PARSONAGE

St. Mary's School
Kitchener, Ont.

In the Berlin Church, the choir of 1884 comprised: the Misses Emma Weaver, Rachel Weaver, Nancy Bowman, Livia Shirk, Mary Shirk, Miss Stouffer, and J. B. Weaver, Fred Sherk, Arthur Bowman, Abram O. Bowman, and Frank Bowman.

Foreign Missions

The Alma Street United Brethren Church has long been active in Foreign Missions. Their activities include the recruitment of missionaries and the support of such denominational work as the Sierre Leone Mission in West Africa. To that barbarous land the local church has sent forth as missionaries those that follow: the Rev. and Mrs. A. F. Stoltz, Will Nash, and the Rev. Lloyd Eby. These shepherds did creditable work until worn out by jungle fever, but lived to return to their homeland.

Nor are the Church's activities confined to West Africa. In part, the local church supports the Canton Chinese School in Canton, China, and the Moy Ling Memorial School in Portland, Oregon. Many Chinese have been trained for religious work among their countrymen in American and Chinese cities. In addition, the local church has contributed to the Chinese field the Rev. Staunton Lautenschlager, Mrs. S. Lautenschlager (formerly Miss Sarah Herner) and the Rev. Roy Lautenschlager.

Furthermore, support is given to the U.B.C.E. Medical Missions. This is a work undertaken by the Young people of the denomination. They make provision for the training of medical missionaries, paying their salaries in the field, and in purchasing supplies for the West African Mission. In Toronto, the denomination has a mission in Bloehm Avenue and another in Silverthorne Street. By earnest co-operation, all the foregoing engagements in the international vineyard have succeeded beyond cavil.

Bishop Wright, father of Wilbur and Orville Wright, the inventors of the aeroplane, often visited the United Brethren Church. But when interviewed would only say that his daughter made the calculations and his sons worked them out.

Church Leaders

A partial list of the ministers who served before and after the division now follows: The Revs. Isaac Sloan, S. L. Downey, George Plowmen, George Waite, Henry Krupp, Wm. Riddle, John Spencer, S. E. Cormany, Samuel Mosher, A. B. Sherk, C. W. Backus, D. B.

Sherk, George Backus, J. B. Bowman, Benjamin Bowman, Israel Bowman, Robert Clark, Isaac Groh, John Groh, G. W. Dinnius; and the Revs. Major, Showers, Nash, Dudgeon, Holtzman, Crowder, Rott, Howe, Hollaway, Pitman, Wm. Gribble, S. H. Schwartz, A. F. Stoltz, A. R. Springer, Moses Clemens, Staunton Lautenschlager, W. C. South, and George Stover Seiple. The Rev. Elmer Becker, who was the pastor for six years, was appointed General Secretary of Christian Education in Huntington, Ind., in August, 1937. The Rev. G. R. Shepherdson of Grand Rapids, Mich., then succeeded the Rev. Mr. Becker.

BIBLIOGRAPHY
Historical Sketch of the United Brethren Church in Early Days. By the Rev. C. W. Backus and Mr. Frank Shantz. 1930. Kitchener.

THE CATHOLIC SEPARATE SCHOOLS

A Separate Catholic School was established by the Rev. George Laufhuber, S.J., in 1859. He was promised teachers by the Sisters of Notre Dame, but when the school was ready the Mother House in Milwaukee was unable to send them. Father Laufhuber therefore had to employ lay teachers. A room in the rectory was set aside for the accommodation of sixty or more pupils and John Berberich of New Germany engaged to teach them. The courses were in English, although German was efficiently taught as a school subject.

Mr. Berberich was followed by another experienced teacher named Joseph Fischer. Mr. Fischer taught about two years and then went to New York City to publish Catholic Church music. He was succeeded by the Rev. Charles Leverman, O.B.S., of St. Jerome's College, who in 1869 withdrew and entered the Montreal Seminary. In close succession the lay teachers that follow were in charge: Edward Yenn, Peter Kaiser, John Zinger, William Obrecht, and Charles Lang, all of whom were graduates of St. Jerome's College.

From 1870 on the number of pupils increased, slowly at first and then faster and faster. A large brick school was built near the rectory in 1874. When it was completed the Sisters of Notre Dame took charge and have conducted primary education ever since. The first principal was Mother Clotilde, with one assistant Sister. The

SACRED HEART SCHOOL.

ST. JOSEPH'S SCHOOL

ST. JOHN'S SEPARATE SCHOOL

THE LATE THOMAS PEARCE
Inspector of Public Schools, 1871 - 1912.

former rectory was converted into a convent for them. In 1885 a new, comfortable convent was built and the old one remodelled as a school. Four years later the school of 1874 was enlarged by the addition of two stories, giving in all six classrooms.

For the first thirty years the School Board was obliged to levy a head tax on Separate School supporters. The reason was that the regular municipal tax was insufficient to defray expenses. After 1889 the rate bill was abolished and the school financed at the same rate as the Public Schools. That change was made in the closing years of the Rev. Louis Funcken's pastorate.

Under the leadership of the Rev. William Kloepfer the school was enlarged in 1897 and provision made for twelve classrooms. Mother Clotilde died in 1902 and was succeeded by Sister Caia, her first companion and assistant. Sister Caia died in 1914 and was succeeded by Mother Damascene, who, in 1916, had seventeen teachers and 750 pupils.

From its inception the school has been kept in a high state of efficiency, both as regards equipment and thoroughness of instruction.

St. Ann's Training School

Subsequently a new interpretation of an old law caused a temporary difficulty. That related to the qualifications of religious teachers and made it obligatory on the Sisters to secure the same qualifications as other Separate and Public School teachers. Besides they were obliged to obtain their training in approved High Schools and in the Provincial Normal Schools. As a consequence the Sisters had either to establish a secondary school for their candidates or give up teaching in Ontario. To surmount the difficulty the School Board, in 1907, purchased the Erb homestead in Weber Street and in September of that year opened "The St. Ann Training School."

An increase of candidates in 1908 created a need for more accommodation. Accordingly the Pearce Terrace in Ontario Street was acquired and fitted up for the purpose. Those enterprises, for which the chief credit belongs to the Rev. William Kloepfer's foresight, have fulfilled all expectations.

The Sacred Heart Ward School

The Rev. A. J. Fischer was appointed pastor of St. Mary's Church in 1909, in succession of Father William Kloepfer. During

Father Fischer's term school accommodation again became a pressing question. Hence a fine new four-roomed building was erected in the North Ward, near the cemetery, at a cost of about $24,000, including the site. In 1915, under the Rev. Father Spetz, the School Board added a second story to the school, at a cost of $13,000. First named "The St. Anthony Ward School," it is now called "The Sacred Heart School." (1)

The Very Rev. A. L. Zinger was appointed rector of St. Mary's parish in 1919. During his regime a second ward school was built on the corner of Albert Street and Courtland Avenue, at a cost of $90,000, and named "St. Joseph's School." In 1925 the Sacred Heart School was enlarged by an addition of four rooms, at an outlay of $29,000.

About Eastertime in 1928 Father Zinger was succeeded by the Rev. M. Hinsberger. While Father Hinsberger was Chairman of the School Board a red brick, eight-roomed school, modern in every detail, was erected in the West Ward at a cost of $60,000 and named "St. John's School."

The Schools of Today

The members of the Separate School Board are: The Rev. C. B. Meyer, Chairman; Lloyd Knipfel, Secretary; George Huck, Clerk; A. C. Wintermeyer, Treasurer; E. F. Donohue, R. Dietrich, Joseph Huck, Henry Krug, John Schmalz, Oscar Lauber, and J. Colombo.

J. C. Walsh, B.A., B.Paed., is Inspector of the Separate Schools. In 1917 Mr. Walsh was appointed Inspector in an inspectorate with Ottawa as headquarters. In 1927, the Department of Education transferred him to Division X, with Kitchener as headquarters.

On the rolls of the city's Separate Schools there are 1,759 pupils. The teaching staff comprises 49 teachers, as follows: 37 grade teachers, Sisters and lay in the four regular Separate Schools, four Sisters in St. Mary's High School, three female supervising teachers for the special subjects of Music, Art and Physical Training, four male teachers for senior boys' classes, Grades VIII and IX located in St. Jerome's College, and one special Shop Work instructor for the preceding boys. Household Science is taught in all the schools.

Separate School pupils have always had good success in passing the Entrance and Lower School examinations. But examination results are not taken as a criterion of the success or otherwise of the work in the schools. Instead success or failure is rather measured by the growth and development of the individual child, varying according to his natural abilities.

In each of the four schools there is a well-stocked library. The value of the books totals $2,915. Whilst the capital invested in the Separate Schools amounts to $340,000, not including $10,000 worth of teaching equipment.

SOURCE

1. *The Catholic Church in Waterloo County.* 1916. By the Rev. Theobald Spetz, C.R., D.D., Toronto.

KITCHENER PUBLIC LIBRARY

CITIZENS OF THE SIXTIES

C. A. Ahrens, I.
Herman Ahrens, Auctioneer.
B. Allendorf, Weaver.
H. Bachman, Photographer.
Carl Becker, Carpenter.
J. Boedecker, Bookseller.
Carl Boehmer, Merchant.
W. Becking, Wagonmaker
J. Blankstein, Carpenter.
H. Bornhold, Shoe Merchant
And. Borth, Cabinetmaker.
A. Brandt, Cabinetmaker.
Henry Braun, Mason Contractor.
P. Breiting, Turner.
Henry Brickner; Cooper.
J. Dauberger, Brickmaker.
G. M. DeBus, Sr., Hairdresser.
Conrad Doering, Weaver.
Conrad Doerr, Carpenter.
J. R. Eden, Financial Agent.
C. Engelhardt, Bookseller.
Jacob Ewald, Contractor.
Mr. Feick, Felt Manufr.
G. Froelich, Potash Mnfr.
Wm. Gastmeier, Builder.
Valentine Gildner, Blacksmith.
W. H. Goetz, Tobacconist
M. Grebenstein, Tailor.
J. Grischow, Carpenter.
John Haller, Hatmaker.
Peter Heins, Merchant.
W. Hertfelder, Weaver.
Henry Hett, Sr.
Joseph Hobson, Surveyor.
Ferd. Hueghlin, Painter.
George Jaeger, Mason
Henry Jaeger, Contractor.
Henry Karn, Mason.
George Klein, Butcher.
Adam Klippert, Foreman.
John Klippert, Detective.
Henry Knell, Sr., Jeweller.
W. H. G. Knowles, Merchant.
John Koch, Baggageman.

J. Koch, Sr., Carpenter.
Jacob Koch, Carpenter.
J. Krug, Carpenter.
"Chicago Jake" Kraemer, Herbs.
Fred Lake, Contractor.
Martin Messner, Tailor.
Alex Millar, Barrister.
Rudolph Mylius, M.D.
Henry Nahrgang, Tailor.
Wm. Niehaus, Shoe Merchant.
Wm. Oelschlager, Manufacturer.
Wm. Pipe, M.D.
George Randall, Tobacco Mnfr.
Fred Rommell, Tailor.
Alexander Roy, Merchant.
Simon Roy, Nurseryman.
Balthasar Schmalz, Weaver.
Milton Schofield, Surveyor.
Bruno Schmidt, M.D.
Henry Schwenn, Brickmaker.
D. Schwenkettel, Tinsmith.
W. L. Schmidt, Merchant.
Louis Seiler, Flour & Feed.
George Seip, Brewer.
Martin Simpson, Weaver.
Henry Sippel, Weaver.
Joseph Spetz, Brewer.
Wm. Stein, Tailor.
C. Stuebing, Importer.
A. Steinke, Tanner.
F. W. Tuerk, Artisan.
Vetter Bros., Painters.
Emil Vogelsang, Button Mnfr.
Charles Vogt, Tanner.
John Walmsley, Agr. Implements.
George Ward, Blacksmith.
Julius Werner, Wagonmaker.
James Whiting, M.D.
Henry Wittig, Hatmaker.
Peter Wolfhardt, Roadmaster.
G. W. Wright, M.D.
Benjamin Ziegler, Blacksmith.

—From a Directory.

NOTES OF THE SIXTIES

Henry Ford's motto: "Cut your own wood and it will warm you twice." In the sixties it was a boy's chore to keep the wood-box full. Eddie Hoffman, the druggist's son, who had been given an improved saw, one Saturday levied a toll of liquorice, marbles and toys on his chums for the chance to try the new blade. Result, enough wood cut to last a week.

Pleasant evenings were spent around those wood-fires. By candle-light or lamp-light, the father cast up his accounts, while the mother sewed, and the children studied their lessons. When the father laid his cash-book aside, the children clambered to his knees and beseeched him to tell them of the Timm family's voyage to America. Complying, he said that their sailing vessel was blown far southward by adverse winds. The ship's supply of water ran low and at last was doled out in spoonsful. Finally, the store of water was used up. The voyagers then preserved their lives with sips of wine.

After the story hour the mother shepherded her flock to their bedroom. It had neither fireplace nor radiator. On a cold winter morning Jack Frost froze the water in their pitcher. The youngsters slipped out of the featherbed, hurriedly dressed, broke the ice, and washed their face and hands. Then scampered down stairs with a candle in a tin holder. Some homes had brass candlesticks, which are now treasured as heirlooms.

Schoolboys played duck-on-the-rock, shinny, and later on, base-ball. Baseball was played with a yarn ball. A batter was out when a fielder caught the ball either on the fly or first bounce. In the winter the lads skated on the ponds in boots that reached to their knees. In the summer they went barefooted. South Ward boys fished Shantz's dam; West Ward bairns, Schneider's pond; and East and North Ward Jungen, the Bridgeport waters. The young sportsmen came back with strings of fish and a flute whittled from a willow twig. Older boys lugged out guns to the woods in the West Ward and shot black squirrels or wild pigeons..

At Christmas, tinkling sleigh-bells and wishes for "ein froe-liches Christfest." The Christmas tree showered down for a boy a Noah's ark, a mouth-organ, and a set of small tools. To this day, boys of German ancestry prefer mechanical toys to any other gift. North Ward boys, before merchants sold toy airplanes, drew planes on the sidewalk with a piece of chalk. Young mechanics made workboxes, inlaid with mosaic, for their sweethearts, with her and his initials on them.

Besides the church festivals of Christmas and Easter, grown-ups set aside the day after Christmas and Easter Monday as holidays. Public balls were usually held on these days. Colloquially, a "Second Christmas" meant a bit of good luck.

The Pennsylvanians brought in grandfather's clocks, a few of which are still ticking away. German families brought over small clocks from the Black Forest or cuckoo clocks.

Of those early families, the male members mostly disappeared after the third generation.

That there were many warm hearts in Waterloo County is made clear by an incident of 1867. The County Council then bought 141 acres of land in outer Frederick Street, from John Eby, for $9,409, and built a House of Refuge at a cost of $3,908. The Home was opened in 1869, with Richard McMahon as manager and Mrs. McMahon as matron. Before the end of that year, seventy-six aged or infirm persons were admitted to the institution. The Waterloo County House of Refuge was the first one to open its doors in Ontario. Today the Old People's Home is managed by Edward A. Amos, and is a much larger institution.

MERCHANTS OF THE EIGHTEEN-FIFTIES - SEVENTIES

In the eighteen-fifties, John A. Mackie, grandfather of Dr. Harry M. Lackner, bought the first store in the village from Mrs. Fred Millar. In 1862 he was appointed Justice of the Peace and served for forty-two years. In 1888, he built the Mackie block. Mr. Mackie was a member of the Public School Board for twenty years and town treasurer for twenty years. When the Economical Fire Insurance Company was founded, he was elected director.

Abram Tyson opened a department store in that decade in the American block. He served the citizens as Reeve and the county as Warden. Of a family of sons and daughters, Mrs. Harriet J. Piper and Miss Lillian Tyson only are now residents of the city.

Frederick Snyder, a silversmith, dealt in stoves and tinware. His first stoves were procured in Albany, N.Y. He made good tinware and sent peddlers out to exchange wares for furs, rags and sheepskins. It was said of him in 1909: "He has kept on turning tin into silver up to now." Mr. Snyder built a block at 51 West King Street in 1859. He served on the School Board and Town Council. He was also an original director of the Economical Fire Insurance Company, of which his son, Fred W. Snyder, is Managing Director.

Henry B. Bowman, second merchant, built a three-story block on the Bank of Montreal corner in the fifties. In the sixties he was succeeded by his son, Israel D., and son-in-law, Peter Hines, a taxidermist. Allan Huber and Alexander Roy afterward occupied the block as merchants. Later on J. B. Fellman occupied the store, but subsequently built the Fellman block, where now the Bank of Commerce stands. Giller & Bowman, and C. Sugarman were among the later lessees of the Bowman block. After a time, the block was purchased by H. L. Janzen and then sold to the Bank of Montreal.

Part of Henry Bowman's block was leased by his son, William H., as a drugstore. Afterward he was appointed C.P.R. Ticket and Express agent, long before the Grand River Railway was built. He sent many young farmers to the Canadian West. His son Fred had the agency for about two years after his father died, then Fred went to Hamilton. W. H. Bowman's son-in-law, A. J. Roos, then bought the drugstore and took over the C.P.R. ticket, express, and telegraph agency, continuing till 1927. The C.P.R. ticket and telegraph office is now managed by Victor M. Wood.

Peter Hymmen the first, tinsmith, opened a shop in the early fifties. He was a skilled mechanic. Once he made a suit of armor out of tin, that he painted to resemble iron, for a youth who wished to go to a masquerade ball at the German Club. He made also jelly bowls with the face of a fish or lion. He was the father of Peter, Henry, and Otto Hymmen.

August Fuchs was an early jeweller and watchmaker. He built the Fuchs block and in town-building had the golden touch. Mr. Fuchs was the father of George Fox, one of Canada's foremost violinists.

John Kimmel, architect, came to Berlin in 1854. As there was little demand for his professional services, he opened a grocery at

20 West King Street. Later on he had a hotel in the same stand. John Kimmel and A. H. Kimmel of the Kimmel Realty Co. are sons, while the late August Kimmel, the oldest boy, became a prominent felt and rubber manufacturer.

Carl W. C. Kranz established a general store at 22-24 East King Street in 1855. His son Hugo became his partner as C. Kranz & Son. When the father died in 1875, the son was mayor of Berlin. In 1876, the latter built the block at 46-50 East King Street, which are respectively owned now by S. R. Ernst and Arnold Brothers, tobacconists. Mr. Kranz continued the store till 1893, when he was appointed manager of the Economical. J. U. Clemens & Co. then leased the premises at 50 East King Street. After Mr. Kranz's death, L. J. Breithaupt said, "Mr. Kranz sacrificed a great deal for the town of Berlin."

Henry Knell, Sr., a goldsmith, emigrated from Toes, Switzerland, to Pittsburgh, Pa., in 1854. He was the only jeweller in that city who could set a diamond. Shortly after cholera broke out and he went to Zurich, Ontario, where he lived for a short time with an uncle, and then came to Berlin. His first store was in East King Street, where afterward the Sachs Plumbing Company located their business. Mr. Knell made his own wedding rings. He built a division of the Germania block; sat in the town council; and for a number of years was a director of the Economical Fire Insurance Company. His brother Frederick was a manufacturer of knitted goods; and his son Henry is Vice-President of the Waterloo Trust and Savings Company, and President of the Economical Fire Insurance Company.

Business Men of the Sixties and Seventies

William Niehaus, shoemaker, came here in 1862 and plied his trade. He was the first tenant in the American block. A few years later he accepted a $100 consignment of factory-made shoes and sold them. Gradually, ready-made footwear supplanted the custom-made shoe and shoemaker. Mr. Niehaus built a division of the Germania block; and soon afterward sold his shoe store to his son William. His son Charles was long postmaster here.

Among Mr. Niehaus' competitors were Wm. Simpson, father of the furniture manufacturer, and Henry Bornhold. Mr. Bornhold built a block near the post-office and numerous houses in the South

Ward. He was a good man for the town. His son Fred was once financially interested in the C. A. Ahrens Shoe Company; and his grandson, K. E. Bornhold, is the owner of a hardware store at 115 East King Street.

John Fennell founded a retail and wholesale hardware enterprise here in 1863, and leased quarters in the Victoria block from J. A. Mackie. Mr. Fennell was one of the first coal merchants in the town. He admitted his son James P. to a partnership and they were for many years lessees of premises in the Royal Bank block. Mr. Fennell, Sr., was the first President of the Board of Trade and for thirty years President of the Economical. In 1923, after his death, the assets and good will of their business were sold by James P. Fennell to C. N. Weber and his father, Karl Weber. The new owners bought the former Randall & Roos block at 66 S. Queen Street and incorporated the Weber Hardware Company Ltd. As retailers and wholesalers, the company specializes in mill supplies, builders' hardware, mechanics' tools, blacksmith and garage supplies, paints, electrical lines, and sporting goods. Hardware figures largely in living, farming, and manufacturing. It is a far cry from the articles of wood and plain materials used by our grandfathers to the present day. In 1863, Mr. Fennell imported most of his hardware. Afterward some lines were made in Canada. In the multiplicity of changes that have taken place in the last seventy-five years, science and technology have put everything on a technical plane, assuring not only improvement but uniformity of manufacture. The Weber Hardware Company has kept pace with that progress. The territory covered by their travellers has a radius of 150 miles, whilst by means of a large catalogue they serve customers from Vancouver to Halifax.

A Family of Brickmakers and Flour-Millers

John Bramm, the first, came here in the early sixties, and opened a brickyard at 58 West Weber Street. Afterward he owned yards in other parts of the town. Mr. Bramm married Miss Elizabeth Wenzel and was the father of six children: Anna, Henry, John, George, Adam, and Marie Elizabeth. "Betty" was married to P. K. Weber, long city roadmaster. Harry once conducted the American hotel. For many years, John Jr.. and George had a brickyard in Wilmot Street. Next they bought the flour-mill in S. Queen

Street, operating it till 1906, when they sold it to Irvin Master. The brothers were noted fishermen and hunters. After the sale of the mill, John lived in retirement. George, four years later, opened a coal-office at 568 S. Queen Street. In 1892 he married Miss Anna (Ash) Huehn, a sister of Christian Huehn, who was accountant for the Breithaupt Leather Co., and who built the Huehn Block in West King Street. Mrs. Bramm has lived at 560 S. Queen Street ever since her marriage. The district east of South Queen Street, between the mill and Schneider Avenue, was then given over to apple orchards and potato patches. Mr. Bramm continued the coal business until his death in 1928. Since then his daughter, Mrs. Kreiner, has managed the office.

Henry S. Boehmer and Associates

Henry S. Boehmer, merchant, began business at 16 East King Street, in a store 16 x 20 feet, in 1868. He and his brothers Charles and Philip erected the Dunke block, and in association with them and his brothers August and Herman, the block at 58-62 East King Street. At various times, his four brothers and P. S. Lautenschlager were partners of the store enterprise; and later on, E. D. Lang, Julius Appel, and his sons, A. O. and E. O. Boehmer. The firm dealt in dry-goods and became one of the chief mercantile houses in the county. Mr. H. S. Boehmer broke ground in Alma Street and built six houses in it. Elsewhere in the town he erected upward of fifty homes. At the time of his death he was President of the Dominion Table Company, and a director of the Berlin Piano Company and J. Y. Shantz & Sons. On his deathbed he was told of the Wellesley Railway by-law, just voted on, having lacked three votes of the necessary majority. "What a pity," said he, "I have three votes that would have carried it."

August and Charles Boehmer in the sixties owned a hardware, stove and tinware store at 58 East King Street. In 1874, they began manufacturing paper boxes, after selling the hardware stock to C. E. Moyer and the tinware shop to Peter and Henry Hymmen. Hymmen Bros. first leased quarters in the Canadian block from J. Y. Shantz, and later on in the Germania block. Hardware and plumbing were added to their lines. In 1892, Peter Hymmen bought his brother's share. In 1906, he opened up West King Street as a business section, erecting a large block at No. 158. Mr. Hymmen was active until shortly before his death in 1930. Prior to his departure, his sons, H. L. Hymmen and Homer Hymmen, had been their father's associates and now direct the enterprise. After Henry Hymmen left the firm he was for four years with H. Wolfhard & Co., and then bought C. E. Moyer's hardware stock. He carried on in the Dunke block until 1900, when he was appointed superintendent of the waterworks. George Potter, who for many years had been with John Fennell & Son, bought Mr. Hymmen's stock, and is still doing business at the old stand.

In the mid-seventies Isaac Hoffman owned the "Golden Lion" store that stood east of his furniture factory on the corner. He sold factory and store to Anthes, Staebler & Co. Afterward this firm sold the store to W. L. Schmidt, a well-remembered merchant. Subsequently William Metcalfe conducted a grocery and liquor store in those premises. Afterward his sons William and George continued the business there and on the Waterloo Trust and Savings Company corner.

Smyth Brothers

Edward and Robert Smyth founded the dry-goods firm of Smyth Bros. in 1877. The brothers imported merchandise from Europe and introduced the cash system. For nineteen years they were lessees of the Ernst block, built by Hugo Kranz. Afterward they leased the Janzen block at 39 East King street from H. L. Janzen. East of the block, on the lower side of the *Telegraph* lane, stood a two-story frame building. Joseph Gorman, grocer, occupied the lower floor, and J. P. Starnaman & Son, makers of picture frames, etc., the upper floor. Smyth Bros. bought the property from Mr. Janzen and in 1909 erected a big block. Edward Smyth retired about 1925 and Robert Smyth in 1928. Both brothers were town-builders.

Other Merchants

Other merchants of the period were: John Kaiser & Co., general merchants; Macfarlane Bros., clothing; Charles Koehn, flour and feed; Fred Sach, monuments; Moffatt & Lang, flour and feed; Charles Mueller, lunch-room; J. W. Krueger, butcher; Gottlieb & Grebenstein, tailors; John Roat, lumber dealer; A. Vanderhart, tailor; and John George Schmidt, shoemaker.

Contractors

Henry Braun, mason, began his career as a contractor in 1864. He continued till 1889, when he was succeeded by his son Casper. The son built some of the principal churches and factories of his time. Later on, he engaged in the monument business on the corner of King and Water Streets. Of late years the works have been situated at 16 Andrew Street. Since Mr. Braun's death in 1937, his son, G. B. Braun, is manager of the estate. Casper Braun gained the lasting esteem of the public.

Jacob Baetz, Sr., came to Berlin in 1868 and learned the mason's trade. Afterward he became a building contractor, beginning with homes and then some of the largest blocks and churches of his day. Mr. Baetz was active for nearly fifty years. During that period, he was for some years a business associate of John S. Anthes in the Anthes Furniture Company. In 1908 Mr. Baetz erected a factory at 264 Victoria Street for his sons Jacob H. and Charles J., in which they founded the Baetz Furniture Company. In 1916, the brothers established also the Baetz Specialty Company to make floor and table lamps. Two years later they purchased an interest in the Anthes Furniture Company (now the Anthes-Baetz Co.) at 242 Breithaupt Street, makers of high-grade furniture. Mr. J. H. Baetz is Managing Director of the three companies, and Mr. C. J. Baetz, Vice-President of the three companies.

A Noted Merchant Tailor

Emil Vogelsang met Matthias Riener in New York City in 1873 and invited him to locate in Berlin. When Mr. and Mrs. Riener learned that there was a Swedenborgian Church here they decided to come over. Mr. Riener had learned the cutter's trade in Vienna and after his arrival here he began business as a merchant tailor in Berges & Shelley's former stand in Frederick Street. In 1893, Mr. Riener rebuilt the structure. The contractor piled 15,000 bricks in the street. One Saturday morning, the farmers' wagons caused a traffic jam. A ruffled citizen summoned Chief Winterhalt, who ordered Wm. Polomski, mason-tender, to remove the bricks. "Ja, Ja," said William, "before you kin valk to King Street und beck the pricks vill be avay."

All the members of the Riener family were musical, and a daughter, Mrs. Miller, often sang in light operas. The father, too,

THE REV.
HERMAN A. SPERLING, D.D.
Pastor, St. Peter's Church

THE FIRST ST. PETER'S
LUTHERAN CHURCH
(1863.)

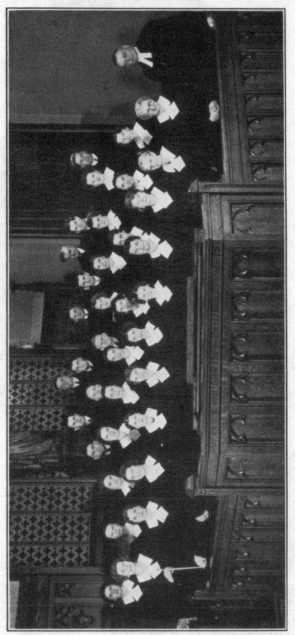

ADULT CHOIR OF ST. PETER'S CHURCH

Front row, left to right: Mrs. A. Bindernagel, Choir Director; Mrs. C. Panhofer, Miss Ruth Cherrie, Mrs. E. Krieger, Miss V. Uhrig, Miss K. Bowman, Miss V. Benninger, Miss M. Kudoba, Miss E. Gebhardt, Miss E. Smith, Miss B. Smith, Rev. Dr. H. A. Sperling, Pastor. Second row: Miss W. Steinke, Miss E. May, Mrs. H. Kraft, Mrs. L. Doelle, Miss A. Schwartz, Miss A. Glady, Miss R. Benninger, Miss M. Seyler, Miss W. Hiller, Mrs. J. Koegler. Third row: H. Bauer, P. Hiller, N. Totzke, Mrs. A. Giller, Mrs. A. Dreger, Miss A. Miglarini, Miss B. Smolinski. Fourth row: J. Rehner, H. Luft, C. Richber, A. Giller, E. Kugler, F. Hiller, C. Stroh, A. Kimmel.

was an active member of the Concordia Society. His closest friends among the members were Charles A. Ahrens, Sr., Louis Bardon, Christ. Meisner, and Herman Rathman.

Mr. Riener's son, Earl Edward, entered the real-estate field in 1907. One of his earliest sales was the northwest corner of King and Gaukel Streets to Hartman Krug. Among later sales were the transfer of the Church of the New Jerusalem to the T. Eaton Company and the purchase of the William Roos property in North Queen Street for the Church of the Good Shepherd. Mr. Riener is a member of the Board of Trade. Of strong faith in the city's future, he expects it will have a population of 75,000 by 1950. With regard to apartments, Mr. Riener admits they are a convenience for elderly people, but is of the opinion that every young couple should own a home of their own.

Charles Quirmbach

Charles P. Quirmbach of Preston leased the Railroad Hotel in Berlin in 1874. It stood opposite Shantz's foundry in West King Street and was a long white building with a verandah in King Street. It got its name from Railroad Street, now College Street. On the lower corner of King and Young Streets then stood Mr. Brueckner's cooper-shop, and next to it, an old frame blacksmith-shop. In 1876 the merchants employed Mr. Quirmbach as a private night watchman, a position that he filled acceptably for nineteen years. He was the father of Emil and Herman Quirmbach, the Rev. Albert Quirmbach, and other sons and daughters.

ST. PETER'S LUTHERAN CHURCH

The Rev. John Bernheim of Elizabethtown, Pa., was the first Lutheran missionary sent to Upper Canada. After travelling 600 miles by stage-coach, canalboat, and on foot, he reached Berlin on August 8, 1835. He visited Lutheran homes in the Dorf and vicinity, preached, baptized, and administered communion. On September 19, 1835, he conducted the first Lutheran confirmation service ever held in Canada and then returned to Pennsylvania.

Later on a group of Lutherans delegated Adam Keffer of Vaughan Township to seek for a missionary in Pittsburgh, Pa. He set out on his 375-mile tramp in the winter of 1849 and pleaded with the Pittsburgh Synod to send them a pastor. In response the Rev. C. F. Diehl was stationed in Vaughan Township. Six additional missionaries soon followed him to the Canadian field. Among them was Pastor Wurster, who settled in Preston, and Pastor Kaesmann, who pioneered in Berlin.

On November 2, 1862, he organized the Berlin Lutherans at a meeting held in the Stadthalle. Ninety-three persons signed the roll. The first trustees were: Johann Kimmel, Sr., John J. Woelfle, Conrad Weber, Henry Jaeger, John B. Hett, Henry Kreutzer (Secretary), and Friedrich Rittinger (Treasurer).

Shortly after a Sunday School was formed. Both school and church services were held in the village hall, but those quarters soon became too small. The members then determined to build a church. A site, comprising 29/100 of an acre, was purchased in North Queen Street, for $178.50, and the materials ordered for a brick building, 36 x 60 feet. The church was built by day labor and nearly every male member gave a hand. Johann Kimmel, Sr., was overseer of the masonwork and John B. Hett of the carpenterwork. The cost of the building was $2,300 and the chosen name, "The Evangelical Lutheran St. Peter's Church." It was dedicated on July 19, 1863.

In 1867 Pastor Kaesmann reported to the Canada Synod 400 communicants and 200 Sunday School scholars. Joseph Hoelscher was a member of his first confirmation class. The Rev. Kaesmann was transferred to another vineyard in 1869. No other pastor was sent in his stead. They extended a call to Pastor Wurster but he was unable to accept it. Of the search for a minister Frederick Rittinger said, "Der Herr moege ihn dafeur belohnen, und die Gemeinde es nie vergessen und ihm zu zeiten manchmal so einen kleinen Stein in der Garten werfen." Afterward the Rev. Mr. Sagehorn of Zurich accepted an invitation and was inducted on March 31, 1870.

A Second Church

The congregation increased in number. In 1872 they bought an acre and a half of land for a cemetery, for $195. The sum of $310 was spent in levelling and fencing the land, after which the heads of families were each assessed $3.05 to pay for the cemetery.

In 1876 they were faced with the quandary of building a confirmation hall or a larger church. It was decided to raze the first church and build a more capacious one, with a basement for the Sunday School and the Confirmation classes. A plan was adopted for a structure 54 x 116 feet, with a spire 180 feet high.

Operations were begun while Pastor Sagehorn was in charge, but before it was completed he removed to Potter, Wisc. Shortly

THE EVANGELICAL LUTHERAN ST. PETER'S CHURCH

after the contractor abandoned the work and left town. His action delayed the completion of the church for two years. Finally it was finished by another contractor and opened for services on October 6, 1878. The church cost $10,140, less $800 received for materials from the old church.

Pastor Sagehorn was succeeded by the Rev. Mr. Manz on November 15, 1877. He did not get on well with the congregation. The services were slimly attended and the contributions fell off. The trustees asked for his resignation in May, 1881. The pulpit was then filled for two months by Professor Thomas Snyder of Watertown, Wisc. Aged Pastor Wurster then came up from Preston and served them till April 1, 1882.

Pastors Since Then

On that date the church procured the services of the Rev. R. von Pirch. He was born in Prussia, the son of a nobleman. After he was graduated from a University he emigrated to America and settled in Florida. Subsequently he enrolled himself as a divinity student at the Lutheran Seminary in Philadelphia. Following his ordination, he was called to Toronto by the Lutheran Church, and while pastor was appointed an examiner of German by Toronto University. When he arrived here, St. Peter's Church had 180 members; five years later they numbered 341. Mr. von Pirch was unfailingly tactful and an eloquent speaker, being equally at home in German or English. Among the improvements made during his pastorate were: redecoration of the church interior; the purchase of a larger pipe-organ and a chime of bells; the organization of several new societies; and the opening of a Saturday School for members' children.

The steeple on St. Peter's Church was struck by lightning on May 12, 1901. The Church Board decided not to replace it. In 1904, a number of families separated from the congregation and founded St. Matthew's Lutheran Church.

For many years the Rev. von Pirch was a member of the Free Library Board and of the Children's Aid Society. He sat also in the Hospital Board. For a time he edited the *Freie Presse*, founded the *Deutsches Zeitung*, and assisted at the grounding of the *Daily Record*. He contracted tuberculosis and died in Cullman, Alabama, on March 19, 1905.

After his death, the Rev. Alexander Oberlander of New York State ministered to the congregation for a span. Later on his son, the Rev. Dr. F. E. Oberlander, accepted a call to St. Peter's. Besides his pastoral duties, he was the pioneer here in combatting tuberculosis. The humanitarian work that he initiated is now carried on by the Waterloo County Health Association at Freeport. Dr. Oberlander received an invitation from a Lutheran Church in New York City, and was succeeded by the Rev. Herman A. Sperling, D.D., when the World War was only a few weeks old.

Extremists tried to have him interned as a German spy. Canadian justice, however, ruled differently, and despite all opposition he began his pastorate. Under the conditions that prevailed, it was more difficult to rebuild than to found a new congregation. Nevertheless he overcame all obstacles and restored St. Peter's to its former eminence. Since his induction, the congregation has installed a new heating system, remodelled the Sunday School, and in 1926 built a large Parish Hall. The handsome building is used as a recreation point by the young people, and as an auditorium by the church societies. A large revolving cross, illuminated at night with electricity, was erected in 1927, and is the only one in Canada. The church interior was altered in 1929 to conform to the Lutheran style. In 1931 the congregation installed a new Baptistry, imported from Italy, as a memorial to Dr. H. G. Lackner, Mrs. C. H. Doerr and son Weyburn, Mrs. Harry Franke, Mr. and Mrs. G. Franke, and Mrs. Wuest.

St. Peter's Frauenverein is more than fifty years old, and its Mutual Benefit Society upward of forty. St. Peter's choirs are renowned for their excellence. Their Young People's Society has a large membership and gives valued assistance. The Church Board is an active body, and the Men's Society a live organization. The Sunday School has a large enrollment. In 1935, Miss Minnie Schultz had attended it without missing a single Sunday for thirty-six years. Others too have records similarly good. The Dorcas Society has existed for many years and cares for the poor and sick. In 1937 the officers were: Mrs. Wm. Knell, President; Mrs. Karl Bornhold, first vice-president; Mrs. Harry Dettmer, second Vice-President; Mrs. E. Ewald, Secretary; Mrs. C. H. Doerr, Assistant Secretary; Mrs. A. F. Schultz, Treasurer; Mrs. Wm. Benninger,

Assistant Treasurer; Mrs. Otto Hiller, Pianist; Mrs. Harold Freund, Assistant Pianist; Mrs. C. H. Doerr, Auditor.

Until January, 1933, Dr. Sperling had for five years been a member of the Kitchener Welfare and Family Relief Board. He was also for more than a decade a member of the Public Library Board, by appointment of the city council. His services were especially valued by the German Book Committee. By request of the city council, he dedicated the Woodland Cemetery and Mausoleum; and for three years conducted the dedicatory service when the aldermanic body held its first session.

TOWNWARD

An outbreak of smallpox in 1860 caused numerous deaths and created a demand for a village cemetery. The council first bought an acre of land from Menno Erb and presented it to the Mennonite Society, to enlarge their burial ground. Subsequently they purchased two acres in the North Ward from John Hoffman and started Mount Hope cemetery. It was thought that two acres would suffice Berlin forever.

The village then had a volunteer fire-brigade of forty-five members. John Winger was chief; Hugo Kranz, secretary of the engine division; Herman Rathman, secretary of the hook-and-ladder brigade; and Jacob Becking, treasurer. The council spent thirty dollars a year in maintenance and paid each volunteer two dollars a year. To swell their receipts the engine crew held a ball on New Year's day and the ladder brigade a dance on Easter Monday.

Berlin then had one constable for every twenty-two inhabitants. The constables were not needed to preserve the peace, but stood ready to serve at the court sittings and thus earn a few extra dollars.

The Ladies' Aid Society of St. John's Church offered in 1862 to donate $150 toward the purchase of a town bell. The conditions were that the council grant an equal sum and the bell be hung in their new church tower. The village fathers however declined to act. Later on they arranged for the ringing of the bell at St. Mary's Church, morning, noon, and night.

After the American Civil War broke out Canadian trade and commerce were invigorated.

The First Incubator

John Winger's pumpshop rested where George Potter's block now stands. Mr. Winger made pumps and broom-handles. In 1860 he leased part of the building to a group of American refugees for a cut-tobacco works. George Randall afterward bought the works and engaged Ralph Chamberlain as manager. Still later Wm. Oelschlager and Henry F. J. Jackson purchased the business and built a factory near the corner of Waterloo and Victoria Streets. Mr. Winger's incubator housed also Simpson & Aldous's furniture enterprise and Matthias Wegenast's sash, door, and washboard works.

The Windmill

In those years Jacob Y. Shantz was engaged in the erection of workmen's homes and mercantile blocks. He built the DeBus, Weaver, and the Canadian block. Afterward he sold the Canadian block to Louis Breithaupt I. In association of H. S. Huber and Fred Rickerman, Mr. Shantz built also a three-storied windmill on the Mecklenburger's hill. It rose near the corner of Church and Albert Streets, had one run of millstones, and was leased to August Boehm. Subsequently the arms of the windmill were broken off in a big storm and never replaced.

The Button Industry

A young German named Emil Vogelsang came to Berlin in 1867 and chummed with Allan Huber, son of H. S. Huber. One day the merchant questioned the youth,

"What can you do, Emil?"
"I'm a button turner."
"Then show us how you make buttons."
"Before I could do that," said Emil, "I'd need a lathe and a batch of ivory-nuts."

Mr. Huber had a lathe made in Waterloo and imported a shipment of nuts for Mr. Vogelsang. The latter leased a room and power from the Simpson Furniture Company and soon was manufacturing first-class buttons. He called his venture, "The Pioneer Button Works." The buttons found a ready sale in Eastern Canada and the United States. His was the first button factory in Canada, if not in America.

Before long Mr. Vogelsang needed a facory of his own. He interested J. J. Woelfle in the enterprise and they awarded Jacob Y. Shantz a contract to erect a $20,000 building on the northeast corner of King and College Streets. Before it was up Mr. Woelfle withdrew. Mr. Shantz then purchased an interest in the button works for a sum equal to the price of the building and entered into a 7-year agreement with Mr. Vogelsang. When that term expired Mr. Vogelsang retired and built another button factory in South Queen Street, which he later sold to the W. G. & R. Shirt Company. (Now occupied by the Fehrenbach Mattress Co.)

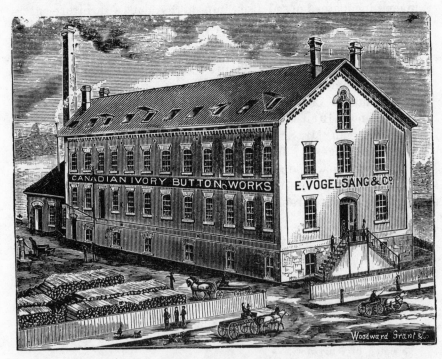

Mr. Shantz had not had any practical experience in the manufacture of buttons, yet did not wish to see the employees deprived of their livelihood. He therefore continued manufacturing and after costly experimenting, during which he was assisted by his son, M. B. Shantz, the factory was placed on a sound footing. Mr. Shantz's sons Dilman and John likewise joined him. Jacob Y. Shantz & Sons became the largest employers of labor in Berlin. For a time there were four button factories in the town and it was widely known as "Buttonville."

Jacob Y. Shantz entered into partnership also with a Mr. Feick and made felt goods in the button-factory basement.

A Troublesome Year

There was a great ado in 1865. A number of farmers who owned lands in East King Street moved to detach 900 acres from Berlin and attach them to Waterloo Township—being one-third of the village's area—and thereby obtain lower taxation. The matter was carried to a session of the United Provinces' government in Quebec City. In the end Berlin kept her territory intact.

A period of hard times followed the close of the American Civil War. In 1866 the U.S. Congress abrogated also the Reciprocity Treaty with Canada, which had been in effect since 1854 and by which Canadian farmers and fishermen had greatly benefitted. To cap the trade slump Fenians invaded Canada in 1866. The Canadian Government, for example, built a drillshed on the English Baptist Church corner and Captain Alex Millar drilled the volunteers. The Fenian raids continued at intervals until 1870, when they were finally quelled.

Early Taverns

West of H. B. Bowman's block in West King Street once stood the "Red Lion Inn," of which Levi Gaukel was proprietor. In the sixties he sold it to B. Brauer. John Roat bought the Western Hotel from James Potter and renamed it the Commercial House (now the Walper) ; in 1864, Robert Gray was lessee of the American hotel; Fred Riegelman owner of the "Franklin Tavern", opposite the little post-office in South Queen Street; A. Nickolaus of the "St. Nicholas," on the Dominion Bank corner; Conrad Schneuker of the "North American," in West King Street; Jacob Weaver of the "Railroad Hotel," nearly opposite the junction of King and Railroad (College) Streets; Casper Heller of the "Royal Exchange," in East King Street; Jacob Kraemer of the "Black Horse Inn," at the southwest corner of Weber and Frederick Streets; and Levi Weaver of the "Weaver House," on the corner of King and Wellington Streets. U. Brinzer owned the first restaurant in Berlin. Years after Jacob Weaver opened the "Terrapin Restaurant."

It seems that men of the sixties were bearded. G. M. DeBus, Sr., hairdresser, said nothing of shaving but advertised that he was prepared "to dye whiskers a permanent color." Mr. DeBus was also the village dentist and extracted teeth without the use of an anaesthetic, unles it was a nip of old rye.

Another Band

For several years Berlin was without a brass band. In 1867, however, the United Band was formed by Leopold Schmidt, W. Fleischauer, John Frick, Mike Knechtel, Louis Seip, Carl Hagen, Conrad Wurm, Fred Hagen, and John Rooke. William Kaiser was the leader and instructed also bandsmen in Waterloo, Preston, Elmira, and New Germany. In Berlin, Noah Zeller was one of his pupils. Mr. Kaiser once owned a frame hotel on the northwest corner of King and Cedar Streets, with a beer garden in the rear. Part of his hotel is still used as dwellings.

Pump-Priming

In 1867 C. F. Brown began the manufacture of furniture in West King Street, next to Simpson & Co.'s warehouse. Afterward he bought Paul Schmidt's house, 200 feet east of Gaukel Street, on the south side of King Street. Up to 1880 Joseph Devitt was his partner; then Menno Erb. Brown & Erb made also mattresses and gloves.

So far as discovered the first instance where Berlin offered an inducement to a manufacturer occurred in 1868. A council minute says,

> Moved by Louis Breithaupt and seconded by Valentine Guildner, That James L. Maude be offered entire exemption from taxation for ten years, provided he will within nine months erect and complete a large foundry and machine shop in connection with his woollenmill in East King Street, between Albert and Cedar Streets.

The Town Hall

In the sixties the council revived the monthly cattle, sheep, and butter fair, with a prize list of $400. The fair was so successful that the council was urged to buy a market-place and exhibition ground. A. Nickolaus and 162 others offered to give $600 toward the purchase of the old Millar store and Lowell's old Queen's Arms (then on the cityhall site) if purchased by the village. King Street merchants above Queen Street then proffered $900 if the council should buy Henry Stroh's property in Schneider's road. The council decided to purchase the Millar-Lowell properties. The electors were asked to approve of the purchase, but defeated the bylaw, because the most of them had gardens.

In 1869 Reeve Hugo Kranz and his colleagues, on their own initiative, bought the Millar-Lowell properties for $1,720. The council received the $600 promised by Mr. Nickolaus and his friends and had Jacob Y. Shantz build a large, two-storied market building and town hall, with a deep basement, for $3,818.

At the municipal election of 1870 an "Anti-Market Slate" contested the seats with the bold councillors of 1869. The town hall was a handsome building and made a strong appeal to the electors, with the result that the members of the old council were all re-elected. The erection of the town hall ranks next to the capture of the county seat in importance. For towns don't grow: they are built.

A local census of 1869 reported a population of 3,056 and the village was incorporated on May 20, 1870.

A Dominion Directory of 1870-1 said: BERLIN: a populous village in the Township of Waterloo. It is the county town. Located in a thickly settled and fine agricultural part of the country, and possessing several mills and factories, it must become an important inland town. The largest button factory in the West is here. There are fourteen churches. An extensive trade is done in grain and produce. Berlin is a station on the G.T.R., at which all trains stop. The Doon branch joins the G.T.R. at Berlin. Mail daily. Population, 2700.

ST. JEROME'S COLLEGE

St. Jerome's College rose from a humble origin in St. Agatha, Ontario. The Jesuit Fathers came to this district in 1847 and opened missions at New Germany and St. Agatha. Later on they planned a college at St. Agatha, New Germany, or Guelph, for the training of a native priesthood. A college was opened in Guelph but on account of an inability to procure professors and the financial condition of the people, it was closed.

The Jesuit Fathers handed over the mission at St. Agatha in 1857 to the Rev. Eugene Funcken of the Congregation of the

Resurrection—a Teaching Order. For youths who wished to pursue an advanced course of religious instruction he supplied the opportunity and originated also the St. Agatha Orphanage. The Rt. Rev. Bishop Farrell of Hamilton sent up David Fennessy, who was preparing himself to enter the Seminary in Quebec, as an assistant teacher. A half-dozen young men assembled in the rectory basement and engaged in the higher studies, including Latin. Mr. Fennessy taught for several years and then removed to Quebec. His leaving halted the work, but Father Funcken determined to resume it.

Accordingly, he invited his brother, the Rev. Louis Funcken, C.R., then in Rome, to join him. The brothers were sons of a German teacher and a Dutch mother and were native in Vanloo, Holland. As a youth Father Louis studied to become a druggist and doctor at Roremund, Holland. Before he had matured his plan he contracted typhoid fever, which left him almost deaf. He then resolved to study for the priesthood and through the intercession of friends was given a six months' trial. At the end of that period he stood first in his class and was permitted to complete the course. He was ordained in Roremund, obtained the Doctor of Divinity

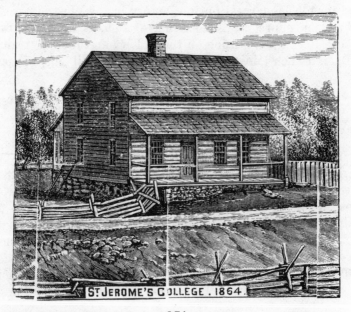

ST JEROME'S COLLEGE . 1864.

Right—

THE REV. W. G. BORHO, C.R.
President of St. Jerome's College

Below—

THE REV. LOUIS FUNCKEN, C.R., D.D.
Founder of St. Jerome's College.

ST. JEROME'S COLLEGE BUILDING IN DUKE STREET

degree in Rome, and was admitted to the Congregation in 1864. Straightway he came to Canada to found a Catholic College at St. Agatha. Before setting out he conferred with the Superior-General of the Order and asked for six assistants. When informed that not a single one was available, he responded, "I will found a college without assistance by multiplying myself."

The First College

His reverence arrived at St. Agatha in the fall of 1864 and leased a vacant log house from Joseph Wey. There, without means or professors, he founded St. Jerome's College. At first the student body consisted of youths who had earlier studied in the rectory basement, one of whom was William Kloepfer. Father Funcken's thorough methods attracted more students and at intervals he received the co-operation of Father David Fennessy and the Rev. Dr. Elena. Ere long the quarters were over-crowded. It was then decided to transfer the college to Berlin, a place of 2,000 inhabitants and the county town.

St. Jerome's in Berlin

Father Louis bought a brick house near St. Mary's Church and built on a wing, 50 x 40 feet. The college was opened in the autumn of 1866 with forty students, drawn from various parts of Canada and the United States, and with six day students. Besides directing the college Father Funcken again "multiplied himself" and governed St. Mary's parish. When he purchased the above-mentioned property he incurred a heavy debt, while the fees for tuition and board were so low that receipts and expenditures refused to dovetail into each other. The resourceful president eased the situation in 1869 by setting out on a lecture tour of the Northern States. Six months later he returned with about $1,000 in his wallet. Subsequently he sent forth the Rev. Edward Glowacki, C.R., on a similar mission, with the result that the college was placed on a stable footing.

When Father Funcken returned from his lecture tour to the college he found that sickness and overwork had made inroads into his staff. Father Fennessy was compelled to leave off work and recuperate in Rome; Mr. Levermann withdrew and went to Beatty, Pa., where he joined the Benedictine Order: Leopold Holzmueller died of tuberculosis; Mr. Cajone suffered a nervous breakdown and left the Congregation; and Carl Lanz lost his health and returned to Rome.

From 1871 to 1878 Father Funcken was the only priest at St. Jerome's. For a time the attendance decreased but the standard was not lowered. He overcame difficulties that would have intimidated anyone else and lived for the day when the students whom he had trained should return from Rome as assistants. The first of his disciples to return was the Rev. Theobald Spetz, C.R., D.D. He came back in 1878 and two years later was followed by the Rev. William Kloepfer, C.R., D.D. Between 1885 and 1887 the Rev. Joseph Schweitzer, C.R., the Rev. Anton Weiler, C.R., Ph.D., D.D., and the Rev. John Steffan, C.R., Ph.D., D.D., returned and joined the Faculty. With the assistance of those earnest coadjutors, Father Funcken's plans were more fully realized.

The number of students steadily increased and in 1881 another story and a wing were built on the college. When it was ready for use his colleagues observed that Father Funcken's long years of toil, "without haste and without rest," had enervated his body. He was persuaded to take a four-month vacation in Europe, the first intermission he had had since 1864. When he returned to the college an abundance of work awaited him. For one thing an increase of the student body necessitated more lecture rooms. A large four-story structure was erected some thirty feet from the first college in 1887.

In the same year Father Funcken celebrated the Silver Jubilee of his entry into the priesthood. The Alumni presented him with a weighty purse of gold. With it he furnished the new building. Cheered up by that demonstration of affection he continued his life's work. The older college building was enlarged by two stories in 1889.

His many years of unremitting labor had, unfortunately, taken a heavy toll. In 1889 his physician constrained him to cease work and seek after health in Europe. He sorrowfully complied, but seemed to know that he would never return. Bidding his colleagues and friends farewell, he journeyed to Roremond, Holland, where, as we have seen, he departed this life on January 30, 1890.

After his demise the Alumni of St. Jerome's began the collection to a fund for a monument to "Father Louis." A bronze figure of heroic size, representing him giving instruction to a student, was unveiled in the college park in 1907. Of him an alumnus said, "Father Louis' coming to Canada was providential. God does not send men like him every day nor every year: perhaps not every fifty years."

St. Jerome's Under Father Spetz

After the founder's death the Rev. William Kloepfer was appointed Superior and Pastor of St. Mary's Church. At the same time the Rev. Theobald Spetz was nominated President of St. Jerome's College. When he assumed the presidency the other members of the faculty were: the Reverends William Kloepfer, Joseph Schweitzer, Anton Weiler, John Steffan, and Hubert Aeymans and Messrs. J. Suddaby, Joseph Ferguson and Francis Meyerhoffer.

Under Father Spetz's direction St. Jerome's continued to advance. His students named him the "Silent Man," for he was of a quiet nature and unassuming mien. In the year in which he became president he founded a congregation in Waterloo and collected a large part of the sum required to erect St. Louis' Church.

A number of young priests returned from Rome in the eighteen-nineties and joined the faculty. The Rev. Joseph Halter, C.R., B.A., the Rev. Joseph Biela, C.R., and the Rev. John Kosinski, C.R., arrived in 1892-3; the Rev. A. Waechter, C.R., M.A., in 1894; the Rev. W. Vincent Kloepfer, C.R., Ph.D., and the Rev. Stanislaus Rogalski, C.R., in 1895; while the Rev. David Fennessy, C.R., and the Rev. Ignatius Perius, C.R., arrived here in 1897.

President Spetz had a basement excavated under the oldest college building for a gymnasium in 1895. The "gym." found favor with the students and was enlarged in 1896 and again in 1901.

In 1899 the Rev. Rudolph Lehmann, a diocesan priest, was appointed a professor and teacher of Music. The same year witnessed the return of three clergymen from Rome who afterward became prominent in St. Jerome's: the Rev. A. L. Zinger, C.R., M.A., Ph.L., the Rev. A. J. Fischer, C.R., B.A., Ph.B., and the Rev. Charles Kiefer, C.R., B.A., Ph.B. In addition the Rev. Francis Pieczinski, C.R., came in and taught for two years.

Meanwhile the wheel of time in its turnings had aged Father Spetz and in 1901 he gave up the presidency. For nine years he continued to teach in the college and act as pastor of St. Mary's and St. Louis' Churches. From 1916 to 1921 he was assistant pastor of St. Mary's.

Father Spetz took a keen interest in public affairs. D. B. Detweiler, before launching the Niagara Power project and setting the St. Lawrence Seaway movement afoot, consulted with Father Spetz. For years Father Spetz was prominently connected with the Children's Aid Society. He assisted also at the organization of the Waterloo Historical Society and was its Vice-President from its inception until his decease.

Father Spetz was likewise the author of *The Catholic Church in Waterloo County*. Therein the arrival of the first Catholic settlers, the origin of its parishes, and the careers of the clergymen who ministered to them are recorded with fidelity. Had he not delved amongst ancient documents and interviewed scores of aged citizens much valuable history would have been lost to posterity.

He suffered a paralytic stroke and passed away at St. Joseph's Hospital, Guelph, on December 1, 1921. His memory is still green.

President Fehrenbach

The Rev. John Fehrenbach, C.R., Ph.D., D.D., was appointed president of the college at the end of the scholastic year 1900-01. He was born in New Germany in 1857 and from 1869 to 1876 was one of Father Funcken's students at St. Jerome's. From 1876 till 1884 he continued his studies in Rome and then joined the Congregation of the Resurrection. Thereafter he was first professor and then President of St. Mary's College in Kentucky.

When he became President of St. Jerome's he had the assistance of a notable faculty. It was comprised of the Reverends Theobald Spetz, A. L. Zinger, Joseph Schweitzer, A. Waechter, W. Vincent Kloepfer, A. J. Fischer, W. A. Beninger, and Paul Sobczak, and Messrs. Suddaby, Didier, Padden, and McKegney. First President Fehrenbach made important changes in the curriculum. Then he undertook to liquidate the debt of the college and deleted the greater part of it. Under his sway the college continued on its forward course. The students said of him, "Father Fehrenbach is not only a priest: he is a man."

He retained the presidency until 1905, when he joined the faculty of St. Stanislaus' College, Chicago. Seven years later he was appointed pastor of St. Agatha Church in Waterloo County and served there until his death on April 2, 1935.

ST. JEROME'S COLLEGE GYMNASIUM

THE LATE SHERIFF JOHN MOTZ

President Zinger

The Very Rev. A. L. Zinger succeeded Father Fehrenbach as President of St. Jerome's. He was native in Teeswater (1874), attended the London Collegiate, and then was enrolled at St. Jerome's College. In 1895 he went to Rome to complete his studies for the priesthood. He returned four years later and was ordained in 1901. After his ordination he was appointed Master of Studies and Vice-President of the College. His elevation to the presidency followed in 1905. When he entered upon his new duties there was no money in the treasury, other than a legacy of $15,000, bequeathed by the Rev. George Brohman.

With that nest-egg he proceeded to erect the magnificent main building in Duke Street. The four-story structure is 154 x 42 feet and was begun in 1907. At the laying of the cornerstone there were present numerous prominent citizens and public men, many priests and prelates, His Excellency Monseigneur Sbarretti, Apostolic Delegate, and the Very Rev. John Kasprzycki, Superior-General of the Order. When the college building was completed in 1908 it was the finest in the city.

Father Zinger established also a Novitiate of the Canadian Province of the Congregation of the Resurrection. It was the first Novitiate of the Order in the Dominion. Quarters were set aside in the three-story division of the college. At daybreak on November 29, 1908, however, the building was destroyed by fire. Only by the strenuous efforts of the fire-brigade and the students were the flames confined to the one building.

A larger structure that conformed to the style of the main building was erected on the site of the destroyed division. On the ground floor provision was made for a swimming-pool; on the second floor, for a gymnasium and five music-rooms; and the remainder allotted for dormitories and washrooms.

In 1909 President Zinger purchased two residences in Duke Street for $10,000 for future requirements. On the other sites there is now a large Novitiate.

At St. Jerome's study and athletics go hand in hand. In spring and summer the students play baseball and tennis; in the fall, rugby; and in the winter, hockey. A gymnasium was erected in 1909, which for size and equipment equals any in Canada. It has an indoor baseball diamond, two basketball floors, a handball alley, and a 100-yard track.

St. Jerome's has numerous student organizations. Among these are: the Athletic Association, the Literary and Dramatic Society, the Glee Club, the College Orchestra, the Alma Mater staff, who edit the college magazine, the Alumni Union, the League of the Sacred Heart, and the Altar Society.

The Very Rev. A. L. Zinger, "the Builder," resigned the presidency in 1919 and was appointed pastor of St. Mary's Church. He was next president of a college in North Bay, Ontario.

Father Zinger was succeeded at St. Jerome's by the Very Rev. W. A. Beninger, C.R., who was President until 1926. Among the betterments of his term was the establishment of a College Infirmary at 64 Young Street. Father Beninger is now Superior of the Provincial Congregation, with headquarters in London. The Rev. Leo J. Seiss, C.R., D.D., was President from 1926 to 1929. Father Seiss especially added to and extended the college courses.

The presidential torch was handed to the Rev. R. S. Dehler, C.R., D.D., in 1929. Father Dehler maintained the high standard set by his predecessors and extended the renown of this international seat of learning. In the summer of 1936 he demitted the presidency and was appointed President of a new Scholasticate in Washington, D.C. His successor at St. Jerome's was the Rev. W. G. Borho, C.R., M.A., the former Vice-President.

In April, 1937, President Borho was advised by the Ontario Conference of Universities that St. Jerome's College had received official recognition as an approved private school. That is, students enrolled at the College will be exempted from writing on the middle and upper school examinations and admitted to Ontario Universities after having passed the college examinations. The College High School Department was also placed in the same rank as other High Schools and Collegiates.

Upwards of seventy years have elapsed since Father Funcken founded St. Jerome's College in a log house at St. Agatha. Yet, with its superior buildings, its facilities, and a staff that outnumbers Father Louis' class roll, the institution is in reality only in its youth.

BIBLIOGRAPHY

History of St. Jerome's College. 1916. By the Rev. Theobald Spetz, C.R., D.D., Toronto.

Building
Occupied
1871-1875
1883-1888

Building
Occupied
1875-1883

Organized 1871. First Board of Directors: Henry F. J. Jackson, Wm. Oelschlager, Hugo Kranz, George Davidson, Frederick Snyder, J. A. Mackie, and John Fennell. Moses Springer, M.P.P., Manager.

EARLY ECONOMICAL OFFICERS

H. F. J. JACKSON
President,
1871 - 1877

W. OELSCHLAGER
President, 1877 - 1880
Manager, 1872 - 1877
Manager, 1880 - 1893

HUGO KRANZ
President, 1880 - 1893
Manager, 1877 - 1880
Manager, 1893 - 1902

UNDER A TOWN CHARTER

The first town council was elected in January, 1871. The mayoralty candidates were Henry F. J. Jackson, John Fennell, and Dr. Wm. Pipe. One of them cooked his own goose by remarking, "There are too many Dutchmen in Berlin." Dr. Pipe was elected. He stood six-feet three in his stockings and was the tallest mayor the city has yet had. William Jaffray was elected Reeve and John Motz, Deputy-Reeve.

Previously the town had been subdivided into wards. The North returned John Aldous, W. H. Bowman, and T. Armstrong; the East, Menno Erb, Henry Schwenn, and Joseph Spetz; the South, John B. Hett, Valentine Guildner, and George Seip; the West Ward, Isaac Hoffman, Samuel B. Schneider, and William Simpson. Israel D. Bowman was the first town clerk and John A. Mackie, first treasurer.

Das Friedensfest

A Friedensfest was held here on May 2, 1871, to mark the end of the Franco-Prussian War, and attracted 10,000 celebrants. The local singing society was assisted by choral unions from Waterloo, Preston, Hespeler, Hamburg, Neustadt, and Hamilton. Dr. R. Mylius acted as marshal, and had twenty-four mounted adjutants. An hour-long procession, with bands and banners, was formed at the town hall and marched to the G.T.R. station to welcome guests from Toronto, Hamilton, Stratford, and other places. At the court house Otto Klotz of Preston afterward delivered an oration, punctuated with hearty "Hochs." Amid the rattle of kettledrums the celebraters then marched to the market square, where a mass meeting was held, with Wm. Oelschlager acting as chairman.

Mayor Pipe delivered a welcome in German. An address, drawn up by John King and Wm. Jaffray, in which they expressed the English residents' admiration of their German neighbors, was next read. A mass choir then sang stirring Lieds. Rousing speeches were delivered by I. E. Bowman, M.P., and Jacob Buchmann of Hamilton, while Consul Widemann of Ann Arbor, Mich., read a poem especially written for the Fest. Afterwards thanksgiving services were held in all the German churches.

After lunch, another procession rode or marched to Waterloo, while the bands played stirring airs. In the long line were thirty-four wagons in which rosy-cheeked girls presented tableaux. Another program of song and speeches followed at Waterloo. The speakers were: Reeve George Randall, Moses Springer, M.P.P., Mr. Williams of Hamilton, the Rev. Mr. Stallinger of St. Jacobs, and Mr. Hart of Toronto. Then back to Berlin, where a commemorative oak was planted. An entertainment was held in the evening in the drillshed, when a chorus of 150 voices rendered the "Mass des Lobes." The day closed with a display of fireworks and a grand ball.

Town Buys a Bell

The vacant Stadthalle was moved to the upper part of the firehall lot and used solely as a firehall. A later council bought a 2,064-pound bell in Troy, N.Y., for $700, and hung it in the firehall tower. It was named "Victoria Bell," and bears the inscription that follows:

Berlin, 1876

Bell Committee: Hugo Kranz, Mayor; Abram Tyson, Reeve; L. J. Breithaupt, Deputy-Reeve; W. H. Bowman, and C. Stuebing. Israel D. Bowman, Clerk; Menno Eby, Treasurer.

MR. SILENCE

Con Gerbig, town constable many years ago, was among the official guardians one day in the court-room. He had been instructed that whenever he heard a name called to hunt up the individual and bring him into court. There was a little hubbub so John Klippert shouted, "Silence!"

Immediately Con hustled out through the corridor calling loudly for, "Mr. Silence."

A Saturday Market

In 1839, Andrew MacCullough of Waterloo announced that he would hold a monthly market in Bridgeport at Jacob S. Shoemaker's mill and on the following day in Berlin. He bought calves and sheep; butter, eggs, and hams; and also fat cattle. That may have been the granddaddy of the Saturday market. John Hoffman returned from Waterloo to Berlin and in 1872 was elected mayor. Adopting J. Y. Shantz's idea, he organized a Saturday market for farm produce. On the first Saturday there was a surplus. He bought it up and gave the produce to his kindred. At the same time he urged the farmers to bring in more the next week and advertised the market. Soon the Saturday market became a fixture.

At first a few tables were placed in the town-hall basement. A long market building was afterward built at the rear of the town-hall, parallel to Frederick Street, and served the town till 1907. The present building was then built, facing Frederick Street, having a frontage of sixty-five feet and extending 225 feet toward Scott Street. The red-brick structure has two floors and 450 growers' tables. When the building was run up, the citizens spent $7,000 weekly at the market; now, according to Louis Sachs, former market clerk, the citizens spend between $20,000 and $25,000 weekly for an almost endless list of offerings from dairy and patch, orchard and yard. The Saturday market is one of the best things the city possesses.

The First Park

In the newly-chartered town the trend was forward. In 1872, a group of men petitioned the council to buy a town park. Accordingly, twenty-five acres of woodland, at the corner of Mill and Queen Streets, were bought from Joseph E. Schneider for $2500. Because the ratepayers disliked debenture debt, the payment was spread over a term of five years. The petitioners then donated $214 to clear off the upper end of trees. The purchase was called "Woodside Park," and James Potter appointed superintendent. Once there was a racecourse in the park that horsemen made at their own expense. The Federal Government moved the drillshed to Woodside. Afterward the lower end of the market grounds was bought from Casper Heller for a Central Park, but the Saturday market soon needed the land.

Birthplace of a Premier

John King, Q.C., at that period practised his profession in Berlin. On December 2, 1872, he espoused Miss Isabella Grace Mackenzie, daughter of William Lyon Mackenzie, the Canadian patriot. Mr. and Mrs. King resided at No. 43 Benton Street, where Grace Tabernacle now stands. In her parlor, Mrs. King displayed a poster of 1837, offering a large reward for the capture of her father, alive or dead. To Mr. and Mrs. King a son was born in their Benton Street home on December 17, 1874, and christened William Lyon Mackenzie King.

Mackenzie King was educated here and at a Canadian and an American University, in which he was especially trained for public life. Later on, North Waterloo, his home riding, returned him as their representative in the House of Commons. Afterward he was appointed Minister of Labor in the cabinet of Sir Wilfrid Laurier. Mr. King succeeded Sir Wilfrid Laurier as leader of the Liberal party in 1919, and in 1921 became Premier of Canada, holding office till 1930. Under his leadership, the Liberal party was again returned to power in 1935. After the Imperial Conference of 1937, Premier King visited Aberdeen, Scotland, when the home of his forefathers conferred on him the freedom of the city, and admitted him "a free burgess and guild brother," for his outstanding achievements in promoting industrial relations and the cause of international peace.

The Concordia Society

Gesangvereine were organized in every American and Canadian centre where any considerable number of Germans resided. The Concordia Gesangverein was founded here in November, 1873, and consisted solely of male voices. Assisted by the Waterloo Liedertafel, their official opening was held early in 1874. The vocalists jointly sang the "Liebesqual," the "Seel-ge Luft," the "Lindenbaum," and the "Treue Liebe."

The Concordia was host to an international Saengerfest in 1875. The society gave the town council $600 toward the erection of a concert hall in Woodside park; and decorated the main streets with twelve arches. Bands from Waterloo, Toronto, Hamilton and Berlin furnished the instrumental music; whilst the Orpheus of Detroit, the Saengerbund and Orpheus of Buffalo, the Harmonia of

RT. HON. W. L. MACKENZIE KING AT HOME OF HON. W. D. EULER

Top Row: Senator Robb, N. Asmussen, M.P.P., J. A. Scellen, W. T. Sass, Hon. James Malcolm, John A. Lang, W. Max Euler.
Second Row: W. J. Motz, Mr. King's Secretary, H. J. Sims, Mrs. J. Cole, Mayor Greb, Premier King, Hon. W. D. Euler, Mrs. Peden Mielke, Mrs. Leonard Oliver, Senator Dr. Rankin.
Bottom Row: Mrs. Max Euler, Miss Rankin, Mrs. W. D. Euler, Mrs. W. J. Motz.

THE KAUFMAN PLANING MILL
Founded in 1877.

Toronto, the Germania of Hamilton, the Teutonia of Lisbon, Ont., the Liederkranz of Preston, and the Liedertafel of Waterloo, assisted the Concordia. Montreal sent up a large delegation, while George Rumpel of Hamilton came up to sing and remained to manufacture felt footwear. The Saengerfest was both a musical and financial success. At intervals the Saengerfests were repeated.

The Berlin Saengerbund was organized in 1889. Shortly after, the Berlin Liedertafel was also former. The Concordia is still active.

A Factory Policy

The town first adopted a factory policy in 1874. Reinhold Lang and Conrad Stuebing, members of the town council, introduced the motion that follows and that was adopted:

> That this council, with the view to fostering and encouraging the coming of manufacturing establishments to this town, offer as an inducement that all manufactories be exempted from taxation for five years and that an annual bonus, equal to the rental of the building required, be granted, provided that the continuous employment of not less than seventy-five hands in each such establishment is guaranteed.

Soon after Henry, Charles and Aug. Boehmer built the Dunke block and manufactured brushes and brooms. Then John S. Anthes, J. M. Staebler, and Samuel Merner bought the Hoffman furniture factory and store, from Isaac Hoffman. Later on the Simpson-Aldous and Anthes & Co.'s furniture factories were united; after which the Anthes plant was removed to West King Street. Mr. Anthes and Mr. Merner then built a block on the Bank of Nova Scotia corner for the Merchants Bank.

In 1877, Henry Ratz and Jacob Kaufman, of Perth County, founded a planing mill in West King Street, near the C.N.R. tracks. Mr. Kaufman was the active partner. He was told he was making a mistake in locating the mill so far out in the country. Soon after he bought his father-in-law, Mr. Ratz's interest. To keep his mill humming, Mr. Kaufman once obtained an order in London for 1000 fanning-mills. Later, when the demand for more houses set in, he enlarged his planing-mill, building the new one around the old one, so as not to halt operations. To feed his mill, he purchased a large timber limit in Muskoka and erected saw-mills at Rosseau Falls and Trout Creek. The Kaufman Planing Mill is now the biggest between Toronto and London, and managed by his son, Milton R. Kaufman.

Mr. Jacob Kaufman established or assisted at the establishment of other enterprises and was called the "Industrial Wizard."

To procure a flourmill the town presented Laurence Doering in 1878 with two acres of land in Schneider's road and gave him other inducements. The mill afterward passed to Bramm Brothers and long after to the Master Milling Co. Shortly after Mr. Doering opened his mill Jacob Shelly and Mr. Lehnen operated, on the northeast corner of King and Cedar Streets, the Berlin Steam Flour Mill. Mr. Lehnen sold his share to a Mr. Shantz, when the firm became Shelly & Shantz. For years they did a thriving trade.

An energetic florist, Henry L. Janzen, came to Berlin in 1878. On the northeast corner of King and Wellington Streets he erected the town's first greenhouse. While by his diligence Mr. Janzen built up a large business, he is chiefly remembered as a searcher after new industries and the builder of city blocks.

Although Berlin had fewer than 4,000 inhabitants, P. E. W. Moyer, M.A., founded *The Berlin Daily News* in February, 1878. It was the town's first daily and first Conservative newspaper. Mr. Moyer was a progressive citizen and the father of the National Policy.

The late J. W. Connor, B.A., said of the town,

> The reader must figure for himself a goodly number of frame houses, here and there; many with pumps at their front door, and nearly all with well-kept gardens. These were strongly fenced. Cows, but not pigs, were free commoners. In preparation for the Saengerfest of 1875, King Street was "ausgeputzt" and a few coal-oil lamps lit on moonless nights.

Councillor David S. Shoemaker planned in 1877 to improve King Street from the Mennonite Church up to Waterloo. A four-foot ridge between Waterloo and the High School was cut down and graded. Next the little sandhills between Scott and Ontario Streets were tackled. While the humps were being whittled down some of the storekeepers fancied the improvement would be their ruination. A man with a club was stationed in the street to prevent them from raising the stakes showing the new level. One merchant who had to lower his floor threatened Mr. Shoemaker with bodily harm. At the next succeeding election enough anti-improvement councillors were elected to thwart the cutting down of the elevation between the railway tracks and the High School.

JACOB Y. SHANTZ, THE COLONIZER

Among his many occupations Jacob Y. Shantz included colonization. The Czar of Russia notified his Mennonite subjects that their age-old rights of religious freedom, use of their mother tongue, and exemption from military service were to be abolished. Thousands of them determined to heed the scriptural injunction, "When they persecute you in this city, flee ye into another." Editor P. E. W. Moyer stirred the Dominion Government to bring them over to Canada. The Government was amenable and asked Mr. Moyer to name a man big enough for the task. He nominated Mr. Shantz, who regarded the invitation as a call from God.

Accompanied by Bernard Werkintin, a Russian Mennonite, Mr. Shantz set out for Manitoba on November 5, 1872. As the C.P.R. had not yet been built they travelled by train, via Chicago, to Pembina and then rode seventy-two miles in a stage to Fort Garry. A quarter of a mile from the fort lay the village of Winnipeg.

Mr. Shantz was instructed to ascertain whether Manitoba was adaptable to agriculture. On wheels and afoot they spied out the land for hundreds of miles east and west and north and south of Winnipeg. One day a military officer blurted out, "Shantz, you'll make a mistake if you send farmers out here. This is not an agricultural country: it's only a fur country." Mr. Shantz responded, "I'm somewhat of a farmer myself and I think, in fact know, that it has great possibilities as an agricultural land."

Another man inquired, "Are you not afraid to go among the half-breeds (more dangerous than Indians)) without a weapon for defence?" Mr. Shantz, who never was afraid of anything that ought to be done, answered: "No. When they see that I do not carry a rifle they know that my purpose is good and become my protectors. Therein lies my safety. I eat and sleep with them without fear."

His Report

To the Government Mr. Shantz reported that the soil was of unsurpassed richness. Mostly a black loam, one to six feet in depth, which he knew would yield abundant crops of wheat and coarse grains. Further, the settler would not require to clear off a forest before sinking his plowshare into the sod. The prairie was well-watered, with woods along the streams, and well-suited for cattle and sheep. He likewise reported on the climate, the rainfall, fur-bearing animals, Indians and half-breeds.

His report was a practical one. He pointed to the 160-acre homesteads the Government was ready to give to settlers and the ease of acquiring more land; advised newcomers to provide for a year's food in advance; and on arrival to build shelters and ware-houses before they erected dwellings. Given $465 a settler could buy a stove, furniture, bedding, implements, a yoke of oxen, build a stable and a house. Given $800 or $1000 he could engage in farming on a larger scale, but $465 was the minimum needful. In short Mr. Shantz covered every point the European would wish light on. His findings were a revelation to the Government, who had them translated into several foreign languages and distributed in Europe.

The Mennonite Colony

Fifteen thousand Russian Mennonites forsook their homeland rather than their principles. About half of them emigrated to the United States and about as many to Canada. On account of the sacrifices the majojrity of them were compelled to make, they reached Canada in straightened circumstances. Mr. Shantz obtained a loan from the Dominion Government and raised a large sum among his brethren in Waterloo County. Those advances enabled the newcomers to carry on till they were self-supporting. To bring over nearly 8,000 settlers was a huge task and consumed three summers. The incomers were settled in two colonies south of Winnipeg, east and west of the Red River.

Before the first shipload arrived in Canada, Mr. Shantz had sheds and warehouses built for them in Manitoba. He purchased wagons, implements, and supplies also for them at wholesale. Since the governmental cheques were not always to hand when needed he utilized J. Y. Shantz & Sons' $100,000 line of credit at the Merchants Bank, passing drafts on his son, M. B. Shantz, who debited his father's personal account. The exodus was fulfilled, and the Mennonites caused the prairie to bloom like the rose.

In time they repaid the sums advanced by their co-religionists and the Government, with interest. Also they repaid some of the money expended by Mr. Shantz in purchasing food and implements. After the Dominion loan was paid off an official said, "Mr. Shantz, this is the first loan of its kind ever repaid." Mr. Shantz remarked, "I knew they were honest and that the country was good."

In the eighteen-nineties overflow colonies were also founded at Swift Current, Osler, and Rosthern, Sask. Mr. Shantz, who was their Abraham Lincoln, made twenty-seven annual or biennial visits to the colonies, the last one when he was in his eighty-fifth year. The Red River colony named one of their villages Shantzenfeld for him, which was his only recompense.

SOURCE
A history of his fathers life, by the late M. B. Shantz.

CERTAIN RESIDENTS OF THE EIGHTEEN-EIGHTIES

Asmussen Brothers, mechanics
Henry Bachman, photographer
August Boehm, windmill
Adam Brandt, cabinetmaker
George Bucher, Sr., mechanic
Wendell Brunner, blacksmith
Edward Buck, telegrapher
Wm. Codlin, tailor
Jacob Cook, cabinetmaker
G. M. DeBus, barber and dentist
Wm. Devitt, harnessmaker
Conrad Doering, weaver
Conrad Doerr, carpenter
John Dotzenroth, mason
David Eby, pumpmaker
Henry Eby, wagonmaker
C. Engelhardt, bookstore
Peter Erb, harnessmaker
Jacob Ewald, contractor
Miss M. Feick, milliner
G. A. Fischer, barber
G. Froelich, potash mnfr.
Robert Furniss, tailor
Wm. Gastmeier, contractor
Wm. Gaul, tailor
Henry Gauntley, harnessmaker
Charles Geddes, seedsman
John Gibson, gardener
Val. Gildner, blacksmith
Henry Glebe, hatter
W. H. Goetz, tobacconist

W. R. Gray, liveryman
Colin Groff, druggist
James Gwynne, lawyer
John Haller, hatmaker
John Haugh, harnessmaker
E. R. Hayne, baker
Wm. Hertfelder, weaver
James Hobson, surveyor
C. Hoffman, spring-wheels
George Klein, butcher
Fred Lake, builder
A. Macpherson, deputy-registrar
M. Messner, musical instruments
Alex Millar, barrister
Dr. R. Mylius, physician
Henry Nahrgang, tailor
Gottlieb Rathmann, tailor
M. Reichert, shinglemaker
Edward Roat, saddler
Fred Rommel, tailor
Alex Roy, clerk.
Balthasar Schmaltz, weaver
Conrad Schmidt, grocer
J. G. Schmidt, shoe dealer
M. Schofield, surveyor
D. Schwenkettel, tinsmith
J. M. Scully, registry-office
Louis Seiler, flour and feed
George Seip, brewer
Martin Simpson, weaver
Simpson & Son, shoe mnfrs.

CERTAIN RESIDENTS OF THE EIGHTEEN-EIGHTIES—Continued

Henry Sippel, weaver
Bruno Schmidt, M.D., doctor
Wm. Stein, tailor
Michael Stoltz, weaver
Henry Stroh, shoe dealer
Joseph Terry, blacksmith
F. W. Tuerk, Jr., mnfr. copper, iron
Abram Tyson, general merchant
John Walmsley, mnfr. cultivators

George Ward, blacksmith
Julius Werner, wagonmaker
James Whiting, M.D., doctor
Henry Wittig, hatmaker
J. J. Woelfle, plow manufacturer
Wm. Young, grocer
Enoch Ziegler, mnfr. carriages
M. Zeale, blacksmith
—From an old Directory.

THE BETHANY MENNONITE CHURCH

At the corner of Chapel and Lancaster Streets stands the Bethany Mennonite Church. The congregation was organized in the early eighteen-seventies. At first the brethren met in the homes of various members, and afterward for a time in the United Brethren Church, now occupied by the Russian Mennonites. The congregation's first church was built in 1877.

Elder Moses Weber was their first pastor. Joseph E. Snyder, Jacob Huber, and David B. Snyder their first deacons; and George Detweiler, the first Sunday School Superintendent. The shepherds who followed Elder Weber in the first church were: the Reverends Peter Geiger, John McNally, John Steckley, C. F. Krauth, Henry Goudie, Christian Raymer, Solomon Eby, Samuel Goudie, A. F. Stoltz, and Peter Cober.

From the outset the church experienced a healthy growth, As a consequence, a larger House of Prayer was in time needed, and the congregation erected a spacious red-brick church in 1908. The Pastors who have served the office in the present church are: the Reverends C. F. Krauth, Cyrus N. Good, Silas Cressman, Ephraim Sievenpiper, William Brown, George Warder, and William Yates. In 1936 a call was extended to the Rev. Sidney S. Shantz, who had charge of the City Mission in Owen Sound, and later on been Conference Evangelist for the Ontario Conference.

The Deacons of the present church have been: David B. Snyder, Daniel Hostetler, and Clayton Cressman. The Trustees are: Vernon Eby, Clayton Cressman, and Gordon H. Good. Now, Vernon W. Cressman is Sunday School Superintendent, in succession of J. H. Sherk.

THE BETHANY
MENNONITE CHURCH

REV. SIDNEY S. SHANTZ
Pastor.

THE RANGERS FOOTBALL TEAM, 1885

Top: R. T. Winn, A. J. J. Thibodo, Sollie Brubacher, Fred Killer, F. Bowman, John Shantz.
Centre: Hugo Rathman, D. Forsyth (Captain), Alex McDougall, Fred Doll.
Bottom row: H. P. Bingham, Alex Gibson.

FIRST HORSE-DRAWN STREET CAR
April, 1889.

Bethany Mennonite Church has a number of active associations. The Senior, Intermediate, and Junior Young People's Societies; the Ladies' Mission Circle; the Home Makers' Society; the Senior and Junior Sunbeams; and five Prayer Meeting Classes. The church has a Young Men's Octette, and the Bethany Choristers who have been heard over station CKCR on Sunday evenings during the winter months.

ASSOCIATION FOOTBALL

For an age the chief sport in Berlin was Association Football. David Forsyth, B.A., ushered it in at the High School in the late eighteen-seventies, when the students took to "soccer" like Galt boys to oatmeal. Other schools, colleges and towns followed the lead and here, on January 30, 1880, the Western Football Association was organized. The first officers were: Hon. President, J. B. Hughes; President, J. W. Connor, B.A.; Secretary-Treasurer, David Forsyth.

Cup holders were sprouted by Berlin, Dundas, Galt, Seaforth, Toronto Varsity, Toronto Scots, Ingersoll, Preston, Windsor and Detroit.

Youths in B.H.S. jerseys won the W.F.A. trophy in 1880-1-2-3. In turn, T. C .Hughes, Edwin Huber and G. H. Bowlby stood in goal; Addison Bowman, Sollie Brubacher, J. Dolph, Tony Kolb, A. Fred Bowman and A. Bowman, backs; George LaCourse, F. W. Sheppard, Fred Killer, C. H. Wilson and H. J. Manz, half-backs; E. N. Hughes, W. Miller, Adolph Mueller, C. Huehnergard, A. Snyder, R. Winn, M. G. Dippel, Tom Gibson, E. Rife, H. P. Bingham and David Forsyth, forwards. Mr. Forsyth, who was one of the best forwards in Canada, captained the teams.

Dundas carried off the cup in 1883-4. About then the "Berlin Rangers," a town club, was formed and won the trophy in 1884-5. The stars were: A. J. J. Thibado, goal; Sollie Brubacher and Fred Killer, backs; John Shantz and Alex McDougall, halves; David Forsyth, Harry Bingham, Tom Gibson, Fred Doll, Alex Gibson and J. Scully, forwards. Football was the only game that moved the Berliners to cheer.

The Berlin and Galt teams were evenly matched. Whenever Galt won here, chubby John Brough, engineer of the "Dutch Mail," shrilled his whistle all the way to Galt. The southerners carried off the trophy in 1885-6, but the Rangers brought it back in 1887 and kept it for three years. Players of that period were: F. W. Sheppard and then Harvey J. Sims, goalkeeper; Fred Killer, Sollie Brubacher, Oliver Shantz, F. W. Sheppard ,J. Brown and A. Eby, successive backs; Carl Kranz, Francis Thibado, J. S. Shantz, H. Snyder and Alex McDougall, David Forsyth, Sollie Brubacher, Harry Bingham, Alex Gibson, Walter Bowman, Edward Dunke, W. Godbold, E. O. Boehmer, Adam Sippel, A. Eby, A. Waggoner and Ben Uttley, forwards. The Rangers won international honors by beating Fall River, Woonsocket, Detroit, St. Louis, etc. For business reasons, a number of players gave up in the early nineties.

A second town team, the Mechanics, rose in 1895 and won the coveted trophy. The winners were: A. G. Heller, goal; N. Asmussen and J. Wagner, backs; W. Seebach, A. Miller and A. B. Snider, halves; Nelson Boehmer, Alfred Scherer, W. Macpherson, Herman Wagner and A. Allemang, forwards.

Later on the Rangers received an infusion of new blood and in 1897-8-9 and 1900 were victors. During the four years Harvey Sims, Dave Brown and Otto Vogelsang in turn guarded the goal; Dr. A. E. Rudell, Dave Brown and George Lackner played backs; H. E. Meinke, John L. Gibson, Harry W. Brown, H. Leslie Staebler and J. H. Bowman, halves; Alfred Scherrer, George Boehmer, Carl Meinke, R. N. Kramer, Otto Vogelsang and A. H. Heller, forwards. A Ranger eleven defeated St. Louis.

Other Clubs

Long before then, the Hough Cup had been given for competition among High Schools and Colleges. The Berlin High School boys won the trophy in 1885-6-7-8. One of their rivals was St. Jerome's College, on which were Michael Jaglowicz and James E. Day, K.C. Once in a match Jimmy Day and Billy King (William Lyon Mackenzie King) had a fight. Michael Jaglowicz was a stellar player and was chosen captain of the Rangers. Footballers generally succeeded in life and a number gained renown. Among these, Father Jaglowicz is Superior-General of the Congregation of the Ressurection, the Hon. W. D. Euler, Minister of Trade and Commerce for the Dominion, and the Rt. Hon. W. L. Mackenzie King, Canada's First Minister.

The younger players competed for the Intermediate Challenge Cup. The II Rangers kicked in the winning goals in 1885-8-9-90 and 1899. In addition the Midgets captured the Junior Challenge Trophy in 1900-01.

A hand-picked company of Canadians invaded the British Isles in 1888. The Rangers whose names follow were members of the team: David Forsyth, Michael Jaglowicz, Carl Kranz, Sollie Brubacher, Walter Bowman, Tom Gibson, Alex Gibson, Harry Bingham and Fred Killer. The Canucks made a good showing against the cracks of Britain. Walter Bowman, a clever dribbler, joined an English club and never came home to stay.

The Rangers' Reunion

A reunion of Rangers was held on August 22, 1900, when the champions of 1886-9 played the champions of 1897-1900. The Young Rangers' line-up: Otto Vogelsang, goal; Dr. Rudell and David Brown, backs; J. H. Bowman, A. Seibert and J. Raymond, halves; A. H. Heller, R. Kramer, George Boehmer, Fred Boehmer and Alf. Scherer, forwards. On the Old Rangers: Dr. G. H. Bowlby, goal; Sollie Brubacher, Carl Kranz and Harvey Sims, backs; F. W. Sheppard, H. Snyder and George LaCourse, halves; David Forsyth, Harry Bingham, Tony Kolb, E. O. Boehmer, Eddie Dunke and Ben Uttley, forwards. The Old Rangers' war cries were: "Carl," "Pete," and "George, vas spielst du den?" The Young Rangers won by 1-0. In the evenings at a banquet, George Bruce toasted the "Absent Old Boys" and named many of the more famous players.

A team of English stars visited Canada in 1905 and played against the Rangers. The defenders were: D. W. Brown, goal; A. E. Rudell and Alf. Scherer, backs; H. Sherriffs, G. Cochrane and J. D. Reid, halves; J. Brinkert, George Wagner, E. Dumart, Will Knell and G. Waterhouse, forwards. Harry Brown refereed the match. The Rangers won by a score of 1-0—the visitors' first defeat in the Dominion.

The
Turning
Point

THE TURNING POINT

In the seventies the town had the industrial firms that follow: Tanneries: R. Lang & Son, and L. Breithaupt & Co. Buttons: J. Y. Shantz & Sons, Emil Vogelsang, E. J. Nordhausen & Co., and S. S. Moyer & Co. Furniture: Simpson, Anthes & Co., and Brown and Devitt. Paper Boxes: A. & C. Boehmer. Rocking Horses: Moriz Lindner. Children's Wagons and Sleighs: Enoch Ziegler. Founders: Nelson & Cairns. Planing Mills: Jacob Kaufman, and H. J. Hall & Son. Slippers: C. A. Ahrens & Co., and George Rumpel. Carriage Works: Bricker Bros., and George Huck. Knitting Works: Philip Boehmer, and Herman Eby. Flour Mills: Shelly & Shantz, and Bramm Bros. Glue Works: Veit Fischer. Felt Works: Shantz & Feick. Cigar Shops: Wm. Meinke & Bro., and Querin & Foersterer. Marble Works: Stroh and Meinke. Altogether they employed 700 persons, of whom 283 were button workers. The weekly wage bill was $4,000.

Canada then had 4,000,000 people and of every hundred twenty were townsmen and eighty farmers. The wheat yield averaged 30,000,000 bushels yearly. There was only one steamship service between Montreal and Liverpool and British Columbia shipped its exportable products round the Horn. Other than grain and pork, Canada's commerce mostly flowed southward and thousands of young Canadians emigrated to the United States.

According to *The Canada Year Book* (1930) the first Canadian tariff law was enacted in 1858. It was objected against, however, by British manufacturers. In the early seventies the tariff was cut down to please the Maritime Provinces, which were commercial instead of manufacturing states. A severe trade slump ensued. In 1878 the electors cast a majority of votes for the protection of home industries.

Next followed the construction of the Canadian Pacific Railway (1881-5). While steel was being laid across the continent a stream of foreign money glided over the Dominion and electrified business. The West was opened to settlement, "sod-busters" poured in, and trade began to course east and west. In Berlin old industries were enlarged and new ones organized. Came a new hum.

George Rumpel bought the felt works from Jacob Y. Shantz and the old tobacco factory at the corner of Waterloo and Victoria Streets. There he became the felt-shoe king of Canada. His sons Oscar and Walter were his associates in the enterprise. C. A. Ahrens & Co. began the manufacture of leather shoes. Prior to Mr. Ahrens's death in 1937, he was the oldest shoe manufacturer in Canada. His son, Fred H. Ahrens, is now head of the company. Frederick Knell acquired Herman Eby's knitting plant and enlarged it . A. Biggs started another carriage works. John S. Anthes withdrew from the Simpson Company and established a furniture factory in E. King Street. Mr. Huber established a glue works in the West Ward. Mr. Wintermeyer afterward bought the property and organized the Atlantic Glue Company.

By now the pioneer manufacturers, with the exception of Wm. Simpson, had departed life. Among them, Jacob Hailer, John Hoffman, Henry Bowman, Reinhold Lang, and Louis Breithaupt. Mr. Lang's and Mr. Breithaupt's sons succeeded their father and respectively organized the Breithaupt Leather Company and the Lang Tanning Company.

The town was in its shirt-sleeves. Often factory proprietors worked at the bench alongside of their men. One owner filed his factory saws before the morning whistle blew. Broadly, where the fathers had used tools, the sons introduced machines.

In 1880, Wm. H. Breithaupt bought two telephone devices and strung a line from his father's office to the family residence in Margaret Avenue. Those were the first telephones in the city. The Bell Telephone Company arrived in 1882 and appointed J. S. Hoffman agent. Their office was in his drugstore. By 1883 there were thirty-eight telephones in the offices and ten in private homes. The spider rapidly spun its web over the town, necessitating new quarters at No. 8 N. Queen Street.

Joseph Hoelscher hauled the first telephone poles into Berlin. A neighbor asked what they were for. Mr. Hoelscher told him what parts the poles and wires play in telephoning. "Are the wires hollow?" the man inquired. "No," answered Mr. Hoelscher. "Then," said his neighbor, "I don't see how they can talk through them."

LOUIS LACOURSE LANG
President,
Lang Tanning Company.
First Vice President,
Mutual Life Assurance Company.
Vice-President,
Waterloo Trust and Savings Co.
Director,
Bank of Montreal.
Etc., etc.

GEORGE C. H. LANG
Organizer, The Lang Tanning Company.
Late President, The Economical Fire
Insurance Company.

THE LANG TANNING COMPANY'S TANNERY

THE C. A. AHRENS COMPANY'S SHOE FACTORY

Established 1880. Fred Ahrens, President.

GEORGE RUMPEL, Felt Manufacturer.

L. J. BREITHAUPT, Ex-M.P.P.

*Past President, Breithaupt Leather Co.
Late Vice-President of The Economical
Fire Insurance Co., of which Mr. H.
Krug was also a Director.*

HARTMAN KRUG, Founder of Furniture Company.

THE H. KRUG FURNITURE COMPANY'S FACTORY

Board of Directors: Rudolph W. Krug, President; H. John Krug, Vice-President; Leonard W. Ruby, Secretary-Treasurer.

Williams, Greene & Rome of Toronto, shirt manufacturers, moved their plant to Berlin in 1884. The firm bought Emil Vogelsang's factory in S. Queen Street. The town gave them $3,000 for moving expenses, spread over five years. That was a good investment, for the company began with seventy-five operators and ran it up to 400.

To get more factories, the townsmen organized a Board of Trade in 1886. A majority of property-owners voted for bylaws to secure new industries, for like Columbus they were not afraid to take a chance. Besides they were proud of their town. Town pride is a powerful force.

In 1887 Hartman Krug established a furniture factory opposite the G.T.R. station, which he built up into a big institution. Mr. Krug was also a charter member of the Interior Hardwood Company, and subsequently purchased the Doon Twine plant and brought it into the city. His son Henry is President of this company and his son Rudolph of the H. Krug Furniture Company.

Daniel Hibner founded also a furniture factory in 1887, adjacent to the railway, at Edward Street. It too was a large enterprise. In recent times Mr. Hibner sold the works to Malcolm & Hill. Mr. Hibner, who died in 1935, was once mayor of the town and long a park commissioner.

Waterloo liked Berlin

Waterloo Town stirred up a hornet's nest in 1887, when they moved to annex 113 acres of Berlin territory in West King Street. Some of those lands were owned by Waterloo citizens, and many of the residents worked in Waterloo. In the end Berlin was allowed to keep the lands.

The Mechanic

Later on Berlin obtained numerous more furniture factories and became known as the "Grand Rapids of Canada." Busy workshops spelled steady employment for workmen, while a mechanic's daily wage rose from seventy-five cents to $1.50. One effect was the replacement of frame houses with neat brick homes. In the eighteen-eighties the population rose from 4,054 to 7,425, while the average amount expended in homes annually was $200,000. Once a Governor-General visited Berlin and was conveyed through the residential sections. After viewing streetful after streetful of substantial brick homes in maple-lined thoroughfares, he inquired, "But where do your workmen live? Have you no poor quarter?"

Actually he had seen the workmen's homes. The town had no slums and fully eighty per cent. of the citizens owned their habitation. How did the mechanic become a property-owner? By work and thrift.

He could build a solid, eight-roomed brick house then for $1200. His lot cost $100 or $200. After saving, say, $300 more, he procured a loan of $900 from a moneyed friend or the Economical Fire Insurance Company for five years. How could a man with a wife and four or five children pay off a mortgage in such a short time on an income of $450 a year?

Father and sons in their early 'teens worked in a factory. Besides, his daughters stitched in button factories or sewed in the shirt factory. Therein they differed from the maids of Galt, Guelph, and Stratford, who stayed at home and were instructed in housekeeping. Not for another decade did their successors enter into a factory. Berlin girls while gainfully employed became adept housekeepers by helping their mothers before and after working hours. In the main the girls', boys' and father's earnings were banked against the day when an instalment of the mortgage fell due.

Parents bought their children's clothes, provided music and song, entertained their friends, and set them an example in church-going.

The core of the story is that every member of a family worked and saved. Yet there is another point that merits attention, namely their method of conserving the cash jointly earned. In a garden, often 60 x 200 feet, they raised vegetables, fruit, and flowers; and generally kept a cow, a flock of fowls, and four or five pigs. Together these yielded the bulk of their foodstuffs, permitting them to lay up the gross of their incomes.

When a son or daughter married, he and she received a nest-egg and went out into the world to repeat the process of acquiring a home by industry and thrift. After their marriage numerous wives sent their little sons to the shirt factory for a batch of sewing and thus earned enough to dress themselves. For a man the ownership of a home was an unwritten law and a yardstick of his worth as a citizen.

Sometimes a mechanic built his own home. A bricklayer, for example, dug a cellar, laid the foundation, and bricked the walls. During its construction he traded work with a carpenter, plumber, and tinsmith, who were also building, getting them to do what he could not do himself. The work was done after hours and spread over two or three years.

THE MOTHER AND HER CHILDREN

"Within bears sway
The modest housewife,
The mother of children—
And governs wisely
The dear home circle—
She teaches the girls,
Restrains the boys,
And finds no rest
For her busy fingers,
Increasing her store
With housewifely lore."

—*Schiller.*

A former building inspector who was born in one of those German homes said of their domestic economy.

"For breakfast we usually had bread, butter, home-made sausage, coffeecake, and a spread. Every week Mother baked coffeecake and six loaves of bread. For dinner we had meat, potatoes, and vegetables. In wintertime we ate pork in various forms, many varieties of sausage, spareribs, ham, and Sauerkraut und Speck. In the summer, beef. If beef was scarce and dear Mother stored a quantity of salted pork. For supper we had cold meat, fried potatoes, and pickles. Pickles gave the food a good taste, and were so generally used that one might have called the town Pickleville. We too had generous slices of pie made of green or dried apples. Although custard pie was my favorite.

"At all meals we drank coffee. Mother bought the green beans, roasted them, and ground them in a coffeemill. Few German families put sugar in their coffee. There was only a little fruit canned. Instead, fruits were dried for winter use. Cakes were seldom seen, excepting at Christmas and when Mother had visitors.

"We youngsters wore dark-colored suits on Sundays and boots that reached up to our knees. In our jack-boots we tramped through the deep snow to school. Boots were greased with lard or fish-oil.

When the first bootblack came to Berlin the roadway in King Street was so far below the sidewalk that he stood in the ditch and shined his customer's shoes. We boys began working in a factory at twelve or fourteen years of age and wore blue overalls.

"Young men wore clothing similar to those of today, and a 'Christie stiff'—a hard, round, black hat. As they strolled along King Street in the evening youths sported a cane to impress the girls. He waited at the church door for his Geliebte and accompanied her home. If her father did not like him they met at a house party or dance. At a party there were games, music and other amusements. We did not know much about shows, for there were only one or two a year in the town hall. While the people worked hard they enjoyed life. Nowadays if everybody worked and saved like them, there would be no hard times, no relief boards, nor so many persons in jail.

"Generally men and women were kind and quiet-spoken. I remember a man who made it a rule always to say something good about everyone. His friends often twitted him about his habit and when a close-fisted, sharp-tongued fellow died one of them exclaimed,

" 'Nu, what kind thing can you say about him?' '

" 'Vell, he vas a gut schmoker.' '

THE PUBLIC SCHOOLS

Until the citizens of Berlin incorporated their village, it was known as School Section No. 5, Waterloo Township. There were then two schools on the firehall lot and a third in the Mennonite churchyard. The first village trustees were: George Jantz (Chairman), Jacob Y. Shantz, Dr. John Scott, Henry Eby, John Eby, and Wm. Davidson (Clerk). Dr. Scott was appointed superintendent of the local schools.

Before incorporation, the farmers objected to spring and fall school terms, for their children were needed in the fields. After incorporation, the school year was lengthened and the course of studies extended. Free schools followed; and soon afterward, the attendance of school children was made compulsory. Miss Eakins was the first female teacher employed by the Board.

D. HIBNER, Ex-Mayor,
Furniture Manufacturer.

LATE C. A. AHRENS
Veteran Shoe Manufacturer.

SHERIFF DR. H. G. LACKNER,
M.P.P.

ARTHUR PEQUEGNAT
Clock Manufacturer.

HENRY L. JANZEN
Florist, City Builder.

CHARLES B. DUNKE
For 50 years a Grocer.

As we have seen, a joint Grammar and Common School was erected in mid-Frederick Street and opened in 1857. The three old schools were then closed. In the new school, the Common School occupied the ground floor. Alexander Young was the first principal, with John Strang and Miss Elizabeth Shoemaker, assistants. Thomas Pearce succeeded Mr. Strang in 1858. There were then 360 pupils on the roll and four teachers. A Separate Catholic School was organized in 1859, withdrawing sixty-eight pupils. Mr. Pearce was appointed principal of the Common School in 1864.

Henry S. Huber, a trustee, was appointed Clerk and served for seventeen years. After Dr. Scott's death, James Colquhoun, the Rev. A. J. Traver, Henry F. J. Jackson, and the Rev. A. Falls successively acted as the superintendent of the school.

Common Schools became Public Schools in 1871. A County Board of Examiners then replaced the earlier Board of Instruction, and a County Inspector, the local superintendents. Mr. Pearce was the first inspector appointed by the County and discharged the appertaining duties until 1912—a span of forty-one years. Donald McCaig followed him as principal of the Central School. His first assistant was W. F. Chapman, while Adolph Mueller taught the German classes.

In 1871, the village became a town. The ratepayers elected the trustees that follow: John A. Mackie (Chairman), Jacob Y. Shantz, W. H. Bowlby, John H. Heller, Henry Baedecker, Enoch Ziegler, and A. J. Peterson (Secretary). In 1873, Israel D. Bowman succeeded Mr. Peterson as secretary.

The Outcast

Meanwhile the school population had increased. To obviate enlarging the school, the Public School Board naively suggested that the High School vacate the upper floor and get new quarters elsewhere. The High School trustees murmured against it, but finally assented.

Mr. McCaig resigned his post in 1872, when Alexander Young was reappointed principal. Mr. Young formed a Junior Horticultural Society among the pupils. Teachers of that period included the Misses Sara Metcalfe, Vestella Weaver, and Lydia Sheppard; Ezra E. Eby, the historian; Alexander Metcalfe, who became an American attorney at law; and James A. Mowat, afterward editor of the *Canadian Magazine*.

The upper floor was soon overcrowded. For a time, classes were held in the firehall and the market building. After filling every available nook, the Board was obliged to enlarge the school in 1875.

A year later, Mr. Mueller was appointed teacher of Moderns at the High School, when U. Brunner was engaged to teach German.

The Model School

The school had good teachers and good material to work on. In 1877, the Department of Education authorized the Board to open a Model School for Teachers-in-Training. When ready, Jeremiah Suddaby was named principal of the Model School. Among his assistants were: F. W. Sheppard, Sylvester Moyer, Richard Reid, Charles Fraser, J. Herman Martin, and Miss Annie Scully. The school then had Fifth and Sixth Forms.

Henry Schwenn and John H. Heller, after they had respectively served as trustees for twelve and fourteen years, retired in 1879. Dr. R. Mylius succeeded Mr. Schwenn and acted for fifteen years.

Louis von Neubronn was appointed German teacher in 1880. In 1882, the first Kindergarten in Canada was opened with Miss Janet Metcalfe instructress. Arbor Day was introduced into the school in 1886 and Professor T. A. Zoellner commissioned to teach Music.

The pupils then numbered 899 and overthronged the twelve rooms. To ease the situation, the first ward school was built in Agnes Street. Miss M. Hyndman was appointed sub-principal. Four years later, a third school was built in Courtland Avenue, with Miss Edith Matheson as sub-principal. A fourth school was built in Margaret Avenue in 1894, with Miss Ada Cairnes as head-mistress.

Among the trustees of that period were P. S. Lautenschlager, H. J. Hall, Arthur Pequegnat, and G. M. Debus. In passing, C. L. Pearson served eighteen years, John Fennell and W. H. Bowlby each twenty-four, and Jacob Y. Shantz, thirty-five years.

At the Central School, Mr. von Neubronn retired in 1893. A scarcity of desk-room suspended the teaching of German till 1895, when W. D. Euler was appointed German master. Four years later, H. W. Brown succeeded Mr. Euler. In 1900, it was decided to teach German in all the Public Schools, and within a decade the enrolment exceeded 1300 pupils who took up that subject. Among the later German teachers were: Miss Ann von Neubronn, Miss E. P. Veit, Miss A. Bornhold, Simon Reid, Theodore Schultz, Miss M. Veit, and Miss M. M. Evans.

Secretary Israel D. Bowman died in 1896. He was followed by his son David, who continued until 1905. Mr. Bowman was succeeded by Edmond Pequegnat, who has ever since capably filled that position.

Manual Training

Chairman G. M. Debus and Trustees C. L. Pearson, Aaron Bricker, John Meisner and J. G. Buchhaupt visited Woodstock College in 1901, to inspect their Manual Training Department. After the delegation had reported their findings, the cry rose: "Put the whole boy to school!" For it was realized that hand-work is the mother of intelligence. In 1902, Chairman Arthur Pequegnat and Dr. H. G. Lackner conferred with representatives from the Separate School and High School Boards about Manual Training and Domestic Science. The upshot was the introduction of those departments at the High School in 1903 and their opening to senior classes of the primary schools. The children took to their respective instruction like strawberry shortcake.

The Model School Closed

Model Schools were superceded by Normal Schools in 1908. Mr. Suddably had then been head of the local Model School for thirty-one years. He was the associate of J. McLellan, L.L.D., in compiling a textbook on *Applied Psychology*. Of him, Mr. McLellan said: "For the chapters on Geography and Kindergarten I am indebted to Mr. J. Suddaby, whose work in the Berlin County Model School has placed it in the front rank of training schools."

Mr. Suddaby died suddenly in May, 1910. The School Board then affirmed: "He was a high-minded, Christian gentleman and a noble representative of his profession." In memory of him the Central School was renamed the Suddaby School.

After the veteran teacher's death, J. F. Carmichael was appointed principal of "Suddaby School."

Trustees of that time included: A. L. Bitzer, Wm. E. Vogt, Dr. W. J. Arnott, C. B. Dunke, W. D. Euler, J. R. Schilling, Martin Schiedel and Charles A. Ruby.

A fifth school was raised in 1910-11 at the head of South Ontario Street and named Victoria School. The trustees then were: Arthur Pequegnat (Chairman), Edward G. Stuebing, Fred Kress, Louis Sattler, Dr. J. E. Hett, W. Hertfelder, Chas. A. Ruby, John E. Vogt, Dr. H. H. Huehnergard, and Dr. J. A. Hilliard. The new school was a handsome building, costing $96,445 with equipment. The merchants in King Street yelled, "Ouch!" and then took off their hats to the structure. Mr. Carmichael was the first principal of Victoria School. After it was ready for use, manual training and sewing classes were introduced into the school.

A Board of Education

The Public and High School Boards organized a Board of Education in 1911. The initial members were: Richard Reid, Chairman; Arthur Pequegnat, Vice-Chairman; Dr. J. F. Honsberger, John A. Lang, Dr. J. E. Hett, D. A. Bean, Dr. H. H. Huehnergard, A. L. Breithaupt, Louis Sattler, A. L. Bitzer, and Edward Smyth. Edmond Pequegnat was appointed Secretary-Treasurer. The new Board bought a lot in Stirling Avenue for a sixth school. Later on the Collegiate wished to introduce Vocational Training and accordingly a High School District consisting of Berlin and Waterloo was formed. Hence the Board of Education was dissolved in 1914.

Principals and Kindergartens

The first Kindergarten teacher at King Edward School was Miss Mary Sherk and the first German teacher, Miss Jessie Kaempf. In 1893 a Kindergarten was opened at the Courtland Avenue School with Miss S. Ayres in charge. At the Margaret Avenue School the Kindergarten dates from 1896. Miss Jessie Thompson was the first Kindergartner, and later Mrs. Pomeroy.

A review of that period shows that Miss Jessie Thompson was the second principal of the King Edward School, and later Miss Stuebing. Succeeding principals were: J. B. Shotwell, J. S. Jackson, Richard Reid, J. D. Weir, Otto G. Smith, S. A. Smithson and W. G. Bain.

At the Courtland Avenue School, Miss M. B. Tier was the second principal. Later principals were Arthur Foster and Peter Fischer.

KITCHENER PUBLIC SCHOOL BOARD

Front Row: F. A. Schantz, K. E. Bornhold, F. H. Schneider (Chairman), D. W. Houston, Dr. C. E. Stoltz, J. E. Vogt.
Back Row: A. F. Klugman, E. C. Schultz, Dr. H. J. Prueter (Inspector), W. V. Siegner, N. G. Shantz, Edmond Pequegnat, (Secretary), J. F. Carmichael (Retiring Principal).

THE SUDDABY SCHOOL STAFF — 1937

First Row: C. Bond, R. Adamson, E. MacLachan, A. Goudie. Second Row: E. Smithson, I. Reeves, A. Welton, F. Ulrich, J. King, A. Knechtel. Third Row: R. Rhodes, M. Rumpel, M. Kirkness, M. Wells, R. Boothby. Fourth Row: H. DeBrusk, D. Bornhold, E. Seibert, M. M. McCormick, A. Hastie, G. Sim.

KING EDWARD SCHOOL STAFF — 1937

Back Row: E. McEwen, R. Gottfried, E. Common, R. M. Gillespie, Alex Fleming (Prin.), M. Struthers, M. Cooper.
Second Row: J. D. Brown, C. Heath, I. Woolner, M. Climie, V. Curtis, F. Stock, G. Gordon, M. Hossfeld, W. H. Taylor.
Front Row: M. Graber, E. Scully, D. Pearen, I. Perrin.

COURTLAND AVENUE SCHOOL STAFF — 1937

Front Row, left to right: Miss E. Mitchell, M. Wettlaufer, R. Smythe, D. Huber, M. Williams (on exchange from England). Second Row: Miss V. M. Asmussen, H. Ellis, P. Pirak, B. Uttley. Back Row: J. C. McClelland, M. Dowswell, W. G. Lovey (Principal), N. Donald, I. M. Kirkness.

J. F. CARMICHAEL SCHOOL STAFF — 1937

Left to right: Miss A. L. Smillie, Miss V. Snyder, A. E. Gillies (Principal), Miss A. M. Burgess, Miss M. Miller.

Miss Janet Metcalfe was the second principal of the Margaret Avenue School. After Miss Metcalfe, the principals were: J. F. Martinson, J. F. Carmichael, and J. B. Pomeroy.

At the Suddaby School, the principals after Mr. Carmichael were J. D. Weir and S. A. Smithson.

The city in 1913 had a population of 17,000, while the Public School children numbered 2,456. There were fifty-three teachers, and the value of the school properties was $264,000.

Sixty Years Ago

Secretary Pequegnat has in his office a portfolio of papers handed down by Miss Elizabeth Shoemaker. It has many samples of writing, which in the eighteen-seventies was one of the chief subjects taught in the schools. She preserved a free-hand drawing of a bird and of a horse by two of her pupils. Mitchell's School Atlas (Philadelphia, 1851) was used in teaching Geography; History lessons were carried back to Abraham; but boys of the seventies thought Grammar had too many moods. Among other things, Miss Shoemaker impressed on her pupils: "Manners make the man;" "To forget a wrong is the best revenge;" and "He that hath not patience, hath nothing at all."

Present-Day Schools

City parents have always desired the best of instruction for their children. Hence they have from time to time elected qualified men to direct school affairs and kept them in office. Board after Board selected able teachers and by fair dealing retained their service. Besides, groups of men and women have taken a lively interest in school activities. As an effect Kitchener schools are not excelled in the Province.

Education here is an important business. For in the last twenty years the city's population has approximately doubled and increased Public School pupils to more than 4,000. Ever since 1916, the Board, nautilus like, has either been enlarging the five schools or building new ones. When the need for more class rooms outstripped the building program, the management staggered classes or used a portable school. An eight-roomed school was built in Sheppard Avenue in 1929, and another eight-roomed one in Patricia Avenue in 1937. A two-roomed school has also been provided for the Westmount area. The teaching staff now numbers 115. Exclusive of equipment, the investment in schools now totals $1,100,000.

At Suddaby School, an auditorium has been provided for gatherings of parents and ratepayers. In other schools the regular class rooms are used for such meetings.

Manual Training and Domestic Science are taught at Victoria, Suddaby and King Edward Schools, while Agriculture Departments are now conducted at the six larger schools.

The Horticultural Society concern themselves in the pupils and the school surroundings. An annual grant of fifty dollars is made to the Society in consideration of seeds supplied to pupils for home gardens. The Home Garden Department, with prizes for the best gardens, trains the boys to make good use of their leisure hours.

The School Board has not lost sight of the need for a vigorous body as well as a trained mind. A beginning in supervised play was made in 1915, when basket-ball sets, teeter-boards, sand-box boards, swings, etc., were purchased for the schools. In the next year, the trustees employed a Cadet and Physical Culture instructor for the boys and a Physical Culture instructress for the girls. Skating rinks were built at the schools and a toboggan slide at three of them.

Soon afterward a City Playground and Recreation Association was formed to supervise play in the summer months. The association set up also a Handicraft Department. The Kiwanis and Rotary Clubs likewise took an active interest in the work. An annual Field Day followed with a trophy for competition among the athletes. The School Board arranged for swimming lessons at Victoria Park and the Y.M.C.A.; the Trail Rangers were formed; and a boys' and girls' Safety Club founded in 1928. A year later the Young Men's Club constructed a wading pool at Suddaby School. Since then they have also installed a wading pool at King Edward and at Margaret Avenue Schools. The Young Men's Club bestows a bulging stocking on needy children at the Community Christmas Tree festival. In 1935, the Public and Separate School Boards took over the summer playgrounds from the Recreation Association.

Free text books and free school supplies are furnished all the pupils who attend the Public Schools.

THE MARGARET AVENUE SCHOOL STAFF — 1937

Back Row, left to right: W. L. Hunter (Principal), T. A. Leishman, J. B. Norman.
Second Row: M. A. Douglas, L. M. Richardson, M. E. Walker, A. M. Forbes, A. M. Bechtel,
D. Russell, R. H. Kleinschmidt.
Front Row: L. M. Detweiler, E. R. Carter, H. B. Schneider, S. G. Bauman.

THE SHEPPARD SCHOOL STAFF — 1937

Back Row, left to right: Dr. Ferguson (School Dentist), H. L. McQuarrie (Principal), Miss E. MacTavish, H. Wildfong. Centre Row: Miss M. Hedley, D. Smith, M. Kirkland, H. Fretz, M. Roedding. Front Row: M. Rennie, R. Snider, L. Shafer.

MISS ALICE COWAN
Art Supervisor of Public Schools.

VICTORIA INTERMEDIATE SCHOOL STAFF — 1937

Back Row, left to right: Chas. D. Fogerty, Harold Ballantyne (Director of Physical Education), Harris Weber, Maynard Hallman. Third Row: Marjorie White, Marjorie Gilmore (Principals' Assistant, Suddaby and Victoria Schools), Jeanette Clarke, Violet Schrag, Bessie Spearin, Jean Bilger, Helen Armstrong. Second Row: George Charlton, Hazel M. Hawkins, Lillian Elsley, Joyce Gardam (English Exchange Teacher), A. Laura Hawkins, Agnes Stock, Harry Hill (Director of Music). First Row: Crawford Mahon, Florence Johnston (Assistant Director of Physical Education), Dorothy Kyle, Helen Christner (Secretary to the Inspector), Mamie Good, Winnifred Cassel, Inu Good, Stanley E. Hodgins (Principal). Absent: Miss Blanche Yates.

E. P. CLEMENT, K.C.

The Friend of Youth.

JOHN FENNELL

First President, the Board of Trade.

LOUIS McBRINE and W. G. CLEGHORN

Founders, The L. McBrine Company.

Special classes have been recently formed for pupils who pass the entrance examination, but do not intend to go to the Collegiate. In the fall of 1937, VIII and IX Grades were introduced.

In behalf of handicapped children, the Board has widened its helpfulness beyond the regulation courses. A school nurse was appointed and an Auxiliary Class for mental defectives formed in 1915. There have since followed a class for sub-normal children, for backward pupils, for shut-ins, for crippled children, and for exceptional pupils and adolescents.

After the appointment of a school nurse, a dental clinic was opened at Victoria School. Although dull parents failed to avail themselves of the service, yet in 1920 the sum of $1,000 was expended in dental work among poor children. The Board of Health, however, has since taken over the dental and nursing responsibilities. In addition, under-nourished tots were supplied with free milk, and moneyless pupils with defective eyesight provided with glasses.

Music

Music has flowered in the schools. Professor Zoellner put in first seeds and tended the plants till 1922. Under his successor, J. L. Yule, the teaching of singing was extended and piano and violin classes set up. School and Home Clubs were formed and entertainments held for the benefit of the public. At King Edward School, for example, seven monthly meetings of the Club and three concerts were held in the winter of 1927-8. Mr. Yule taught Music also in the Collegiate and Waterloo Public Schools.

Harry Hill, the present supervisor, came after Mr. Yule and discharged similar duties. Art and Entertainment sessions have been held in the schools; community concerts arranged for, and also the broadcasting of Christmas carols. In 1928, twenty-eight Public School pupils were invited to sing before the Ontario Educational Association. The members of the association were so pleased with their efforts that a second invitation followed. Mr. Hill uses the radio to broadcast programs and teach Music.

Inspectors

Fred W. Sheppard, inspector of urban and rural schools, chiefly in North Waterloo, gave up his position in 1928. In appreciation of his services here, the School Board named the school in East

Weber Street, "Sheppard School." In 1929, Dr. H. J. Prueter of Toronto, an experienced educationist, was appointed inspector of Kitchener Public Schools. That has been an advantageous change, since Dr. Prueter devotes his entire time to the advancement of the seven schools.

Chairmen

For nine years Arthur Pequegnat was chairman and for twenty-seven years a member of the Board. In town days the schools were of plain design. Mr. Pequegnat's artistic nature found expression in the erection of Victoria School, which became an exemplar in subsequent school construction. After his death in 1927, a bronze tablet was unveiled in that school as a memorial to his efforts in behalf of education.

The chairmen who followed Mr. Pequegnat were: E. D. Lang, G. M. DeBus, H. Leslie Staebler, E. G. Stuebing, J. E. Bilger, H. J. Graber, D. W. Houston, and at present, Fred H. Schneider.

Lack of space debars mention of the many useful men who have sat in the Board. One of them, however, the late Louis Sattler, had a score of 17 years. Of the teachers, Mrs. Ada Eby and Miss Ann von Neubronn were long members of the staff; Miss Mamie Woods was for thirty years Kindergartner at Suddaby School, while Miss Annie Scully taught for thirty-one years. Of the principals whose ship has reached the Haven, J. D. Weir, W. G. Bain, and S. A. Smithson served long and well; while J. B. Pomeroy was for twenty-one years superior of Margaret Avenue School.

Miss Alice Cowan was a member of the teaching staff from 1900 to the fall of 1937. Illness obliged Miss Cowan to retire as Art Supervisor of the Public Schools. She had then served the schools for a longer period than any other member of the staff.

Mr. Carmichael ably filled the role of principal for thirty-three years. He retired in June, 1937, when the School Board thoughtfully named the new school in Patricia Street, the "J. F. Carmichael School."

Here's to education and little Jack Horner!

WEST KING STREET IN 1880
Right side: M. Kiefer's hotel, Simpson's Warehouse, Swedenborgian Church.
Left side: Corner Simpson factory, Shantz clubhouse, High School on hill.

THE TOWN HALL OF 1869

THE McGARVIN TRUNK FACTORY — NOW DOMINION BUTTON WORKS

THE TEMPO QUICKENED

From 1875 till 1882 Berlin was for custom purposes an outport of Guelph, with Samuel S. Weaver the sub-collector. Amasa L. Bowman succeeded him in 1880. Two years later Berlin was raised to a customs port, with Mr. Bowman as collector.

The town council had Yost Kimmel erect a market building in 1882. It was placed in the rear of the town hall, parallel to Frederick Street, was 30 x 70 feet and cost $1825.

Cows were allowed to run at large. One day a "bossy" chased the station-master's wife in King Street. She fell and hurt herself. In 1882 a bylaw to prohibit cows grazing in the streets was submitted to a vote. After a hot campaign it was carried by a majority of twenty-five. The result cast gloom over the wards.

The California block was burned down in the same year. It was a long frame building extending easterly, on the south side of King Street, and owned by Sheriff Davidson. The lessees were: Henry and Philip Boehmer, dry-goods merchants; Daniel Freeman, oysters and cigars; George Schaefer, furniture; John Seyler, saddler; C. H. Ziegler, dentist; Oscar Becker, barber; and Wm. Hundeshagen, tailor. The citizens declared that it was the most successful fire Berlin ever had. Afterward Joseph Spetz, J. B. Fellman, Henry Knell Sr., Wm. Niehaus, and John B. Hett built the Germania block on its site, each owning a part.

Previously M. B. Shantz had introduced gas-lighting into J. Y. Shantz and Sons' button factory. Taking a leaf from his book a group of capitalists organized the Berlin Gas Company. The directors were: M. B. Shantz, President; L. J. Breithaupt, Treasurer; J. M. Staebler, Secretary; W. H. Breithaupt, Hugo Kranz and Ward Bowlby. The officers each invested $5,000 in the venture. The council then installed twenty-five street lights. For the first time the town hall was illuminated with gas on January 23, 1883, for a firemen's ball.

A Horticultural Society was also formed in 1882. The directors were: John Motz, President; Richard McMahon, Vice-President; Alexander Roy, Secretary-Treasurer; H. L. Janzen, Louis Koehler, E. F. Gassion, P. H. Good, H. J. Hall, C. R. Lundy, Simon Roy and G. S. Howard.

Conrad Stuebing, a forward-looking citizen, died in 1883. He came here in 1857 and, with J. Boedecker as a partner, bought Christian Enslin's bookstore. Later on Mr. Stuebing purchased his partner's interest in the firm and ramified into the wholesaling of fancy goods and stationery. John S. Smith, the bandmaster, subsequently became a partner, trading as Stuebing & Smith. After Mr. Stuebing's death, Mr. Smith continued the business until his own death.

Scottish Canadians formed the Berlin Curling and Skating Company in 1883 and built a frame rink in Gaukel Street. One of the chief promoters was James Gibson, father of the football stars. On the main sheet of ice youth cut the figure eight on wooden skates.

The Post-Office

Soon after Hugo Kranz, M.P., induced the Dominion Government to erect a post-office and customs building in Berlin. The site chosen lay on the northwest corner of King and Benton Streets and was purchased from Casper Heller, proprietor of the Market Hotel. The building was completed in 1886, at a cost of $20,000.

The Board of Trade

Twenty-one merchants and manufacturers met in the American House on April 29, 1886, to organize a Board of Trade. After a canvass sixty-three business men signed an application for a Dominion charter. The survivors in 1937 were: L. J. Breithaupt, John C. Breithaupt, Henry Hymmen, D. B. Shantz of Buffalo, N.Y., and W. A. Greene of Chatham, N.J. In their application Alexander Millar, Q.C., said that Berlin had more than 5,000 inhabitants. A charter was issued by the Hon. J. A. Chapleau, Secretary of State, on May 31, 1886.

Officers were then elected. John Fennell was chosen President; L. J. Breithaupt, Vice-President; H. W. Anthes, Secretary; and J. B. Fellman, Treasurer. The choices for the Board of Trade Council were: George C. H. Lang, W. R. Travers, J. M. Staebler, W. A. Greene, J. S. Hoffman, P. S. Lautenschlager, George Rumpel and Robert Smyth.

The organization was completed on June 8, 1886. Before June ended the Board had negotiated with the Crompton Corset Company to remove their plant to Berlin. The company was given a free

CAIRNES & McBRINE FACTORY
Gloves and Valises.

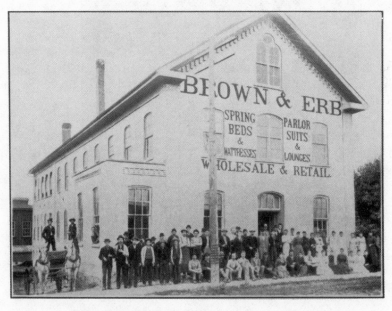

BROWN & ERB'S FACTORY — *West King Street.*

THE SCHUETZENVEREIN

Joseph Zuber, Karl Harttung, J. M. Staebler, M. Grebenstein, M. Huehnergard, Mr. Boneweis, R. Wegener, Karl Mueller, George Klein, George M. Schmidt, Mr. Kalb, caretaker, Mr. Lynden, photographer.

site, exemption from taxation and a bonus of $10,000. The corset men built a factory in North Water Street, on the Dominion Button Company site, and within a year had 250 hands on their payroll.

The Street Railway

John B. Snyder, Simon Snyder and Daniel Bowman of Waterloo had procured a charter for a street railway between Berlin and Waterloo in 1883. The line was not immediately built. The Board of Trade then put their shoulder to the wheel and had the Berlin council grant the company a franchise in 1886. The line was eventually built by local and New York capitalists, with T. M. Burt of Boston as manager. In 1901-2, Mr. Ford S. Kumpf was manager. The company was permitted to use horses, mules, or electricity; to operate cars at intervals of not more than an hour for twelve hours a day, excepting Sunday; requested to carry signal lights of different colors on the front and rear ends of their cars; and always have a bell attached to the lower hame-straps of their horses. The service was begun with horse-drawn cars in 1888. The carbarns were in Waterloo. Two well-remembered employees were Harry Clemens and Jacob Peppler.

A Try for a Second Railway

Berlin then had only the G.T.R. service. The Board of Trade conceived a plan to have a branch of the C.P.R. constructed from Dumfries station to the sister towns. Berlin voted the company $80,000 and Waterloo $40,000. Although the charter was kept alive for a decade, the branch was never built. It seemed that the two railways had an agreement not to invade one another's territory.

Meanwhile trouble had broken out in the corset factory. A walking delegate induced the girls to strike for higher wages. Straightway the Board of Trade offered to arbitrate the matter, but the company refused mediation and shipped its machinery back to Toronto. In 1889, the Board induced the McGarvin Trunk Co. of Acton to take over the vacant factory. This company stayed three years and then closed up.

One of their foremen was Louis McBrine, who remained here, and in 1893 formed the partnership of Cairnes & McBrine to manufacture gloves and valises. Two years later, the glove department was purchased by W. Cairnes and Karl Mueller. Mr. McBrine continued the other department, and in 1895 was joined by W. G. Cleghorn. Four years later the firm was manufacturing trunks and bags in S. Ontario Street. In 1903, the enterprise, by now the L. McBrine Company Ltd., was installed in a big factory in S. Water Street. There, about 200 mechanics make the company's famous "Around-the-World Baggage" for the domestic and foreign markets.

After the McGarvin Company vacated the building in N. Water Street, it was purchased by J. Y. Shantz & Sons. Ever since it has been the headquarters of the Dominion Button Company. David Gross is now President of the company and his son Mervin, Manager.

As is well known, the Board of Trade was the principal agent in the conversion of a town into a city. The Board mixed the dough and the Council baked the loaf. If at least one new factory was not bagged in any twelvemonth that year was counted lost.

Past Presidents: John Fennell (1886-8) ; George C. H. Lang (1889) ; Hugo Kranz (1890) ; L. J. Breithaupt (1891) ; W. R. Travers (1892) ; J. S. Anthes (1893) ; H. L. Janzen (1894) ; J. C. Breithaupt (1895) ; J. M. Staebler (1896-7) ; C. K. Hagedorn (1898-9) ; S. J. Williams (1900-1901) ; Robert Smyth (1902-03) ; C. H. Mills (1904-05) ; D. B. Detweiler (1906) ; H. J. Sims (1907-08) ; Edward Smyth (1909) ; J. A. Scellen (1910-11) ; H. L. Janzen (1912) ; L. J. Breithaupt (1913-14) ; W. M. O. Lochead (1915- part 1916) ; W. D. Euler (part 1916-1917).

Secretaries: H. W. Anthes (1886-8) ; P. E. W. Moyer (1889-90) ; J. S. Hoffman (1891-8) ; H. J. Sims (1899-05) ; J. A. Scellen (1906-09) ; Solon Lutz (1910) ; W. M. O. Lochead (1911-13) ; W. P. Clement (1914) ; George M. DeBus (1915-17).

The Public Library

The Mechanics Institute carried on till the early eighteen-eighties. In 1884 the town, under the leadership of J. M. Scully and Hugo Kranz, adopted the Free Libraries Act and established a Public Library. The first Board of Management consisted of: Thomas Pearce (Chairman), the Rev. R. von Pirch, the Rev. William Kloepfer, J. M. Staebler, P. E. W. Moyer, Alexander Macpherson, I. D. Bowman, Charles Crookall and Mayor Alexander Millar. The library started off with 2,855 volumes and was located on the first floor of the town hall. Miss Carrie Weaver was the first librarian, acting for two years. She was followed by Miss Ida McMahon, who continued for thirteen years. In 1899 the Board appointed Miss Effie Schmidt, who acted till 1908, when she was succeeded by Miss Mabel Dunham, B.A.

The Board purchased a lot on the corner of Queen and Weber Streets for a building, in 1897, from the Israel D. Bowman estate, for $1900. Acting on a suggestion made by D. B. Detweiler in 1902, Mayor Eden applied to Andrew Carnegie for a grant and obtained $15,000. The Rev. W. A. Bradley (Chairman), the Rev. Joseph Schweitzer, and David Forsyth were named a Building Committee. The library was erected in 1903 and opened in January, 1904. Further grants—$40,900 in all—were obtained from the Carnegie Foundation and the building completed as it now stands.

In 1933 the library had 51,582 books, pamphlets, etc., including works by German, Polish and French authors. The circulation of books was then nine per capita. The estimated value of the library is now $100,000.

Upward of fifty prominent men have since its inception served the library as directors and generally for long periods. The chairmen since 1884 have been: Thomas Pearce, the Rev. von Pirch, I. D. Bowman, the Rev. J. Schweitzer, Alexander Millar, John Motz, J. K. Master, David Forsyth, the Rev. J. W. German, Adolph Mueller, the Rev. W. A. Bradley, Karl Mueller, W. M. Cram, the Rev. A. L. Zinger, W. H. Breithaupt, Peter Fisher, J. J. A. Weir, John Wellein, the Rev. W. A. Beninger, H. W. Brown, W. J. Motz, George Bray, J. F. Carmichael, the Rev. H. A. Sperling, H. M. Cook, A. L. Breithaupt and the Rev. R. S. Dehler.

Among the full-time or part-time assistants have been: Mrs. Edith Simpson, the late Mrs. Homer Hymmen, Miss Irmgard Bitzer, Mrs. M. C. Herner (Winnipeg), Miss Hazel Bowman, Miss Alma Foreman, Miss Jessie McEwan (Toronto), Miss Ethel McNally, Miss Margaret Detweiler, Miss Olive Brubacher, Mrs. Fred Light (Chicago), Mrs. Rev. David (Philadelphia), Miss Hardy (Mimico), Miss Jessie Beatty (Blair), Mrs. E. J. Hawley (Peace River, Alberta), the late Miss Constance Banting, Miss Ruth Bond, Miss Berith Bond, Miss Arthura Bond, Mrs. Keith Staebler, Miss Audrey Buchanan, Miss Jean Hermiston, Miss Dorothy Schwalm, Miss Geneva Wanklyn, Miss Dorothy Shoemaker, Miss Ruby Wallace, Miss Nellie Weseloh and Miss Hazel Woolcott.

Fred Martin was the first caretaker. After his death Michael Heintzman succeeded him and still fills the position.

Miscellaneous Notes

Little standard life insurance was then sold in Berlin. Instead husbands joined one or more of the dozen fraternal societies that had lodges here and whose rates ran from sixty cents to one dollar a month for a $1000 policy.

To assist Waterloo Township to stretch a bridge across the Grand River at Breslau in 1886 the town granted the township $4,000. It opened a new source of trade for the local merchants. In that year the council gave the Berlin Gas Company a franchise to generate electricity and set up four electric street-lights between the townhall and Waterloo.

Back in 1856 Berlin had offered to unite with Waterloo but the northerners declined the bid. In the decade under review Waterloo proposed that the two municipalities form a union. Mount Hope cemetery was the only obstacle. Waterloo was prepared to purchase a burial-ground elsewhere, remove the organic remains and, if Berlin did likewise, to convert Mount Hope into a Union Park. In Berlin there was a deal of opposition to disturbing the dead and they shelved the plan.

Afterward a Town Park Association as formed here to deck Woodside park. The directors were: J. M. Staebler, President; John Moffat, Vice-President; Adolph Mueller, Secretary; J. S. Hoffman, Treasurer; C. R. Geddes, P. H. Good, J. S. Anthes and Emil Vogelsang. The society sold fifty-five memberships at one dollar each and expended fifty dollars in trees and shrubs; while the council expended a like sum in grading a driveway and building a grandstand. Boys played lacrosse, baseball and football there but soon agitated a central park.

The town still had a Landwehrverein in 1887. The officers were: Charles Mueller, Hauptmann; G. Hartmann, Lieutenant und Secretary; E. H. Meisner, Feldwebel und Schatzmeister; and Trustees: F. Welz, J. Bojanowski, J. Liftmann, August Frost, and E. Rosengartner.

Under the direction of Theodore Zoellner, the Philharmonic Society produced Mendelssohn's "Lobesgesang" and Handel's "Messiah," in 1887. Berlin had also a Mozart Club, a Guitar and Mandolin Club and the Dilettanenverein. The Berlin Orchestral Society held a number of concerts and bought a piano for the town hall. Many households then had either a piano or organ, but in 1888 Edison's phonograph invaded the musical field. One year the Berlin Dramatic Society presented two playlets: "A Cup of Tea" and "Papa Hat's Erlaubt." Balls were often held in the townhall or at Woodside park. There were two Debating Clubs, who debated: "Closer Relations with Great Britain,' "Capital Punishment" and "Commercial Union with the United States."

The Button Industry

Up to the mid-eighties the button industries held the foremost place. The four factories did an extensive trade and exported a deal of their output to the United States. Then our southern neighbors clapped on a stiffer duty, crippling the local factories. Emil Vogelsang closed up his factory and removed to Port Elgin; J. Y. Shantz & Sons opened a branch factory in Buffalo, shipping over partly-finished buttons and completing them there. M. B. Shantz, the manager, went to and fro for a number of years. In 1887 he established a factory of his own in Rochester, N.Y., and numerous Berlin mechanics went with him, including Wm. Asmussen and Jacob Mohr. Several years later E. J. Nordhausen & Co. too moved to Rochester. The fourth Berlin factory, of which S. S. Moyer was a principal, seems to have discontinued operations.

Those losses were felt, but the Board of Trade sought after replacements. The spirit of the time is made clear by two incidents. In 1889 a group of manufacturers sent Allan Huber to Japan to make commercial connections. After he came back another group sent him to Jamaica on a similar mission.

A knot of business men erected a grain elevator near Hartman Krug's furniture factory. The directors were: Hugo Kranz, Jacob Kaufman, P. S. Lautenschlager, George Rumpel and John Fennell. About the same time the street-railway was partly double-tracked and steel laid to the G.T.R. station.

Heins & Halliday opened an animal park in the West Ward in 1889.

A Salvation Army platoon came over from Guelph in 1884 and held meetings in the town hall. Their drum, tamborines and banner with the "Blood and Fire" device generally displeased the citizens. As a consequence they were restricted to the market place. A newspaper item of the time said,

> Dr. Jacob Kraemer, the widely-known manufacturer of hair-oil, eye-water, etc., had to appear in police court on Tuesday to answer a charge of having disturbed the Salvation Army on Saturday evening. He was accused of having beaten a tin kettle and of singing while the army members were praying in front of the market building. The doctor claimed that he had beaten his drum to attract a crowd to buy his specialties. But he failed to support his claim with witnesses and was fined $1.00 and costs.

Opposition made friends for the army. For some years they occupied the third floor in the Dunke block; then leased a barrack in Wilmot Street. Later on they built a citadel in South Ontario Street. Now they possess an attractive brick structure in Gaukel Street, which cost $30,000.

The Schuetzenverein

A Schuetzenverein was organized here in 1887. The first officers were: Dr. R. Mylius, Schuetzen Hauptmann; George C. H. Lang, II Offizier; John Peters, III Offizier; Karl Mueller, Sekretar; Martin Grebenstein, Schatzmeister; E. B. Reinhardt, Exerziermeister; E. Mueller, Schiesmeister, and Louis Zimmer, Gendarm. The Verein bought 2.75 acres of land east of Woodside park and held weekly meets. The members wore Tyrolese costumes and in the summer held a Schuetzenfest. Afterward, at a dinner, the winner was crowned Schuetzenkoenig. The evening was concluded with a ball.

Subsequently a farmer entered an action against the club to prevent them from engaging in shooting. To avoid injuring anyone the Verein constructed an underground gallery. The club continued until 1899, when they disbanded. There were then six active members: George Klein Sr., Karl Mueller, G. M. Schmidt, Karl Harttung, Herman Jaeger and N. Wegener. A silver trophy was placed in the care of the oldest member—probably Mr. Klein—to be retained until his death and then handed to the next oldest. At last the trophy was to become the property of the sole survivor. George Klein, George Schmidt, Herman Jaeger and Karl Mueller have gone

J. M. SCHNEIDER
Founder of
J. M. Schneider, Limited,
one of Canada's largest
Packing Companies.

THE FIRST PLANT
1890 - 1912

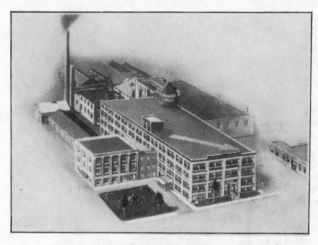

J. M. SCHNEIDER'S PRESENT PLANT
President, J. M. Schneider; Vice-President, N. C. Schneider;
General Manager, F. H. Schneider; Secretary; H. H. Schmidt.
Directors: C. A. Schneider, H. A. Voelker, Mrs. W. V. Siegner.
(Company incorporated in 1912.)

THE L. McBRINE COMPANY'S FACTORY
"Around the World Baggage"

to the Happy Hunting Ground, while Mr. Wegener's whereabouts are unknown. Mr. Harttung survives but does not know what became of the trophy.

A Poetical Plea

Thirty ratepayers in the North Ward petitioned the council for a street-light at Badke's corner and for a sidewalk. With the petition they attached the verse that follows:

> "Hier in Berlin ist es gar schoen;
> Da darf man Abends nicht aus dem Hause gehn—
> Dann sinkt man 'nein
> Bis um das Bein,
> Und Niemand hoert sein Flehn und Schrein.
> Drum lieber Stadtrat hilf geschwind,
> Denn wir sind doch kein Weisenkind."

THE BUSY NINETIES

In the eighteen-nineties, the town obtained a sheaf of new industries. Most of these made commodities not before manufactured here, such as wood-working machinery, pork products, pianos and organs, trunks and bags, chemical preparations, biscuits and confectionery, racycles, and rubber footwear. This centre thus became a town of diversified industries, employing many more mechanics. The fruits were more brick homes, better stores, and an increased municipal assessment. The gain in tax receipts spelled improved streets, a sewage-disposal system, and the first venture upon municipay ownership of a public utility. As wealth increased the town acquired numerous community services.

Fresh Factory Smoke

J. M. Schneider, pork products.
Jackson & Cochrane, wood-working machinery.
Cairnes & McBrine, gloves and valises.
Brown-Whiting Co., leather shoes.
Foster Shoe Co., leather footwear.
The Alpha Chemical Co. (David Moody), chemical products.
J. T. Huber, glues.
The L. McBrine Co., trunks and bags.
Joseph Bingeman, gloves.
The Messett Shirt Co., shirts, etc.
The G. V. Oberholtzer Co., leather footwear.
The Berlin Shirt & Collar Co., shirts and collars.

C. H. Doerr & Co., biscuits and confectionery.
The Mitchell Button Co., pearl buttons.
J. R. Stauffer & Co., covered buttons, etc.
C. K. Hagedorn, suspenders.
Kreiner & Co., household furniture.
The Diamond Furniture Co., household furniture.
The Star Whitewear Co., women's blouses.
The Lippert Furniture Co., household furniture.
The Berlin Furniture Co., (later the Jacques Co.) furniture.
I. E. Shantz & Co., furnaces and founders.
C. E. Hoffman, covered buttons.
The Casper Braun Monument Works, monuments.
Tuerk Bros., fine tools and gasolene engines.
The Berlin Racycle Co., bicycles.
Chris. Huether, lager-beer brewery.
The Berlin Rubber Co., rubber footwear.
A. G. Schreiter, upholstering.
The Daily Record and the Daily Telegraph.

In 1893, numerous citizens visited the Chicago World's Fair, and there for the first time saw a typewriter. Soon replicas of it were to be seen in factory offices.

The First Rubber Factory

The change of the town into a city was mostly owed to the manufacturers. As a rule, they began on a modest scale. The secret of their success was given out by the late George C. H. Lang: "Our men are trained for their business and aim to make better commodities than anyone else."

Up till then, on what was the town chiefly nourished? Boxes, buttons, chemical preparations, confectionery, furniture, leather, pianos, pork products, racycles, shirts and collars, felt and leather shoes, suspenders, trunks and bags, and woodworking machinery. Then in came Miss Rubber Latex.

In the winter of 1898 George Schlee and Nelson Good visited the chief rubber centres of the United States. Mr. Schlee, on his return, set about the forming of a company to manufacture rubber footwear. He had earlier been a building contractor and experienced in tackling big things. He succeeded in interesting Jacob Kaufman, A. L. Breithaupt and Louis Weber in a venture to make rubber footwear. The company was named: The Berlin Rubber Company, Mr. Schlee was appointed manager, and they erected a factory in Margaret Avenue, near the railway. In January, 1900,

FOUNDERS OF FIRST RUBBER COMPANY

GEORGE SCHLEE

JACOB KAUFMAN

A. L. BREITHAUPT

LOUIS WEBER

THE BERLIN RUBBER COMPANY'S WORKS

THE H. A. LIPPERT FURNITURE COMPANY'S PLANT

Mr. Schlee came down town wearing the first pair of rubbers turned out by the plant. Soon, they were making between 800 and 1000 pairs a day.

Three years later, Mr. Kaufman organized the Merchants Rubber Company to make rubber footwear, and erected a giant factory in Breithaupt Street. One of his executives was T. H. Rieder. Mr. Kaufman sold that industry in 1906 to the Dominion Rubber Company. A year later his son, Alvin R. Kaufman, induced him to form the Kaufman Rubber Company to make rubber footwear. Situated at the corner of King and Francis Streets, it is one of the city's largest industries, and is headed by Mr. A. R. Kaufman. With regard to Mr. Jacob Kaufman's life work, he never asked for nor received any bonus or concession from the city.

Mr. Schlee stayed with the Berlin Rubber Company until 1906, when he sold his shares to Mr. A. L. Breithaupt. Mr. Schlee then organized the company now known as Kitchener Buttons Limited, to manufacture vegetable ivory buttons. His associates were his three sons: Ervin, Eden and Wilfrid. A large factory was built on the corner of Edward and Victoria Streets. Eden and Ervin have since identified themselves with other businesses. In recent years the company began the manufacture of furniture knobs and radio-control knobs. In 1932, Mr. Wilfrid Schlee opened a market for those specialties and the Yo-Yo Stop in Great Britain. Mr. George Schlee, now in his 80th year, has done his full share for the advancement of the city.

The First Sewage-Disposal System

In 1889 West Ward citizens asked the council to stop the flow of sewage into Schneider's creek. In 1891, Wm. H. Breithaupt, C.E., and H. J. Bowman, C.E., devised a separation system that was approved of by the Provincial Board of Health. Twenty-five acres of land in lower Mill Street were picked out and $25,000 set aside for the system. Its construction was directed by Mayor J. M. Staebler, John C. Breithaupt, George C. H. Lang, Jacob Kaufman, P. S. Lautenschlager, J. S. Anthes, and H. J. Hall.

The work was done with day labor. While digging a main in King Street, the workmen struck a spring and uncovered an old corduroy road that had been laid down in 1842.

At the sewer farm, the committee constructed a series of beds that ran from Mill Street to the railway embankment. Rows of large half-pipes were laid level with the beds, and the beds underdrained with tiles leading to Schneider's creek. The sewage overflowed onto the beds and after filtration the effluent was clear and odorless. In passing, the committee completed the work for $17,000.

It was hoped to make the sewer-farm self-sustained. Beds at rest in the summer were planted to mangels, peas, onions, and cabbage. In 1893 the committee raised eight acres of cabbage and vended 25,000 heads at two cents apiece. Optimists fancied that the crops would pay off the debenture and the farm suffice for a city of 30,000 people. For a time the system handled the load with ease. Then, as the number of factories and population increased, difficulties arose. Finally a septic tank was built at the discharge point in the creek. In the meantime the cabbage patches had disappeared.

DR. J. F. HONSBERGER

Later Systems

Soon the farm became too small to treat daily 450,000 gallons of sewage. Five farmers, whose lands abutted the creek, entered

JOHN ROAT'S COMMERCIAL HOTEL

Courtesy, J. M. Snyder.   Photo by Sebastian Fischer.

NORTH QUEEN STREET
From American House corner.

TOURIST CAMP AT VICTORIA PARK
——Courtesy, Allan A. Eby.

SOUTH QUEEN STREET
From Walper House corner.

an action at law against the town for polluting the stream. To abate the nuisance, Dr. J. F. Honsberger, who had given years of time and thought to the problem, had the Ross Government send up Dr. J. A. Amoyot and Professor Robertson to find a solution. Those experts said that in all America there was only one other city that had such complex sewage to treat. After experimenting for six months, they recommended the town to buy a sandy farm, put in septic tanks, and lay out beds for an intermittent filtration system.

The Gens farm of seventy-two acres was bought in 1904 for $5,000. To carry out the recommendations, the council named a Sewer Commission, the first in Canada, with the members that follow: Dr. Honsberger (Chairman), J. M. Staebler, Arthur Pequegnat, and John Cochrane.

Before the system was completed, Dr. H. G. Lackner, M.P.P., had the Whitney Government spend $4,000 more in experiments. That system, after completion, handled its load for upwards of two decades. Then, since the population has trebled, difficulties mounted therewith, and the city was obliged to build a $500,000 system, with a plant on the Grand River at Doon. City Engineer Stanley Shupe supervised the construction. Mr. Shupe is a Trustee of the Canadian Institute on Sewage and Sanitation.

Since then, the old Genz farm has been converted into a municipal golf course.

The Walper House

John Roat's Commercial Hotel was destroyed by fire in 1892. It was a white, frame hotel and stood on the northwest corner of King and Queen Streets, first built by Fred Gaukel in 1835. That corner has been a hotel site ever since the days of Phineas Varnum. After the destruction of the landmark, Abel Walper of Zurich, Ont., bought the site for a large red-brick hotel. Before he began operations, he offered to sell the town a triangular strip, with a fourteen foot base in King Street, to straighten the jog at the intersection of King and Queen Streets, for $500. The council accepted his offer but there was so much public criticism of the price that the plan was dropped. Two generations have since worn out shoe leather going around the corner. Mr. Walper completed his hotel in 1893 and named it the Walper House. At first the big hotel was managed by his son, C. H. (Currie) Walper. Long afterward it was purchased by Joseph Zuber and by him enlarged.

When the Walper House was opened, King Street was paved with wooden blocks and had plank sidewalks. In its entirety, King Street is possibly the only thoroughfare in the world said to run east and west and north and south. On early maps it appears as a diagonal running southeasterly from Erb's mill in Waterloo to the First Mennonite Church. Here, the villagers used the terms: "Southeast King Street," and "Northwest King."

Martyrs to Duty

The street-railway company electrified its horse-car line in 1895. Previously, the Messrs. Breithaupt had purchased the bulk of shares. The conversion was made under the direction of Ezra C. Breithaupt, E.E. For a number of years, T. E. McLellan was superintendent of the street railway. After the line was electrified, Mr. Ezra Breithaupt was elected general manager of the Street Railway Company and the Gas and Electric Company. Late in the evening of January 26, 1897, there befell at the gas works the most shocking accident in the town's history.

There was a tank in the ground, empty of oil, but full of highly inflammable vapor. The oil supply had been exhausted and before a regular tank of oil could be received by rail, it was proposed to use barrels of coal-oil to keep up the supply of gas for the town. The tank-cover had been taken off and Manager Breithaupt, William Aldrich, electrician, and William Woeller, lamplighter, were about to empty a barrel of oil into the tank when an unguarded lantern, seemingly held over the opening, caused an explosion and blast of fire. Mr. Breithaupt, who was standing on the tank, was hurled high into the air and dropped on a roof, sustaining injuries from which he died before morning. Mr. Woeller was severely burned but recovered and is still living. Mr. Aldrich was thrown against a building and burned to death. The citizens mourned the deaths of the two martyrs to duty. Mr. Breithaupt was a young electrical engineer of great promise.

After the fatality W. H. Breithaupt, C.E., of New York City, succeeded his brother Ezra as manager. Under his direction the street-railway was extended to Albert Street and a power house there built. The Berlin and Bridgeport Railway Company was also organized by Mr. Breithaupt and a service to Bridgeport begun on July 14, 1902.

Wayside Notes

English-Canadians who joined the Board of Trade found the town-building spirit as contagious as laughter.

The bicycle was then in its heyday. On a holiday a cyclist might pedal 100 miles to a celebration. Magistrates thundered, "Don't scorch!"

Senator Samuel Merner built the Brunswick Hotel—now the Windsor—and leased it to Samuel Dopp.

In 1896 the furniture manufacturers of Ontario held their first exhibition at the Toronto Fair.

There was then a demand for houses that would rent at five dollars a month. The electorate adopted the Frontage Tax Act upon persuasion of G. M. DeBus and Aaron Bricker. Shortly afterward A. W. Feick fathered a garbage-collection system for the central part of the town.

A New Station

The Board of Trade finally induced the G.T.R. to build a new passenger station. First the moguls asked the town to buy a strip, 50 x 250 feet, to straighten the jog between West Weber Street and Gzowski Street (Upper Weber Street). The station was built by Casper Braun and completed in 1897. Its erection was a feather in D. B. Dover's cap.

Cigar Manufacturers

Cigar-making was then of importance. Among the manufacturers were: Fred Stephan, Wm. Meinke, Joseph Winterhalt, Charles Blankstein, Fred and Alex von Neubronn. It was the day of nickel smokes: the "Canadian Belle," the "C. B.," "Joe's Prime," "Meinke's Special" and "Fritz's Favorite." Well-to-do men smoked a "Rich Uncle" or other dime cigars.

The Day of Public Balls

Because of its numerous doctors, South Queen Street was dubbed "Materia Medica Lane." The mid-nineties introduced the citizens to "La Grippe." Local farmers organized a rural telephone company, with an office in V. F. Weber's store and after in John

Querin's Delmonica Hotel. One Easter Monday there were four balls aswing: the fire-brigade's in the townhall; the Concordia's in Fuchs' block; the Saengerbund's in the Canadian block; and the Landwehrverein's in the American block.

The Saengerfest of 1898

Under the auspices of the Saengerbund, a Saengerfest was held in 1898. The officers were: Hon. President, Joseph E. Seagram; Hon. Vice-Presidents, Senator Merner and George Randall; President, Dr. H. G. Lackner; Vice-Presidents, Wm. Roos and John Motz; Corresponding Secretary, Otto Schmidt; Treasurer, Fred H. Rohleder; Manager, Frank von Neubronn. Committee of Management: George M. DeBus (Chairman), Mayor George Rumpel, August R. Lang, F. G. Gardiner, C. L. Pearson, Phil Davey, D. Hibner, George Bramm, Alois Bauer, J. C. Breithaupt, W. R. Travers, H. M. Andrews and W. S. Russell.

Musical Committee: W. H. Schmalz (Chairman), Wm. Forder, John F. Stumpf, the Rev. F. W. Tuerk, George Ziegler, Sr., Wm. McCullough and W. S. Russell. A feature of the international Fest was the production of the opera "Snow White," with Miss Racie Boehmer in the titular role.

First Opera House

Abel Walper built an opera house in 1896. It was attached to the hotel, with an entrance in Queen Street. George O. Philip was the first lessee. Among the plays he brought in were: "The Old Homestead," "Pinafore," "Richelieu," and "Charley's Aunt." Mr. Philip, a professional actor, produced also plays with local talent. Mrs. Philip, a talented actress, assisted him at coaching the cast. An outstanding success was the production of "Faust," with Oscar Rumpel taking the part of "Mephisto." Mr. Philip brought in also the first moving picture.

Hockey

The world's first hockey-match was played at Kingston, Ont., in 1888, by teams from the Military College and Queen's University. Eddie Wettlaufer, travelling salesman for the Alpha Chemical Co., saw a number of hockey games and caught the fever. There were then a cluster of bank clerks in the Twin-City who had played in Montreal. In 1890, Mr. Wettlaufer was the means of forming a hockey club here. Ten young men joined the club and practised in

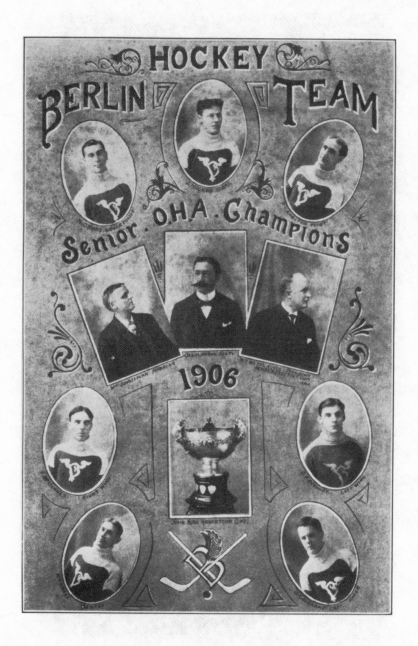

AN EARLY FIRE BRIGADE

Courtesy, Hugo Rathman.

GEORGE O'NEILL
Police Chief 1902 - 32

N. ASMUSSEN
Former Mayor and M.P.P.

H. R. STEPPLER'S HOTEL
Where "The House of Lords" met.

FAMOUS BERLIN BAND

Back row: H. Snider, Louis Moebus, G. Garlick, E. Hinsberger, S. Ferrier, W. R. Travers, President, O. Ziehm, G. M. Schmidt, E. Hammel, J. Keyes, M. Morosky, E. Badke, John Hett, A. Schwenn, R. Hintz.
Middle row: F. Rattenbury, H. Illing, Secretary, A. Vanderhart, W. Forder, leader, W^m. Roos, Treasurer, F. Dushinsky, F. Hett.
Bottom row: G. Albrecht, A. Steinke, F. Crowley, T. Mueller, F. Slumkowsky, W. Hulmes, E. Treusch, E. Hamel.
—Photo by courtesy of J. C. Moebus.

the old Gaukel Street rink. The game gripped the youths, and later on the club joined the Ontario Hockey Association. David Forsyth once said: "Hockey is the most interesting game to watch and curling the most interesting one to play." Local matches attracted only small gates, and the players had to pay their travelling expenses out of their own pocket.

The first scheduled game was played at Stratford in 1892. The home pucksters consisted of: Lorne Bricker, goal; F. G. Oliver, point; J. Barry, cover-point; Eddie Wettlaufer, Herb Snyder, Mr. Waud, and Alf. Snyder, forwards. Of that match the *Stratford Herald* said: "Hockey is a polite name for bankers' shinny. If the public does not patronize the game and enjoy it, there's no fun outside of a keg of lager, a ring of sausage and a few bretzels. A rink of curlers tried to curl while the game was on, but though they arrived at seven o'clock not a stone was played before nine. In the meantime a string of bald-heads were mounted on the guarding, yelling like schoolboys or whooping like Sioux Indians." The score: Berlin 15 goals, Stratford, 5 tallies.

Berlin was the first winner of the Intermediate Series, and in 1906, the club won the senior championship. These pucksters were: Nelson Gross, Will Knell, Peter Charlton, Carl Schmidt, Jim McGinnis, and John Mickus.

Other stars were: Goldie Cochrane, E. F. Seagram, Jack Gibson, Nelson Schell, "Butch" Trushinski, and George Hainsworth.

A professional team was formed in 1907. Among the players were Hughie Lehman, Cully Schmidt, Nelson Schell, Billy Knell, and Goldie Cochrane. Since then numerous local players have worn the uniform of the biggest clubs in Canada and the United States.

Hockey, like the measles, attacked every family that had boys big enough to wield a stick. In Chief Frank Seibert's family there were seven sons who in 1906 met the King family septette of Guelph and won the match by a score of 5 to 4 goals. Later on the late John H. Schnarr's sons formed a team and won many matches.

The Horseless Carriage

E. J. Philip, on August 16, 1898, rolled along King Street in the first automobile ever seen in the town. Accompanied by his mother, he left Toronto after dinner and reached Berlin in the evening. The car was called a "horseless carriage," weighed 1400 pounds, and had pneumatic tires. The roads were bad, hence his speed was only fourteen miles an hour. Hundreds of citizens viewed the marvel that was to cause a social revolution.

Dr. J. E. Hett purchased the first automobile owned by a Berlin resident. In 1903, the Ontario Legislature enacted a law forbidding motor-cars being driven at more than ten miles an hour in country roads, because they scared the farmers' horses. The "gas-buggy" was then looked on as a rich man's plaything and generally disapproved by the public.

Nelson Gross was the city's first automobile salesman.

Fire Chiefs

The fire-brigade has advanced from two-score volunteers to thirty regulars, and from water-buckets to motorized equipment. The chiefs have been: George Stahle (1879-81) ; Wm. Ryder (1881-86) ; Herman Rathman (1886-89) ; George Huck (1889-1894) ; Louis Timm (1894-97) ; Frank Seibert (1897-1906) ; J. Howard (1906-07) ; Jacob Cook (1907-15) ; and Chief Harry Guerin from 1915 up to the present.

Herman Rathman was secretary of the brigade for twenty-five years. Other veterans were George Scharlach and Dan Boettger, while Hugo Rathman has served since 1910.

Police Chiefs

In the eighties, Joe Atkinson was the police chief, but was let out in 1887 because he did not keep order when the Salvation Army came in. He was succeeded by Chief Henry Winterhalt, who served for twenty-five years. Mr. Winterhalt tactfully kept the peace as the only policeman in a town of about ten thousand inhabitants. Chief George O'Neil was appointed in 1902 and served the city for thirty years. Mr. O'Neil was a born leader of men, cool and courageous. As the population mounted, he gradually formed a police staff, with the sanction of the Police Commission. One of his stand-bys was Sergeant-Detective James Blevins, who is still a member of the force. The present chief is William J. Hodgson.

Customs Collectors

Amasa L. Bowman was customs collector till 1895. A. Shaw then acted for a year. In 1896, Frederick Colquhoun was appointed and served ten years. Martin Schiedel capably filled the post from

1906 to 1931. From then to now, Louis Feick has been at the head of this service.

In 1882 the amount of duty collected was $3,899. In 1929 it was $2,902,494.

THE MUSICAL SOCIETY'S BAND

For sixty years the band has been a city asset. A group of players organized the Berlin Musical Society in 1876, with the performers that follow: Fred Kress, Matt Stricker, Harry Moebus and Carl Venselow, Altos; Charles S. Smith, Alex Mackie, Joseph Zeller, Astor Weaver, Henry Schaefer and James Scott, Cornetists; John S. Smith, Noah Zeller, A. H. Ziegler, J. W. Fuchs and Noah Ziegler, Clarinetists; Dennis Scharlach, A. J. Peterson and John Schaefer, Tenors; George Lippert, Trombone; J. W. Hett, Saxophone; Archie Chamberlain, Piccolo; George Huck, Wm. Fleischauer and A. Jantz, Basses; George M. Schmidt, Bass Drum, and John Poure, Snare Drum.

John S. Smith acted as bandmaster till 1878, when he was succeeded by Noah Zeller. The organization was chosen as the 29th Battalion Band in 1879. Mr. Zeller continued until 1882, when he was appointed leader of the Waterloo band. Harry Hunt then led the Berlin band. At that stage there was an older organization, the United Band, of which Wm. Kaiser was bandmaster. With two bands in a town of 3,000 it was difficult to finance them. The Musical Society, to raise funds, joined the Concordia, the Firemen, the Western Football Association or the Philharmonic Society and held holiday celebrations. After William Roos removed from Waterloo to Berlin, in 1884, the society gained a staunch friend. Mr. Roos was a gifted cornetist and for a spell acted as bandmaster. He made the band a hobby and contributed generously to its maintenance.

The two bands were united in 1887. The first directors were: Wm. Roos, President; Wm. Jaffray, Vice-President; Joseph Bury, Secretary; and Henry Gildner, Treasurer. Citizens' Committee: John S. Smith, H. W. Anthes and A. L. Bowman. Players' Committee: Bandsmen Howe, Bickert and L. Moebus. A year later a Mr. Cline was employed as teacher and remained a twelvemonth.

W. R. Travers was elected Vice-President and Harry Illing, Secretary, in 1889. Subsequent members of the Citizens' Committee were Adolph Mueller, David Forsyth and George Huck; and of the Players' Committee, J. W. Hett, Harry Illing and Julius Gerbig. Drum majors of that period were: George O. Philip, George M. Schmidt and Jacob Fricker.

H. C. Heinicke was appointed bandmaster in 1890. There were then only fifteen players, but within a few months he enrolled twenty-two more. The band won laurels in Hamilton, Galt and other centres, which so pleased Mr. Roos that he presented Mr. Heinicke with a cheque for $100. Soon afterward Mr. Roos gave up the presidency, when he was elected Hon. President for life.

Mr. Heinicke retired in the middle nineties and was followed by Wm. Forder, a former leader of military bands. Mr. Forder continued till 1900. In those years there was a keen rivalry between the Berlin and Waterloo bands. When Mr. Forder withdrew, Noah Zeller, who had led the Waterloo band for eighteen years, was appointed leader of the Berlin band. He brought the society's band up to a high pitch of excellence. It was averred: "Mr. Zeller's musicians play a Beethoven symphony or a Wagnerian overture with as much skill as any popular air." Engagements were filled in numerous Canadian and American cities. The 29th Battalion Band accompanied the First Canadian Contingent to the Quebec Centenary in 1908 and acted as guard of honor to the Prince of Wales, later King George V. Once, after an engagement in Toronto, *Saturday Night* commented: "Of all the bands which visit Toronto, except professional bands, it is the best."

W. H. Schmalz was elected president in 1901 and served until 1921. After him Robert Ritz, a veteran player, acted till 1933, when he was succeeded by W. M. O. Lochead, the current president

On account of poor health Bandmaster Zeller resigned in 1913. He was followed by J. H. Stockton, who had a wide experience in England, the overseas Dominions and the United States. Professor George H. Ziegler succeeded him in 1925. Under him the band has advanced from a high to a higher standard. Mr. Ziegler has also organized a Ladies' Band, an entire Brass Band of twenty-nine members and a Boys' Band.

KITCHENER LADIES' BAND

One of the largest and best on the continent, with more than eighty players.

KITCHENER BOYS' BAND

Lieut. George Ziegler is conductor and Nathaniel Stroh associate conductor of the Boys' Band. The band were winners of a competition at the Canadian National Exhibition, and of the trophy at the Canadian Musical Festival in London in 1937.

BAND OF THE SCOTS FUSILIERS.
KITCHENER, ONT.
1935

LIEUT. GEORGE ZIEGLER, Conductor.

Other Bands and Musicians

The Philharmonic Society produced the oratoria "St. Paul" in 1896, with a cast of 160 male and female voices and its own orchestra. Professor Zoellner was their director. A group photograph of the ensemble rests in the Historical Society's museum.

Active then was also the Philharmonic Maennerchor. The Rev. Mr. Tafel was President; Karl Harttung, Vice-President; E. E. Warner, Secretary; Henry Hymmen, Treasurer; E. W. D. Tuerk, Librarian; and Theodore Zoellner, Musical Director.

In bygone years Mr. Howd organized a creditable band among W. G. & R. employees. Once the mechanics employed by Hartman Krug had also a meritorious band. The Berlin Bugle Band appeared in 1904. Floyd Bricker was President; Will Beyer, Vice-President; Walter Stuebing, Secretary-Treasurer; Kirk Huehnergard, Bandmaster; and E. Shantz, Drum Major. In the same year the Berlin City Band was organized, with J. W. Huehnergard, Bandmaster, and C. E. Moyer, Secretary-Treasurer. Those four organizations have since ceased to function.

The town gave America two cantatrici—Miss Detta Ziegler and Miss Racie Boehmer—who by merit won professional rank.

George Fox likewise gained an exalted reputation as a violinist. He was instructed by Joseph Bauman of Hamilton, also native in Berlin, who studied in Leipzig, Germany. When Mr. Fox died, Mrs. A. B. Pollock said: "I was grieved to hear of George Fox's death. As a musician he was wonderful. I have heard Ysaye and Kubelik, but in that eloquence of expression that touches the soul, George Fox was the equal, if not the superior, of them all."

A. J. Smith, son of John S. Smith, became a professional violinist and rose to prominence in the United States. Another native son, Maurice Poure, son of John Poure, made his mark also as a violinist. His patrons assisted him to go to Belgium and complete his studies. Maurice never returned to the city as a resident.

A Musical Club was organized here in 1910. The officers were: Professor Zoellner, Hon. President; H. Leslie Staebler, President; Mrs. Racie (Boehmer) Pollock, first Vice-President; Charles A. Ruby, second Vice-President; and Charles B. Clement, Secretary-Treasurer. The club increased the love for classical music in the community.

Among noted teachers of music are: Miss A. R. Bean, Professor A. H. Heller, and Professor George Ziegler and his staff at the Conservatory of Music.

C. Harry Boehmer early evidenced that he possessed a tenor voice of wide range and power. After studying in Canada and New York City, he went to Italy to complete his musical education. There his advancement was so marked that the Maestro urged him to enter upon a career of Grand Opera. Adopting that suggestion he gained eminence in his art and adopted the name of Carlo Bemer. When the World War hurtled through Europe grand opera was relegated to the background. Mr. Bemer then returned home and engaged himself in business.

THREE PUBLIC INSTITUTIONS

A General Hospital

As more wealth was accumulated by the townsmen they gave slices of their income to philanthropic undertakings. A project to build a community hospital was launched in 1893. Dr. J. S. Minchin, J. S. Anthes and W. R. Travers collected $10,000 from men in easy circumstances; in Waterloo a committee received $5,000 in subscriptions and about fourteen acres of land in the Greenbush, for a site, from Joseph E. Seagram.

The first members of the Hospital Trust were: George Randall, President; John Fennell, Vice-President; Adolph Mueller, Secretary; Dr. Minchin, Assistant Secretary; W. R. Travers, Treasurer; and L. J. Breithaupt, August R. Lang, J. S. Anthes, William Hendry, J. M. Staebler, Christian Kumpf and James Lockie.

The cornerstone was laid on September 19, 1894, by the Hon. J. M. Gibson, Provincial Secretary. Before the roof was on a Ladies' Hospital Auxiliary was organized, with the officers that follow: Mrs. George Rumpel, President; Mrs. George C. H. Lang, Vice-President; Mrs. Catherine Breithaupt, Treasurer; Mrs. (Dr.) A. F. Bauman, Assistant Treasurer; Mrs. (Dr.) H. G. Lackner, Corresponding Secretary; and Mrs. E. P. Clement, Recording Secretary. Succeeding secretaries were: Mrs. George Wegenast, Miss L. Oelschlager and Mrs. C. A. Ruby.

THE KITCHENER-WATERLOO GENERAL HOSPITAL

A Modern, Well-Equipped Institution.

—Courtesy, The Waterloo Chronicle.

KITCHENER-WATERLOO HOSPITAL COMMISSION

Top row: Mayor W. McKersie, Waterloo; C. N. Weber, Treasurer; Mayor J. A. Smith, Kitchener.

Bottom row: E. A. Strasser, Waterloo; Ernest Tailby, Chairman; J. H. Franks, Secretary. (County representative: A. Heer.)

THE CITY ORPHANAGE

The Auxiliary supplied the hospital with linens, bedding and other furnishings. To raise funds they held garden parties, balls and produced plays in the opera house. One day they manned a daily newspaper, writing the articles and canvassing the merchants for advertisements. The Women's edition netted them $559. A branch Auxiliary was also formed in Elmira and urban and rural households invited to make donations of cloth, fruit and vegetables.

On July 12, 1895, the hospital was opened, with Miss J. Duncan filling the role of superintendent. Primarily the hospital was a philanthropy. A yearly membership was sold for five dollars and a life membership for $100. Small grants were also obtained from the municipal councils. Patients who lived in good homes at first preferred being treated at home to going to the hospital. Yet there was soon wardsful of free patients. As a consequence the income did not always balance the outgo. One year the hospital would have been closed up had the Ladies' Auxiliary not wiped out a deficit.

The Board sustained a distinct loss in 1898, when Secretary Adolph Mueller suddenly expired. In memory of him they planted a Colorado fir in the hospital grounds. The late W. H. Schmalz succeeded Mr. Mueller and served many years as secretary and also as president.

In 1913 the Board of Trustees consisted of: J. B. Hughes, President; Allan A. Eby, Secretary-Treasurer; E. P. Clement, S. B. Bricker, George Diebel, W. H. Schmalz, G. M. Wedd, L. D. Merrick, A. J. Roos, Robert Smyth, A. J. Kimmel, F. W. Sheppard, Walter J. Strub and Drs. Minchin, J. A. Gillawee, G. H. Bowlby, G. E. Chapman and W. T. Wallace. By then the accommodation was overtaxed. The Trustees built a large wing to relieve the congestion, with one of the best operating-rooms in the Province. To furnish the operating-room the Dr. D. S. Bowlby estate donated $1300. The hospital then contained seventy beds. Mrs. Mary Bowman was superintendent and Miss Virginia McSweyn, assistant-superintendent.

Various wards were furnished by public-spirited citizens. Thus the James Livingstone (Baden) Ward; the Catherine Breithaupt Memorial Ward by her descendants; another by Mrs. George Lang, Mrs. John A. Lang and Mrs. A. R. Lang; and additional ones by Mrs. W. H. Bowlby, the Elmira Hospital Auxiliary, Mr. and Mrs.

Oscar Rumpel, Schreiter & Sons and the Twin-City Hospital Auxiliary. The Young Women's Auxiliary of Waterloo likewise furnished a ward and a nurses' lecture-room.

Mr. and Mrs. Jacob Kaufman, who were ever ready to help a good cause along, in 1917 bestowed upon the institution a $50,000 Nurses' Home. The handsome structure afforded much needed quarters for the hospital staff.

Hospital Now Municipally Owned

Kitchener and Waterloo assumed into the ownership of the hospital in 1924 and jointly maintain it. To operate it a Hospital Commission was appointed. The first commissioners organized on May 15, 1924. Arthur Foster was chosen Chairman; E. O. Weber, Vice-Chairman; and Erwin Greb, Secretary-Treasurer. The ex-officio members were: Mayor L. O. Breithaupt of Kitchener, Mayor William Henderson of Waterloo, and Mr. John Herber representing Waterloo County. A yearly grant was received from the County Council. Dr. J. J. Walters was Superintendent in 1924 and continued for five years. Miss Barabe was appointed Assistant Superintendent.

An X-ray machine was installed in 1924 at a cost of $3,000. In 1925, an Obstetrical table was purchased; a playground opened at the corner of King and Park Streets for children; and a clinic for crippled children held under the auspices of the Rotary Club. In 1926 a roentgenologist was employed. In 1929, a Medical Advisory Board was appointed. In 1930, a morgue was built, a Kesson machine for administrating anaesthetics installed, and a dietician engaged. A year later, an outdoor clinic was held. In 1933 Miss Stephanie Seagram founded a library at the hospital. The standardization of the hospital was undertaken by the Commission in 1934 under the Chairmanship of Ernest Tailby, with the full co-operation of the Medical Advisory Board and the Medical Staff. For this purpose new By-laws were enacted on December 18, 1934.

Yearly the demands on the institution and its value to the community increased. There was then a need for a three-story wing capable of treating seventy-five patients, including twenty-five children. Anticipating its construction, the Shriners' Order created a fund to provide furnishings for the children's divisions.

E. O. Weber was chairman from 1925 to 1929, inclusive. E. E. Ratz succeeded him in 1930 and continued until the end of 1933. Ernest Tailby was elected chairman in 1934. J. H. Kennedy was secretary in 1927, E. D. Lang in 1928, and E. E. Ratz in 1929. J. H. Franks followed in 1930 and still fills the position.

Miss K. W. Scott is Superintendent and Miss L. McTague, Assistant Superintendent. Miss Edith Quickfall is Assistant Secretary and Miss A. Buchanan, stenographer. The institution then had fifty nurses. In 1933 it treated 1,885 patients. The operating expenses range between $6,000 and $7,000 a month. There has been $7,000 invested in X-Ray equipment.

Members of the Commission in 1935 were: from Kitchener, Ernest Tailby, C. N. Weber, J. H. Franks and Mayor J. A. Smith; from Waterloo, E. A. Strasser and Mayor H. E. Ratz; and from Waterloo County, W. Hostettler.

Steps were taken in 1935 to build a three-story maternity hospital. The new building is on the west side of the main buildings. Mr. B. A. Jones was appointed architect. There provision was made for about fifty children's beds, obstetrical cases, and a new, complete X-ray department. The Kitchener Shrine Club donated $9,000 for furnishings. In recognition of their benevolence, the Hospital Commission have named the children's wing, "The Shrine Club's Endeavor." The total cost of the building was $65,000, and was opened in April, 1936.

Later on in that year the Nurses' Home was also enlarged. The capital invested in the institution approaches $400,000.

Kitchener Ladies' Hospital Auxiliary

The present officers of the Kitchener Ladies' Hospital Auxiliary are: President, Mrs. C. C. Hahn; First Vice-President, Mrs. C. A. Pollock; Second Vice-President, Mrs. E. S. Smyth; Third Vice-President, Mrs. E. O. Weber; Fourth Vice-President, Mrs. G. P. Nash; Recording Secretary, Mrs. D. J. Emery; Corresponding Secretary, Mrs. H. P. Hamilton; Treasurer, Mrs. R. I. Gordon; Assistant Treasurer, Mrs. W. McDonald; Work Committee, Mrs. R. E. King, convenor; Telephone Committee, Mrs. F. R. Pollock, convenor.

The Young Men's Christian Association

In 1895 E. P. Clement, K.C., addressed a Bible Class of Trinity Church and suggested that they found a Young Men's Christian

Association. The class approved of the idea and gained the cooperation of other churches. In "Tonti" hall, above the Bank of Hamilton, T. S. Cole, of the Provincial Y.M.C.A., on June 7th, gave an informative talk on the work before a gathering of interested citizens. A Board of Directors was chosen on July 19th and consisted of: E. P. Clement, President; L. J. Breithaupt, Vice-President; T. M. Turnbull, Secretary; E. D. Lang, Treasurer; and Robert Smyth, Arthur Pequegnat, C. B. Dunke, Conrad Bitzer, E. S. Hallman, J. U. Clemens, John Bristol, W. H. Schmalz, George Rumpel, J. A. Good and J. S. Levan.

The two upper floors at No. 24 N. Queen Street were leased from the Louis Breithaupt Estate for a home. At a cost of $2,000 provision was made for an office, lecture hall, parlor, reading and games rooms, a gymnasium and shower baths. The Y.M.C.A. was dedicated on November 1, 1895, and J. W. Ridgeway appointed General Secretary. Social, religious and educational labors were then set going among the youth of the town. In addition baseball, tennis, hockey and camera clubs were formed, attracting scores of young men. Soon after inauguration day a Ladies' Auxiliary was organized and gave the "Y" excellent service.

Later on the Association bought the building for $5,000 from the Louis Breithaupt Estate. The Estate contributed $1,000 toward the purchase price and the Mutual Life Assurance Company advanced $4,000 on mortgage. Yearly thereafter the membership increased and the quarters became too small. By 1906 the task of financing the "Y" had become burdensome. Hence the directors sold the property to L. J. Breithaupt for $8,000. The mortgage was paid off, the furnishings sold and the net sum banked as the nucleus of a fund for a larger Y.M.C.A.

In the eleven years of activity the secretaries that followed Mr. Ridgeway were: John Page (1897-9) ; George Elliott (1899-05) ; and Mr. Cutler (1905-6).

The Present Y.M.C.A.

Eighteen years ago steps were taken to procure a Y.M.C.A. correspondent to the needs of the Twin-City. Friends of youth assembled in Zion Evangelical Church in February, 1919, when the Provisional Committee that follows was appointed: A. R. Kaufman, Dr. E. D. Heist, A. E. Pequegnat, Charles A. Ruby, R. D. Lang,

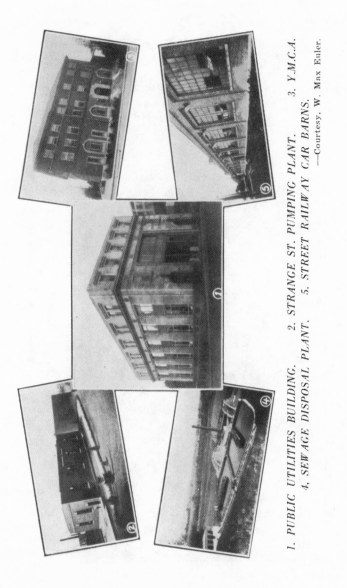

1. PUBLIC UTILITIES BUILDING.   2. STRANGE ST. PUMPING PLANT.   3. Y.M.C.A.
4. SEWAGE DISPOSAL PLANT.   5. STREET RAILWAY CAR BARNS.

—Courtesy, W. Max Euler.

KITCHENER MUNICIPAL MARKET.

This is a well organized, well patronized institution and is one of the largest in Ontario.

—Courtesy, W. Max Euler.

N. B. Detweiler, C. K. Hagedorn, H. E. Wellein, W. H. E. Schmalz, the Rev. J. P. Hauch, and J. H. Baetz. The committee resolved on buying a site and erecting the first home-unit. All the money in hand was the nest-egg of $3,755 from 1906. Subsequently Mr. A. R. Kaufman announced that his father, Mr. Jacob Kaufman, would donate $25,000 provided that enough members were obtained to meet running expenses.

F. J. McKellar was appointed General Secretary in July, 1919.

The Provisional Committee fixed upon the Rittinger property at the corner of N. Queen and Weber Streets as a site. The Rittinger Estate set on it price of $25,000, less a contribution of $5,000. The Breithaupt Leather Company thereupon purchased the property for $20,000 and presented it to the Association.

The International Y.M.C.A. Building Bureau prepared a plan for the new building that was on a much larger scale than the original one. Consequently a campaign was launched to raise $250,000, with Dr. J. F. Honsberger as General Chairman. The Dominion Rubber Company donated $10,000, which with hundreds of other subscriptions swelled the total to $243,753. That was less than the sum aimed at, but through the liberality of President A. R. Kaufman the structure was completed according to plan, and all the requirements of a modern Y.M.C.A. provided for. The new "Y" was officially opened on April 19, 1922, by Lord Byng, then Governor-General of Canada.

A fruitful fraction of the "Y's" work is a summer camp for minors. Through the good-will of the Kiwanis Club they are yearly given the use of the Paradise Lake Camp. There with the co-operation of the Knights of Columbus and other Catholic Societies, 500 boys and girls camp out in the holiday months. Y.M.C.A. officers and Reverend Fathers of the Catholic Church supervise the camps.

Y.M.C.A. fees are so low that few boys need forego its benefits. Then, too, the Kiwanis and Rotary Clubs pay the dues of lads who cannot. For a number of years Paul Sampson was Boys' Secretary. He was followed by Don McLaren. For a time Jack Carley was Physical Instructor. His successor was Tom Armour. On certain days of the week the members of the Young Women's Christian Association use the "gym" and the swimming pool.

Milton Harlow succeeded Mr. McKellar as General Secretary in 1933. Mr. Harlow was followed by Rev. L. A. Buckley in 1935. The maintenance of the Y.M.C.A. is owed to the perennial interest of thoughtful men. Among them, Dr. Honsberger, E. D. Lang, and Jacob Kaufman were members of the first "Y." Mr. Kaufman was a helpful friend until his death in 1920. Since then, Mr. A. R. Kaufman has redoubled his interest in the work and been a generous supporter of the association.

SOURCE

Excerpts from a sketch of the Y.M.C.A. by Dr. J. F. Honsberger.

The City Orphanage

The City Orphanage was organized and incorporated in 1896. The first officers were: Aaron Bricker, President; Samuel B. Snyder, Treasurer; and Mrs. (Dr.) L. B. Clemens, Secretary. Various committees were appointed to oversee the functioning of the institution.

A home on the southwest corner of King and Wilmot Streets, known as the old Cressler place, was purchased for $1500 and re-modelled. Mrs. A. F. Stolz was employed as matron and soon had fifteen children under her care. To date, upward of 1500 children have been cared for. Some of them were orphans, but the most of them were unfortunates who had been bereaved of either a father or mother. After receiving the Christian training provided for them, a large majority of the inmates have gone out into the world and become good citizens. Scores of philanthropic citizens have made their welfare one of their chief interests.

The orphanage in King Street was sold in 1920 to T. H. Rieder for $20,000, and the present property at 98 Charles Street purchased. The institution owns also eleven acres of land in Sheldon Avenue. Should the need arise for one, this land was acquired for a future rural home. The orphanage's assets now amount to $56,000, of which $23,000 are invested in carefully selected bonds and stocks.

Since its inception the matrons have been: Mrs. A. F. Stolz (1896-1902); Mrs. Hannah Roat (1902-04); Miss Mary Snyder (1904-26); Mrs.-Hill and Miss Payne (1926-27); Mrs. Hyatt (1927-28); Miss E. Good (1928—and ever since).

Presidents: Aaron Bricker (1896-1900); G. V. Oberholtzer (1900-04); A. S. Hallman (1904-6); Peter Shupe (1906-11); Edward Stuebing (1911-21); M. S. Hallman (1921-32); H. B. Brubacher (1932-34).

The officers for 1934-5 were: H. B. Brubacher, President; A. R. Kaufman, Vice-President; Frank A. Shantz, Secretary; and M. C. Cressman, Treasurer. Auditors: W. H. E. Schmalz and H. B. Brubacher.

CITY PARKS

On Sunday afternoon, long ago, J. R. Eden, G. M. DeBus and William Vogt strolled along David Street. Pointing to the right, Mr. Vogt said, "There'd be a fine spot for a central park. It has land, water and woods." His companions agreed the fact and Mr. Eden inserted an item in the press recommending the idea. Soon a plan was evolved to buy the athletic grounds and part of Samuel Schneider's lands up to the railway track. In the fall of 1894 a bylaw was introduced into the town council to adopt the Public Parks Act. Six councillors voted Nay and eight, Yea. The progressives were: J. R. Eden, J. M. Staebler, Aaron Bricker, Jacob Baetz, Ephraim Bricker, F. G. Gardiner, Alex Roy and J. Stadelbauer.

At the election public opinion was about evenly divided for and against the bylaw. Opponents declared that if an artificial lake should be excavated its waters would be shrivalled up by evaporation and smell to heaven; while a cartoon, portraying a cow drinking the lake dry, was placed in Smyth Bros.' window. Nevertheless the bylaw was carried by a majority of 275 votes. The first Board of Park Commissioners was named in October, 1894, and was comprised of: C. F. Brown (Chairman), William Roos, L. J. Breithaupt, August R. Lang, J. S. Hoffman, Thomas Bridger (Secretary) and Mayor D. Hibner.

The Athletic Association agreed to accept $2500 for their grounds and Mr. Schneider to sell twenty-eight acres at $125 an acre. Three commissioners thought that fifteen acres of the Schneider lands would suffice their needs, but the proprietor asked $200 an acre for the smaller area. Rather than pay this price, Commissioners Breithaupt, Lang and Bridger proposed that an equivalent sum be spent in improving Woodside park. A motion to that effect was submitted to the Board, when the three supported it, but Commissioners Brown, Roos and Hoffman voted Nay. The mayor was not at the meeting. At a later session he was present when Commissioners Brown, Roos, Hoffman, and Mayor Hibner voted for the purchase of the David Street lands.

The athletic grounds and the lands bought from Mr. Schneider cost $6,000. Mr. Ricker, a landscape engineer of Buffalo, N.Y., approved the Park Board's plan to convert the Schneider lands into a park and the construction of a five-acre lake in Schneider's creek. A debenture of $12,000 was issued and the work begun. In December, 1895, the new recreation grounds were named Victoria Park, the larger island, Roos Island in honor of Mr. Roos, and the smaller one, Swan Island.

When $11,000 had been spent, a councillor criticized the Board's alleged extravagance. Chairman Brown then offered to buy the park from the town for the sum already expended. His offer, however, was not taken up. The work was continued and Richard Cowan appointed superintendent. Mr. Brown died in February, 1896. His successor was J. M. Staebler, who as chairman left an impress of his artistic nature on Victoria Park.

John S. Hoffman was appointed secretary in 1896 and faithful Fred Kruse employed as caretaker. From the Devitt Estate the Board purchased a 60-foot strip of land and extended Courtland Avenue from Queen to David Street, and had Reuben Bowman build the boathouse.

Victoria Park was officially opened on August 27, 1896, with music, speeches, bicycle-races, tub-races, and a regatta.

It will be recalled that at the Friendensfest of 1871, the celebrants planted a memorial oak. The tree, however, withered. After offering to subscribe an equal sum toward a monument of Queen Victoria, a group of citizens erected a bust of Emperor William I in Victoria Park in 1897. During the world war, the bust disappeared.

Year after year the park was improved. A pavilion was built and Dr. D. S. Bowlby's lots in David Street purchased to enlarge the athletic grounds. Meanwhile a zoo had been started for the benefit of the children. The woods became a bird sanctuary. One summer, Frank Shantz, Naturalist, counted upward of eighty different feathered visitors.

The Daughters of the Empire collected a large sum and in 1909 had a Governor-General unveil a monument of Queen Victoria.

Natural Parks

Later on the Park Board bought woodlands in the outskirts and converted them into natural parks. The Louis Breithaupt Estate donated ten acres of woods in the North Ward to the city, while the Board purchased an equal area of woodlands from the estate, and also adjoining woods from other owners, in all sixty-three acres. In honor of the Breithaupt family, the purchases were styled Breithaupt Park.

Afterward the commissioners bought the Poor House bush for $3,900. Park lands as a whole then embraced 154.96 acres, costing $105,000.

Hibner Place and Knell Place

Before Victoria Park was in existence, Wm. Aldrich and George M. DeBus moved to acquire a triangle of land for a parklet. It is bounded by West Weber, Young Street, and Margaret Avenue. Mr. Aldrich collected $350 for the purchase, while Mayor Hibner gave them a cheque toward the buying of a fountain. The parklet was then named Hibner Place.

Frederick Knell gave the city a point of land at the intersection of Water and Victoria Street that was named Knell Place.

Park Lands

Mr. A. R. Kaufman, a number of years ago, presented the city with a park in East King Street, once part of the George Rumpel Estate. In 1935, the areas of the city's parks were

Victoria Park	57	acres
Breithaupt Park	66	"
Woodside Park	9.5	"
Hibner Place	0.5	"
Knell Place	0.1	"
Springwood Park	24.0	"
Lancaster Park	28.5	"
Knollwood Park	12.5	"
Kaufman Park	9.0	"
Total:	207.1	acres.

The value of the city parks was then $400,000.

Since 1921, the Park Board has received one-mill annually from the City Council, which has enabled them to make numerous improvements. The Municipal Swimming Pool, for example, was constructed in 1931, and in 1937 attracted upward of 4,000 swimmers, old and young.

Superintendents

George M. DeBus was appointed manager in 1912. In 1914, Bernard Koehler became superintendent and served exceedingly well until his accidental death in 1926. C. D. Pequegnat filled the position about one year, when C. Kress succeeded him.

Secretaries

C. E. Hoffman followed his father in 1907. Mr. DeBus acted from 1908 to 1912. Oswald S. Leyes was then appointed and continued till 1921. C. G. Lips, now city clerk, filled the post about two years, when he was succeeded by Louis J. Albrecht, who kept on till 1924. In March, 1924, Arnott L. Hanenberg, the present secretary, followed him.

OSCAR LAUBER
Chairman.

Chairmen

Among the chairmen not yet mentioned were: August R. Lang, Karl Mueller, George Rumpel, L. J. Breithaupt, William Roos (who sat in the Board for sixteen years), Daniel Hibner, A. W. Feick, Homer Ford, D. A. Bean, S. J. Wellheiser, W. O. Knechtel, Charles Smith, and since 1933, Oscar Lauber.

Many of the city's brightest minds have served as commissioners.

Victoria Park is a bewitching spot. For citizens and thousands of visitors it is a perennial delight. From time to time outside park commissioners come in to learn how the Park Board have achieved its beautification.

The Park Board of 1937

Oscar Lauber (Chairman), A. R. Kaufman, H. L. Staebler, L. Knipfel, W. Malcolm, W. H. E. Schmalz, and Mayor J. A. Smith.

THE KIRMES

St. Peter's Church initiated a Kirmes on August 11, 1894. It was held in the rink in Gaukel Street and lasted five days. A description reads: You step inside and find yourself in another country, for it is a reproduction of an ancient German village. On either side, the main street is flanked by quaint buildings and decorated booths, and is thronged by a multitude of citizens and guests from neighboring towns. Flitting to and fro among them are gaily-dressed Frauleins and holidaying Frauen and Maenner, while a German band plays sweet airs.

The Kirmes was officially opened by Chairman Conrad Bitzer. Standing on the stone steps of the Court House—its prototype four centuries old—he explained that the Kirmes is a representation of a German village during the Jahrmarkt. Mr. Bitzer invited the patrons to make a tour of the Dorf and see some truly German scenes. Mayor D. Hibner then extended the host a civic welcome. He was followed by Dr. H. G. Lackner who delivered a congratulatory speech in German, praising the Rev. R. von Pirch and the Church. In concluding he said: "Those of you who have attended a Kirmes in your native land will note the omission of the dance and the social glass of beer, but you will be able to procure numerous savory German dishes."

The guest speaker was C. A. Howland, M.P.P., of Toronto. He smiled, "I felicitate your friendly citizens on the marked progress that of late Berlin has made. The success of this Kirmes stamps you as an enterprising town. Your guests will go away indelibly impressed by all they have seen and enjoyed. The spirit that animates you flows from a loyal German fountain. As a Canadian, I am proud of your accomplishment, knowing that the skilful reproductions are actually German work, yet the work of German blood in Canadian veins. The imaginative German handicraft and the imaginative pictures of German life, people, dress, and mode of celebrating important events have been faithfully portrayed. The part that the young people are playing reminds me of Goethe's poem, wherein he tells of a lion that escaped from its cage into the street; of the villagers sallying out to capture or slay the beast; and how the savage animal was subdued by the song of the keeper's child. It is a pretty legend and gives a good estimate of the power of song, beauty, and innocence; all of which we have here today."

The Review

After Mr. Howland's address a venerable Schutzmann appeared. With a wave of his staff he opened a passage-way for the groups in character. First came a line of matrons and maidens in the gowns and head-dresses of a dozen different German principalities. Next a company of boys and girls in old-world attire; then a bevy of brunettes in bright colors and spangles, followed by coveys in attractive costumes. In succession of them the Kirmes Grenadiers, forty-five strong, under the veteran Captain Schmidt, singing a martial song as they marched. Then sequent, a marriage procession just coming out of an ancient church. The bridal role was taken by Miss Alice Tiedt. She wore handsome apparel, decked with roses and wore a crown. Will Faber acted as the groom. He wore a short, dark coat, black knee-breeches, low shoes with silver buckles, and carried a silk hat. As the bridal party emerged from the church the Kirmes band, led by George Ziegler, played a wedding march, while at intervals a troop of children, bearing flowers, sweetly sang a wedding song. Heralds, in by-gone century attire, and bearing garlands, succeeded the children. Following the heralds, came two appropriately-vestured youth holding aloft a bridal arch, under which the young couple passed. The band then played a lively air, bringing the review to a close. In its entirety, the parade made a fascinating living picture.

Guests were now at liberty to stroll about the village. Free to sip coffee in the Kaffeegarten or watch the busy Frauen in the Spinnstube; to cross the Wahrsagerin's palm with a piece of silver; to linger at the Zuckerwarenhaendlers' booth, where the confectionery is tempting; to enter into the Sun Inn and partake of Rye Brod, Wienerwurst, Kartoffelsalat, Sauerkraut, and other delicacies; to pass over to the Blumengestell, where flowers are on sale and a voting contest to decide who are the most popular gentlewoman and gentleman in Berlin; to attend the weiblische Handarbeit stand, admire their work and doubtlessly to buy; to swing into the tide to the Fischteich and try your luck; to call at the Postamt, where a letter awaits you; and to register at the Musee, where there are mysteries beyond the telling. Nearby is the Rathaus, whose tower clock looks down the ages with a glance of assurance on its wise old face. Adjacent to the Rathaus are the Puppen and other booths, and the tents of the Zingari.

The Kaffeegarten

In the Kaffeegarten, Mrs. Hugo Kranz and Mrs. Hailer, handsomely gowned, preside over a staff of charming assistants. Miss Annie Knell wore the costume of a maiden from the Isle of Ruegen; Miss Quirmbach, Miss Kalbfleisch, and Miss Janke appeared as Frauleins from Hesse; Miss Boecking as an Austrian peasant; Miss Wuest as a coy Alsatian maiden; Miss Pinke as a Maedchen from Schwalmar; Miss Morley as a girl from the Tyrol; and Miss Euler as a Fraulein from Hesse-Darmstadt. Their gowns were of bright colors. Each miss wore a diminutive headdress, no two of which were alike.

The Zuckerwarenhaendlers' Stall

The candy booth typified a sweetmeat shop of the Spreewald. Here Herzkuchen, Lebkuchen, Sauermorsell, and Bretzels made by Miss Dora Mylius and Miss Franzeska Kranz, were as appetent as those of Brandenburg. The young ladies were dressed as Hessen brides. In their booth is a large wedding-cake, decked with orange blossoms, and a myrtle tree, such as is seen in every German home after a young couple are betrothed. If the tree flourishes it signifies that the affianced will have a happy married life. Mrs. David Forsyth and her daughter Dora were also members of staff. Miss Forsyth wore a costume which her grandmother, Mrs. (Dr.) R. Mylius, had worn when a girl in Germany, and a feature of which was a small bonnet. Miss Dittmer of London, Eng., was likewise a member of the candy-booth staff.

Schurtz & Co.'s Kramladen

The Ladies-Work booth is under the direction of Mrs. R. von Pirch. She was becomingly attired. Her assistants included Miss Kimmel, dressed as a Swiss embroidery girl; Miss Bachman, as a maiden from Brunswick; Miss Geiger as a miss from Schwalmar; Miss Frost as a Bavarian Fraulein; Miss Peters as a Maedchen from Wuertemberg; and Miss Walper as a Swiss peasant. At this booth were numerous articles on sale, ranging from the useful to the beautiful.

The Musee, Fishpond, Etc.

The Musee is housed in a log-cabin made of rough slabs, bark outward. Edward Stuebing is the manager and with him is his brother Henry as "Professor Herman." The latter entertained the visitors with a select performance of magic. Mr. H. Stuebing had also on view a collection of curios and art objects. The Musee attracted large audiences.

Close to the Musee is the popular fishpond. It is under the management of the Misses Tiedt, Vetter, Scherer, and Hopp. They were garbed to represent girls from various German villages. Callers paid a fee, cast a line into the pond, and drew up whatever the girls, unsight, unseen, elected to attach to the hook. The catches made by young men often caused bursts of merriment.

Next the Fishpond, Julius Knauff and Miss Oelschlager are charged with the Prize Booth. Here are displayed the various gifts for the contests and prize drawings. Miss Oelschlager was gowned as a maiden from Hesse-Breitenbach. After leaving the Prize Booth the traveller reached the end of the village street and faced the Alsfeldt courthouse.

Das Gerichtshaus

Of all the buildings the ancient court house is most interesting. It is of quaint construction, having odd-looking windows, iron-hinged doors of rare pattern, and, as mentioned, a clock in the bell tower. From the tower top floats a Canadian and a German flag.

Near the courthouse a Punch and Judy show is entertaining the young folk, while the Nachtwaechter, in his ancient uniform, carrying a wooden alarm in one hand and a battle-axe in the other, and with a bunch of keys and lanthorn attached to his girdle, calls the hours.

The Gypsy Tent

Beyond the Rathaus is a grove in which a band of gypsies have camped. Its members wear gaily-tinted Bohemian dress. The gypsy king and queen are clothed in particularly brilliant colors. The king and his henchmen are out selling or bartering jewellry and tinware. A dark-eyed beauty bends over a large pot, suspended by a tripod over the camp-fire, preparing the evening meal. Within a tent the gypsy queen and Princess Pritosi are lifting the curtain that conceals the future for a pair of lovers, while other anxious couples await admission to the fortune tellers' presence. The gypsy pony, "Joe," is nibbling grass near a two-wheeled cart, and over all comes the echo of song and laughter. The role of gypsy king is taken by Oscar Rumpel and that of gypsy queen by Miss Annie Knell. The gypsy princesses are Mrs. George Potter, and the Misses L. Huehnergard, L. Kimmel, M. Gildner, and E. Gorman; and that of the gypsy princes, Walter Rumpel and Otto Miller. For the occasion R. Baulder is acting as musician.

The Doll Booth

At the Doll Booth prizes are offered for the best dressed doll, the oldest doll, the largest doll, and for collections of dolls. Miss Margery Dopp won the first prize for her family of dolls; Miss Jennie Brandt for the largest Puppen on view; Miss A. Hett for the oldest doll (thirty years), named "Hulda;" Miss Dora Forsyth for the best-dressed "German-bride" doll; Miss E. Roos for the finest group of dolls; and Miss G. Rummel for the homeliest doll.

Edwin Huber, Henry Knell Jr., and G. D. LaCourse were the judges of the doll exhibits. The Misses L. Kruse, L. and M. Goulich, Kessig, and M. Bluhm are managers of the booth and are assisted at the display by the Misses Bluhm, Peters, Hoelscher, and Reitz. The maidens are gowned as Bohemian Frauleins.

The Spinnstube

The Spinning-room is presided over by Mrs. George Rumpel. If you cross the doorkeeper, Henry Oswald's palm, with a piece of silver, you will be admitted into a neat German kitchen, with a large fireplace and bakeoven; see a table set with old blue china— every piece an heirloom—and yonder a curiously-cut wooden cradle. The kitchen's small windows are high up from the floor and their broad ledges filled with flowers in brown earthenware pots. On a wall is a cuckoo-clock, wound with weights, whose chains almost touch the floor, and whose musical ticking heightens the home-like air of the kitchen. On a high wooden rail, suspended from the beams, hang strings of apple cuttings, which are being dried for winter use by the frugal Hausfrau. Near the apples are bunches of asparagus to catch the inquisitive fly.

There is an atmosphere of comfort in the ancient kitchen and every inch of it is spotlessly clean. One of the most attractive features is the rosy-cheeked housewife, who is seated beside her spinning-wheel and who sings as she spins. She wears a plain, home-made frock, whose lines proclaim her skill with a needle. Love and contentment shine in her eyes. To make the scene more realistic Mrs. Rumpel invited eight Canadian-German women to assist her at the Kirmes and to bring their spinning-wheels with them. This is to show the younger generation how their grand-mothers spun yarn from wool and flax. The spinners were: Mrs. Hoelscher, Mrs. Slumkowski, Mrs. Witte, Mrs. Draeger, Mrs. Stecho, Mrs. Maas, Mrs. Neils, and Mrs. Marklewitz. Mrs. Schmidt sits also in the kitchen making lace on a home-made block, with an odd-looking set of needles or bobbins. The Spinnstube is a reproduction of a kitchen in Saxony by Mrs. Rumpel. On the wall is the quotation that follows,

> "Ehret die Frauen,
> Sie flechten und weben
> Himmlische Rosen in's irdische Leben;
> Flechten die Liebe geheiligten Bund."

The Flower Booth and Postoffice

The Flower Booth is in the capable hands of the Misses T. Kimmel, E. Scherer, L. Tiedt, A. Rathman, C. Kimmel, May Lackner, Grace Kimmel, and Leonie von Pirch. They wear attractive, old-age costumes and transact a flourishing trade.

Die Post has two postmistresses: Miss Rathman and Miss Tiedt. The Postamt is an early-century building, with a tall round tower. Set in the tower is a large clock with a cheerful face. At the wicket there is a Brief for everyone, written while you wait. The Postgeld varies according to the popularity of the citizens: the better he or she is known, the higher the fee.

The Sonne Gasthaus, Etc.

The Sun Inn is an interesting building, with its long verandah and skilfully wrought lattice work. In one of its ancient gables is a stork's nest; and swinging back and forth a signboard bearing a rising sun. In the doorway stands George Klein Sr., rotund and jolly, enveloped in a white apron, and his long-stemmed meerchaum agoing, as he welcomes his guests.

A voting contest was held to determine who are most popular lady and gentleman in Berlin. Mrs. George C. H. Lang was declared to be the most popular gentlewoman and Dr. H. G. Lackner the most popular gentleman.

Every character and feature in the Kirmes were replete with interest, and permit of no comparisons. Mature minds, however, dwelt upon the Spinnstube, and youth upon the heavily-laden wagon bearing the household effects of the "newly-weds," whilst atop sat the handsome bride, crowning the whole. Alongside the vehicle marched the Gatte, keeping an eye on his precious freight.

THE GRAND RIVER RAILWAY

Galt and Preston obtained an electric-railway service in 1894. Preston and Berlin capitalists then organized the Preston & Berlin Railway Company to build a line to Berlin. The town gave them a franchise to operate their cars in East King Street. One difficulty was to bridge the Grand River at Freeport. While they sought for more capital John Patterson of the International Radial Co., of Hamilton, announced that his company would build a radial to Berlin and transmit electric power from DaCew Falls. A week later the Port Dover Railway Co. offered, for a consideration, to build an electric line from Port Dover to Berlin and Waterloo. With regard to Mr. Patterson's proposal to transmit power from DaCew Falls, his rivals shrugged, "It'll likely end in talk. Electrical engineers pooh-pooh the idea."

Mr. Patterson insisted that his plan was feasible, but his company was not prepared to build at once. The Port Dover Co.'s chief inducement was lower coal rates and the town granted them a bonus of $21,000. Straightway the Preston & Berlin Railway laid rails in East King Street—a checkmate. The Port Dover Co. finally agreed to hand over $14,000 of the sum just voted to them for the privilege of using the track in East King Street. However, when this plan was submitted to the ratepayers for their approval, they defeated the bylaw. The Port Dover Co. afterward brought in a revised plan, one feature of which was to transmit electric power to the town, but it was also rejected and they withdrew from the field.

Under Manager Martin Todd the Preston & Berlin Co. built a bridge across the Grand at Freeport in 1903. A year later their cars shuttled back and forth between Preston and Berlin. The company bought also a right-of-way through the South and West Wards, and up to Waterloo, in 1905, for a freight and passenger service. The line is now known as Grand River Railway and its cars no longer roll up to the centre of the city.

FLYING LEAVES

A Town of Homes.

Ten thousand inhabitants and only one policeman.

Fifty factories and more than one hundred travellers.

A widow without kin died and left $345. Her friends expended the sum in a grand funeral for the old lady.

An auctioneer between sales frequented the Grand Central hotel, where a joker labelled him, "Busy Berlin."

C. Herman Quirmbach volunteered for service in the South African War. His brother Albert went later on to China as a missionary.

After their curling games, a group of young men lunched at the "Last Chance" hotel and were dubbed the "House of Lords."

The Rev. D. B. Sherk took heed of time. In middle age, he ceased wearing laced shoes and wore gaiters to save a few minutes each day.

When the last surviving parent dies, the children sometimes disagree with the alloting of their parent's effects. One family avoided heart-burnings by holding an impromptu auction sale, when coveted articles went to the highest bidder.

Chris Huether bought a half-acre of land at the corner of King and Victoria Streets, for $500, from John 'A. Mackie. On the site he built a brewery and thus forestalled the erection of another in South Queen Street by George Sleeman of Guelph.

The Canada Furniture Manufacturers Limited was organized with a capitalization of $3,000,000, and merged nineteen furniture factories. In the group were the John S. Anthes Co. and the Simpson Company. In 1906, Mr. Anthes and Mr. J. C. Breithaupt founded the Anthes Furniture Co., at 242 Breithaupt Street, to make high-grade furniture.

Mr. Anthes' son, J. I. Frank Anthes, was the associate of his father in furniture manufacturing. Afterward he was a director of the Canadian Consolidated Rubber Company for ten years. From 1915 to 1919 he was the company's General Purchasing Supervisor in Montreal. Mr. Anthes espoused Cyrena H., daughter of the late L. W. Simonds, long connected with J. Y. Shantz & Sons. In 1919, Mr. Anthes founded Anthes & Sons, Agents and Importers, in Montreal. Since his recent death, his sons, Leonard J. and Herbert H., direct this company.

A citizen inherited $50,000. Before the probation of his father's will, his lawyer asked him whether he would like an advance of cash. The heir was agreeable. "How much shall I give you?" the lawyer inquired. "Oh, vell," said the heir, "you can gif me fiftee cents."

There was then music in the air. High-School boys chanted, "Tenting on the Old Camp Ground;" College boys hummed, "There'll be a Hot Time in the Old Town To-night;" and town youths warbled, "Ach du lieber Augustin." As the band played selections from "William Tell" or "Cavelleria Rusticana," a duchess in print exclaimed, "Isn't it heavenly?"

In 1900 the centenary of Joseph Sherk's arrival in Upper Canada was celebrated by his descendants at the old Doon homestead. His six generations of descendants then numbered 920 persons, of whom 350 attended the celebration. When the pioneer came over, he brought with him six three-year-old apple-shoots and planted them. A century later there were five trees still bearing fruit. A number of his offspring picked apples from the trees and on reaching home, "cloved" them. The sixth tree had died shortly before the reunion. Members of the family cut off pieces from the tree and took them away as·mementos.

THE BOARD OF HEALTH

The municipality has been long served by a Board of Health. One problem was to get a sewage-disposal system. Dreaded diseases then were smallpox, diphtheria, tuberculosis, and influenza. Exclusive of the County's Sanitorium at Freeport for tubercular patients, the Board has three Isolation pavilions. Their Health Department includes a Medical Officer of Health, a Sanitary Inspector, a Food and Meat Inspector, a Baby Clinic, a Chest Clinic, a Venereal Disease Clinic, and a well-organized Nursing System.

FIRST CHURCH OF CHRIST, SCIENTIST

The year 1892 signalled the inception of the Christian Science movement in this locality. At first, a few of those interested met in private residences on Sunday for the study of the Quarterly Bible Lessons. Then a Sunday School was started. The First Church of Christ, Scientist, was organized with twelve members on December 25, 1894. In a small office-building in North Queen Street, that stood on the present Y.M.C.A. site, the first public meeting was held. The average attendance was about twenty, but at the end of ten months larger quarters were needed. A commodious room in the Court House was placed at the disposal of the church. That was occupied for almost a year, when a move was made to a new house in Roy Street that a member had built, leaving the upper story without partitions. This provided a large room for the services, while the Reading Room was below. By that time the average attendance had increased to eighty, showing a steady growth.

The year 1899 was an important one. On April 4th, the church had the privilege of receiving its first lecturer, Mr. Carol Norton, C.S.D., of New York City, who inspired the members to build a church home for themselves. For that purpose, a member donated a lot near the corner of Water and Francis Streets, while through

THE LOCAL BOARD OF HEALTH

Upper row: H. W. Sturm, Alderman; Dr. J. W. Fraser, Medical Officer of Health; Charles G. Lips, Secretary.

Bottom row: Mayor J. Albert Smith, Edward F. Donohoe, Chairman; Alderman Eugene A. Berges.

THE FIRST CHURCH OF CHRIST, SCIENTIST

KING STREET BAPTIST CHURCH

THE REV. EWART G. HINDS
Pastor

the kindly spirit of the Town Council, the triangular lot adjoining was given to the church by the town.

The first spadeful of soil was turned on July 27, 1899, a historic event. For it was the first instance in the British Empire of a church edifice being entirely built from the ground up and dedicated to the cause of Christian Science. The corner stone was laid on October 12, 1899, being of New Hampshire granite, quarried in Concord, then the home of the Rev. Mary Baker Eddy, the discoverer and founder of Christian Science. Fifty-two members built this church, which was formally opened on August 5, 1900, with two members of the Christian Science Board of Lectureship, the Rev. W. P. McKenzie and the Rev. Arthur R. Vosburg, taking part in the services.

About twelve years after the dedication of the church, a fine pipe-organ, a Casavant, was installed. In the fall of 1937 the basement of the church was remodelled for Sunday School purposes, making in every detail an edifice adequate for the needs of a growing congregation.

THE KING STREET BAPTIST CHURCH

On June 25, 1895, a number of English Baptists met in the German Baptist Church to consider the question of forming a congregation. It was decided to proceed and to begin as a home mission. The Rev. E. T. Fox ministered to them from October 13 to November 10, 1895. Among the church leaders were: W. H. Joyce, J. Kennedy, R. D. Lang, E. D. Lang, John Cummings, W. C. J. King, J. Cation, Oliver Master, Mrs. Moffatt, Mrs. Whitehead, Miss Pritchard, Miss Geddes and Miss Alice Joyce. The flock of twenty-five chartered members completed an organization on November 10, 1895. Miss Joyce was appointed Clerk and Mr. King, Treasurer. The members of the German Baptist congregation gave them wholehearted assistance at easing the ship down the ways.

The young congregation's first regular pastor was the Rev. P. A. McEwan. For a time they worshipped in the original Y.M.C.A. The Church Board purchased a large plot of land on the southwest corner of King and Water Streets, on May 3, 1896, for $1200, as the site for a church. The congregation received $400 from the

Home Missions Board toward their undertaking. In 1897, a Sunday School was built, utilizing it also for church services.

After eight years of labor in behalf of the congregation, the Rev. Mr. McEwan resigned his charge, and was succeeded by the Rev. J. T. Marshall. The church proper was commenced in 1906 and finished in 1907. To procure a pipe-organ the Board sold a portion of the church land not required for building purposes.

The members realized the debt of gratitude owed to the Revs. Mr. Marshall and McEwan for their sustained endeavors during the church's infancy.

From the outset the value of missionary work was impressed on the members' minds. The first son of the church to obtain a preacher's license was Paul Medlinger. Besides, Miss Susie Hindman entered the missionary field in India and Miss Alice Clark and Miss Euphemia Hebel in Bolivia. The congregation, since its inception, has contributed $180,000 to the spread of Christianity. Five young men have also become Baptist ministers: the Rev. William Watson, the Rev. Harold W. Lang, the late Rev. Henry Good, the Rev. Don Cameron and Captain Charles Sim.

Today the church has 292 members. Since organization the church has been served by six pastors: the Rev. P. A. McEwan (1895-1903), the Rev. J. T. Marshall (1903-09), the Rev. Joseph Janes (1910-15), the Rev. P. C. Cameron (1915-22), the late Rev. J. R. Webb (1922-35) and the incumbent, the Rev. Dr. Ewart G. Hinds (1935——).

THE STORY OF THE WATERWORKS

Had Lake Ontario jutted into the East Ward the city would probably now be another Hamilton. As it is the municipality has always had to take thought about the water supply, especially for fire protection. In the city's budding stage householders depended on wells in their yard. Every good man was expected to keep two water-buckets in reserve and, when Hoffman's bell clanged, to rush to the scene of a fire.

In the eighteen-fifties the village relied on wells and later on tanks sunk at the principal street corners. The tanks were filled from Schneider's creek with a pumper-engine by sweating firemen.

That procedure continued until the place had 2700 inhabitants. In 1871 the Fire and Water Committee reported that,

> With a view of finding a strong spring of water to be conducted in pipes to the market square, for the supplying of tanks on the line of King Street, we have sunk a well on what is known as Adi's hill on St. Peter's Street. The well is down 13 feet and a strong spring has been struck. There is 4½ feet of water in the well and your committee is of the opinion that it will hold out for all time. . . . Your committee would recommend that a pipe be laid leading toward Church Street, so as to have the strength of the spring tested before incurring any considerable expense.

That, however, was an abortive scheme. Soon afterward the firm of Anthes, Staebler & Co., owners of the furniture factory on the Bank of Nova Scotia corner, offered to remove their factory to a point on Schneider's creek and install a plant to fill the tanks. The expense involved, however, seemed too great and the matter dropped.

A Toronto firm proposed in 1878 to build a system of waterworks for the town, but the council decided to act itself. Savage & Palmer of Petrolia were awarded a contract to sink an artesian well at the Royal Bank corner. A five-inch well was bored to a depth of 350 feet, striking water, which did not rise to the top. To raise the water, three plans were considered: (1) to set a steam-pump at the well, at a cost of $800; (2) to place a pump in Simpson & Co.'s furniture factory in West King Street, at an outlay of $600; (3) to buy a portable steam-engine for $1425. The council favored a trial of either the second or third idea, but public opinion coursed strongly against them and they abandoned the well.

For a time no further effort was made to relieve the situation. In 1885, however, L. Breithaupt & Co., predecessors of the Breithaupt Leather Co., offered to install a pumping plant in their tannery and supply the town with water. The firm planned to draw on its source of supply or if necessary to tap the Grand River. Again the matter of cost deterred the council from accepting the offer. A year later a bylaw was introduced into the council to expend $35,000 in constructing a municipally-owned water plant. Two proponents of the proposal were L. J. Breithaupt and J. M. Scully. But few, if any, Ontario towns then owned a waterworks system. The proposal seemed too bold and was turned down.

The Nut Cracked

A solution was found in 1887. First the council appointed a committee to study the town's needs. The members of it were: Reeve L. J. Breithaupt and Councillors P. E. W. Moyer, H. L. Janzen, J. M. Staebler, William Hendry and Enoch Ziegler. After a thorough investigation they recommended that tenders be called for the installation of a suitable system. Moffatt & Hodgins, an American firm, were the successful bidders. Before the contract was actually signed, W. H. Breithaupt, C.E., and Ward Bowlby, Q.C., offered to form a local company and build the works. The council, however, felt that they ought to close with the American company, which was done. As the Berlin Waterworks Company, the firm was given a ten-year franchise, dated from July 9, 1887. The contract called for a pumping-plant at Shoemaker's lake, a mile-and-a-half southwest of the townhall; the erection of a stand-pipe in St. George Street; the laying of six and a half miles of mains and a provision for sixty-three hydrants at an annual rental of $3,000. The town then had say 6,000 inhabitants. It was thought it might eventually reach 10,000 and the system was planned for this number.

The company leased thirty-two acres of land surrounding a spring lake near Shoemaker Avenue. Water was turned on in the forepart of 1888. The plumbers then took off their vests and busied themselves installing watertaps and bathtubs. Exit the "tin Lizzie." In time Berlin had more bathtubs than any other town in Canada. After the water service was begun the company was permitted to supply Waterloo for ten years. The water was drawn from Shoemaker's lake, which was open to the rains and floods and which was not treated in any way. In the springtime or when a heavy demand arose the fluid was often turbid. The consumers kicked, but unavailingly.

The Town Buys the System

Time passed and the day approached when the company's franchise would expire. To buy or not to buy was the question. In 1897, when John C. Breithaupt was mayor, the question was considered well. Mr. Breithaupt was one of the first openly to recommend the purchase of the waterworks and their operation as a public utility. As a consequence, in November, 1897, a special committee was appointed to investigate the subject. The members were: Mayor

THE FIRST COMMISSION

Back row, left to right: Wm. Mahlon Davis, C.E.; Herbert J. Bowman, C.E.; an employee; Mayor J. R. Eden; P. S. Lautenschlager; Chairman J. C. Breithaupt, on horseback.
In the foreground: John S. Anthes.

SHOEMAKER AVENUE PUMP HOUSE

MEMBERS OF COMMISSION — 1934

Left to right: J. Hainsworth, C. Braun, P. Gies, H. W. Sturm, Mayor; J. C. Breithaupt,
Chairman; M. Pequegnat, B.A.Sc., Supt. and Treasurer.

PLANT OF DOON TWINES LIMITED
Henry C. Krug, President.

MARCEL PEQUEGNAT, B.A. Sc.
Superintendent and Treasurer.

JOHN C. BREITHAUPT
Chairman of Water Commission.

LATE JOHN S. ANTHES
Prominent Furniture Manufacturer.

LATE T. H. RIEDER
Leading Rubber Manufacturer.

VIEW OF A HORTICULTURAL SOCIETY'S SHOW

Breithaupt, John S. Anthes and George Rumpel. Mr. Rumpel succeeded Mr. Breithaupt as mayor in 1898. Mr. Breithaupt then offered his services as a councillor and was elected. In the ensuing months he devoted his energies to the furtherance of purchase. An expert opinion of the plant's physical worth was procured. After a long negotiation with the company, they agreed to accept $102,000 for the property. At that stage J. E. Skidmore was manager of the waterworks and a town councillor. He was a likable man but wished to see the company's franchise renewed by the town, questioning whether any commissioners chosen under municipal ownership would be capable of making the system earn even engine-grease.

Considerable opposition arose. As often happens a number of prominent men were opposed to the purchase because they disliked someone who favored it. Other ratepayers stood aghast when it was proposed to invest $100,000 in a utility and run the gamut of attendant risks. Moreover, the company, in its efforts to get the franchise renewed, offered to reduce its water-bills by twenty per cent.; to furnish free water for flushing the streets, for the schools and firehall, and to lower the hydrant rental charge from $4,500 down to $3,000 per annum. Those inducements appealed to the fainthearted.

Mayor Rumpel countered the company's stroke by an announcement that if the town did not buy the waterworks he would do so himself. Then, as the tide continued to run against the bylaw, Jacob Kaufman, John A. Lang and Hartman Krug made it known that if the bylaw should be carried they were willing to take the purchase off the town's hands, make all the concessions offered by the company, pay the instalments of principal and interest and hand over one-half of the profits to the municipality. Their confidence in the venture assisted the council to carry the bylaw.

Municipal ownership in Canada was then in its infancy. Besides, for a town of fewer than 9,000 population, the sum involved was a large one. Friends of the hazard realized that the successful operation of the system would depend on the capacity of the men selected for the task. Fortunately, on nomination day there was no dearth of capable candidates and in January, 1889, the electors chose John C. Breithaupt, John S. Anthes, P. S. Lautenschlager and Herbert J. Bowman, C.E., while by virtue of office Mayor John R.

Eden was the fifth commissioner. At the initial meeting of the Water Board, Mr. Breithaupt was appointed chairman, in recognition of his services in purchasing the plant and his ability to guide the undertaking.

Primary Difficulties

When the commissioners took possession of the system they faced a succession of difficulties. The winter of 1899 was unusually severe, freezing long stretches of piping that had not been laid deep enough; in the following spring, floods submerged the flat land between the pumping-house and the road, filling the lake from which most of the supply was pumped with a discolored fluid; in the summer there was a protracted dry spell that threatened to cause a water famine. To cap the climax, the commissioners had undertaken to supply Waterloo's needs until they had completed their own waterworks. "This here municipal-ownership," klucked a disgusted elector, "mebbe ain't so good."

Yet there were a few rays of sunshine shining through the clouds. The Water Board sunk several artesian wells near the pumping-station and from their combined flow obtained 1,000,000 gallons a day, which exceeded the daily consumption; chased away the consumers' frowns by offering to lay service-piping up to their property line and adjusted rates downward. While Berlin and Waterloo agreed to assist each other in case of a water shortage or a conflagration.

At the end of the first year the commissioners had laid two miles of new water mains and the number of takers had increased from 732 to 803. When the town purchased the works, only twenty-eight percent of the consumers were metered and seventy-two percent on flat rate. The Board persuaded these to install meters, pointing out that the flat-rate customer helped to pay for the careless consumer's water. The raisin in the commission's cake, however, was a cash surplus of $4,845.

A year's operation disclosed that the pumping facilities would either have to be reconstructed or replaced. The equipment was eleven years old, and since its installation in the eighteen-eighties the population had about doubled. From then to now, the Water Commissioners have had to provide for the needs of a fast-growing city. Their chief difficulty, of course, has been to procure an adequate supply of potable water. On account of there being no strong, flowing spring or lake in the vicinage, they have always had to face the possibility of a water shortage. At various times it seemed they would have to draw on the Grand River, and lands were purchased there. So far they have obviated a necessarily large investment in that quarter by boring artesian wells in new neighborhoods in the city and thus keeping a jump ahead of consumption.

Thirty-Five Years of Progress

	1898	1933
Number of equipped stations	1	2
Power used	steam	electricity
Reserve Power	steam	gas and oil
Capacity of pumps	2,000,000 gals.	6,500,000 gals.
Capacity of reserve pumps	none	3,500,000 gals.
Source of supply	lake	artesian wells
Storage capacity	none needed	2,000,000 gals.
Tower capacity	60,000 gals.	1,333,000 gals.
Available daily supply	500,000 gals.	5,000,000 gals.
Average daily consumption	500,000 gals.	2,540,000 gals.
Population	9,642	31,328
Daily per capita consumption	50 gals.	81 gals.
Feet of Mains	67,300	348,232
Miles of Mains	12.75	65.95
No. of Hydrants	103	425
No. of Consumers	732	6,798
No. of Meters	177	6,695
Hydrant Rental per annum	$45.00	$35.00
Minimum House rate per Quarter	$2.02	$1.44
Metered Rate per 1,000 gals.	27c	17.3c
Rate for largest consumers	6c	6.5c
Value of Plant	$102,000.00	$802,971.39
Debenture Debt	$102,000.00	$197,713.17

At the end of 1936, the distribution system consisted of 68.38 miles of mains. These to feed 438 fire hydrants and 6,876 households and factories. The average daily consumption per capita was 94 gallons and the total average consumption 3,079,580 gallons.

There were then two water towers and two reservoirs. In 1937, the Commission had the Dunker Construction Company build a third reservoir at the Shoemaker Avenue plant, with a capacity of 2,000,000 gallons. The Board has an artesian well at Bridgeport. This year they began laying 3,000 feet of 18-inch main to connect the well with the system. Their best well is in the Shoemaker lake field and has a daily flow of 2½ million gallons. Not since 1922 have they issued a single debenture, notwithstanding many rate reductions to consumers.

In his report of 1936, Superintendent Marcel Pequegnat said: "From a small beginning, entirely financed by the revenues from the sale of water, the waterworks, at the end of thirty-eight years of municipal ownership, now consists of a plant in which we have an equity of well over half a million dollars after proper allowance for reserve, depreciation and debts have been made."

The Commissioners

As has been seen, Mr. Breithaupt was elected commissioner in 1899, and has continuously served the city for thirty-nine years. With the exception of one year when he courteously stepped aside for Mr. George Rumpel, Mr. Breithaupt has been year after year chosen chairman, which is probably a Dominion record.

Among the early commissioners, H. J. Bowman, C.E., acted for fourteen years. P. S. Lautenschlager served nine years; George Rumpel, three years; and J. S. Anthes, George Buchhaupt, D. B. Detweiler, C. E. Cowan, S. J. Williams, and R. Gofton each for two years; and Dilman Shantz, one year.

Casper Braun was elected in 1908. He was a man of sound judgment, and sat in the Board continuously until his death in March, 1937. The city council then appointed Albert E. Dunker to fill out Mr. Braun's unexpired term. Philip Gies was returned as a commissioner in 1909 and has without a break given the city good service ever since. John Hainsworth was elected in 1920 and has been biennially re-elected up to the present time, a testimonial of his worth. Since 1899, the mayors have also had seats in the commission.

Superintendents

Wm. M. Davis, C.E., after the purchase of the utility, acted as superintendent until 1901. He was then succeeded by Henry Hymmen, the first full-time superintendent, who discharged the duties well for nineteen years. Mr. Hymmen was followed by Marcel Pequegnat, B.A., Sc., in 1920. Mr. Pequegnat has ever since ably filled the position for the larger city.

Officials

In the waterworks office, the Misses Rose and Georgina Huck were successively accountants till 1904. Since then, R. Lautenschlager, F. Walter Snyder, H. Bricknell, and Miss Edith McMeekin have filled the position. In 1922, A. C. Shantz was appointed accountant and has ever since been in charge of the office.

Among the engineers at the pumping plants have been: Wm. Collard, Joseph Walker, and his sons Ivan, Ralph, and Cecil. Also Theodore Schreiber. Cecil Walker is now meter reader.

Leander Klem was appointed foreman in 1912 and served the commission creditably for decades. His successor was Nelson Klem, who is still in charge of mains' construction, etc.

THE EULER BUSINESS COLLEGE

The Euler Business College was founded in 1900 as a unit of the Federated Business Colleges of Ontario. The college was located on the third floor of the Woolworth building. The Hon. W. D. Euler was principal and Miss McDiarmid taught shorthand and typewriting. Then the typewriter was a comparatively new device and the college had only four machines.

Later on the Federated Business Colleges were dissolved. Mr. Euler purchased the local school and renamed it the Berlin Business College. Soon afterward he removed the college to the Whyte Packing Company's block, on the site of the Waterloo Trust and Savings Company's office. The best business methods were taught and the keynote was thoroughness. It was one of the first schools in Ontario to adopt the Gregg system of shorthand. Steadily the student body increased. To accommodate the students Mr. Euler leased the top floor of the Pequegnat block in Frederick Street. More classrooms were again required in 1916. Accordingly, larger quarters were procured from Mr. H. L. Janzen in West King Street and the school's name changed to The Euler Business College. Among other early teachers, former students will remember Mr. Brent, Mr. Marks, Mr. Robinson, Miss King, Miss Power, and Mr. Phelps.

Mr. Euler was elected to a seat in the Dominion Parliament in 1917. Since then W. H. Nixon has been principal of the college.

Mr. Nixon is recognized as being one of the ablest business educators in the Province and once was chosen Chairman of the Business Educators' Association of Canada. At present the college is functioning at No. 44 South Queen Street.

MERCHANTS OF THE EIGHTIES AND AFTER

Henry Stuebing was a city grocer for some forty years. When a youth, Martin Schade of Waterloo sent him out into the country to sell fur-caps, and mitts. But it was hard sledding. So he gave a concert at the home of a friend. The neighbors came in and were pleased with the entertainment. Afterward he opened his pack and sold them eighty dollars worth of his wares. That experience led him to open a grocery store at German Mills. In 1881, he began business in Berlin. Mr. Stuebing was also a Naturalist, collector of antiques and coins, and a sleight of hand performer.

Randall & Roos

In 1884, George Randall and William Roos of Waterloo established a wholesale grocery and liquor warehouse in Ahrens' block. Randall & Roos occupied the ground floor and the C. A. Ahrens & Co., the upper floor as a shoe factory. These quarters are now the home of the Fischman Spring Co., of which Joseph Wuest is manager. Later on Aaron Bricker built a large block opposite the auditorium for Randall & Roos. Two of their travellers were H. Brown and Michael Roos. As a Park Commissioner and President of the Musical Society, William Roos gave the city good service.

Charles B. Dunke

Charles B. Dunke, grocer, began business in 1887 at 61 E. King Street. His father, Reinhart Dunke, joined him in 1888 and continued till 1900. Charles conducted the store himself for nineteen years. In 1919 he formed a partnership with his brother Edward, who had been his accountant. Charles bought the "Incubator" in Hall's lane and the Boehmer block, now the Dunke block. Henry and Philip Boehmer once made brushes and brooms there on an upper floor; there P. S. Lautenschlager and Amos Weaver founded the Maple Leaf Button Co.; there G. V. Oberholtzer once manufactured shoes; and there the Berlin Shirt Co. made shirts and collars. Mr. Dunke helped a number of industries to start. For thirteen years he sat in the council. Dunke & Co. sold their stock in 1937 to Dominion Stores, at the point when Charles had been a merchant for fifty years.

Philip Gies

Philip Gies, in the seventies, learned the hardware and tinsmithing trade at Hymmen Bros.' establishment. The first year he received his board and twenty-five dollars; in the second, thirty-five dollars in cash. In the summer of both years, he was given two weeks' holiday to go out to a farmer's and earn enough to buy his clothes. In the third year, the cash payment was sixty dollars. Afterward he gained further experience in other towns, and then bought the right to manufacture a patent steam-cooker in Ontario. Later on Hymmen Bros. re-engaged him. When he left their employ, he was the highest paid mechanic in Berlin, receiving eleven dollars a week.

In the mid-eighties, he entered into partnership with Henry Wolfhard and Wm. Mickus to launch a hardware store and tinsmithing shop. Mr. Gies put in $400, Mr. Wolfhard, $350, and Mr. Mickus, $650. A store was leased in the Canadian block. After a few years, Mr. Mickus sold his share to George Meisner. Three years afterward, Mr. Wolfhard and Mr. Meisner sold their shares to Mr. Gies, Peter Itter, and Henry Hymmen. Philip Gies & Company leased quarters in the new Walper block. Finally, Mr. Gies bought his partners' interests and engaged Thomas Cowan as store manager.

Meanwhile he had taken on plumbing and heating. In 1902, he sold his retail departments to Henry Wolfhard, George Sehl, and W. K. Weber. He then built a foundry in South Water Street to manufacture heaters and fill orders for castings, etc. Later on he started a plumbing and heating service in J. M. Staebler's block, at 45 West King Street, which five years after he sold to Hollinger & Durst. Mr. Gies subsequently bought an imitation leather enterprise for son Harry, that has since been sold to an American company. In 1922, he purchased the gasoline-pump department from V. O. Phillips. His son Harry is manager of this undertaking.

The Pequegnat Family

Ulysse Pequegnat, a member of the Watchmakers' Guild in Chaux-de-Fond, Switzerland, came to Berlin in 1874. He was accompanied by his wife, by Mrs. Arthur Pequegnat, and by thirteen sons and daughters. The sons were instructed of fine tools and adopted their father's vocation. At one period eight brothers each owned a watchmaker's business in as many different Canadian centres. The eldest son, Arthur, began at Mildmay, Ont., while Paul started in the Canadian block. Afterward, for ten years, Arthur and Paul conducted a jewelry store in Mr. Lautenschlager's block, at 68 E. King Street—the premises long occupied by Oscar Boehmer, jeweler. Later on, Mr. Arthur Pequegnat located a store in the Wunder block. In 1897, when cycling was at its height, he built a four-story block at 53-61 Frederick Street and manufactured racycles, turning out thousands of wheels. The automobile afterward encroached on the bicycle, and in 1903 Mr. Pequegnat ceased making racycles and founded the Arthur Pequegnat Clock Company to manufacture "Canadian Time"—good clocks of the pendulum type. His brother Paul was president, and his brothers George and Philemon associated with the company. Mr. Arthur Pequegnat was active in its behalf until his death in 1927. Since then his son Edmond has directed the enterprise. In closing, this clock company was the second ever established in Canada and the first to make substantial headway.

Clothing Merchants

Samuel R. Ernst began business as a clothing merchant and men's furnisher in 1892. His first store was in the American block. Afterward he purchased the block at 46 E. King Street. Mr. Ernst has built up a large trade by selling only dependable goods at fair prices. Other merchants recognize his merits as a buyer of merchandise. Thirty years ago the average youth spent forty dollars a year for clothes. Mr. Ernst's sons, Vorwerk and Harold, are with their father, who has well served the public for forty-five years, and who is the oldest merchant in the city.

Soon after Mr. Ernst began, Solomon Sauder started a similar store in premises nearby Mr. Ernst's. Mr. Sauder was successfully engaged in merchandising for about twenty-five years. He then sold his stock to his son, Eugene A. Sauder, and lives in retirement.

John Peters and V. M. Berlet were the contemporaries of the two foregoing merchants. Mr. Berlet is now manager of the Barrie

SAMUEL R. ERNST
City's Oldest Merchant.

A. K. JANSEN
Optometrist.

HENRY W. SHOEMAKER
Prominent Druggist.

M. C. CRESSMAN
Retired Merchant.

DAVID KNIPFEL
Founder, Pearl Laundry, Ltd.

LIEUT. GEORGE ZIEGLER
Founder, Conservatory of Music.

H. LESLIE STAEBLER
Insurance Broker, Musician.

EX-ALD. LLOYD KNIPFEL
Manager, Pearl Laundry, Limited.

Glove & Knitting Co.'s clothing department. Later on Herman Lippert and A. H. Kabel & Co. established men's furnishing stores.

Merchant Tailors

Merchant tailors of the nineties included George Harrison, Harry Balzer and Mr. Washburn. The latter business is now conducted by J. W. Washburn in the Royal Bank block. Another leading firm of that period was Stumpf & Stieler. Mr. J. F. Stumpf of that firm is now manager of the Walper Cigar store. Mr. Stieler formed a partnership with Mr. Seibert. The house of M. Wildfang & Co. is still remembered, while F. Tylinski still carries on. George Hoelscher, of 65 E. King Street, has seen the town of 10,000 expand into a city of 33,000 and kept pace with its requirements.

Grocers and Flour Merchants

J. A. Good, now office manager for the Janzen Realty Co., opened a grocery in 1891. Later John Steiss became his partner. S. A. Brubacher bought their stock in 1896. Five years afterward, Mr. Brubacher sold his grocery to Beck & Schell. "Sollie" was a Board of Trade stalwart. Schell Bros. purchased Mr. Beck's interests and for a generation transacted business at 16 E. King Street. Now the firm is Schell & Englert.

Valentine F. Weber was a clerk in Simon Yost's grocery in the mid-eighties. In 1888 he started a grocery himself at 18 Frederick Street. There he built up a yearly turnover of $75,000. Mr. Weber sat in the town council sixteen years, and was active in fraternal societies.

Two of the earliest neighborhood stores were those of H. J. Ahrens at the Five Points and from 1893, J. H. Schnarr's opposite the High School. In 1925, Mr. Schnarr sold his grocery and bought the Iler hot-house, which is now conducted by his sons at 784 W. King Street. To that period belongs also George Faber of 108 W. Weber Street, who enjoys a wide patronage. A little later on, Walter & Moser, George E. Zettel, Fred Wunnenberg, and J. M. Hoelscher began business. Mr. Zettel was for years a member of the City Council, while Mr. Hoelscher was a long-time school trustee and chairman of Courtland Avenue School. A. S. Hallman and J. R. Hallman were likewise well-known grocers.

In the flour and feed line were Pat Scully, J. B. Detweiler, and Mr. Eidt, now the Weber Feed & Seed Co. of Benton Street; J. Kennedy & Son, Shirk & Snider, the Wm. Snider Milling Co., and the Master Milling Co.

Hardware

A number of years ago, H. Wolfhard & Co. sold their premises to the S. S. Kresge chain store. George Sehl then purchased Mr. Wolfhard's and Mr. Weber's shares and located the business at 62 E. King Street. Since Mr. Sehl's death, his sons, Clayton and Jerome, conduct the enterprise.

Druggists

Three early druggists were C. E. Hoffman, who afterward purchased a covered button activity, J. H. Landreth, and J. E. Neville. In 1905, E. O. Ritz bought Mr. Neville's stock, then in the Glueck block. In 1917, Mr. Ritz leased the American House corner, where he has since conducted his well-patronized drugstore. In 1907, J. H. Schmidt began business at 57 E. King Street and has occupied the same premises ever since. Mr. Schmidt specializes in the filling of prescriptions, has a registered nurse in attendance, and has an I.D.A. drugstore. Henry W. Shoemaker is a contemporary of the two druggists just mentioned and serves his customers in the Twin City from No. 72 W. King Street. His is also an I.D.A. Drug Service. Mr. Shoemaker was the first to suggest that the city apply to the Dominion Government for a new federal building, that is now under construction.

Milliners

Among the milliners of that period, and this, were Miss S. Fehrenbach, Mrs. Brechbill, Alex Rose, Miss Cowan, and Miss A. F. G. Lowes. In hats, the ladies of the city have always been up-to-the-minute.

Carpenter Contractor and Merchant

As a youth George Bucher was employed by Henry Dunker, carpenter contractor. After seven years Mr. Bucher launched into the contracting business for himself, continuing for twelve years. He had thirty-five contracts one year for building homes and employed twenty-five mechanics. After his son had learned the hardware business, Mr. Bucher opened a hardware store in the Grand Central block. After the untimely death of his son, six years later,

Mr. Bucher sold the store to Karl Bornhold. Mr. Bucher was an alderman for seven years and for twelve years a member of the Board of Health. In 1927, he was appointed Building Inspector, continuing until a few years ago, when the peak of the depression arrived.

Photographers

Photographers of the early days included Mr. Schneuker, George Seiler, A. S. Green, S. J. Yost, A. A. Perrin and H. A. Huber. Since their day, color photography and motion-picture cameras have come in. Among the prominent houses of today are the Binning Studio, the Denton Studio, and the Suffolk Studio.

Once a clairvoyant and her husband stationed themselves in Casper Heller's Market hotel. She claimed that when she went into a trance a number of celestial spirits surrounded her. Dr. Minchin heard of the claim and smiled at it. Approaching the husband, he suggested that they photograph the spirits. The man was willing. Dr. Minchin consulted with Mr. H. A. Huber. On the evening before the day set for the photographing, a large chair in which the clairvoyant was to sit was placed in a central part of the room and around it four men with flour on their faces and in long white sheets, who were photographed. The next evening the woman was placed in the chair and the negative again exposed. Result: a lady and four spirits around her. Both husband and wife were delighted with the picture. He sent it to an American spiritualistic paper, which published it. New York papers copied the story. There was much excitement over it. Scientists, however, laughed at the claim. Reporters were sent here to interview the Doctor and from him learned that it was a practical joke.

China Hall

For thirteen years Louis D. Merrick was a travelling salesman for Nerlich & Co., wholesale china, etc., of Toronto, and visited Berlin. Here he made many friends. In 1899, he resolved on opening a China Hall and leasing a store at 30 E. King Street. Instead of buying his stock from the wholesale houses, Mr. Merrick imported it from Europe, often making personal visits to the largest glassware and pottery firms in England and elsewhere. One of his wellwishers was Mrs. George Rumpel, who said to him: "You sell toys. Why don't you gather up all the tin cans in the alleys and make them yourself? You'll get your raw material for nothing."

Knell Bros.' Hardware and Plumbing House

Wm. G. Knell learned the plumbing trade with Philip Gies and later on was in the employ of H. Wolfhard & Co. His mother was a daughter of George Seip, the brewer. She told her son that when the railway was built in the fifties there was a big bush along the tracks. Indians came in and traded baskets and beads for food. One of the earliest bakers was named Bamberger, one of the best pretzel makers.

Mr. Knell was a journeyman for thirty-five years, after which he started a plumbing business on the old brewery property in Queen Street. Charles H. Doerr was his silent partner. Three years after they bought the four-story Staebler block at 45 W. King Street and continued in plumbing and heating. Subsequently they added 150 feet to the block. Mr. Knell's brother, Fred L. Knell, joined the firm in 1910, when they entered into the retailing and wholesaling of hardware. Three years later the brothers bought Mr. Doerr's interest. In 1920, their brother-in-law, J. W. Fraser, became a partner.

Fred says that on the 24th of May he and his brother were each given a nickel and cautioned not to waste the money. Fred used to get his nickel changed into coppers and spent a cent at a time.

Bakers

The late Louis Bardon founded the Bardon Bakery in 1889. Mr. Bardon was a prominent member of the Concordia Society and well liked. This business is now managed by his son, Fred. About the same time as Mr. Bardon Sr., H. A. Dietrich founded a bakery. Mr. Dietrich was for many years a member of the council. His son, R. A. Dietrich now manages the business. Another early baker was Mike Massel, who was an adept bretzel maker. Phil Davey too conducted a bakery before leasing the Walper House.

Shoe Merchants

Old timers will remember the years when E. K. Snyder was a shoe merchant. Afterward A. Weseloh began and was followed by his son. Wm. Moore sold footwear and small wares. His stock was purchased by W. H. Leeson. Walter Ziegler was also an early shoe merchant.

Bookstores

Among the early booksellers were Joseph Bingeman, M. S. Hallman, W. H. Becker, F. I. Weaver, Mr. Swaisland, and J. P. Bender. Since then the J. C. Jaimet Company and R. B. Russell have been founded.

House Furnishings

J. Derbecker has been long established at No. 8 Frederick Street as a dealer in house furnishings.

Coal Merchants

Among the earliest coal merchants was A. A. Pipe, with an office and yard in South Ontario Street. Mr. Pipe took a lively interest in his town and in sports.

In the early nineties, Kloepfer & Co. had an office in George LaCourse's ticket-office in E. King Street and a coal-yard in Breithaupt Street. Genial August P. Frank was appointed manager and built up a large business. Many years ago their office was removed to No. 8 N. Queen Street. Late in 1936, while on a motor-trip to Toronto, Mr. Frank was seriously injured in an automobile accident and died of his injuries in March, 1937. He was then the oldest coal merchant in the city.

Reinhart Boehmer is one of the six brothers who helped to convert the town into a city. As a boy on his father's farm, he hauled logs to Hoffman's saw-mill. When he was twenty-one, he bought a farm. "If you start up small," said Mr. Boehmer, "it takes a lot of scratching to pay for a farm. But, if you work hard and make spare, you'll prosper. The Saturday market helped me to pay for mine."

In 1893 Mr. Boehmer bought a coal and builders' supplies venture, with an office near the city hall waiting room. A story-and-a-half house could then be built for $700. In 1921, he sold his business to his brother Herman and retired. Mr. Herman Boehmer had previously been a dry-goods merchant for twenty-five years. The new proprietor in 1923 opened an office, coal-yard, and builders' supplies depot in South Ontario Street. Of his four sons, Edward, Robert, Herbert and William, the eldest, Edward and Robert, were their father's business associates. Since his death in 1925, the two young men have successfully conducted the enterprise, sparing time to promote the city's interests.

Mr. Reinhart Boehmer and his only child, Miss Angeline Boehmer, reside at 79 Benton Street. Mr. Boehmer, who is in his 84th year, goes to bed at eight o'clock in the evening and rises at five, taking a cold bath, winter and summer. Then he goes through a set of exercises, including exercises for his eyes.

Jewellers

The citizens of that generation were especially thrifty, for most of them were paying for a home. A young man carried a watch and when he married a wife, bought a ring. But that ended his buying of jewelry. Their children, however, wanted engagement rings, necklaces, and what not. Among the jewellers of that period were Heller Bros., Henry Knell Jr., A. J. Gabel, who manufactured collar buttons, and Arnold Jansen. Mr. Jansen, while at the Horological College, made a gold watch which he still carries. He had also a post-graduate course at the Opthalmic College and after 1915 confined himself to optical work. Oscar Boehmer was for many years a jeweller at 68 E. King Street, but recently sold his business to Edward Becker. Present day jewellers include Albert Heller and Edward Heller & Co.

Optometrists

A century ago, persons who needed spectacles sent to Boston for them and waited three months for their arrival. Now young men graduate from the college in connection with Toronto University and supply the citizens with scientific lenses. Among the well-established optical houses are those of H. E. Heller, A. Jansen & Son, and G. W. Gordon. Mr. Gordon was for a number of years an alderman and Chairman of the Finance Committee.

Miscellaneous

George Wanless was an early dealer in sewing machines and musical instruments. Frank Gardiner sold pianos and organs and helped to found the Berlin Piano Co. Joseph Fehrenbach was a prominent saddler, and an alderman. Louis Sattler was also a leading saddler, a friend of trees, and a school trustee. His son, R. G. L. Sattler, now deals in leather goods in his late father's stand at 49 S. Queen Street. One of the fur merchants was the late Wm. Kaufman. The enterprise is now a company with M. Kaufman at its head. George O. Philip and J. J. A. MacCallum opened tobacco stores in the first years of the nineties. Mr. Philip was for a time lessee of the Walper House, but returned to the tobacco business. This year he sold his stand to Norm Davison. Mr. MacCallum has continued until the present day. He was one of the first merchants to found a tobacco chainstore, with three stores here and others in Preston and Woodstock. He also founded the Imperial Wholesale Co.

BANKS AND BANKERS

The Bank of Upper Canada opened a branch here in 1853. Seven years later it departed and was followed by the Commercial Bank. In 1868, the Commercial Bank was taken over by the Merchants Bank.

The first three managers of the Merchants Bank were Robert Rogers, Charles Crookall, and W. R. Travers. When Mr. Travers came here in 1886, old industries were enlarging and new ones springing up. The requests for loans exceeded the local supply of funds and outside money had to be brought in through the bank's branch system. During Mr. Travers' stay here, he loaned out $42,000,000, and the Merchants Bank became known as the manufacturers' bank.

W. E. Butler was appointed manager in 1900. Mr. Butler capably discharged his duties for a number of years and was then assigned the position of Bank Inspector. The Merchants Bank had then been for a long period lessees of the Merner block, on the southeast corner of King and Ontario Streets. Mr. Butler was followed here by Harry P. Bingham. He too was an experienced banker, and as an old Waterloo boy had played with the Rangers football team. A. Harvey Devitt was the successor of Mr. Bingham and well served his customers until 1914, when he was appointed first inspector and then Supervisor of Agencies by the Economical Fire Insurance Company.

D. A. MacMillan followed Mr. Devitt in 1914. A broad-gauged banker, Mr. MacMillan contributed weightily to the upbuilding of the city. In 1922, the Bank of Montreal absorbed the Merchants Bank, and in 1926, the Molsons Bank. Meanwhile the company had erected a handsome banking house on the corner of King and Queen Streets. Mr. MacMillan directed the larger service until 1936—a record of twenty-two years—when he retired.

When the Bank of Montreal absorbed the Molsons Bank, J. R. Kirkpatrick was manager of the Molsons. He entered the service of the Bank of Montreal and was stationed at Woodstock. After Mr. MacMillan's retirement, Mr. Kirkpatrick was appointed manager of the Kitchener branch.

The Canadian Bank of Commerce

The Canadian Bank of Commerce initiated its service here in 1879, with an office at the corner of King and Ontario Streets. Afterward for many years the bank occupied premises at the corner of King and Frederick Streets. Their first local manager was J. Young. He was followed in 1889 by D. B. Dewar, an able banker, curler, and supporter of football. Then, as now, the bank had numerous manufacturers' accounts and more mercantile customers. Mr. Dewar was transferred to Hamilton in 1893. At that stage it was said that the farmers roundabout had one million dollars deposited in his Savings Department.

Successively, Mr. Dewar was followed by W. C. J. King, E. P. Gower, George M. Wedd, and W. H. Collins. Besides performing their social duties that quartette was especially active in Board of Trade work. Two early accountants who rose in the Bank's service were C. W. Rowley and Thomas Turnbull.

The Bank of Hamilton

The Bank of Hamilton came in 1893, and leased quarters on the southwest corner of King and Queen Streets. O. S. Clarke was the first manager. After him J. P. Bell was in charge. Mr. Bell was afterward General Manager of the Bank of Hamilton. Here, he was followed by Thomas Haines, Mr. Laing, and J. H. Dobbie. In 1927, the Bank of Hamilton was merged with the Canadian Bank of Commerce, which also acquired the Standard Bank. The Bank of Commerce then purchased the former Bank of Hamilton building, and appointed Mr. Dobbie manager. The present manager is Mr. J. L. Thompson.

The Bank of Nova Scotia

The Bank of Nova Scotia was established here in 1900 in the Canadian block, with A. E. Williams at the managerial desk. From 1901 to 1916, the managers were: R. C. Wallace, E. T. Hammett, H. V. Cann, V. D. McLeod, and G. H. Montgomery. In

1916, Mr. A. J. Cundick became manager and ably filled the role until November, 1937, when he retired. In 1926 the bank was removed to the corner of King and Ontario Streets, after the old Merner block had been enlarged and remodelled. This bank has grown with the city. Mr. Cundick is on the Board of Trade executive council, and for years has given commendable service in the Family Relief Board.

The Bank of Toronto

The Bank of Toronto entered the local field in 1906 and leased premises in the Potter block. Ground was broken by J. K. Ball. After Mr. Ball, E. W. Lamprey directed the bank for nine years, when he was assigned the superintendency of the Bank's branches in British Columbia. Mr. Lamprey was followed by efficient George B. McKay, who left in 1927 and was followed by W. D. McCrirrick. The Bank of Toronto has since purchased the block at No. 19 East King Street. The present manager is Mr. J. C. Wolfraim, who has been here since 1930, succeeding Mr. McCrirrick.

The Dominion Bank

In June, 1907, the Dominion Bank, in an office in the corner building next the post-office, made its bow to the public. The first manager was T. H. Scott. Two years later he was followed by Karl Bergman, who continued till 1913. Then for four years the berth was filled by Norman Evans. R. D. Boughner succeeded Mr. Evans. In 1925, the Dominion Bank opened a city branch at the corner of King and Wilmot Streets, with George D. Hynes in charge. In turn, Mr. Hynes was succeeded by R. J. Conrad and A. E. Brown. Mr. P. Kennedy is now manager. In 1926 the main office was transferred to the former Bank of Commerce office. The Dominion Bank has widened its services and is the city's banker. Mr. H. S. Lancefield is the present manager.

The Royal Bank of Canada

The Royal Bank of Canada is one of the "big three" Canadian banks. Their branch was established here in 1919, with Fred H. Boehmer at the helm. The Bank purchased the former Economical block on the corner of King and Ontario Streets. In 1925 they acquired the Union Bank, which had had a branch here, with, successively, Mr. Anderson, Mr. Sheldon, and Mr. Milne, managers.

Mr. Boehmer acted as manager until 1928, when A. E. Brundrett succeeded him. In 1934, Mr. Brundrett was followed by the present manager, Mr. J. R. Dier. The Royal Bank, with its many domestic and foreign branches, serves a considerable number of the city's 160 manufacturers.

The Imperial Bank of Canada

The Imperial Bank of Canada has had a branch in the city since 1926. The bank then purchased from Lang Brothers the former Snyder property at 51 King Street West. Their service was begun by manager T. R. Richardson, who stayed here until 1929, when he was followed by J. B. Thompson. Mr. Thompson died in 1931, and the branch was then placed under the management of J. W. Thomson, who came here from Fort William. On Mr. Thomson's removal to the Dundas and University branch in Toronto, the present manager, Major D. G. P. Forbes, was placed in charge in 1936.

The Clearing House

In 1916, the city's banks jointly organized a Clearing House. The weekly clearings now amount to about $1,000,000.

When the Commercial Bank opened a branch here, its capitalization was below a million dollars. Now the banks represented in the city have capitalizations and reserves exceeding $227,000,000.

Savings Banks

In 1912, the Waterloo Trust and Savings Company was organized in Waterloo. Soon afterward they opened a branch in Kitchener, which is now their executive office. This thriving institution has been capably managed since its inception by Mr. P. V. Wilson.

In 1935, the Ontario Government opened a Savings Bank in the Walper House Block. Its deposits are increasing under the management of Mr. W. A. Neill.

SOURCE
The Chartered Banks in Kitchener. 1927. By Mr. D. A. MacMillan.

Twentieth
Century

THE TWENTIETH CENTURY

The Canadian Northern, National Continental, and Grand Trunk Pacific Railways were begun in the beginning of the twentieth century. A billion dollars were expended in their construction. Before 1920, 3,300,000 newcomers settled in Canada—mostly farmers and their families. The Western prairies were broken to wheat and prosperity set in. Among the new town industries then organized were:

The Anthes-Baetz Furniture Co.	The Interior Hardwood Co.
Baetz Bros. Furniture Co.	Jacques Furniture Co.
The Bauer Shoe Co.	The Kaufman Rubber Co.
The Beaver Furniture Co.	A. Kimmel Felt Co.
D. B. Betzner's Woodenware Co.	G. J. Lippert Table Co.
Bullas Art Glass Co.	The Merchants Rubber Co.
Canada Furniture Co.	A. W. Niergarth, Furn. Specialties
Canada Gasolene Pump Co.	The Norton Drinx Co.
DeLuxe Upholstering Co.	The Ontario Glove Co.
Diamond Grate Bar Co.	Ott Brick & Tile Co.
Reorganized Dominion Button Co.	Ontario Sugar Co.
Dominion Shirt Co.	Onward Manufacturing Co.
Doon Twines Limited	Arthur Pequegnat Clock Co.
Dumart Packing Co.	Pollock-Welker Corporation
John Forsyth Shirt Co.	Ritchie Button Co.
Forwell Iron Pipe Co.	The Robe & Clothing Co.
Galt Shoe Co.	Geo. Schnarr, Buttons, etc.
Philip Gies Foundry	George Schlee Button Co.
The Greb Shoe Co.	The Superior Stone Co.
The Grimes Phonograph Co.	Harry Tolton Shirt Co.
G. H. Hachborn Upholstering Co.	The Mitchell Button Co.
Hamblin-Metcalfe Candy Co.	Walker Bin & Fixture Co.
The Huck Glove Co.	J. E. Wiegand Shirt Co.
The Huether Brewing Co.	Woelfle Bros., Fine Tools
The Hydro City Shoe Co.	Wunder Furniture Co.

Boys in humble homes can draw inspiration from the lives of the early manufacturers. The President of the J. M. Schneider Co. cased his first wieners on a kitchen table. The head of the C. H. Doerr Confectionery Co. at first drove about the district in a horse-drawn vehicle seeking for orders. The President of the Interior Hardwood Co., in beginning, only allowed himself $1.25 a day. As a boy the President of the Dominion Button Co. got work in Shantz's button factory, and had his shoes laced with pieces of

J. D. C. FORSYTH
President, John Forsyth, Ltd.

THE FORSYTH SHIRT FACTORY

string. One day a Mr. Detweiler gave him a nickel to buy a pair of shoe laces. Those leaders all had what it takes. Like the postage stamp, they stuck to their job until they reached their destination.

BEET SUGAR

Canada's first beet-sugar mill was built in Berlin. Reports of sugar being made from beets in Bay City, Michigan, reached here in 1900. Several citizens went over to see how it was done. On their return they said that a sugar factory was a good thing for both the growers and the town. Soon, at the Saturday market, Dan Detweiler was talking of sugar-beets to every farmer who would listen. Interest mounted.

In 1901, L. J. Breithaupt, M.P.P., had the Ross Government send up Dr. A. E. Shuttleworth of the O.A.C., to select twenty-five test plots. The Board of Trade then appointed D. B. Detweiler, H. L. Janzen, Wendel Shantz, J. E. Shantz, Isadore Snyder, H. Herner, J. L. Umbach, and Allen Shantz to induce twenty-five farmers to make the experiment. Although doubting Thomases declared that the short Canadian summer would never store sufficient sugar in home-grown beets to warrant a factory, the required number of experimenters were rounded up.

To encourage the erection of sugar-mills in the Province the Ross Government, in 1901, offered a bonus of $75,000. The velvet was spread over three years, on sugar actually manufactured: half a cent a pound in the first two years, and one-quarter cent, in the third. Sugar companies were required to pay growers four dollars a ton for beets testing twelve per cent in sugar content, and proportionately more for higher values.

When the beets grown in the experimental plots were lifted they fulfilled all expectations. Straightway the Ontario Sugar Company was organized in Toronto, to build a mill either in Dunnville or Berlin. The company sent representatives here to seek for inducements. It was proposed to invest $500,000 in buildings and plant; to slice 60,000 tons of beets yearly; to pay the growers at least $240,000 annually; to employ 300 men for three months during the run; and to expend $260,000 a year in wages and supplies.

THE MERCHANTS RUBBER COMPANY'S WORKS

A. R. KAUFMAN
President, The Kaufman Rubber Co.

W. T. SASS
Founder, The Interior Hardwood Co.

The company asked the town for a bonus of $25,000 and exemption from taxation for ten years. The offer set the heather afire.

Board of Trade members rolled up their sleeves, and arranged for an excursion to Bay City. Hundreds of townsmen and farmers went over. There they saw wagonloads and trainloads of beets being unloaded at the sugar-mill; followed the process of sugar-making from the slicers to the final machine where white granulated sugar poured into bags, ready for shipment to the grocer; and interviewed American growers and merchants regarding the worth of a sugar-mill to a municipality. The delegation returned home determined to net the sugar factory.

A bylaw was submitted to the property-owners, and, under President S. J. Williams' leadership, every available vote was brought out. The law required that of every five votes three must be favorable. The evening's count showed a majority of 661 for the factory, or fifteen more than the needed three-fifths.

Meanwhile Dunnville seemed to have put in some good licks. For after the Berlin bylaw had been carried, the company said it would not come here unless the citizens purchased $75,000 of their stock. Quickly the amount was subscribed. Even a washerwoman bought a share. Later on, the company requested the purchase of a further $25,000. Mr. Williams personally bought the extra block to nail the factory.

Growing Sugar-Beets

For his work, Mr. Williams was banquetted and offered the mayoralty. But he was unable to accept the chair, because he had been appointed manager of the sugar factory.

The next duty was to induce growers to plant 5,000 acres of beets. Local farmers played Scotch, agreeing to plant only from one to five acres, or what they could till without hiring outside help. To prevent a shortage of beets from occurring, a number of townsmen formed acreage companies. It was even proposed that the town itself buy 200 acres of land near Bridgeport and grow sugar-beets. Finally, without committing the municipality, the acreage was signed up. Dr. A. B. Campbell was one of the growers.

A site for a mill was purchased between Berlin and Bridgeport. Afterward it was annexed to the town, and gave it a footing on the Grand River. The company awarded the contract for erecting a sugar-mill to the Dyer Construction Co. of Cleveland, O. The factory was ready for its first run in October, 1902.

Meanwhile the amateur growers found that sugar-beets need summer-long hoeing. Even school children were pressed into service. When the hoeing fell in arrears, scores of Six Nations Indians were imported from Caledonia. The Indians came in groups of twenty or twenty-five, and mostly were related; lived in tents; and set up frame cook shacks. During the season they initiated S. J. Williams, Dr. Shuttleworth, and John Peters into the Indian brotherhood at Victoria Park. The initiation was performed by Chief Robert Davey, aged eighty-four, Captain William Bill, Tim Warner, Charles Williams, Joe and John Hill. The formality was marked with ancient rites, including the war dance and the corn dance.

After the beets had ripened the next stunt was to pull them before Jack Frost's arrival. To assist the growers companies of Chinamen were brought in from Montreal. Even so some of the acreage companies' beets were blanketed with snow. However, a tonnage sufficient for a three-months' run was stored. The yields were as high as fifteen tons to the acre, while the sugar content averaged fifteen percent.

In the next season most of the amateurs dropped out, and left beet-growing to more experienced hands. After a decade the farmers asked for a higher price for beets, and when it was not forthcoming many of them discontinued raising the sweet-root. Subsequently the factory was sold to Wallaceburg capitalists, who since have closed the mill.

NIAGARA POWER

We are all familiar with the tale from the *Arabian Nights* in which Ala-ed-Din "arose, fetched the Lamp, and rubbed it, and there appeared the Slave." The Lamp, however, pales beside "Hydro." It lights up a myriad homes, dispels darkness from countless streets, and turns thousands of factory wheels.

The Niagara Power achievement is linked to the Twin City. At a Board of Trade banquet in Waterloo, on February 11, 1902, said the *Berlin Daily Telegraph*, E. W. B. Snider advanced the idea that follows:

E. W. B. SNIDER
The Father of "Hydro"

D. B. DETWEILER
Organizer of "Hydro"

SIR ADAM BECK
Constructor of "Hydro"

THE BIRTHPLACE OF "HYDRO"
24 North Queen Street

C. K. HAGEDORN
First Chairman of Light Commission.

GEORGE LIPPERT
Chairman, 1912 - 1922.

AUGUST R. LANG
Chairman, 1922 - 1934.

DAVID GROSS
Chairman, 1934 - 1937.

NOTE—Mr. A. L. Breithaupt, Chairman from 1905 to 1912, appears with the founders of the Berlin Rubber Co.

That as Toronto was discussing the use of power from Niagara Falls, Waterloo should seek for the co-operation of the Boards of Trade in Berlin, Galt, and Guelph, and the Mayors of Preston and Hespeler to investigate the matter.

Mr. Snider's winged seed was carried to Berlin and lodged in the mind of D. B. Detweiler, who asked him to amplify his idea. On February 14, 1902, Mr. Snider wrote to Mr. Detweiler from Toronto, saying:

> It is the company engaged at present to put in a power plant at Niagara Falls I had reference to, not a government undertaking. The city of Toronto is making efforts to secure power from this company, and I thought it a good time for several towns like Waterloo, Berlin, Preston, Hespeler, Galt and Guelph, as a "hive of industries," joining hands, and with a united effort, in conjunction with Toronto, might in that way secure some special privileges, which might not be secured later on.

> Possibly something better might be accomplished with the Cataract Power Company. These are matters the joint committee of the towns mentioned could with advantage take up and investigate. I believe it would have a tendency to facilitate greatly the locating of new industries in the midst of our several towns if electric power were secured on a satisfactory basis. The sooner the better.

Afterward the two outstanding men, who were like David and Jonathan, met and planned a campaign. Mr. Snider, who was a former M.P.P., undertook to win over the Ontario Government, and Mr. Detweiler to line up the manufacturers of the district.

For three months, at his own expense, Mr. Detweiler button-holed business men, usually jogging to and fro on a bicycle. Steam-power then cost from forty to $100 a horsepower. He felt certain that Niagara power would cut down power bills from thirty to sixty percent.

On May 8, 1902, Mr. Detweiler placed the question before the Berlin Board of Trade. Nearly all the local manufacturers then had steam units, while the furniture factories and tanneries had a deal of waste to burn. It was felt that they would never instal electric motors. Shirt and whitewear companies, however, might so do. The town itself did not own the gas and electric plants. Hence the lighting up of homes and streets did not enter into the discussion. In sum, it seemed to be wholly a manufacturers' nut to crack.

Of that session, the News Record said,

Vice-President Detweiler introduced two important questions. First, the transportation problem, the proper solution of which he said could only be found in the nationalization of the railways and their operation by a committee of experts, instead of politicians.

Secondly, the advisability of appointing committees by the various inland towns to take steps to procure power from Niagara Falls.

S. J. Williams followed him and said,

I do not think Mr. Detweiler's suggestion will receive the support it deserves. Toronto tried to get just what is under consideration and was fired from the Legislature. Then the Toronto Street Railway asked for a franchise and got it. If the towns interested were to put up $5,000 as an expense fund it would not be a drop in the bucket when they ran up against the lobbyists of such corporations as the Toronto Street Railway and the Electric Light Company.

Mr. Williams' views did not dampen the ardor of "D.B." He held that the facts would convince manufacturers that Niagara Power would effect big savings. But he was not able to swing the Board of Trade into line. The members said, "Let Dan do it!" So he was appointed a Committee of One to investigate Niagara Power.

Engages Mr. Mitchell

Mr. Detweiler's favorite saying was: "Where there is no vision the people perish." Next morning he telephoned Mr. Snider and then wrote to Charles H. Mitchell, C.E., Consulting Engineer of the Ontario Power Company, and engaged him to address a gathering of manufacturers in Berlin.

The First Conference

Mr. Detweiler personally journeyed from centre to centre to induce prominent manufacturers to attend a conference in Berlin on June 9, 1902. Before setting out, he called on his friend, August R. Lang, who was engaged in supervising the construction of a tall tannery building. Mr. Detweiler climbed up several ladders and asked Mr. Lang to buy some natural-gas securities from him in order that he might defray his travelling expenses. Those who attended the conference included the following:

From Waterloo: E. W. B. Snider, Mayor David Bean, Wm. Snider, and R. Roschman. From Guelph: Christopher Kloepfer and Lincoln Goldie. From Preston: George A. Clare, M.P., S. J. Cherry and Thomas Hepburn. From Bridgeport: Peter Shirk. From Toronto: Frank Spence.

From Berlin: D. B. Detweiler, Mayor J. R. Eden, George Rumpel, Rev. Theo. Spetz, Carl Kranz, C. H. Doerr, J. M. Staebler, J. S. Anthes, Senator S. Merner, Dr. J. F. Honsberger, John Fennell, Dr. G. H. Bowlby, C. A. Ahrens, G. M. DeBus, J. W. Davey, N. B. Detweiler, J. Luft, the Rev. A. B. Francisco, Dr. R. W. Schnarr, Graham Jackson, M. E. Shantz, Louis McBrine, Harry Peters, John A. Lang, F. Tylinski, C. E. Moyer, August Boehmer, H. S. Boehmer, C. Sugarman, A. W. Feick, J. U. Clemens, A. Williams, Judge Chisholm, C. K. Hagedorn, A. Weseloh, S. E. Moyer, and others.

E. W. B. Snider was chosen chairman and D. B. Detweiler, secretary. Mr. Snider pointed out that American cities were already using Niagara Power and said Canadians should have enough enterprise to utilize the great heritage that Nature has placed before their door. He then laid before them two suggestions: (a) to ask the Ross Government to develop power and sell it at a trifle over cost to the municipalities; (b) to organize a company among manufacturers within a radius of 100 miles with a capitalization of $5,000,000—the power to be sold to shareholders. Later on legislation might be obtained to allow municipalities to buy shares.

Highlights of Mr. Mitchell's Speech

Mr. Mitchell was then called on. He said there were several companies on the American side that had developed power at the Falls. One, the Niagara Falls Power Company, generates 50,000 horsepower, has operated eight years, and sells its current chiefly in Buffalo. On the Canadian side, the Canadian & Niagara Power Company was developing 50,000 h.p., while the Ontario Power Company was building a plant to generate 60,000 h.p.

Mr. Mitchell asserted that the transmission of electricity from the Falls to Berlin, a distance of 92 miles, was feasible. If Niagara Power were brought in, the company supplying it would build a trunk line to Berlin, with arms reaching to other towns, and transmit say 10,000 h.p. The power line would be in duplicate. In transmitting the curent there would be a loss of from sixteen to eighteen percent. Power will be available at the Falls for eighteen dollars a h.p. and could be sold here for thirty dollars.

After Mr. Mitchell's speech the delegates adjourned for lunch. Two dozen business men subscribed two dollars each to banquet the delegates at the Walper House. There was enough money over to pay Mr. Mitchell a fee of thirty dollars.

Frank S. Spence

After lunch, Frank S. Spence of Toronto was heard. Six months before he had unsuccessfully contested the mayoralty in his city on a public-ownership platform. Mr. Spence said,

> Electricity will be the power of the future. Niagara Power should do for Ontario what coal and iron did for England. I was interested in a movement to buy and transmit Niagara Power to Toronto. We made an application to the Legislature for the rights of producing as well as transmitting power. But the request met with such strong opposition from other constituencies, notwithstanding that Toronto was willing to serve other municipalities, and from private power companies, that our bill was bowled down. Later on a private company was given a franchise by the Government and placed in a position to tax the whole city for its profit. Instead of Toronto getting as much as possible of the benefit, a private company is charging as much as it dare.
>
> I recognize that the problem is a big one and that there are many difficulties in the way. Owen Sound and other northern constituencies, for instance, will never consent to the Government developing power for the benefit of Western Ontario. A commission appointed by the Lieutenant-Governor might solve the problem. I suggest that a committee be formed to interest a sufficient number of persons, so that they could go before the Legislature with prestige and influence strong enough to overcome the opposition that will be met with.

A Resolution Adopted

On motion of Christopher Kloepfer of Guelph and Samuel Cherry of Preston, the resolution that follows was then carried,

> That a committee be appointed, with power to add to their number, to prepare a co-operative plan for procuring a supply of electrical energy for the manufacturing interests on the most favorable terms; the committee to call a convention of the representatives named by Municipal Councils, Boards of Trade and Manufacturers' Associations to consider such plan and take steps to carry out the plan agreed upon.

The conference named the committee that follows: E. W. B. Snider, D. B. Detweiler, John A. Lang, C. K. Hagedorn, Wm. Snider, R. Roschman, Frank Spence and P. W. Ellis (Toronto), George A. Clare, George Pattison, Robert Scott, Joseph Stauffer, and R. Mc-Gregor (Galt), Mayor Wood and Lloyd Harris (Brantford), Christopher Kloepfer and Lincoln Goldie (Guelph), W. A. Kribs and George Forbes (Hespeler), and Peter Shirk.

To interest manufacturers, a second conference was held in Galt in October, 1902.

The Die is Cast

A third convention was held here on February 17, 1903. The delegates assembled in the basement of the old Y.M.C.A. building, 24 N. Queen Street. The select committee then presented their report, saying that electric power could be purchased in large quantity, at a low price, by a group of users or a group of municipalities, from a private company in Niagara Falls. The committee favored having the municipalities joining together and erecting a distribution system, and perhaps later on developing power as well. To do so, special legislation was necessary. Prompt action was recommended to obtain such authority from the Legislature. The cost, in their opinion, would be apportioned according to municipal population.

That was the crucial conference. The sixty or seventy delegates had to determine whether to go ahead or drop the proposal. One new face was that of Mayor Adam Beck of London, who said that he had come to learn.

Mayor Urquhart of Toronto made a proposal. Namely, that the conference ask the Government to build transmission lines and deliver power to the cities and towns of Ontario. Mr. Spence moved an amendment that the municipalities, instead of the government, erect the power lines and bear the expense. The Urquhart motion, however, was adopted in its original form, thereby committing the municipalities to the enterprise.

Toronto City Council made the first move. On March 13, 1903, they begged the Government to build a plant at the Falls and deliver power to a group of municipalities.

Berlin Buys the Lighting Plants

In June, 1903, Berlin bought the local gas and electric-light works for $90,000. The first light commissioners were: C. K. Hagedorn (Chairman), S. J. Williams, H. J. Bowman, C. H. Mills, and Mayor J. R. Eden. W. H. Cone was appointed superintendent of the works and George H. Clarke secretary-treasurer.

When the plants were taken over, the sale of electric current was seventy h.p. The Niagara Power project was then a chrysalis and two commissioners questioned whether it would ever reach the winged state. Since the demand for current was increasing, the commissioners bought four gas-engines, each with two vertical gas-benches of six retorts, and two 200-k.w. generators, to make electricity from coal-gas. Their spokesman said, when asking the town council for $70,000 to buy the equipment,

> It is not the intention to beat Niagara Power at once, but eventually it will be done. In Batavia, N.Y., Niagara Power has been thrown out and gas-engines put in.

The Government Acts

The Ontario Government acted on June 12, 1903. Legislation was then passed that enabled a union of municipalities to do any one of three things: to develop, transmit, and distribute Niagara Power through a commission appointed by a bench of judges; to buy power and have the vendors deliver it to users; or to buy power delivered at their door and distribute it themselves.

A fourth conference was held in Berlin on July 9, 1903, to weigh the Power Act. At it, a Committee of Seven was chosen to get light regarding the purchase and delivery of power. The members were: E. W. B. Snider (Chairman), R. McGregor of Galt, Adam Beck of London, P. W. Ellis of Toronto, C. H. Waterous of Brantford, George McLagan of Stratford, and Lincoln Goldie of Guelph.

At that conference a Municipal Power Union was also shaped, with J. W. Lyon of Guelph as secretary. Mr. Lyon proved to be a tower of strength.

Shortly afterward the Government set up the Western Ontario Power Commission to delve among the roots. The members were: E. W. B. Snider (Chairman), Adam Beck, P. W. Ellis, and W. F. Cockshutt of Brantford. The commissioners employed Robert A.

Ross, E.E., of Montreal, and R. G. Fessenden, Technist, of Washington, D.C., as consultants; while James C. Haight of Waterloo was selected as secretary of the commission. The study began in the fall of 1903. Toronto, London, Guelph, Brantford, Stratford, Woodstock, and Ingersoll agreed to share the cost of the investigation, not to exceed $15,000.

THE BOWLING CLUB

A lawn bowling club was set up here on April 12, 1902. Judge Chisholm was elected President; Dr. G. H. Bowlby, Vice-President; and J. J. A. Weir, Secretary-treasurer. The club's capital was fixed at $600, in five-dollar shares, and a lot in the rear of the court-house bought for $325 from D. B. Detweiler. The first Committee of Management were: A. H. Devitt, E. P. Gower and E. T. Hammett —three bankers—and the Grounds Committee: H. F. Pearson, John McDougall and David Forsyth.

The annual fee was four dollars. Eight rinks were formed of the fifty-seven active members, with the skips that follow: W. E. Butler, A. H. Devitt, David Forsyth, E. T. Hammett, J. J. A. Weir, Martin Schiedel, C. E. Hoffman and E. P. Gower. On July 26, 1902, two rinks were sent to Galt, where they were trimmed by a score of 34-20.

In 1905 the club joined the Ontario Lawn Bowling Association and the Western Lawn Bowling Association.

Seven British rinks toured Canada in 1906 and played here against an equal number of rinks drawn from the county. The Berlin skips were Martin Schiedel, W. D. Euler and J. A. Richards; Waterloo: E. F. Seagram and A. H. Snyder; Galt: Dr. McKendrick and J. Patrick. The islanders were strong in the draw and won the match by 140 to 121 points. Among their skips was a parson. On one end, when he had built up a huddle of bowls round the kitty, W. H. Leeson made a running shot and trailed the jack. His play nettled the visitor, who blurted out: "It takes an artist to paint a good picture, but any fool can put his foot through it."

In those rosy days the bowlers of the county engaged in friendly contests, usually in the afternoon and travelling by trolley. On the way home the local trundlers sang "La Compagnie" and other choruses.

Yearly tournaments were held by the Berlin and Waterloo clubs, open to the Province. Joseph E. Seagram and the Kuntz Brewing Company each presented a trophy. Later on, the Berlin club furnished a cup for the consolation award. Tournaments lasted three or four days and were first cousin to the six-day bicycle races. Now one-day tournaments are the rule and evening tilts the more popular.

A Home Rink Wins the Highest Honors

The Ontario championship was won by a Berlin rink at Niagara-on-the-Lake on July 16, 1909. The winning rink consisted of: W. G. Cleghorn, lead; Herman Boehmer, second; Harvey J. Sims, third, and W. D. Euler, skip. In the final contest they foiled a Brantford rink by a score of 24-16 points. The Twin-City gave the victors a public reception with band music, and dined them at the Walper House. In celebration of the victory, Colonel W. M. O. Lochead wrote the annexed poem:

1. When bowling is played anywhere near the town,
   You can always find Euler somewhere peeking around.
   'Tis his favorite game, every point he can name,
   For him touchers, o'er tees and fast runs are the same.
   Hence Billy got nervy, for big game butted in,
   We'll now raise his salary for he belongs to Berlin.
   Of scalps he peeled dozens; poor Turnbull was slain,
   It was a tough battle but victory came.

   Chorus:
   Euler, Cleghorn, Boehmer and Sims,
   You're the boys,
   You made them all "Tremble" and "Turnbull" was seen
   To turn pale at the stunts you pulled off on the green.
   EULER you're the hero to-day,
   So we'll all join in three hearty
   Cheers for your rink,
   Hip, hip, hip, hooray!

2. When Harvey from tennis to bowls took a turn,
   How all the cracks shivered at how he did learn.
   Hence his place on the line-up was honestly won,
   And now he's still wondering how it was done.
   Ask Woodyatt the tale, you will get but a groan,
   "For this loss of my rep. I can never atone."
   The sting of this ad. hits the Indians full deep
   "Eight useless old bowls we've for sale very cheap."

3. You've all heard of Herman, his tale about coal,
   But say as a second who says he can't bowl?
   He said for the outing I'll gladly be bumped,
   And at Euler's bid he did quickly jump.
   They say 'twas the music of the cataract's roar,
   That tuned Herman's bowls to lick Whitehead some more.
   Poor Whitehead's still wailing may the falls o'er me roll
   E'er again I'll get bumptious and think I can bowl.

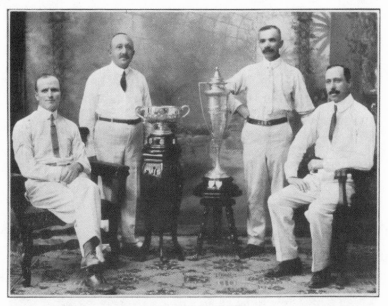

THE EULER RINK
Left to right: W. D. Euler, Herman Boehmer, W. G. Cleghorn, Harvey J. Sims.
Winners Ontario Bowling Association Trophy (1909 and 1913), and
Dominion Bowling Association Trophy (1913).

CLUB OF THE MUNICIPAL GOLF COURSE

HEAD OFFICE OF THE ECONOMICAL FIRE INSURANCE COMPANY

Officers: Henry Knell, President; Carl Kranz, Vice-President; F. W. Snyder, Managing Director; W. W. Foot, Secretary-Treasurer; A. H. Devitt, Superintendent of Agencies; L. J. Shantz, Inspector.

Directors: L. O. Breithaupt, Hon. W. D. Euler, M.P., Henry Knell. Carl Kranz, Henry C. Krug, Reinhold A. Lang, W. J. Motz, M.A., H. J. Sims, K.C., F. W. Snyder.

4. With Cleghorn, wee Scotty, this tale we must close,
'08 saw him enter the arena of bowls.
His nerve is well judged by the size of the trunk,
That he took in his car to bring home all the junk.
His eyes were e'er peeled to "Harass" his man,
Poor Lloyd couldn't stand it and hence bit the sand.
And Scotty has joy since the Dutchmen's lone four
Did shut out all comers, got covered with lore.

Afterward the same quartette repeated their Provincial victory and won the Dominion championship at Toronto.

General

The annual meetings were the crown point of the year. When the club was flush, they dined at the Berlin Club. One year, Secretary Weir set down in his minutes: "Mr. (Scotty) Cleghorn, the president, occupied the chair and in his novel, impressive manner called the meeting to order—when there was no disorder. He told of all he had done for bowling and the bowling club—which didn't take him long."

Among bowling greens, the local grounds rank with the best. Martin Schiedel made a hobby of their upkeep for many years. Once a green pea complained of his inability to make a toucher every time. "If you could," said Skip Middleton, "no-one would play against you."

The late Eddie Wettlaufer, a prince of amateur sport, accompanied a Canadian team to Great Britain in 1913. He and Harvey Sims likewise toured the Isles in 1924 and 1926. For more than twenty years Eddie skipped a rink at the International tournaments in Buffalo, N.Y. One of his partners from 1913 on was the late J. J. A. Weir, and from 1920 onward, Clarence E. Cornell.

In 1926, the club had ninety-five members. Forty-seven of them went to other places, sixteen died, and thirty-two still play. In 1934, the club had ninety members. That year, the Hon. W. D. Euler, Harvey Sims, and W. G. Cleghorn took part in the British Empire games in London, England.

Among the secretaries after Mr. Weir were E. J. Payson, E. A. Wismer, and L. H. Dahmer.

, The officers in 1937 were: Vincent Thiele, President, and C. E. Shantz, Secretary-Treasurer.

In the old clubhouse there was once posted up beside the telephone, "Life is not holding good cards, but playing a poor hand well."   ,

ST. MATTHEW'S LUTHERAN CHURCH

St. Matthew's Lutheran Church was founded on February 23, 1904. Several hundred Lutherans, who had severed their congregational connection, invited the Rev. E. Hoffmann, D.D., of Hamilton, to confer with them on the advisability of establishing a new congregation. As a result it was determined to organize one, to designate it St. Matthew's Lutheran Church and affiliate with the Canada Synod. The first Church Council consisted of: C. Meisner, August Tobian, Karl Mueller, Jacob Baetz, Adam Sippel, Louis Sattler and H. A. Hagen. Dr. Hoffman, who was then President of the Canada Synod, was appointed pastor. The first regular service was held in the court house on March 6, 1904.

Shortly afterward the congregation purchased an unoccupied Methodist Church in North Queen Street and a parsonage at No. 43 Alma Street. In Queen Street abundant harvests followed, necessitating a larger church. The preparatory steps to that end were taken in 1912. Soon thereafter Dr. Hoffman accepted a call to the First Lutheran Church in Toronto. He was succeeded at St. Matthew's by the Rev. C. R. Tappert, D.D., of Meriden, Conn., in January, 1913. Subsequently so many persons attended the services that not infrequently one or more fainted away in the auditorium, which led the church council to hasten the preparations for building.

A site was purchased at the corner of Benton and Church Streets, from Charles B. Dunke, for $5,000. Spier & Gehrke, architects, of Detroit, designed the edifice. After its inception, the first church was sold for $14,000. Besides the members contributed $8,000 to the building fund and raised $3,500 more by a mortgage. The cornerstone was laid on May 24, 1914. Several months later the World War broke out, bringing chaos in its train. As a consequence the members debated whether to suspend building operations until after the restoration of peace. However wiser counsels prevailed and the work was proceeded with. The church as it now stands was consecrated to the worship of God on March 7, 1915, in the presence of 2,000 persons. When completed there remained a debt of $25,000 on the property. The church historian says of those trying years: "Meantime war's alarum spread. It invaded the peaceful precincts of the sanctuary and Pastor Tappert was its victim. His last confirmation service is graven indelibly upon

ST. MATTHEW'S LUTHERAN CHURCH

THE REV. JOHN SCHMIEDER, Pastor

the memory of a congregation that will ever hold him in grateful remembrance as the builder of her beautiful church, as a scholarly preacher and a cultured Christian gentleman."

After Dr. Tabbert's retirement he was appointed editor-in-chief of the *Lutherischer Herold* and abode in Philadelphia. The Rev. C. Zarnke followed him at St. Matthew's and "guided the church ship safely through the storms that threatened without and within, gave courage to the faint-hearted—inspiring the congregation with hope and confidence." At the end of 1917 ill health compelled Pastor Zarnke to accept a less arduous charge. He successively became pastor of Sullivan Parish, of the Conestoga Church and of Zion Church at Pembroke. The Rev. M. G. W. Arendt, pastor emeritus, then supplied St. Matthew's pulpit for four months. On May 1, 1918, the induction of the Rev. John Schmieder, formerly of Philadelphia, as regular pastor, followed. Pastor Schmieder is the incumbent. Under his able leadership St. Matthews Church has advanced in every department.

The Sunday Schools

A German Sunday School was organized in a hall over the old Bank of Hamilton on February 28, 1904. It began with thirty-six teachers and 120 children. The first officers were: Hon. President, Dr. Hoffman; President, John E. Vogt; Superintendent, Conrad Boettger; Secretary, Carl Emmerich; Assistant Secretary, A. L. Bitzer; Treasurer, Adam Treusch; Financial Secretaries, the Misses Erica Veit and Rose Berner. For a time the school was in the Queen Street church. Quarters for this department were set aside in the present church on November 14, 1914. Mr. Boettger acted as superintendent until 1915, when he was succeeded by C. S. Smith. Mr. Smith served until February, 1928, when the incoming leader was William Weicker. In 1933 the officers were: Edward Westphal, Superintendent; John E. Vogt, Secretary; William Vogt, Librarian; and Miss Ruth Otterbein, Pianist.

An English Sunday School was organized in 1919 with 100 scholars. The first teachers were: Jacob H. Eydt, Superintendent; the Misses Emma Berner, Eleanor Smith, Florence Treusch, Hilda Sattler, Irene Heldman and Clara Berner. In 1933 this school had an enrollment of 794 pupils, teachers and officers. The officers were: Mr. Eydt, Superintendent; George Hoelscher, Assistant Superintendent; W. H. Schaefer, Secretary; and Miss E. Schaus, Treasurer.

A Cradle Roll was formed in 1921 and is directed by a bevy of ladies. Periodically they visit the tots' homes to become acquainted with the mothers, leave booklets on Christian child-training and send out birthday cards. A picnic is also held in the summer and an entertainment at Christmas. There were 245 names on the Cradle Roll in 1933. The officers then were: Mrs. A. H. Eaton, Superintendent; Mrs. A. F. Klugman, Assistant Superintendent; Mrs. George Hoelscher, Secretary; Mrs. H. Doerr, Treasurer; and Mrs. A. Heldman, Roll Keeper.

When the Sunday School was founded the number of scholars at the end of 1904 was 315. In 1933, the number, including the Cradle Roll, was 1200.

St. Matthew's Choir

St. Matthew's choir was organized concurrently with the church. The primary conductor was Conrad Boettger and the members: the Misses Elizabeth Wuest, Christina Koch, Lovina Oswald, Emma Hertel, Ida Smith, Ella Steen, Augusta Neigel, Phoeba Haymaker, Sopranos; Anna Wuest, Marie Smith, Clara Steen, Margaret Zimmerman, Elizabeth Meisner, Altos; Erich Messerschmidt, Casper Oschmann, Carl Linke, Tenors; Adolph Scharlach, Alfred Lindner, John Steifke, John Meisner, George Treusch, Wm. Keil, Wm. Oppermann and Jerry Steiner, Bassos. Mr. Boettger, who was a gifted teacher, continued until 1915, when Otto G. Smith succeeded him as choirmaster. At intervals his choir delighted large audiences with cantatas and sacred concerts. A convocation on Church Music, for example, was held in St. Matthew's on June 15, 1921, under the auspices of the U.L.C. Thirty-five choirs drawn from the Canada Synodal churches took part and formed a massed choir of 125 voices. St. Matthew's choir was augmented by the choirs of St. Peter's and St. John's Churches. Among the prominent visitors present were: the Rev. J. F. Ohl, Mus.D., D.D., the Rev. L. D. Reed, D.D., the Rev. G. C. Rees, D.D., and Wm. Benbow, Mus.D. The committee said of the choir's singing, "The choir was in splendid form. . . . The deep impression made by the service will not soon be forgotten. It was worship in the truest sense—a revelation of the potent influence the best type of church music can have in inciting the human heart to genuine devotion."

Mr. Smith was obliged on account of business demands to retire in 1922. On March 1st, of that year, he was followed by F. K. Thiele of Toronto. Mr. Thiele received his musical training in Germany and was a man of lofty ideals. Two years later he accepted a position in New York City. Mr. Otto Smith was again pressed into service and continued from September, 1924, till February, 1929. When he resigned the leadership he was elected an honorary life member of the choir. Clarence Totzke was chosen choirmaster in succession of Mr. Smith and faithfully discharged his duties for five years. Early in 1934 Mr. Totzke voluntarily gave up the position and was succeeded by W. H. Bishop, F.R.C.O. Mr. Bishop is a specialist as regards voice production and an experienced director of choirs.

Der Frauenverein

Der Frauenverein of St. Matthew's was grounded on April 4, 1904, with sixty-four members. In that year fifty-seven more members were added to the Ladies' Aid Society. The women raised money for the building fund and missions, supplied flowers for the altar and visited the sick. At Christmas they called on the oldest members, bearing gifts. In 1933, Mrs. (Pastor) Ramthun, the Secretary, recorded that der Frauenverein had 175 members, including twenty-nine surviving charter members.

In June, 1920, Pastor Schmieder and his council undertook to wipe out the church debt. The campaign closed on August 1, 1920, and all the subscriptions were paid up on or before April 30, 1921.

The Women's Missionary Society

A Women's Missionary Society was organized in 1927 and in 1933 had seventy members. The officers then were: Mrs. W. Strahl, President; Mrs. A. Meyer, First Vice-President; Mrs. (Rev.) John Schmieder, Second Vice-President; Mrs. C. Musselman, Recording Secretary; Mrs. H. Hollinger, Financial Secretary; Miss H. Heldman, Treasurer; and Miss L. Prast, Pianist. The society promotes the interests of Home and Foreign Missions, visits the sick and despondent and at Christmas distributes hampers among the needy. Foreign missionary donations included a shipment of hospital garments to India and fifty dollars for the maintenance of a Bible Woman in that distant land.

St. Matthew's Luther League

A St. Matthew's Luther League was formed a number of years ago and serves the church socially and spiritually. In 1933, for example, a Life Service Programme was held in May and on Labor Day the League was host to the first Workers' Conference of the Luther League of Canada. The officers in 1934 were: Ralph Buschert, President; Miss Marie Barker, Vice-President; Miss Helen Haas, Secretary; and Miss Valeria Steiner, Treasurer.

St. Matthew's Bell

St. Matthew's Church has the largest swinging bell in Ontario. It weighs 5,747 pounds and at the mouth is five feet, five inches in diameter. The bell was cast by Heinrich Ulrich of Apolda, Thuringia, and is a masterpiece. The inscription on the bell consists of Psalm 95: 6, 7, and, "This bell was dedicated to the Glory of God A.D. 1923, by Christina Berlet and by the members of St. Matthew's Congregation of Kitchener, Ontario."

Since February 23, 1930, Pastor Schmieder's morning sermons have been broadcast by station C.K.C.R. "Kirche Daheim" is a vast unseen audience comprising the aged, the sick and infirm, most of whom are shut-ins. "Fan Mail" has come in from many places in Ontario, Michigan and Pennsylvania. In 1934 the Rev. R. Mosig composed a fine poem, "Lied Einer Kranken," expressing his gratitude for this good-will offering.

When St. Matthew's Church was founded it had 579 souls. In 1933 the congregation had reached the 3,000 mark.

In 1934 St. Matthew's Church Council was comprised of the Rev. John Schmieder, President; A. F. Klugman, Vice-President; A. W. Sandrock, Recording Secretary; Adolph Damman, Financial Secretary; Emil C. Schultz, Treasurer; Elder Rudolph Kraemer, Elder Wm. G. Roth, A. H. Eaton and Albert Schiefele.

SOURCES

The Twenty-fifth and Thirtieth Annual Reports. By the Rev. John Schmieder and Church Officers.

EXPERIMENTS

Nelson and Milton Good and Isaac Neuber founded the Le Roi Motorcycle Co. in 1902. In addition to motorcycles they made a number of automobiles. Sales of autos in Canada, however, soon passed to American companies, for they could export motor-cars at a lower price than Canadian concerns could manufacture them.

Two years later Wm. Redpath and Andrew Reid of Toronto came in and organized the Redpath Motor Company. Among the local shareholders were: T. A. McLellan, David B. Bowman, and George Seiler. The company leased the "incubator" in Hall's lane from C. B. Dunke, and set out to manufacture a replica of a one-cylinder French car.

The main difficulty was to hire mechanics who could build gas-engines and who could properly cast aluminum parts. Their scrap-pile rose higher and their capital-sum fell lower. Moreover, their cars were excessive in price, and in time the attempt was given up.

While they were engaged in their experiments, R. R. Olds of Detroit came over to compare notes, while the guest of Oscar Rumpel. He had just organized the Oldsmobile Company to make a one-cylinder car with a chain drive. After his visit he abandoned the one-cylinder car and made first a two-cylinder and then a four-cylinder car with a shaft drive.

After he had gone the rumor spread that Henry Ford had been here. It was whispered that he might buy an interest in the Red-path Company and remove to Berlin. To clear up the point, a letter was written to Mr. Ford in Detroit. Through his secretary he answered on January 7, 1931, and said,

> Referring to your letter of December 5th.
>
> Mr. Ford paid a visit to Kitchener in the year 1920, which is the only visit he recalls every having made. This was long after the Ford Motor Company was in existence. His visit to Kitchener was only a result of passing through on his way to the Toronto Exposition.

Eventful 1905

Prince Louis of Battenburg, vice-admiral of the British fleet, anchored in Quebec harbor in 1905. He was born in Hesse, the birthplace of many Berlin citizens. The "Hessens" invited him to visit the town, and he accepted the invitation. At the Berlin club, Mrs. Charles Mueller prepared a typical Hessen Freustueck. The prince particularly relished the sour roast. After the luncheon a public reception was held in Victoria Park. Prince Louis fell in love with the park and the band's musical skill.

Berlin then had seventy factories, and sent out 165 commercial travellers. To bag more industries a part of Woodside park was set aside. Tuerk Bros. built a gasolene-engine works there; and later on Forwell Bros. erected an iron-pipe foundry. Others followed. Now the ancient recreation ground is chiefly factory footings.

In that year Charles A. Ahrens and A. W. Feick suggested that the town erect a hive for manufacturers and lease its divisions to beginners. The provincial laws, however, were not elastic enough to allow its being done.

The population had mounted to 11,705 souls, and there was a brisk demand for homes. The county sold off seventy-five building lots from the Poor House farm, and Martin Dunham subdivided and marketed five acres adjoining the House of Refuge.

The market value of urban property rose. John S. Schwartz and Frank Heiman amazed the public when they bought the Fellman block for $20,000; and citizens marvelled when Charles B. Dunke purchased the Berlin Shirt & Collar block for $26,000. To cap the climax, the Rev. J. E. Lynn of Berhen, N.Y., bought nine of the ten apartments in Courtland Avenue as an investment.

Longo Bros. of Sunny Italy, opened a wholesale and retail fruit store on the corner of King and College Streets. The Longos were the first merchants to illuminate their premises with electric light on a full measure.

Louis Sattler was a lover of trees, and as a school-trustee used to take boys out into the woods and impart tree lore. He applied also to Mrs. Mary Kaufman for the wherewithal to buy eighty trees for the Courtland Avenue school. The saplings included walnut, oak, and butternut.

Made-in-Berlin Exhibition

Under the auspices of the Musical Society, the Best Town in Canada held a "Made-in-Berlin" exhibition in October, 1905. Visitors spoke of it as "Berlin and her 57 varieties." Among the exhibits were:

Automobiles, Aluminum Ware, Automatic Switches, Aprons and Cuffs.
Buttons, Biscuits, Bicycles, Beet Sugar, Brick, and Brooms.
Cigars, Clothing, Cement Tile, Carriages, Confectionery, Collar Buttons, Covered Buttons, and Chemical Preparations.
Electric Meters.

Felt Footwear, Rubber Footwear, Leather Footwear, Household
Furniture, Upholstered Furniture, Furnaces, Foundry Castings
and Boilers.
Glues, Gloves, Gauntlets, and Gasolene Engines.
Ivory and Pearl Buttons.
Harness Leather, Sole Leather, and Lager Beer.
Monuments and Cement Work.
Paper Boxes, Pianos and Organs, Pivotal Bin Store Fittings, Robes
and Clothing.
Trunks and Bags.
Women's Wear, and Woodworking Machinery.

The exhibition was opened by Premier J. P. Whitney of
Toronto. He said,

> Today Berlin stands at the head of the procession in the
> Dominion. Such an occasion has never been known before in
> Canada. I will tell people to come here for lessons in enterprise
> and progress.

A SHOE STORE AND SHIRT COMPANIES

Soon after the Williams, Greene & Rome Co. began here, Harry
A. Hagen learned shirt cutting under Horace Messett. Later on,
Mr. Messett patented an improved shirt, which with the aid of
friends he manufactured in Galt. Mr. Hagen joined them, but the
venture came to grief. The assets were purchased by Henry S.
Boehmer and his son A. O., who then formed the Berlin Shirt &
Collar Co., with quarters in the Dunke block. Some time afterward
Mr. Hagen was appointed manager. Finally he bought the ma-
chinery and made shirts for Aaron Erb on a jobbing basis. Wiegand
Brothers operated the laundry. Subsequently the plant was moved
to 22 N. Queen Street, and purchased by J. E. Wiegand & Co. Ltd.,
who have since built up a large shirt, collar, and underwear pur-
suit. The heads of this company are M. E. Wiegand and H. A.
Wiegand.

Mr. Hagen, in association of John A. Lang, David Knipfel,
and Philip Ringler, then organized the Hagen Shirt & Collar Company. Four years later Mr. Hagen sold his interest and with his
brother C. W. Hagen opened a shoe store for men and another for
women in Henry Knell's block. Charles Hagen went out to the
Canadian West, when Adam Sippel joined Harry Hagen. Charles
is now local representative for the Canada Life Assurance Co.

When Harry Hagen was head of the Berlin Shirt & Collar Co., the late John Forsyth, manufacturers' agent for tailors' trimmings and buttons, sold some of his shirts. In 1906, Mr. Forsyth began the manufacture of shirts and engaged Mr. Hagen to make them. From that seed has sprung the nationally known house of John Forsyth Ltd., makers of shirts, collars, neckwear, pajamas, and underwear, of which the founder's son, J. D. C. Forsyth, is President.

The Lang Brothers

R. D. Lang and E. D. Lang have been lifelong residents of this community and were engaged in retail business for forty years. The brothers were born on their father's farm in the South Ward. From their doorstep little could be seen of Berlin except a few houses in Albert Street and the windmill on the Mecklenburger hill. As boys they walked 1½ miles to the Central (now Suddaby) School, carrying a dinnerpail, and often wading through the deep snow before a team had broken the road. Threshing-day interested them, and the crew, including a Negro named Charley Jones, who

E. D. LANG

R. D. LANG

had been raised by the Kolb family and could talk Pennsylvania-Dutch like a streak. The brothers attended the Friedensfest of 1871, and remember Detective John Klippert, whose stern face and robust voice struck terror in every evil-doer's heart. When he drove his bay pacer along the country road, every boy, bad or good, took to cover. That neighborhood was then entirely German and included such well-known names as Schmalz, Shelley, Stuckhart, Meyer, Kehl, Kramp, Karrow and Richert.

Mr. R. D. Lang, in the eighteen-nineties, had a house-furnishing store at 58 E. King Street. Later on he was manager of the house-furnishing department at Smyth Bros.

Mr. E. D. Lang's early experience was gained in H. S. Boehmer's store at 62 E. King Street. There was then much credit extended and a deal of bantering between buyer and seller, while due-bills were used as a means of exchange. Store due-bills were popular and negotiable almost everywhere, excepting at the tax collector's office. After passing through many hands, the due-bills found their way back to Boehmer's store, which redeemed them in merchandise. When the first street-car came down from Waterloo, merchants threw up their hat for joy, for it heralded more trade from the sister town.

Afterward Mr. E. D. Lang was for a number of years with G. B. Ryan & Co. of Guelph, who opened a large dry-goods house at 34 E. King Street. Mr. Lang was sent to Europe a number of times to buy merchandise for the company. In 1904, he and his brother, R. D., bought the premises at 63 W. King Street and established a dry-goods and house-furnishing business, trading as Lang Bros. Subsequently they incorporated the enterprise and admitted W. C. Treacy, C. H. Germann, M. H. Schmitt, and F. A. Shantz to partnership. The Lang Treacy Co. Ltd.'s principles were: good value and good service; and was one of the most successful in Ontario. Several years ago the Canadian Department Stores Ltd. bought their stock. Mr. Schmitt is now manager of this store; and Mr. Germann of the Brodey-Draimin Fur Co.

Since the sale of that business, the Brothers Lang have lived in retirement. Mr. R. D. Lang, who has long been a member of the Board of Trade, has of late years been actively connected with the Red Cross Society. He has been also treasurer of the King Street Baptist Church almost since its organization.

Mr. E. D. Lang was for nearly twenty years a member of either the Board of Education or the Public School Board, and twice chairman. During his term of service, nearly all the schools were built or rebuilt. He was one of the first to introduce organized play into the playgrounds. The Social Welfare Society has for many years had his support, and during the late depression he sat in the Family Relief Board. For a long period, Mr. Lang was superintendent of the King Street Baptist Sunday School. He is a member of the K.-W. Kiwanis Club and enjoys their good fellowship, and appreciates the opportunity to give vocational guidance to twin-city youth. In his opinion, a young man is not likely to succeed in life unless he chooses a suitable vocation, for most failures are the result of a wrong start or a lack of application.

A. R. Goudie

As a boy, A. R. Goudie sold vegetables from the home garden to the housewives in his native town of Hespeler. Next, newspapers, soap, stationery, and everything a lad could sell, for he was a born salesman. As a youth he apprenticed himself to Smyth Bros., here, and learned the dry-goods business. In his first year he received $100. Afterward he was with M. C. Cressman, Lang Bros., and G. B. Ryan & Co. Mr. Goudie has the faculty of being able to think a matter through to the end. He is likewise practical and thorough, while his ability as an organizer accounts to a large degree for his success as a merchant. As a citizen, Mr. Goudie has taken a keen interest in needy persons. He was for fifteen years Secretary of the Mothers' Allowances Board, and for many years a member of the Children's Aid Society, serving at one time as its President. He is now President of the Retail Merchants Association of Canada. The big store's silver jubilee was observed in 1934. His staff then presented him with a bronze plaque bearing a sculptured likeness of himself and an inscription attesting their high esteem.

Lippert's Home Furnishing Co.

Lippert's Home Furnishing Co. was started in 1905 by the late Edward Lippert. Previously, Mr. Lippert had been buying and selling real estate in Calgary. Here he built the Mayfair Hotel. His growing retail establishment is now managed by Edward Lippert and A. J. Reinhart.

IMPORTERS OF
DRY GOODS & HOUSEFURNISHINGS

CARPETS   CURTAINS   LINOLEUM   WALL PAPER

LANG BROS. & CO.

GOUDIE'S DEPARTMENT STORE AND ITS FOUNDER

In 1909, with a staff of four, A. R. Goudie laid the foundation of the Department Store at 42 E. King Street. A disastrous fire swept away his stock in 1918. Five years later he purchased the former John Querin hotel property, facing King and Queen Streets, from F. W. Snyder, and in 1925 built the first unit of the present department store. In 1934 the store was enlarged, giving it a selling floor space of more than 50,000 square feet, which is the largest of any store outside of the biggest cities in Ontario. The staff now averages 100.

G. H. Schnarr, Button Manufacturer

George H. Schnarr began the manufacture of covered buttons in 1908. Since then he has branched also into a general line of buttons and specialties. In his thirty years of business life, Mr. Schnarr has built up an extensive connection throughout the Dominion. His diversions are bowling and golf.

WM. H. BREITHAUPT AND GRAND RIVER CONTROL

Wm. H. Breithaupt, C.E., has long been in touch with the Grand River. As a boy it drew him and his fishing-rod; as a youth, spots appealed to him as sites for summer homes; and as an engineer he saw a stream that runs wild in the spring, that if bridled would serve where it now lays waste. *The Berlin Daily Telegraph* said in September, 1906,

> Mr. W. H. Breithaupt, who has gone over the Grand River from its sources to its mouth, says that not ten percent of the available power is being used. By a most injurious piece of legislation its natural reservoir, Luther swamp, was obliterated thirty years ago. Reservoirs along the river are unknown. Without authority from anyone, individuals and municipalities are making it an open sewer and garbage receptacle.

Mr. Breithaupt made further studies of the river. In 1908 he spoke to the Engineers Club of Toronto and showed the necessity of conserving the waters and regulating their flow. His fellow engineers approved of his plan. Next he tried to rouse the Grand River Valley. The river towns, however, were like the man whose roof leaked: "When it was wet he couldn't fix it; when it was dry it didn't need it." Berlin, for example, had plenty of artesian-well water, while a sewer-farm and Schneider's creek set the sewage. Why worry?

Nevertheless Mr. Breithaupt was seized of the danger and urged the valley to take action. Nature gave his design a fillip in 1912, when the river's rampage was the worst in forty-two years. Hart-hit Galt mustered up a conference to hear Mr. Breithaupt speak on "River Physics and the Recent Flood Flow of the Grand." He stressed the fact that the woods were disappearing—in Waterloo County only one-eighth was then under bush—leaving no natural means of holding back spring freshets. The unbridled waters sally out and flood the valley, causing much damage. He counselled the formation of a flood-prevention alliance and an appeal to the Provincial Government for aid in controlling the river. As a result the dripping towns set up a Grand River Improvement Association.

The association held its first convention in Galt in July, 1912. Mr. Breithaupt told them they could avert floods by storage basins at chosen points. Given these, the stored waters could be let out in the dry months to increase the river's flow. Among those who sanctioned his plan were: R. Thompson and U. Richardson of Elora, Mayor Hartman and F. Cockshutt of Brantford, and J. H. Fisher, M.P., of Paris. H. F. Jones, City Engineer of Brantford, said that between 1887 and 1912 his city had spent $114,000 in trying to protect itself from floods. Mr. Cockshutt agreed that the cause of floods is because there are only fingers of forest left and held that Ontario should as surely have a river policy as a road policy.

In August, 1912, two-score delegates met the Whitney cabinet. The Berlin envoys were Mr. Breithaupt, D. B. Detweiler and George M. DeBus. Mr. Breithaupt told the cabinet that the Grand River in its meanderings is about 170 miles long and drains an area of nearly 2600 square miles. When the stream was in flood, 24,000 cubic feet per second passed a given point and 40 cu. ft. per second at summer ebb. Storage basins afford the solution. The impounding of 15,000 cu. ft. per second during a flood will create a reserve of more than 2,000,000,000 cubic feet.

The flux of the stream in 1912 was probably equal to what it was before deforestation. But with most of the trees gone and the swamps dried up, the run-off was speeded up and caused heavy losses. The benefits of conservation would be two-fold: (a) the prevention of damage by assaults of the floods; (b) the provision of a method to ease out the stored waters in the dry months, which would enable water-driven mills to run for a longer time and at greater capacity.

The Reaction

Although the plea was a novel one, the cabinet were impressed by the facts laid before them. The Hydro-Electric Power Commission was soon afterward asked to make a topographical survey of the Grand River Valley. From 1913 to 1919 Hydro Engineers surveyed the river to a point above Elora, including the Nith and

WM. H. BREITHAUPT, C.E.
Father of Grand River Control.

MAYOR J. ALBERT SMITH, M.P.P.
Member, Ontario Hydro-Electric Power Commission.

Ex-MAYOR C. MORTIMER BEZEAU

Ex-MAYOR EDWARD E. RATZ

A FEW KITCHENER HOMES

These are typical of the class of home occupied by the average industrial employee.

—Courtesy, W. Max Euler.

Conestoga Rivers. The investigation was then taken over by the Dominion Powers Branch. In 1931 the Provincial Department of Lands, Forests and Mines assumed the probe. Meantime the Grand River Boards of Trade had been hammering on river control, and in 1932 the Provincial Government appointed a Grand River Conservation Commission with the members that follow: William Philip, Galt, President; F. P. Adams, Brantford, Secretary; Marcel Pequegnat, Kitchener, E. T. Sterne, Brantford, Robert Kerr, Fergus, and George Thompson, Caledonia.

Since Mr. Breithaupt inducted Grand River Control, Kitchener has become more deeply interested in its vagrancies. For the Water Commissioners have bought land near the river, at Bridgeport, as a future source of supply, and the City Council has built a $500,000 sewage-disposal plant at Doon, on the stream.

In October, 1933, Hydro Engineers offered a Grand River Drainage Scheme. It is planned in four stages: (1) to build dams at Luther and Waldemar, at a cost of $673,000; (2) to raise a dam at Hollen on the Conestogo tributary, at $686,000; (3) to erect Conestoga dam No. 2, to cost $791,000; (4) and to hatch the Elora Development, at an outlay of $805,000. Total estimated cost of the scheme, $2,955,000.

In the summer of 1936 the valley suffered a two-months' drought. Wells dried up and the Grand became a runnel, with a flow at Doon of only 13 cu. ft. per second. Hugh Templin of Fergus says: "Eighty years ago the Grand River was a navigable stream which allowed steamboats to ply between Buffalo and Brantford. Canoes and rafts were also plentiful for another 75 miles, as far as Elora, carrying produce and people. From the saw-mills of Grand Valley, Fergus and Elora, logs were floated down the river to Galt in the spring—square timber cut in the bush during the winter. Today it is impossible for even a canoe to travel over the course. In August, 1936, the Grand River, from its source near Dundalk to Fergus, was a dry stretch of fifty miles."

The long drought of 1936 opened the eyes of the 270,000 inhabitants of the Grand River Valley to the need for river control. Since then the Conservation Commission has appealed to the Ontario and Dominion Governments for assistance. Marcel Pequegnat, Waterworks Engineer, gave valuable service to the preparation of the appeal and Mayor J. Albert Smith to the presentation of the adverse situation to the authorities.

As a result of their pleas, Premier Mitchell Hepburn promised to bear a large share of the cost. In October, 1937, the Mackenzie King Government likewise assented to shoulder a similar share, to provide work for the unemployed.

The commissioners asked for the construction of two dams. The one at Waldemar and the other in the Conestoga River, a tributary of the Grand, near Hollen. The estimated cost of the two dams is $1,500,000. The Dominion Government agreed to bear 37.5 percent of the cost, provided that the Provincial Government passed legislation at its next session authorizing the work and contributing also 37.5 percent of the expense. The remaining 25 percent is to be borne by the municipalities of the Grand River Valley.

Thus Mr. Breithaupt will have the satisfaction of seeing his vision realized.

THE ARNOTT INSTITUTE

Forty years ago, Dr. W. J. Arnott founded an institute for the cure of stammering. The institute was for many years situated in the late Dr. R. Mylius's residence in Frederick Street. The Arnott Institute's method of treatment is a scientific one, and in the course of time attracted patients from many parts of Canada and the United States. Afer the Doctor's death in 1905, the direction of the institute devolved on Fred S. Krug. Now the institution is at 515 South Queen Street.

CLUBS

The Berlin Club was formed in the eighteen-nineties with quarters above what is now the S. R. Ernst store. In 1907 they had 115 members. A decade after this the fraternity was renamed the Lancaster Club.

A Canadian Club was organized on January 28, 1908. The primary officers were: C. H. Mills, President; W. M. Davis, first Vice-President; Dr. J. F. Honsberger, second Vice-President; Solon Lutz, Secretary; Wm. H. Breithaupt, Treasurer; and H. W. Brown, Literary Secretary.

The Grand River Golf and Country Club was established by Berlin and Waterloo men of affairs on September 28, 1909. The first officers were: Wm. H. Breithaupt, President; Jacob Hespeler, first Vice-President; W. M. Cram, second Vice-President; and W. M. O. Lochead, Secretary-Treasurer. Executive Committee: Edward F. Seagram, C. E. Hoffman, and Dr. Wallace.

The club was capitalized at $40,000. Sixty-one men and women purchased shares. Forty-four acres known as the Hamel farm, lying east of the Sugar factory, were acquired; and in 1910 a handsome clubhouse and 9-hole course laid out.

Then only midirons played. Now their sons and daughters begin at ten or twelve years. Saturday matches for men were popular. Three hours of play in the sunshine, followed by a shower and dinner, put the turf-cutters atop the world. Town lads who served as caddies usually saved their 40-cent fee. One niblick banked $500.

For competitions among the playing members of both sexes, E. F. Seagram, T. W. Seagram, the Mesdames Seagram, W. M. O. Lochead, and others presented trophies.

The clubhouse became a focal point for social diversions and the entertainment of prominent visitors.

A European, while playing a round of golf, said: "Canadians do not yet know how to dress nor how to live."

At Bridgeport the nineteenth hole was a favorite putting place. On hearing a player say that two swallows do not make a summer, a wit remarked, "But three do."

In recent years, the members purchased a large area of land between Kitchener and Waterloo for an 18-hole course. It was named the Westmount Golf and Country Club, and has a well-appointed club house.

A private company bought the Bridgeport links and still operates that club. The city has become golf-minded.

THE PENTECOSTAL TABERNACLE

The Pentecostal Tabernacle, an outgrowth of the Mennonite Church, was founded in 1907, with twenty-five charter members. Among the founders were C. R. Miller, Aaron Shoemaker, W. H. Hilborn, and Nathaniel Eby (Secretary). The members convened in two combined rooms above the old China Hall and Schell Bros.'

grocery, in East King Street. Two years later, larger quarters were procured in a building beside the firehall in Frederick Street. There a Sunday School was organized, with between twenty-five and thirty-five pupils in four classes, and with Milton Shantz as superintendent.

The congregation steadily increased in number and influence. Presently, a move was made to a building in Scott Street, near King Street. There progress was continuous until 1927, when the present edifice in Benton Street, near Church Street, was erected at an approximate cost of $30,000. The Tabernacle seats 650 worshippers.

One hundred and sixty-five families attend the church services. Instead of a choir, the Tabernacle has a twelve-piece orchestra, under the leadership of Mr. James Tupman. During the last three years, the congregation has donated $7,018 to Missions. In 1934, the Sunday School had an average attendance of 185 children, grouped in seventeen classes. Mr. Tupman is the superintendent. The children's contributions in 1932-33-34 amounted to $1,840.

The ministers who have served the congregation since its foundation are: the Rev. Mr. Edwards, prior to 1912; the Rev. G. A. Chambers, 1912-16; the Rev. R. E. McAllister, 1916-18; the Rev. Mr. Adams, 1918-21; return of the Rev. Mr. Chambers, 1922-25; the Rev. W. L. Duffin, 1925-33; and the Rev. F. R. Jolley, from May, 1933, to the present day.

In the religious life of Kitchener, Waterloo and Bridgeport, the Pentecostal Tabernacle is taking a prominent part.

THE STREET RAILWAY AND NIAGARA POWER

Early in 1905, the first Light Commissioners, and the superintendent, retired. The second commission consisted of A. L. Breithaupt (Chairman), Jacob Kaufman, August R. Lang, and George Lippert. The new commissioners thought well of the Niagara Power project and nursed the electric plant on producer-gas for five years.

On the advice of the commissioners, the town bought the Street Railway in 1906, and kept the services of Victor S. McIntyre, manager. The eight cars and eight trailers were run on the 3.2

miles of trackage by steam-power generated in an Albert Street power-house, with storage batteries to handle peak loads.

The Power Investigators Report

The Western Ontario Power Commission, headed by E. W. B. Snider, published its report on March 28, 1906. The commission recommended the Whitney Government, then in office, to develop and transmit or buy and transmit Niagara power for the Union of Municipalities. In passing, the commissioners served without compensation.

Mr. Detweiler straighway urged the interested municipalities to send a monster deputation down to Toronto to plead for action. At that point the local superintendent of the lighting plant publicly said that Berlin was the poorest town in Canada into which to introduce Niagara power, since so many factories burned refuse for fuel and heating. In reply, Mr. Detweiler said that of the 2,566 h.p. used by local factories only 589 h.p. was produced with offal. Furthermore, steam-power averaged $48 a h.p., while the Light Commissioners' charge for electric current was $90 a h.p. A host of nearly 1500 strong and mostly from Waterloo County invaded Queen's Park and called on the Government to act. Premier Whitney said the situation teemed with difficulties, but the Government would settle the question.

Quickly, Niagara Falls, St. Catherines, and other towns in the peach belt presented a counter petition. A hundred men wearing badges with "Niagara Falls objects to the Transmission or Development of Power by the Government," appeared before the cabinet. The bluff Premier told them that other places beside those in the Niagara Peninsula had the right to secure power at the lowest cost, and they would get cheap power whether it meant government ownership or not.

The Hon. Adam Beck, a member of the cabinet, introduced into the Legislature a Bill on May 6, 1906. It was entitled: "An Act to provide for the Transmission of Power to the Municipalities." After much opposition within and without the House, the measure became law.

The Ontario Hydro-Electric Power Commission

On June 7, 1906, the Government appointed an Ontario Hydro-Electric Power Commission. The members were: the Hon. Adam

Beck (Chairman), the Hon. J. S. Hendrie and W. K. McNaught, M.P.P. The commission made a forty-year contract with the Ontario Power Company, agreeing to buy 25,000 h.p. at $9.40 a h.p., or if the load increased to 100,000 h.p., to pay $9 a h.p. Next they set out to sell power to the interested towns. These were required to guarantee proportions of the costs entailed in erecting power stations and lines. If the venture failed, each contracting municipality would be liable for its share of the loss. A baker's dozen, including Berlin, passed the necessary bylaws covering the capital guarantee. Here, the town council acted after Commissioners Jacob Kaufman and August R. Lang fathered a motion recommending the step.

In 1908, the McGuigan Construction Company was awarded the contract for building the power lines, 293 miles in all. The system was planned by Peter W. Sothman, a Danish engineer. By 1910, the steel towers were up and the copper wire strung.

Arrival of Niagara Power

A test of the power lines was made on September 1, 1910, and a load of 120,000 volts turned on. The copper wires stood up without a break.

The Government decided that Berlin should be the first municipality officially to receive Niagara power. The day chosen was October 11, 1910. The town sent invitations to the power municipalities, prominent Canadians and Americans to attend a 3-day celebration. Among the guests were Premier Whitney, the Hon. Adam Beck, E. W. B. Snider, D. B. Detweiler, and Colonel Greene of the Ontario Power Company.

Four thousand guests and townsmen assembled in the auditorium to greet the new Slave. The interior was pitch dark. A second after 3.30 p.m., Premier Whitney placed his hand over Adam Beck's and taking the Power Minister's finger in his own, pressed a key. Instantly the auditorium was flooded with light, while the throng cheered themselves hoarse.

Mayor C. C. Hahn next read a civic welcome addressed to the Premier and Mr. Beck. Mr. Whitney signalled Mr. Beck to respond first. The Hon. Adam said in part,

> The event we are about to celebrate marks the inception of the greatest municipal enterprise on the continent. It is befitting that

Niagara Power should be first turned on in Berlin, for it is the home of men of vision. They called the first meeting of representative men together to consider ways and means of procuring electric power for manufacturing and other purposes. Of the dozen original contracting municipalities, six are in Waterloo County.

The work of the Ontario Hydro-Electric Power Commission is just begun. We shall not rest until we have no more coal-oil, no more gas, and, I hope, no more coal.

Premier Whitney, following Mr. Beck, said among other things:

This is a great day for Berlin and a great day for Ontario. For an experiment has been brought into practical operation. It is one of the most important of modern times. Without hesitation, I say that no Government in Canada ever took such risks on behalf of the people. We have been attacked, vilified and slandered. Men from the lowest in the land up to the Prime Minister of Great Britain were approached by our opponents to destroy our power legislation. Men who pretended to be friendly to the Hydro-Electric project made secret efforts to have the Laurier Government disallow our legislation. All their plans, however, failed.

We can now breathe easy. Looking on the accomplished fact, it is no disparagement of the men who labored early and late for this service, to express our appreciation of the heavy sacrifices and services rendered by Mr. Beck. We, his fellow ministers, can never forget his confidence in the outcome and the pluck with which he stood up against all attacks.

Among the mottoes in the auditorium was the one that follows: "Berlin, Ontario, the first city in the world to receive electric power transmitted at 110,000 volts. October 11, 1910."

When the Power Bund Received Niagara Power

NAME	DATE	QUANTITY
Berlin	Sept. 29, 1910	604 h.p.
Guelph	Nov. 13, 1910	248 "
Waterloo	Nov. 13, 1910	167 "
Preston	Nov. 29, 1910	134 "
Woodstock	Nov. 30, 1910	450 "
London	Dec. 2, 1910	805 "
Stratford	Dec. 25, 1910	54 "
Hespeler	Jan. 5, 1911	87 "
Hamburg	Feb. 3, 1911	100 "
St. Thomas	Feb. 22, 1911	134 "
Galt	Mar. 15, 1911	80 "
Toronto	Mar. 24, 1911	805 "
Ingersoll	Apr. 1, 1911	—
St. Marys	Apr. 21, 1911	135 "

From official reports.

The City of Kitchener now purchases 20,000 h.p.

Light Commissioners

Mr. Kaufman voluntarily retired from the Light Commission at the end of 1910. In 1911, the commissioners were: A. L. Breithaupt, George Lippert, Dr. R. W. Schnarr and Dr. J. J. Walters. Mr. Breithaupt retired in 1912. Carl Kranz and August R. Lang then took seats in that Board, and Mr. Lippert was chosen chairman, acting till his death in February, 1922. D. B. Detweiler served from 1914 to 1919, when he was succeeded by Charles H. Doerr. David Gross followed Mr. Lippert in 1922. Mr. Lang was elected chairman in 1922, serving till 1934, when he was followed by Mr. Gross, who acted as chairman until 1938. Mr. Kranz served until the end of 1936. Eugene Sauder was elected in 1934 and re-elected in 1936. Harvey Graber was the successor of Mr. Kranz in 1937.

In that period the car-barns in East King Street and the handsome "Hydro" office building were built. Chairman Lang was the moving spirit in the erection of the office.

For many years Mr. McIntyre has managed the three utilities, while since 1904 William Sinclair has had charge of the car-barns, and Geo. S. Schmidt, been roadmaster.

WOMEN'S ACTIVITIES

"In the sixties," said a grandmother, "nearly every one had a vegetable garden, with fruit trees and flowers. Cellar bins in the fall bulged with good things. There were few cakes, ices and salads. Houses were heated with wood. Ironing beside the kitchen stove on a hot summer day verily tried one's patience. The breadpan and washboard were in use and taxed a woman's strength, but nothing seemed overly hard to those homemakers.

"Women's everyday dresses were of cotton, wool or muslin and Sunday gowns of merino, velvet or satin. Later on, plaid dresses with a lace collar were worn. Girls' clothing was of similar materials. Cloths were then more serviceable than those of to-day. Dame Fashion bid women wear hoops or crinolines, and afterward, the bustle. In the winter we wore velvet bonnets or hoods, and in the summer, straw hats with a long feather or flowers. Commercial travellers said that Berlin women were better dressed than those of any other town. Mothers and daughters wore their hair long and

MEMBERS OF THE PUBLIC UTILITIES COMMISSION — 1937

Left to right: Eugene A. Sauder, Harvey Graber, Mayor J. A. Smith, Miss M. Shantz, Secretary-Treasurer; David Gross, Chairman; V. S. McIntyre, Manager of the Utilities; Charles H. Doerr, Vice-Chairman.

THE FREEPORT SANATORIUM

B. A. Jones, Architect.

"CHICOPEE," RESIDENCE OF MR. AND MRS. H. J. SIMS

THE YOUNG WOMEN'S CHRISTIAN ASSOCIATION

1861 · 1911

"How ridiculous you look, my dear!"

either braided it or bound it in a knot. Pink-cheeked wives were the rule, and only gypsy women smoked.

"Christmas day was the Fest of the year. Children never tired of hearing about Santa Claus. Of his coming from the Northland on Christmas eve in a sleigh drawn by reindeer with gifts for good boys and girls. A girl usually received a doll, a set of dishes, and gay ribbons. A godfather and a godmother too remembered their goddaughter and godson at Christmas. The day was spent in entertaining kinsfolk with good cheer, music and song.

"At school, we played handball and skipped the rope. At our house parties, we played 'Drop-the-Handkerchief,' 'Spin-the-Plate,' and a game with a strip of paper and a pencil on which each little one wrote a sentence. The writings were afterward read aloud, amid the hawhaws of the boys and the chuckles of the girls.

"In the middle sixties, mother bought a Howe sewing-machine. The first kind were run by a hand-wheel and the second by foot. The machine did away with much sewing by lamplight and lessened eyestrain. I recall too that the women of that day were great knitters.

"Concord abounded in the town. For the people were a fold of friends, jolly and sociable. Town happenings, so to say, were reported by wireless. Days before the carrier boy flung the weekly paper onto the porch, we wives had told each other the news over the garden fence. We knew everyone else's business and they knew ours. Friendship beamed brightest whenever sickness or death overtook a family."

The Bachelors' Ball

In the nineties, a Bachelors' Ball was annually held in the Walper House. One year the patronesses were: Mrs. J. E. Seagram, Mrs. Jacob Hespeler, Mrs. W. H. Bowlby, Mrs. George Rumpel, Mrs. Dr. Bowlby, Mrs. Hugo Kranz, Mrs. Alex Millar, Mrs. Dr. Mylius, Mrs. Wm. Roos, Mrs. Wm. Jaffray, and Mrs. W. R. Travers.

The Stewards were: George A. Bruce, E. F. Seagram, O. S. Clarke, Dr. W. J. Arnott, J. P. Fennell, Harry Bockus, Oscar Rumpel, Henry Knell, G. D. LaCourse, W. A. Colson and C. W. Rowley.

Twin City Red Cross Society

The Twin-City Red Cross was formed on January 17, 1900, in connection with the South African War. The officers were: Mrs.

J. E. Seagram, Mrs. C. Breithaupt, and Mrs. W. H. Bowlby, Hon. Presidents; Mrs. George C. H. Lang, President; Mrs. D. S. Bowlby, Mrs. George Rumpel and Mrs. Hugo Kranz, Vice-Presidents, Mrs. C. E. Hoffman (Mrs. Heather), Secretary; and Mrs. H. L. Janzen, Treasurer.

The directors were: Mrs. Charles A. Ruby, who acted also as secretary for ten years, Mrs. J. P. Jaffray, Mrs. Alex Millar, Mrs. A. W. Robarts, Mrs. J. Suddaby, Mrs. C. H. E. Smith, and Mrs. T. E. McLellan. The Society sent $1500 to soldiers wounded in the Boer War. The Red Cross Society is still active and at present is contributing to the relief of destitute families in Western Canada.

The Princess of Wales Chapter I.O.D.E.

The Princess of Wales Chapter of the Daughters of the Empire was organized at the home of Mrs. C. E. Hoffman (Mrs. G. A. Heather) on March 1, 1902. The primary officers were: Mrs. D. S. Bowlby, Regent; Mrs. J. E. Seagram and Mrs. J. Barton Taylor, Vice-Regents; Mrs. C. E. Hoffman, Secretary; Mrs. J. Suddaby, Treasurer; and Mrs. Mahlon Davis, Standard Bearer. The Councillors were: Mrs. Wm. Roos, Mrs. D. Chisholm, Mrs. H. M. Andrews, Mrs. W. H. Breithaupt, Mrs. J. H. Landreth, Mrs. H. G. Lackner, Mrs. J. C. Falls, Mrs. C. H Mills, Mrs. W. H. Bowlby, Mrs. G. H. Bowlby, Mrs. J. H. Hespeler, Mrs. John Fennell, Mrs. J. P. Fennell, Mrs. Alex Millar, Mrs. E. Bricker, Mrs. H. J. Sims, and the Misses May Lackner, Margaret Roos, Annie Dunn and L. M. Bruce. Mrs. Charles A. Ruby was one of the charter members.

Her Majesty, the Queen Dowager, for whom the chapter was named, sent the order an autographed photograph of herself. Afterward she accepted a life-membership badge, which was presented to her personally by Mrs. Heather, Hon. Regent.

The Chapter raised $6,000 and procured a monument of Queen Victoria for Victoria Park. It was graven by Raphael Zaccanini of Rome, and is a heroic figure of bronze, with a height of 10.5 feet, and resting on a pedestal 16.5 feet high. The monument was unveiled in 1912 by Earl Grey, then Governor-General of Canada, who said: "It is fitting that Berlin, the City of Homes, should be crowned with a statue of Queen Victoria—the Good—and the presiding genius and guardian angel of the home all over the world."

Three additional chapters have since been organized in the city: the Queen Anne Chapter, of which when this was written Mrs. J. D. C. Forsyth was Regent; the Tommy Atkins Chapter, with Mrs. David Weber, Regent; and the Municipal Chapter, with Mrs. Vorwerk Ernst, Regent.

The Daughters of the Empire have a company of Girl Guides. Mrs. G. A. Heather was then Divisional Commissioner for Waterloo County; Mrs. H. J. Sims, the Hon. President of the District Commission; the late Mrs. J. P. Fennell and Mrs. W. G. Weichel were District Commissioners, and Mrs. D. Shannon Bowlby the Secretary. Major and Mrs. Heather go to England and Ireland every summer and share in the work of several committees that deal with Empire affairs, and occasionally attend League of Nations' conferences in Geneva.

Stitches

In 1902 the Women's Christian Temperance Union presented the town with a drinking fountain for the civic square.

Two active organizations of the time were the Monday Club and the Emerson Club. Both made systematic studies of the best literature.

Miss L. Lackner was a skilful writer. After removing to Western Canada, she wrote: "The gold-gleaming West will nurture a people whose proud boast will be,

> Not Saxon nor Dane,
> Norman nor Celt,
> CANADIANS WE.

The Young Women's Christian Association

A group of women met in Zion Church on April 14, 1905, and organized a Young Women's Christian Association. Their purpose was to provide girls from other towns, who were employed in offices or factories, with a home having a Christian atmosphere. The first officers and directors were: Mrs. Mary Kaufman, President; Mrs. W. H. Becker, Vice-President; Mrs. C. L. Laing, Recording Secretary; Mrs. E. P. Clement, Corresponding Secretary; Miss Alice Moyer, Assistant Secretary; Mrs. W. H. Breithaupt, Treasurer; and Mrs. Dr. J. F. Honsberger, Mrs. George Harrison, Mrs. W. A. Bradley, Mrs. W. M. Cram, Mrs. W. L. Schmidt, Mrs. J. C. Breithaupt, Mrs. E. D. Heist, Mrs. W. H. Bowlby, Mrs. George Rumpel,

Mrs. H. L. Janzen, Miss Zoellner, Miss Stella Boehmer, Miss R. Weaver, Miss Breithaupt, Miss Collard, Miss A. A. Uttley, and Miss M. Tier, Directors.

A house at 79 Frederick Street was leased from J. P. Bender for classrooms, and space in Concordia Hall for Physical Culture. Miss J. Dingwall was the first General Secretary; while Miss Lough was engaged in visiting the factories to invite girls to the rooms. Miss Chand was the first housekeeper. By February, 1906, the Y.W.C.A. had 133 supporting members. Later, Mr. Jacob Kaufman fitted up his building in South Queen Street, opposite St. Paul's Church, for the association.

Socials were held to interest young women. Nearly all the factories were visited and the girls invited to attend entertainments at the "Y". Among the public entertainments arranged to raise funds, were "The Carnival of Nations", "A Dream of Fairyland", bazaars and tea-rooms.

A library class, reading, writing and spelling classes were introduced, while Dr. D. J. Minchin and Dr. W. T. Wallace gave instruction in first-aid work. Later on, household science, dress-making and millinery classes were added.

In 1911, nearly $40,000 was raised for a Y.W.C.A. building. A year later, a Building and Site Committee were appointed and they bought a lot 66 ft. by 190 ft. at 84 Frederick Street, from C. Meyer for $6,000, after which a building was erected, which was officially opened on May 15, 1915, when Mrs. R. D. Lang was President and Miss J. Rolston was General Secretary. In their new building the Y.W.C.A. more than doubled their usefulness. The institution has more than two score boarders, while hundreds of young women benefit by classes and recreations.

Mrs. Mary Kaufman, who was President for the first nine years and has been a director ever since, recently donated a large and commodious new wing for the Y.W.C.A. On the main floor of the wing, there is an auditorium accommodating about five hundred people, to be used primarily as a gymnasium. The stage, with four dressing rooms at the end of the main floor, will be satisfactory accommodation for plays and concerts.

The basement provides a small auditorium, shower baths, class-rooms and an especially equipped room for household science classes. The top floor has bedrooms, and also a flat roof, suitable for gymnasium classes and games.

Mrs. Kaufman laid the cornerstone of the new wing on June 12th, 1937, while Mrs. L. O. Breithaupt presided at the ceremony.

The Advisory Board consists of: W. P. Clement, K.C., A. R. Kaufman, E. D. Lang and M. B. Shantz.

Directors and Officers

The officers and directors in 1937 were: Hon. President, Mrs. Mary Kaufman; Past President, Mrs. A. E. Pequegnat; President, Mrs. L. O. Breithaupt; Vice-Presidents: Mrs. H. G. Mistele and Mrs. M. B. Shantz; Recording Secretary, Mrs. C. L. Beck; Corresponding Secretary, Mrs. A. E. Pequegnat; Treasurer, Mrs. E. D. Lang; Assistant Treasurer, Miss Alice Moyer. Additional directors: Mrs. H. J. Ahrens, Mrs. C. B. Augustine, Mrs. E. W. Clement, Mrs. W. P. Clement, Mrs. H. M. Cook, Mrs. A. K. Cressman, Mrs. H. Holmes, Mrs. F. H. Illing, Mrs. C. H. Janzen, Mrs. H. J. Haviland, Mrs. T. H. Rieder, Miss O. Snyder, Mrs. S. C. Tweed, Mrs. James Valentine, Miss A. Weber, and Miss O. Woelfle.

Miss Ruth M. Low is General Secretary; Miss K. Renton, Girls' Work Secretary; Miss Ruth Srigley, House Superintendent; Miss Elizabeth McCammon, Physical Director; and Miss Margaret Knechtel, Office Secretary.

The Young Women's Christian Association is a Kitchener-Waterloo institution, with a charter dating from 1913. There are at present eight hundred and sixty members.

Women Missionaries

Among the young women who have or are serving as missionaries are those that follow. In the Argentine: Miss Vera Hallman, Mrs. Litwiller, Mrs. Schwartzentruber, Mrs. McLean, and Miss Alice Clark. In China: Miss Alvina Schierholtz, Miss Cora Heist, Mrs. Elmer Morrison, Miss Vera Schweitzer, Mrs. Homer G. Brown, and Miss Evelyn Lackner. In India: Miss Rodebough, Mrs. Alexander Lindsay, Mrs. Jessie Clark, and Miss Susie Hindman. In Africa: Miss Dorothy Richardson, Mrs. L. A. McAllister, Miss Ethel Bingeman and Mrs. Joseph Blakeney.

When a Civic Improvement Association was formed in 1913, Mrs. J. A. Hilliard was a member of the Committee of Twelve. That committee drafted a course of procedure and aimed at a City Beautiful.

The Women's Canadian Club

A Women's Canadian Club was organized at the Public Library by the women of Berlin and Waterloo on October 3, 1910. The founders of the club were Miss B. Mabel Dunham and Miss L. Lynn. A Canadian Club fosters patriotism, develops an interest in Canada's history, resources and institutions, discusses the questions of the day—both domestic and foreign—brings in eminent men and women to speak on weighty subjects and assists at the Dominion's advancement.

The local club began with 115 members. Their primary officers were: Mrs. J. C. Lynn, President; Miss A. R. Bean, first Vice-President, and Mrs. Clark, second Vice-President; Miss Annie Scully, Secretary; Miss McIluraith, Literary Secretary; and Miss M. Hockey, Treasurer. Miss Devitt was appointed convenor of the Speakers' Committee, Mrs. J. F. Honsberger of the Reception Committee and Mrs. R. Wood of the Entertainment Committee.

Since then many prominent personages have addressed the members. Among these Dr. Helen McMurchy, the Rt. Hon. W. L. M. King, Dr. Falconer, Canon Cody, Professor Wrong, Bliss Carmen, Peter McArthur, Wilson McDonald, Judge Mott, Francis Nickawa, Lady Poynter, Miss Agnes McPhail, Dr. Blatz, Miss Edith Groves, Rabbi Eisendrath, Miss Jennie Lee, Denton Massey and Rajah Singham.

Between 1914 and 1918 the club did extensive war work. Now its chief concern is to bring in lecturers to address Twin-City women. The Women's Canadian Club is an influential society and has an enrolment of 220 members.

The officers and directors in 1935 were: Mrs. O. W. Thompson, President; Mrs. H. G. Mistele, first Vice-President and Mrs. A. J. McGanity, second Vice-President; Mrs. G. Eastman, Secretary; Mrs. J. H. Smyth, Assistant Secretary; Mrs. K. Staebler, Treasurer. Mrs. M. R. Kaufman was convenor of the Social Committee, Mrs. Russell Murray of the Entertainment Committee, and Mrs. G. Harper of the Speakers' Committee.

The Victorian Order of Nurses

A branch of the Victorian Order of Nurses was formed in the city in 1912. Their object is to care for the sick who cannot afford a full-time nurse. This at a comparatively small expense. Or, if the patients are unable to pay, the order gives its services gratis. For this purpose the city makes a grant yearly. The service, of course, is not confined to the needy, being available to anyone.

The members of the first executive were: Mrs. A. Foster, President; Mrs. W. H. Breithaupt, first Vice-President; Mrs. W. H. Schmalz, second Vice-President; Mrs. George Rumpel, third Vice-President; Mrs. J. E. Lynn, fourth Vice-President; Mrs. E. D. Lang, Secretary; Miss Bowers, Treasurer; and Mrs. B. K. Robinson, Assistant Treasurer.

Miss Tolton was the first visiting nurse and began her duties on May 21, 1912. That year she made 897 visits to patients, giving hourly nursing service. The income amounted to $412.80 and the outgo to $733.54. The city council made a grant of $150. In 1914, a second nurse was engaged. Four years later Mr. and Mrs. Jacob Kaufman bestowed on them their first motor-car. Since then the service has been widely extended. In 1933 the V.O.N. had three nurses, enrolled 1,000 patients; made 8,000 professional calls; received $2418.79 in fees; and disbursed $7,000. The city grant in 1934 was $3,000. Miss J. Whiteford, the superintendent, is assisted by Miss O. MacQueen and Miss M. Craig—a capable trio.

At present the officers are: Mrs. H. M. Cook, President; Mrs. W. H. Breithaupt, Treasurer; Miss Alice Moyer, Recording Secretary; and Mrs. Kenneth Sims, Corresponding Secretary. From the inception of the order, Mrs. W. H. Breithaupt and Mrs. C. A. Ruby have taken a deep interest in the work. Mrs. Ruby was president from 1915 to 1925.

Miss Emma Kaufman

In far away Tokyo, Miss Emma Kaufman is engaged in "Y" activities. Miss Kaufman went to Japan in 1913 and after she had acquired a knowledge of the language was appointed Associate Secretary of the Tokyo Young Women's Association: a position she has filled ever since.

Y.W.C.A. work was begun in Japan in 1905 in a dormitory housing fifteen girls. In 1935 the Association had erected in Tokyo the Surugadai Central Activities building which accommodated 900 girls; two summer camps; the Tokyo Suburban Recreation House; three Dormitories; a Secretary's Apartment; and a Settlement Branch.

At the Dormitories were 52 regular boarders, 2,004 guests; 14 Nationalities. Their Hota Business Girls' Camp on Tokyo Bay had an average attendance of 120 girls. The Nojiri High School Girls' Camp attracted 115 girls for three weeks each and was held at a lake in the mountains, eight hours from Tokyo. The Recreation House enrolled 2,698 girls. From Hakusan, one of Tokyo's poorest districts, 70 children were registered at the Vacation School in the Botanical Gardens; while 119 tots were in the "Y" Clubs, 57 factory girls in classes, and 2,044 girls and women attended meetings. At the Surugadai School, 1,455 girls were enrolled in the day or night classes.

Miss Kaufman, as her parents and brothers and sisters, is an organizer and builder. Fourteen years ago 500 Japanese and Canadian women assembled in the Tokyo "Y" to congratulate her on having been presented with a silver cup, having the imperial chrysanthemum crest in gold, by the Emperor of Japan. The gift was made in recognition of Miss Kaufman's services to Japan as an educator and social worker, and for having found shelter for thousands of refugees after the great earthquake of 1923.

Miss M. Edna Breithaupt

As an artist Miss M. Edna Breithaupt of Toronto has reflected credit on her native city. The critics especially praised her illustration of "The Taoist Pearl" (Albert Quentin). Miss Breithaupt helped to found the Art Students' League. It was through this organization that Art Education was made available to all children in the Social Settlements of Toronto. She too assisted at the organization of the Guild of All Arts of Scarborough, and while serving in the Board of Representative Educational and Social Welfare Organizations was able to extend the first opportunity of direction in the Arts and Crafts, at the Grange Studio, to many unemployed citizens of Toronto. More recently, she was likewise instrumental in forming the Kitchener-Waterloo Centre of Community Arts.

Miss Breithaupt is also President of *Wakunda*, which will be known as the National Art Centres of Canada. The purpose of this movement is to provide all the people with an opportunity for greater expressional life, aiming to supplement the work of other institutions and organizations. A feature of Wakunda is a plan to permit a greater number of Canadians to spend a season in the creative atmosphere of the National Parks. The outcome is expected to be more expressive and original work and a happier citizenship. The National Parks of the Dominion will thus become focal points for the development of Canadian talent in Music, Drama, Painting, Sculpture, Writing, and other liberal arts. The Parks Branch of the Federal Department of Mines and Resources have approved of this project, and the first centre is being developed at the Georgian Bay National Park, north of Midland.

Mrs. Muriel R. Cree

British Columbia is the home of at least one of Kitchener's native daughters who has carved out for herself a career in that distant and beautiful Province.

Muriel R. Cree, daughter of the late Principal Suddaby and Mrs. J. Suddaby, left Berlin for Fernie, B.C., in 1907, after her marriage to Arthur Hamilton Cree. After five years of residence there they moved to Victoria, B.C., with their two small sons.

When the Great War broke out in 1914 the Archives of the Province were being catalogued and indexed. She joined the Department in 1915, and has seen the work grow up until it is known from one end of Canada to the other. B.C. has a great wealth of historical material, which is now used extensively by students from both Canada and the United States.

The B. C. Historical Association was organized in October, 1922, to promote the preservation of historic sites, buildings, documents, relics and heirlooms, and to publish historical studies and documents. The Association actively co-operates with the Provincial Library and the Archives Department, in which Institution are housed many interesting records of Colonial days in B. C. Mrs. Cree is Hon. Secretary of this Society and also of the Provincial body, which this year bestowed upon her a life membership.

The Geographic Board of Canada has also named an island in Barkley Sound, on the West Coast of Vancouver Island, after Mrs. Cree, for her furtherance of interest in things historical in the

West. Her desire is, "to keep one hand on the traditions of the past, and green the memory of our illustrious dead."

Specials

Miss Waimel, daughter of Mr. and Mrs. George Waimel, is a young sculptress. Her strong faculty has been further developed under experts in Europe.

American Women, the feminine who's who of America, contains the sketches of two Kitchener women, namely, Miss B. Mabel Dunham, B.A., the authoress of three historical works, and Mrs. E. D. Heist, an officer of National and International Osteopathic Associations and office-bearer in the Y.W.C.A.

Mrs. Keith Staebler has blossomed as a playwright. For her play, "The White Waistcoat," this year, Mrs. Staebler won first place in the Kitchener-Waterloo Little Theatre writing competition. She received a handsome shield, the donation of Mrs. Henry Krug, and a prize of twenty dollars from the executive of the organization.

ST. LAWRENCE SEAWAY

This city was the birthplace of the St. Lawrence Seaway. After the Niagara Power project was afoot, D. B. Detweiler fathered a plan to bring the Atlantic to the heart of the Continent.

His studies showed him that the Great Lakes and their links stretch from Lake Superior to the Gulf of St. Lawrence. The flood loops and zigzags for 1900 miles and drops down 630 feet to sea level. Its course, however, is marked with falls, shallow straits, a thundering cataract, and angry rapids.

The first canal was made beside the Lachine Rapids, above Montreal, by Sulpician monks in 1700. *Voyageurs* then sweated their *bateaus*, loaded with traders' packs, up the St. Lawrence, and later on headed their fur-flotillas down stream, shooting the rapids. Other small canals followed. The second Canadian canal was dug at Sault Ste. Marie, to circumvent St. Mary's Falls, by the Northwest Fur Company in 1797-8. The canal had a single lock of 38 feet and nine-foot depth. To get around Niagara Falls, a little canal for schooners was built in 1829. In the eighteen-fifties, the American Government constructed a canal with a lift of nine feet on their lateral. In 1895, the present canal on the Canadian side was built, 900 x 60 feet, with nineteen feet of water on the sills.

In the meantime, the canals to surmount the six rapids in the St. Lawrence, below Lake Ontario, had been deepened to fourteen feet. The Welland Canal was likewise deepened to 14 feet. The United States afterward built four modern canals at the "Soo," having a depth of 22 to 25 feet, and handling boats up to 19 feet. Our neighbors deepened also the channels in Lake and River St. Clair, and the crossings in the Detroit River.

In 1907, when Mr. Detweiler opened his campaign, a mass of freight passed through the "Soo" canals. The cousinly systems locked through 58,000,000 tons valued at $760,000,000. Wheat formed a large part of the cargoes. The whaleback, U.S.S. *Lemoyne,* once carried down 572,000 bushels of grain. Canadian wheat was carried down and stored in Buffalo elevators, then shipped by rail to New York and loaded onto sea-going ships, because the Welland and other canals would not permit large vessels of more than 14-feet to pass.

Mr. Detweiler visioned a 30 or 35-foot seaway from Lake Superior to the Gulf. Given either one, ocean craft could load grain at Fort William or Duluth and, without breaking bulk, steam to Liverpool. While for return cargoes every lake port would become an ocean port. He estimated that on a yearly export of 200,000,000 bushels of wheat, the Canadian growers would receive $10,000,000 more for their crop. U.S. Army Engineers say that on 13,000,000 tons of freight the savings would be $70,000,000.

Moreover the potential volume of electric power in the international rapids is a magnet. Mr. Detweiler was informed by engineers that 3,000,000 h.p. could be developed there, and that the income would carry an investment of $300,000,000.

Mr. Detweiler saw that the seaway would require to be a joint undertaking on the part of Canada and the United States. This because they jointly own the waterway from the Lake of the Woods to the tip of Lake St. Francis in the St. Lawrence, and by an early treaty each country may use the waters of the other on equal terms.

General Bixby of the U.S. War Department told Mr. Detweiler there were no obstacles that could not be overcome. That the opening of the Great Lakes is only a matter of money.

Arousing Interest

Our planner then buttonholed leaders on both sides of the line. At first it was hard to awaken interest in the plan, but he persisted in his purpose. Then too, before long, a company was formed to build the Georgian Bay Canal as a short cut from the Bay to Montreal. The promoters said that a 10,000-ton vessel would be able to cruise the 442 miles in one day less than via the lower lakes and St. Lawrence River; that it would lie wholly within the Dominion, and that in case of war with the United States it would afford a safe outlet for western grain.

Mr. Detweiler showed that in event of such a war the United States could bar the egress of boats at the "Soo". That the proposed route would have 116 curves, and that in rounding the shorter curves, a 10,000-ton vessel could not move more than two miles an hour. He quoted Dominion engineers and showed that there would be a shortage of water for locking purposes at the height of land and that the company would require to install gas-producer plants to conserve water out of the summit reach, although in no large canal had such a principle been resorted to for supplementing the water supply.

After his joust with the Georgian Bay Canal, he gained more adherents to the St. Lawrence Seaway. Great Lake cities in both Canada and the United States organized bodies to further the project. U.S. Senator Townsend of Michigan was a strong ally, while Minneapolis rolled up its sleeves.

An International Joint Commission was appointed by treaty in 1909. The commission was given full control of the boundary waters and have the final say on all questions that arise.

Senator Townsend introduced a resolution into the American Senate on June 27, 1911. In it he asked that the President be directed to make an agreement with the Dominion of Canada for a seaway of sufficient depth to serve sea-going vessels for the common benefit of both countries.

A Canadian Waterways Union

Here, on January 11, 1912, a seaway conference was held to promote the project. At it, a Great Waterways Union of Canada was set up. The Executive Committee consisted of D. B. Detweiler, Chairman; George C. H. Lang, J. W. Lyon and Alex Stewart of

Guelph, George Pattison of Preston, secretary; Aloyes Bauer of Waterloo, Mayor Graham of London, Mayor Scott (Treasurer) and G. A. Dobbie of Galt; W. B. Burgoyne of St. Catherines, G. B. Ryan of Guelph, and Thomas Church of Toronto.

The conference protested against the construction of the Georgian Bay Canal; petitioned the Dominion Government to investigate the merits of the St. Lawrence Seaway; and urged them to deepen the Welland Canal and the other Canadian canals, and to develop the water powers along the river concurrently with the navigation works.

Shortly afterward, the Government determined to deepen the Welland Canal to a depth of 22 feet. Mr. Detweiler interceded by persuasion for a deeper channel, quoting the engineering maxim that a public work begun by one generation only serves the generation that began it; and the words of Captain Tom Conlon of St. Catherines, who said that in his sixty years he had seen the old cut deepened twice. The upshot was that the Government began a 25-foot canal in 1913, with 30-feet of water on the sills, at a cost of $131,000,000. In all, Canada has sunk $250,000,000 in its canals.

Later Developments

The first international seaway conference was held in Minneapolis on January 10, 1918. Mr. Detweiler was invited to address the delegates, but was too sick to travel. Yet from his sickbed he continued to promote the seaway until his death in 1919. Through the efforts of Mr. August R. Lang, and a group of admirers, a commemorative cairn has been reared to his memory in his birthplace at New Dundee, Ontario.

The International Joint Commission appointed a Joint Board of Engineers on December 19, 1921. On April 9, 1932, they reported an agreement in which they recommended the construction of a waterway of at least 27-foot depth. On July 18, 1932, a St. Lawrence Deep Waterway Treaty was signed by the United States and Canada in Washington, D.C.

By its terms, Canada agreed to complete the Welland Canal, and of the canals in the Soulanges and Lachine areas of the Canadian section of the St. Lawrence River which will provide essential links in the deep waterway to the sea.

The American Government undertook to complete the works in the Great Lakes System above Lake Erie.

With respect to the international rapids section, each nation agreed to construct works for navigation and power development in their respective areas.

In 1935, of 50,000,000 tons eased through the Soo Canals, only 9,000,000 tons passed through the Welland cut. Of the nine million tons, only 7,000,000 tons were carried down to Montreal.

The world-wide depression delayed the approval of the foregoing treaty by the U.S. Senate. Canada awaits their decision.

SOURCES

Canada Year Book. 1926.
St. Marys Falls Canal, Michigan. 1934. By U.S. Army Engineers.
St. Lawrence Deep Waterway Treaty. 1932. King's Printer, Ottawa.

THE WATERLOO HISTORICAL SOCIETY

Steps were taken here to form a historical society on April 11, 1912. A discriminating group who were interested in the generations which have gone before and bequeathed a priceless heritage, met in the Public Library and discussed the advisability of organizing a society. On motion of W. H. Breithaupt and H. W. Brown, a committee consisting of W. J. Motz (Chairman), Miss B. Mabel Dunham, and the Rev. F. E. Oberlander was appointed to formulate a plan and to invite President Williams of the Ontario Historical Society to deliver an address. He came in from Collingwood and gave an assembly of about fifty persons an outline of the work being done by the Huron Institute and the Ontario Historical Society. As a result the Waterloo Historical Society was organized on November 12, 1912. At its inception the officers were: W. H. Breithaupt, President; the Rev. Theobald Spetz, Vice-President; and Robert G. Wood, Secretary-Treasurer. An Executive Committee was likewise elected and consisted of the officers and W. J. Motz, Dr. G. H. Bowlby, H. J. Bowman, and C. H. Mills. Mr. Wood removed to Toronto early in 1913, when Peter Fisher succeeded him as Secretary-Treasurer.

The purpose of the society is the collection and preservation of archives and historical objects pertaining to the primal days of

Waterloo County. With rare perseverance the officers and members have traced and acquired a store of ancient books, family histories, maps, photographs, newspapers, pieces of furniture, and devices used by the pioneers. Many of these are irreplaceable. The articles and historical lore are housed in the basement of the public library. Yearly hundreds of persons from near and far visit the museum and gaze at the treasures, while for school children the exhibits are as magnetic as a travelling menagerie. A wealth of material there awaits the student, the biographer, and the future novelist.

The principal officers and members have served continuously for more than twenty years. As a consequence the museum's coat has become too small. The time has come when the historical society should have a commodious building of its own.

Annually the society publishes a Year Book. From time to time within its covers are to be found transcripts of official documents, descriptions of historical events, and sketches of men who laid the county's foundation and of those who have gained prominence in its service. In another direction the society has placed name plates on historical buildings and industries.

Under the society's auspices a Waterloo County Pioneers' Memorial Association was formed on July 13, 1923. The officers were: Hon. President, W. H. Breithaupt; President, D. N. Panabaker (Hespeler); Secretary, Allan A. Eby; Treasurer, David B. Betzner; A. C. Hallman, and Benjamin Brubacher (Waterloo). Its object was to commemorate the arrival of the first settlers in Waterloo County. A memorial tower was constructed near Doon on the lands purchased in 1800 by Joseph Schoerg and Samuel Betzner, two Mennonite pioneers from Pennsylvania. The Historic Sites and Monuments Board of Canada officially recognized those first clearings and contributed to the tower a tablet bearing a suitable inscription.

Through fat and lean years the Waterloo Historical Society carries on. In the opinion of the Ontario Historical Society it is one of the best local societies in Ontario. In 1933 the Council was comprised of: D. N. Panabaker, President; H. W. Brown, Vice-President; Peter Fisher, Secretary-Treasurer; W. H. Breithaupt, W. J. Motz, Miss B. M. Dunham, and C. W. Cressman, city; J. E. Kerr, Galt; Dr. C. W. Wells, Waterloo; Wellington Keffer, Hespeler;

Anson Groh, Preston; George Klinck, Elmira; A. R. G. Smith, New Hamburg; Miss E. D. Watson, Ayr; and W. W. Snider, St. Jacobs; J. M. Snyder, Curator.

After eleven years of commendable service, Mr. Panabaker retired as President in 1937. Mr. H. W. Brown was then elected President and Mr. W. W. Snider, Vice-President. The Executive Committee comprises: Mr. Panabaker, Mr. Wm. H. Breithaupt and Miss B. Mabel Dunham. New local Vice-Presidents are: Miss Ann McRae, Galt, and Mr. M. M. Kirkwood, Preston.

BERLIN BECOMES A CITY

Berlin was proclaimed a city on June 10, 1912. The Dominion census of 1911 had credited it with 15,195 inhabitants. It was the first town in Canada to wait until it had the statutory fifteen thousand before applying for a city charter.

The proclamation was read one second after midnight on June 9th. Six thousand citizens, including a group from Bridgeport and 500 well-wishers from Waterloo, had assembled in the square. On the town-hall steps stood Mayor W. H. Schmalz, Reeve W. D. Euler, Aldermen E. W. Clement, C. H. Mills, Wm. Pieper, C. B. Dunke, J. R. Schilling, H. A. Dietrich, Carl Kranz, Joseph Winterhalt, H. A. Hagen, F. H. Rohleder, W. O. Knechtel, J. S. Schwartz, J. H. Schnarr, George Bucher, David Gross, N. Asmussen, N. B. Detweiler, and other prominent men.

When the twelfth stroke of the post-office clock had ceased reverberating, the mayor read the official notice. The announcement was hailed with a mighty cheer and a band melody. Mr. Schmalz then congratulated the citizens on having entered into the charmed city circle. Church bells pealed and cannon-firecrackers detonated. Afterward the band and lines of rejoicing citizens marched up and down King Street until cockcrow.

On the day when the town became a city, a daughter was born to Henry and Lavina Koch of 120 Edward Street. The council gave the child a locket bearing the municipality's new crest, in commemoration of having been the firstborn of the city.

W. H. SCHMALZ

First Mayor of the City.

*Served The Economical Fire Insurance Company for fifty years,
and was its Manager from 1902 to 1933.*

HARRY LINCOLN
President, McDowell & Lincoln.

F. W. SNYDER
Managing-Director, "The Economical"

CHARLES H. JANZEN
President, Horticultural Society.

A. W. SANDROCK
President, Schreiter-Sandrock Ltd.

C. N. WEBER
President, Weber Hardware Co., Ltd.

L. O. BREITHAUPT
President, Breithaupt Leather Co. Ltd.

WATERLOO TRUST AND SAVINGS COMPANY
Directors:
F. S. KUMPF, *President*
LOUIS L. LANG   HENRY KNELL
Vice-Presidents
George A. Dobbie, Galt   H. J. Sims, K.C., Kitchener
Fred Halstead, Waterloo
P. R. Hilborn, Preston   R. O. McCulloch, Galt
W. L. Hilliard, M.D., Waterloo
Thos. W. Seagram, Waterloo   W. H. Somerville, Waterloo
J. E. F. Seagram, Waterloo
Hon. W. D. Euler, Kitchener   W. J. Motz, Kitchener
Allan Holmes, Galt   Wm. Henderson, Waterloo
P. V. Wilson, Managing Director
Kitchener, Ont.

W. H. DUNKER
Of Dunker Construction Ltd., Contractors.

F. G. BALL
Of Ball Bros., Ltd., Contractors.

H. J. BALL
Of Ball Bros., Ltd.

A. E. DUNKER
Of Dunker Construction, Ltd.

A Cityhood Celebration was held from July 15 to the 20th. Its features were a Made in-Berlin exhibition and an Old Boys' and Girls' Week. On July 17, the council banquetted 150 guests at the Grand River Country Club. At the dinner, Mayor Lees of Hamilton presented Berlin with a silken flag to mark the tie of friendship uniting the two cities. In turn, Mayor Schmalz bestowed on Hamilton an artistically illuminated address, which was his own brushwork.

The Hamilton delegation motored up to Berlin. On the way they punctured a tire. At the hands of Carl Kranz the young city presented Mayor Lees with a Berlin "wheel-shoe," as tires were then called, and a pair of made-in-Berlin rubbers.

Congratulatory speeches were made by George A. Clare, M.P., of Preston; W. G. Weichel, M.P., of Waterloo; Dr. H. G. Lackner, M.P.P., of Berlin, the Hon. Adam Beck of London, and others. The "Minister of Power" said in part,

> This district of Ontario was the adopted land of our forefathers. Today it is the native land of their sons and daughters, and grandchildren.
>
> Let me pay you a tribute. It is owing to the City of Berlin that the waterpowers of the Province have been nationalized. We, as a country, must thank Berlin for it.
>
> Moreover, in the conduct of your public utilities, you have become an object lesson for the world.

THE LEAVEN OF PROGRESS

After the municipality procured a city charter the leaders aspired to a population of 50,000 before 1920. To secure its goal it was sensed that more factories were essential. Among the additional ones obtained early in 1912 were the Jesse Hallman Shirt Co., the Colonial Shirt Co., the Woelfle Shoe Co., and John Walter & Sons, furniture ornaments works.

In that year, the Dominion Rubber Company, which had been manufacturing automobile tires in Montreal, decided to build a factory somewhere in Ontario. The Board of Trade determined to land it. Fortunately, two citizens, T. H. Rieder and A. J. Kimmel, were directors of the company and friendly to Berlin's aspirations. Following negotiations with the company they agreed to erect a factory here if exempted from taxation for ten years and given a sum towards moving expenses. The property-owners sanctioned the agreement. The company then built a tire factory and machine shops in the West Ward, investing a million dollars in buildings and plant. Thus the young city made a hole-in-one. Incidentally, the company after five years voluntarily gave up their tax exemption concession.

For a number of years Mr. Rieder managed the tire works. He then withdrew, when he was followed by John A. Martin. Later on, Mr. Rieder organized the Ames-Holden Tire Co., and built a large factory at the corner of King and Wilmot Streets. After his death in 1922, these works were acquired by the Canadian Goodrich Co., a subsidiary of the Goodrich Tire Co. of Akron, Ohio.

Up to 1900, a factory that employed 100 to 150 persons was accounted a large concern. Then came the rubber footwear and tire factories with staffs of between 800 and 2,000 hands. These have materially contributed to the doubling of the city's population and wealth.

To attract still more industries, three leaders offered free factory sites to new companies. H. L. Janzen proffered lots in the North, West, and East Wards; J. M. Schneider tendered plots in the South Ward; and A. J. Kimmel several sites near the G.T.R. station.

DOMINION TIRE COMPANY

The City Council and Board of Trade then formed a joint Industrial Committee, and appointed George Rumpel chairman. The committee contacted the Buffalo Blower Forge Co., of Buffalo, N.Y., who had a branch in Montreal. For a gift of five acres of land in Woodside park the company removed its Canadian plant to Berlin. At first the Park Board wanted $6,000 for the site, but by appealing to their civic pride, the price was whittled down to $1,000. Of this sum, the council granted $600, Mr. Janzen, $300, and Mr. Rumpel, $100.

Subsequently, the committee brought in also an automobile concern.

More factories: more employees. Workers were drawn in from other towns, causing an infiltration of further English families. Fathers came in the more readily because their sons and daughters could also obtain positions. Still there was a shortage of day laborers, for the second generation of Canadians side-stepped the pick and shovel. One parent said, "If you once let your son put on a white collar, you'll never get it off." Rough work was therefore done by immigrants.

A Civic Improvement Association

Activities were not confined to the search for new factories. Men spurred the city on to get a city plan. Then places of 50,000 or upward only might appoint a Planning Commission. To extend the right to others a convention was held here on December 11, 1912, with delegates from Toronto, Ottawa, Oshawa, Peterboro, St. Catherines, St. Thomas, Galt, Guelph, Parkhill, Sarnia, St. Marys, Ingersoll, Preston, Hespeler, and Waterloo. Towns were then like Topsy, they "jes growed."

The convention organized a provincial association to obtain a Town Planning Act. Afterward a Civic Improvement Association was organized in Berlin, whose aim was a City Beautiful. C. E. Levitt of New York City was engaged to make a survey for a civic center, at an outlay of $1,000. Afterward a Federal Square, to extend from Frederick to Scott Streets, emerged from the association's discussions. The city was expected to buy thirty-five feet east of the cityhall grounds and to build a handsome city hall; while the Dominion Government consented to buy fifty feet below for $50,000, and erect a $200,000 post-office. The government placed

$50,000 in their estimates for the purpose, but the property-owners defeated a bylaw to purchase the city's share of the lands and private buildings.

Workmen's Compensation

By then Berlin had gained a wide reputation as an organizer of public movements. A group of Toronto men suggested that local leaders make a study of the American Workmen's Compensation Acts, with the view of having Ontario pass a similar law. One hundred and seventy-five manufacturers convened here, and James H. Boyd of Toledo came over and explained the workings of the Ohio Compensation Act. Previously manufacturers had carried liability insurance. If a workman was injured while on duty his only recourse was to sue his employers, when the insurance company defended the action. Often an injured employee was afraid to sue his bread and butter. When he did so, the amends were small, and a considerable part eaten away by expenses.

The assembly approved of the Ohio law, and soon after had the Ontario legislature enact a similar law. Now, when an employee sustains an injury or loses his life, he or his family receive fair amends without resort to litigation. From a social standpoint, the Ontario Workmen's Compensation Act is one of the most important advances of the present century. To illustrate: in the first half of 1933 employees to the number of 17,009 received from the fund the sum of $1,802,609.

THE FIRST ENGLISH LUTHERAN CHURCH

Canadian Lutheranism dates from 1749, when a church was erected in Halifax, N.S. In 1783, numerous German U. E. Loyalists emigrated from New York State to Upper Canada, settling on the banks of the St. Lawrence. In 1789, they built St. John's Church at Riverside. That was the first Protestant Church in Ontario. In 1793, a number of Germans from Pennsylvania settled in York County and grounded churches at Buttonville, Unionville, and Sherwood. In Zion Church, Sherwood, the Canada Synod was instituted in 1862. Today, this body has eighty-seven congregations, fifty-six parishes, 42,000 members and adherents, and is served by some

THE ROCK GARDEN

THE REV. A. G. JACOBI
Pastor.

THE REV. J. MAURER, D.D.

THE FIRST ENGLISH LUTHERAN CHURCH

sixty pastors. The Canada Synod supports the Theological Seminary and Waterloo College in Waterloo, Ontario.

Under the Synod's auspices, the First English Lutheran Church was organized here on February 2, 1913, by the Rev. M. J. Bieber, D.D. He was Field Missionary of the General Council (English Division), and represented the Home Mission Board of the Evangelical Lutheran Church. When organized, the congregation had eighty-seven members and convened in Concordia Hall.

A call was extended to the Rev. H. J. Behrens on April 6, 1913, the first permanent pastor. He ministered to the congregation from June 25, 1913, till July 15, 1918. There were about thirty children in the Sunday School. The primary superintendent was Mr. S. W. Gartung, then a student of the Theological Seminary at Waterloo, and now pastor of the Evangelical Lutheran Church in Welland, Ont.

From St. Matthew's congregation, the young organization purchased the church property in North Queen Street for $14,000. Possession of the building was taken on June 10, 1914. At the same time a parsonage was acquired at No. 47 Irvin Street, for $4,000. The necessary repairs of both buildings swelled the amount to $25,000. Thus a congregation of eighty-seven members began its life under a heavy financial obligation.

The next pastor, the Rev. J. Maurer, M.A., D.D., took charge on December 1, 1918. He was born at Erbsville, Waterloo County. After graduating from the Stratford Collegiate, he entered the Arts Department of Thiel College, Greenville, Pa., where he obtained his B.A., and subsequently his M.A. degree. In May, 1888, he was graduated from the Lutheran Seminary in Philadelphia, Pa. On May 28, 1888, he was ordained a minister of the Gospel at Zurich, Ont., by the Rev. F. Veit, D.D., President of the Canada Synod.

The Rev. Mr. Maurer's first parish was at St. John's, Mahone Bay, N.S. He was the first President of the Synod of Nova Scotia, 1903-4, and a pioneer in the formation of the Synod of Central Canada, and was its President from 1912 until it was merged with the Canada Synod in 1926. The degree of D.D. was conferred upon him in 1920, by Thiel College, from which seat of learning he had graduated in 1885. He is a charter member of the Waterloo College and Seminary and served on the Board of Governors from the year of its organization until 1928. He had also served on the English Home Mission Board of the General Council and is a member of the American Missions of the United Lutheran Church.

When he took charge of the First English Lutheran Church of Kitchener, it had seventy-five members and a heavy debt. In 1935, the average attendance at the Sunday morning service was between three and four hundred worshippers; while the indebtedness on the church property has been reduced to $4,600. The congregation has under consideration plans for a new church. Similar progress has been made in the Sunday School. It now has forty officers and teachers and an enrolment of 380 scholars.

Music plays an important role at the school and church services. The church choir consists of twenty-five voices. Mr. J. Mahn is choir-master and Mr. F. Linke, organist.

Auxiliary organizations likewise render good services. Among the church societies are the Ladies' Aid, the Women's Missionary Society, the Clover Leaf Society, the Light Brigade, the Brotherhood, and the Intermediate and Senior Luther Leagues. In missionary and local work, the congregation has always shown a marked interest. It has been, and at present is actively engaged in family-relief work, especially looking after the needy of the congregation.

The Rev. Dr. Maurer resigned his pastorate in May, 1935, and was succeeded by the Rev. A. G. Jacobi of Rose Bay, N.S.

Since then the congregation has purchased the Roschman property on the corner of King and Green Streets. At present, Sunday School services are being held in the residence, and regular services in the Queen Street Church. Later on, the congregation plans to erect a fine edifice on the Roschman property.

BIBLIOGRAPHY

The First English Lutheran Church Year Book. 1930. Kitchener, Ont.

THE FREEPORT SANATORIUM

Early in the twentieth century, a boy whose parents were members of St. Peter's Church contracted tuberculosis. The pastor, Rev. Dr. Oberlander, now of New York City, built a shelter and had him cared for. Moreover, within a few years, a mother and six children died of the disease. Those deaths aroused Dr. Oberlander's sympathy and he interested physicians and others in a movement to combat the scourge. In 1908, at a public meeting called by him, Dr. J. F. Honsberger and other physicians, an "Anti-Consumption League" was formed to awaken interest in the threat and in the need for an institution in which to isolate and treat sufferers.

In a historical sketch of the Sanatorium, Dr. Honsberger tells of the steps taken. A committee was appointed at a public meeting in March, 1909, to select a site suitable for a hospital and solicit the help of other municipalities, for in one year there were seventy deaths from tuberculosis in Waterloo County. The "Berlin Sanatorium Association" was formed at St. Peter's parsonage in November, 1911. The committee recommended the purchase of the Shantz property at Freeport, containing a large stone house and fifteen acres of land—an ideal spot on the right bank of the Grand River. There was also a creek running through the property and an ample water supply. The site was bought for $2800 by the town council, after which the property-owners sanctioned a bylaw to raise $15,000 for the undertaking.

The house was remodelled and a boiler-house, laundry, and caretaker's dwelling built on a lower level. The entire cost of the improvements was about $28,000, which was met with a second by-law of $6,000 and a Government grant of $4,000. In May, 1915, the property was conveyed to the City of Berlin, but, while preparations were being made to receive patients, the Military Hospitals Commission asked for its use as a Sanatorium and Convalescent Home for soldiers who had contracted tuberculosis in the World War. The city granted the request. During the term of military occupancy some changes were made in the stone house and a large frame pavilion built as an adjunct for additional patients.

In 1920 the institution was handed back to the City of Kitchener. All the municipalities of Waterloo County joined together in that year and organized the Waterloo County Health Association, leasing the Sanatorium at a nominal rental for ninety-nine years. Since then a Medical Superintendent's residence and Nurses' Home have been built on more land purchased by the association. Plans for a new modern Sanatorium were developed in 1930. Half of this building was constructed that year, and the remaining half in 1932. There is accommodation for 103 patients, and administration and dining-room areas. A new modern power plant was built in 1932. Separate residences for male and female employees were completed in 1935-6. The old building was then used for children and adults. At the present time, a new wing of fifty beds is being added to the Sanatorium.

Dr. E. N. Coutts was appointed Medical Superintendent in 1921, and is still head of the institution. At present he directs the treatment of 138 patients. Miss A. E. Bingeman is Lady Superintendent, with a staff of fifteen nurses.

Sanatorium Auxiliaries function at Ayr, Blair, Conestoga, Elmira, Hespeler, Preston, Waterloo, and Kitchener. When this was written, the officers of the Kitchener Auxiliary were: Miss Lillian Breithaupt, President; Mrs. O. W. Thompson, Secretary; and Mrs. A. Bauman, Treasurer. Mrs. Frank Haight of Waterloo was then President of the Central "San" Council.

Directors

In 1937, the directors of the County Health Association were: Hon. Presidents: Dr. J. F. Honsberger, Mr. C. Dolph, Preston; and Mr. A. D. Pringle of Preston; President, Mr. W. H. Somerville, Waterloo; Vice-President, Mr. P. R. Hilborn, Preston; Secretary, Mr. T. R. Richardson, Galt; Chairman of Finance Committee, Mr. L. L. Lang, Galt; Chairman Property Committee, Mr. P. R. Hilborn, Preston.

Medical Superintendent, E. N. Coutts, M.B., F.A.C.P. Visiting Consultant in Medicine, W. E. Ogden, M.D., F.A.C.P. Visiting Consultant in Surgery, R. I. Harris, M.C., M.B., Toronto. Visiting Consultant in Eye, Ear, Nose and Throat, C. C. Ballantyne, M.B., F.A.C.S., Galt.

The late Dr. Honsberger said of the Sanatorium: "Great credit is due the various Boards and Auxiliaries for the institution's existence, and to the Medical Superintendent and Nursing Staff. Also to those who at a time now long past had a vision of the usefulness such an institution would serve in the prevention and cure of that dread disease, tuberculosis. The Sanatorium will ever serve as a testimonial to their efforts in this behalf."

THE REV. U. K. WEBER
Pastor.

STIRLING AVE. MENNONITE CHURCH

ONTARIO

BEFORE AND AFTER THE GREAT WAR

The city was like a watch: wheels within wheels. The factories were the great wheel; industry, the mainspring; the Council, the balance heel; and the Board of Trade, the hair-spring. All the parts, named and unnamed, clicked.

The Board of Education opened night classes to Canadianize new-comers. A Home Reunion Association was set up to bring over their wives and children. Dr. J. E. Hett advocated public baths. N. B. Detweiler proposed to have the Counties of Waterloo, Perth, Brant, Oxford, Norfolk, and Elgin buy 400 acres of idle farm land and have jail inmates convert them into an improved farm, to regain their lost manhood.

Another group supported the purchase of Cressman's Woods near Doon. The City Council sent a deputation to Buffalo, N.Y., to investigate Commission Government under a city manager. D. B. Detweiler prompted the Board of Trade to petition the Dominion Government to approach the Government of the United States and suggest that the two nations connect Fort Erie and Buffalo, N.Y., with an international bridge, in remembrance of 100 years of peace, and in 1915 to celebrate the centenary of amity.

However, "The best laid plans of mice and men gang aft agley." On July 14, 1914, a Serbian student assassinated the Austrian Grand Duke Ferdinand and his Duchess at Serajevo. That fell deed put match to powder. Within a month the principal nations of Europe were divided into two hostile camps. On August 4, 1914, Great Britain declared war against Austria and Germany, and Canada was drawn into the conflict.

The pick of Canadian youth obeyed the Dominion Government's order to shoulder arms. Sectional enlistments in the Canadian

Expeditionary Forces were as follows: in the First Battalion, 8; in the 18th, 61; in the 34th, 81; in the 7th Battalion of Mounted Rifles, 86; and in the 118th Battalion, 813—a total of 1,049 men. Of that number 112 Twin-City soldiers were killed in action or died of wounds or disease.

At home, the great upheaval changed the lives and living conditions of the citizenry. Many thought that the war would not last more than three months and laid in stores of foodstuffs to forestall high prices. For a time the factories filling war-orders only were busy. However the departure of 418,000 members of the C.E.F., the expenditure of two billion dollars by the Canadian Government, and a similar sum for munitions, etc., by the British Government in Canada, soon created a demand for workmen. Since so many men had gone overseas, employers had to fill their place with young women. During the four-year war, there was a scarcity of drugs and materials needed by manufacturers, necessitating the use of substitutes.

For the majority of citizens, war-time was a period of trial, yet stamped with exemplary conduct. Per capita, the citizens gave as much or more than other Canadians to patriotic drives. In 1916, reports of the criticisms levelled at Sir Adam Beck on account of his German parentage reached the city. Fearing that Berlin might be next, two hundred business men petitioned the council to change the name of the city. That was finally done. They chose "Kitchener," in remembrance of Lord Kitchener. Of the break, native-born citizens said in effect, we deplore the change but must accept it.

Since then, Kitchener has become a large, modern city. The first white man to set his foot on the area covered by the city is said to have been George Eby, who purchased Lot No. 1, G.C.T., in 1804. If he could return, would he not marvel at the progress attained? In passing, the city has made greater advancement since 1916 than in the previous century.

The City Planning Commission

The Ontario Legislature passed a Town Planning Act in 1917. Kitchener was the first municipality to appoint a commission under that Act. The body was comprised of those that follow: Wm. H.

Breithaupt, C.E., Chairman; August R. Lang, W. H. Schmalz, Martin Huenergard, Walter Harttung, Sam Brubacher, and Mayor David Gross. Norman C. Helmuth was appointed Secretary.

In 1922, the commissioners recommended the city council to engage Thomas Adams of Ottawa, planning expert, to make a city plan. He came in and surveyed the city and its environs, making a plan. Waterloo likewise had experts draw up a plan for its commission. Both bodies work hand-in-hand.

The Kitchener Commissioners have passed zoning regulations, set street lines, encouraged the opening of alleys, extended streets, rounded corners, placed the seal of approval on new parks and recreation grounds, and made many other noteworthy improvements.

Mr. Breithaupt acted as chairman until the end of 1920, and sat in the Board until the thirties. Mr. Huenergard was chosen chairman in 1921. He was followed in 1922 by Mr. A. R. Kaufman, who has filled that position ever since.

The members of that commission in 1937 were: A. R. Kaufman, Marcel Pequegnat, W. H. Dunker, L. O. Breithaupt, Harold Ball, Aaron Bricker, and Mayor J. A. Smith.

The Kitchener Orphanage Board

In 1937, the members of the Kitchener Orphanage Board were: H. B. Brubacher, President; A. R. Kaufman, Vice-President; F. A. Shantz, Secretary; M. C. Cressman, Treasurer; A. C. Slumkowski, Assistant-Secretary; W. H. E. Schmalz, W. W. Foot, Mrs. G. Bray, Mrs. H. J. Haviland, Mrs. Louise Jaeger, Mrs. Mary Kaufman, Mrs. Mary Learn, Mrs. A. Bott, Miss A. S. Weber, and Mrs. Max Euler. Miss E. R. Good is matron.

Children's Aid Society

Hon. Presidents: Mayor J. A. Smith and A. R. Goudie; President, H. D. Huber; 1st Vice-President, R. H. Sanford; 2nd Vice-President, Mrs. Mary Kaufman; Treasurer, W. H. Woods. Miss E. H. Reist, Secretary; and A. P. Pullam, Inspector.

Mothers' Allowances Commission

Chairman, E. E. Ratz; Vice-Chairman, W. J. Motz; Directors: Mrs. C. J. Massel and Mrs. P. J. McGarry. Secretary, M. H. Phillips.

MAYOR, ALDERMEN AND CITY OFFICIALS — 1937

Left to Right: Standing—Wm. Hodgson, Chief of Police; M. E. Bollert, Assessment Commissioner; Stanley Shupe, City Engineer; Fred F. Mullins, Alderman; H. W. Sturm, Alderman; Ivan A. Shantz, Alderman; Clarence Seibert, Alderman; John Walter, Alderman; Reuben V. Alles, Tax Collector; Harry W. Guerin, Chief Fire Dept. Sitting, left to right—Albert Brubacher, Alderman; Jos. Meinzinger, Alderman; Alex.Schafer, Alderman; His Worship Mayor J. Albert Smith; Irvin Bowman, Alderman; Eugene A. Berges, Alderman; Charles G. Lips, City Clerk; Louis M. Dahmer, Treasurer.

KITCHENER'S $500,000 CITY HALL — 1924   —W. H. E. Schmalz, Architect.

Family Relief Board

Chairman, C. C. Hahn; Vice-Chairman, A. J. Cundick; Treasurer, J. R. Dier; and A. N. Farries. Secretary: Miss M. Feick.

Reeves and Mayors Since 1854

The Reeves of the Village were: John Scott, (1854-6); Henry S. Huber (1857); Israel D. Bowman (1858); H. S. Huber (1859-1864); Ward H. Bowlby (1865-68); Hugo Kranz (1869-70).

Mayors of the Town

Dr. Wm. Pipe (1871); John Hoffman (1872-3); Hugo Kranz (1874-8); Louis Breithaupt I (1879-80); John Motz (1880-81); J. Y. Shantz (part 1882); Wm. Jaffray (1882-3); Alex Millar (1884-5); Dr. H. G. Lackner (1886-7); L. J. Breithaupt (1888-9); H. L. Janzen (1890); J. M. Staebler (1891); Conrad Bitzer (1892); Dr. H. G. Lackner (1893); D. Hibner (1894-5); J. C. Breithaupt (1896-7); George Rumpel (1898); J. R. Eden (1899-1900); Dr. G. H. Bowlby (1901); J. R. Eden (1902-3); Carl Kranz (1904-5); Aaron Bricker (1906-7); Allan Huber (1908); C. C. Hahn (1909-10); W. H. Schmalz (1911). Dr. G. H. Bowlby was the first native son ever elected mayor.

Mayors of the City

W. H. Schmalz (1912); W. D. Euler (1913-14); Dr. J. E. Hett (1915-16); David Gross (1917-19); J. R. Eden (1920); Charles Greb (1921-22); L. O. Breithaupt (1923-4); N. Asmussen (1925-6); E. E. Ratz (1927-8); W. P. Clement (1929-30); C. Mortimer Bezeau (1931-2); H. W. Sturm (1933-4); J. Albert Smith (1935-6-7). Mayor Smith was for three years returned by acclamation. In 1937, he was elected member of the Ontario Legislature by North Waterloo. In October, 1937, the Hepburn Government appointed Mr. Smith a member of the Ontario Hydro-Electric Power Commission.

City Officials

C. G. Lips, City Clerk; L. M. Dahmer, City Treasurer; M. E. Bollert, Assessment Commissioner; R. V. Alles, Tax Collector; S. Shupe, City Engineer; Dr. J. W. Fraser, M.O.H.; Dr. C. K. Mader, Food Inspector; Dr. R. H. Ferguson, Public Health Dentist; W. H. Rau, Sanitary Inspector; Scully & Scully, Auditors; P. J. McGarry, Building Inspector.

Suburban Road Commission: J. S. Schwartz, Chairman; Marcel Pequegnat, Secretary; Allan Shoemaker.

Police Commission: Magistrate J. R. Blake, Chairman; Judge E. W. Clement, and Mayor J. A. Smith. Secretary: L. D. Leyes.

Public Library Board: H. J. Graber, Chairman; H. M. Cook, Treasurer, J. C. Walsh, W. J. Motz, H. W. Brown, Mrs. Mabel E. Fraser, Dr. Olive Matthews, J. E. Bilger, Mayor J. A. Smith, Secretary: Miss B. Mabel Dunham.

Growth

In 1900, the town's population was 9,696. In 1937, the city's population numbered 32,862. Meanwhile the taxable municipal assessment had risen from $3,344,920 to $26,122,591.

In Retrospect

Primarily, Canada's prosperity depends on the price of wheat. From 1909 to 1913, says the *Canada Year Book of 1926*, the average price was 69 cents. Russia was then selling 400,000,000 bushels of that cereal yearly to European countries. In 1917, the Russian Revolution occurred, causing a famine in that empire and her disappearance as an exporter of breadstuffs. In Canada, wheat rocketted. In 1919, it zoomed to $3.43 a bushel. In 1920-21, there followed the greatest period of industrial activity ever known till then in the Dominion. In 1920, the output of manufactured goods rose to $3,772,250,057. The average wage, contrasted with 1913, increased 92.9 percent. The cost of living, however, kept pace. In 1913, the average weekly family budget was $14.10; in 1919 it had risen to $25.90. Well-managed manufactories reaped a golden harvest in 1920-21. The greatest gains were made by men who in the third year of the war, when the future was vascillating, took long risks and bought large quantities of raw materials.

While the war raged, factory and office employed an additional 100,000 young women. During the two-year period of luxury, those wage-earners purchased fifteen-dollar shoes, and clothes to match. To furnish a home, a young man contemplating marriage, had to first lay up $2,000 to furnish it.

After the war, the automobile began its revolution of transportation in earnest. The "gas-buggy" ushered in the concrete highway and lengthened a day's journey to 300 miles. Its big brother, the truck, for short hauls, seriously competed with the steam railway. Its cousin, the airplane, predicted flights through the stratosphere at 500 miles an hour and a day when winged craft would be more numerous than automobiles.

To resume the story of wheat, it dropped to $1.17 a bushel in 1921. From July on, trade and commerce wilted and prices declined. Soon there were 200,000 unemployed breadwinners in Canada. Unrest was rampant. In other Canadian cities there were 285 strikes. The big inning was over.

Then England and the United States loaned European nations huge sums for reconstruction. Exports of Canadian products increased greatly. Until 1929, trade and commerce reached its zenith. Prominent men said that prosperity was here to stay. Stock speculation spread over the Continent like influenza. In October, 1929, the bubble burst, ruining a myriad and fathering the worst worldwide depression in history.

This city did not escape scot free. Factory orders almost dried up, causing much unemployment. By way of illustration, the Canadian furniture industry's peak year was in 1929, when it employed 11,899 persons and paid them $11,997,435 in wages. The number of employees dropped to 7,120, according to the Furniture Association, and the payroll to $4,634,757. In Kitchener, in 1932, when the depression was at its nadir, the output of furniture, in round numbers, fell from $11,000,000 in 1929 to $1,000,000.

Other industries too felt the prolonged squeeze. During the seven lean years the highest number on relief was 4,434, when the city's share of the burden rose to $130,304. That experience was wholly foreign to the carefully conducted city. Building operations were also at a standstill and tax arrears were high. But it weathered the storm. Since 1936, conditions have improved much. In 1929, building permits amounted to $1,645,350. In 1936, they had risen to $449,123 and this year will probably reach a milion. The number on relief now is only 849.

For the mayors and aldermen the direction of the civic ship through the shallows during the years in mind was an onerous task. Perhaps the best illustration of their financial forethought is to say that the city council has reduced the debenture debt down to $3,588,000, the lowest since 1922. The headache is gone, and the city again striding forward.

THE BOARD OF TRADE

After the Great War the Board of Trade discussed soldiers' insurance, vocational training, the rationing of food, and city planning. In 1919, they advocated a Technical and Vocational School, Grand River Control, and a new City Hall. In that year Kitchener obtained a second tire factory, and soon after a third tannery. The Dominion Government were memorialized in 1919 to dig a deeper Welland Canal, while the Board approved a National Research Council. The Four-Wheel Drive Co. of Clintonville, Wisc., established a plant here in that year.

In 1926, they organized a Retail Section of the Board. An appeal was also made to financial and industrial concerns to encourage young Canadians, and especially graduates of educational institutions, to stay in Canada and assist at the upbuilding of the Dominion. In the following year, the Kitchener Export Association was formed. One reason why Kitchener withstood the depression of the thirties so well was because of its volume of exports. Today, there is scarcely a single world market in which Kitchener production cannot be purchased.

Early in 1928, the Board recommended the City Council to install traffic signals in King Street, and discussed an inter-city airport. A year later, the Kitchener-Waterloo Airport Commission was set up and they bought a flying field near Lexington. The first Kitchener commissioners were: Norman C. Schneider, Chairman, Robert A. Dietrich, Alex. Schaefer, and Mayor W. P. Clement. In 1930, while President of the Board of Trade, Mr. Schneider had

THE GRANITE CLUB
Curling, Badminton, Skating

1937 EXECUTIVES OF THE KITCHENER BOARD OF TRADE

The membership of which was increased this year from 247 to 332.

Reading left to right: Front row—A. J. Cundick, Treasurer; N. C. Schneider, Past President; C. N. Weber, Past President; H. J. Ball, President; W. M. Euler, 2nd Vice-President; N. Riffer, Secretary.

Second row: Directors—Wm. Milner, T. H. Kay, L. A. Galloway, A. H. Kabel, L. M. Dahmer.

A. S. CAPWELL
Past President

J. W. SCOTT
Director

R. A. DIETRICH
Director

A. W. BOOS
Director

HARRY WOLFHARD
Manager, Merchants Rubber Company.

WALTER P. ZELLER
Founder, Zeller's Limited.

THE CENOTAPH
(Corner King and Frederick Streets)

LEO D. LEYES, J.P.

KITCHENER, ONTARIO, FROM AN AIRPLANE

the Board procure aerial photographs of the city for Mr. McColl, Trade Commissioner to South America, and other Canadian Trade Commissioners. One outcome was a visit by a group of business men from the Argentine. At present, the Airport Commissioners from Kitchener comprise: Messrs. Schneider, Dietrich, Schaefer, and Mayor J. A. Smith of Kitchener, and Messrs. H. E. Ratz, Ald. W. D. Brill, and Mayor W. McKersie of Waterloo. Gradually the youth of the Twin City are becoming air-minded.

In 1930, the Horticultural Society was commended for their unique flower show, which proved a good advertisement for the city. A survey of the Grand River Valley was made in 1931, in conjunction with the Grand River Valley Board of Trade. The Board of Trade approved too of a cross-town bus, uniform Provincial Daylight Saving regulations, and a Downtown Business Men's Association. To commemorate the services of Sir Adam Beck, the Hydro Knight, the Board was one of the prime movers to erect a tower on the Baden hill, near his birthplace. Kitchener and Waterloo Boards of Trade requested the Ontario Government to include also thereon the names of E. W. B. Snider, the father, and D. B. Detweiler, the organizer, of the Niagara Power movement.

The worst year of the trade slump was in 1932. Western growers, in the hinterland, then received only twenty-five cents a bushel for their wheat, and ranchers only one cent a pound for their cattle. Here, unemployment increased, while the dearth of trade nipped the merchants. To move his stock of goods, one dealer offered to allow a customer five dollars for his old suit or overcoat, if he bought a new one. To ameliorate conditions, the Board of Trade introduced a "Give-a-Man-a-Job" campaign.

There were only a few industries founded in that period. But, when the Board was unable to attract new ones, they made Kitchener a convention city. In 1933-4, twenty-seven outside organizations convened in the city. Tourists from south of the line find that Kitchener has many attractions. One year, city bankers reported that, in July and August, $107,702 in American currency had been deposited in their strongboxes. The diversified points of interest in the City of Flowers, plus a warm welcome by the friendly citizens, sent tourists away well pleased with their sojourn in the city.

The Board of Trade was actively engaged in furthering Grand River Control in 1933. Its representatives on the Grand River Valley Board of Trade then were: President C. N. Weber, L. O. Breithaupt, N. C. Schneider, and Allan A. Eby. The City Council also warmly supported river control. The Board of Trade had the Provincial Highways Department take over the Elmira high road as a provincial highway, and approved of highway officers being equipped with first-aid kits.

In 1934, it was announced that, among cities from 15,000 to 50,000, Kitchener had been the winner of the Dominion Health and Safety Contest of 1933. It again captured first place in 1937.

A full-time Secretary was engaged in 1933, with headquarters in the city hall. From the outset, especial attention was given to export trade and inquiries passed on to city manufacturers. As a consequence, ever since then, overseas commerce has increased in volume. This important work is being continued by Secretary Riffer.

In the early thirties, notwithstanding adverse conditions, a number of new companies were established. Among them, the Mansfield Shirt Co., an enlarged Swiss Knit Co., a Wooden Heel Co., the Marley Freres Cosmetic Company, the Venetian Gardens Cosmetic Company, and the J. H. Kennedy Furniture Company. In December, 1937, a Montreal Wooden Heel Company opened a branch in Kitchener, beginning with 75 hands.

Presidents

Since 1917, the Presidents of the Board of Trade have been: A. S. Capwell (1917-18); N. M. Davison (1919); Erwin C. Greb (1920-21); W. T. Sass (1921-24); R. D. Boughner (1925-27); W. W. Breithaupt (1928-29); N. C. Schneider (1930-31); E. J. Capling (1932); C. N. Weber (1933-34); and Harold J. Ball (1935-36-37).

Past President C. N. Weber is Second Vice-President of the Ontario Boards of Trade and Chambers of Commerce.

Vice-President L. O. Breithaupt has been elected a director of the Canadian Chambers of Commerce, the first time that a Kitchener citizen has been thus honored.

Mr. Breithaupt is also Chairman of the Kitchener Committee in connection with the Dominion's Home Improvement Plan. Up to October 30, 1937, 197 loans had been advanced to Kitchener citizens, totalling $80,400.

Secretaries

Included in the list of Secretaries since 1920, are: N. C. Helmuth, A. J. Cundick, E. J. Payson, Allan A. Eby, W. W. Foot, R. D. Boughner, and Norman Riffer, the incumbent.

ADDITIONAL INDUSTRIES

1. Household Furniture, Radio Cabinets, and Specialties:

Beaver Furniture Co.	Luxury Upholstering Co.
F. H. Bechtel & Company	Murawsky Furniture Co.
Bogdon & Gross	A. W. Niergarth
Dom. Electrohome Industries	Lipperts Ltd., George J.
Galloway Furniture Co.	Woeller Upholstering Co.
J. A. Hallman	Guelph Wood Products
Hallman Carving Company	

2. Shirts, Underwear, and Textiles:

Cluett Peabody & Co., Ltd.	Dominion Shirt Co.
Doon Twines Limited	Mansfield Shirt Co.
Swiss Knit	Barrie Glove & Knitting Co.

3. Boots and Shoes, Leather and Leather Products:

E. S. Shoe & Slipper Co.	John A. Lang Leather Co.
Dunbar Pattern	Lasch & Co.
Galt Shoe Mnfg. Co.	Ontario Glove Co.
Greb Shoe Company	Ontario Shoe Ltd.
Huck Glove Company	Western Shoe Co.
Hydro City Shoe Co.	Dependable Cut Soles
Jones Pattern	Twin City Shoe & Slipper Co.
Kitchener Shoe Company	

4. New Rubber Products:

Bi-Lateral Fire Hose Co.	Canadian Goodrich Co. Ltd.

5. Meat Packers:

Kitchener Packers Limited	A. W. Morrison
E. Gronau	

6. Beverage Industries:

Blue Top Brewing Co.	Coca-Cola Company
B. Huehnergard	Kitchener Beverages

7. Metal Industries:

Campbell Machinery Co.
Canada Skate Co.
Canadian Transformer
Canadian Bell Foundry
C.-K. Industries
Dom. Truck & Equipment Co.
Kitchener Brass & Aluminum Co.
Globe Stamping Co.
Rubber Machinery Shops
Sehl Engineering Co.
Woelfle Bros.

McDowell & Lincoln
National Cash Register Co.
Sutherland & Schultz
United Shoe Machinery Co.
United Typewriter Co.
Dom. Electrohome Industries
Depew Welding Co.
O.-K. Electric & Acet. Welding
Kitchener Burner Co.
Superior Tinning Co.
Zapfe Machine & Repair

8. Additional Lumber Companies:

J. M. Card Lumber Co.
Kitchener Lumber Co.
Siegner Lumber Co.

Robert Stewart Limited
Houde-Hill Veneers
Penrod, Jurden & Clark Co.

9. Dairy Products:

L. A. Burkhardt Dairy
Model Dairy
Purity Dairy
Rickert Dairy
Rosemount Farm Dairy

Silverwoods Dairy Co.
Fisher's Dairy
Twin City Dairy
West Side Dairy

10. Bakers and Manufacturers of Confectionery:

Berges & Shelley
Hamblin-Metcalf Ltd.
Feil's Bakery

Fischer's Bakery
Fromer's Bakery
Vienna Bakery

11. Glass, Stone, Cement, Tile, Flooring, etc.:

J. Bullas Glass Co.
Bernardo Terrazzo & Tile Co.
Ott Brick & Tile Co.
Gypsum Lime & Alabastine Co.

Kitchener Concrete Block Co.
John Schultz
Twin City Monuments
Tait Plate & Window Glass Co.

12. Medicines:

Kitchener Tonsilitis Co.
McDonald Medicine Co.

Walter R. Wilson

13. Horticulturists:

Cowan's Gardens
J. L. Colombo
Downing Steen & Co.

C. H. Janzen, Springbrook Farm
Kitchener Horticultural Society
Ben Warren

14. Printing and Publishing Trades:

Allison Press
Bender Printing Co.
V. L. Cober Printing Co.
Commercial Printing Co.
Keystone Printing Co.

Kitchener Stamp & Printing Co.
Merchants Printing Co.
News Record Limited
Nelson Press
Peerless Press

15. Miscellaneous:

Canada Auto Top Co.
Dodds Paper Stock Co.
Diamond Grate Bar Co.
Eureka Vacuum Cleaner Co.
Fischman Spring Co.
Fehrenbach Mattress Co.
Hogg Roofing Co.
Galt Roofing Co.
Gould-Leslie Signs Co.
Johnston & Keys Dental Co.
R. W. Ripley Dental Co.
Kahen Optical Co.
K. and W. Optical Co.

Kitchener Public Utilities
Kitchener Water Commission
Kitchener Wiping Products
Lippert Custom Trailers
McPhail Engraving Co.
Master Milling Co.
Schmidt & Kramp, Bookbindery
J. C. Lehman, Bookbindery
A. T. Schiedel Broom Co.
E. C. Kimmel, Awnings
Weiss Bag & Burlap Co.
Zinger & Geiger, Auto Springs
Carton Corp'n of Canada

16. Felt Manufacturers:

W. G. Rumpel Commercial Felts   Industrial Felts—Hair & Punch

17. Furriers:

Barrie Glove Co.
Brodey-Draimin Fur Co.
Langleys Ltd.
Hofstetter & Ruppel

J. M. Graf
Kaufman Furs
Feldman Furs

18. Signs and Show Cards:

Twin City Signs
Kitchener Signs

J. W. Schroeder
George E. Schlee

19. Dyers, Cleaners, Launderers:

Pearl Laundry Limited
Burtol Cleaners
Kitchener Dye Works

Twin City Dollar Cleaners
Langleys Limited

Industrial Notes

The Greb Shoe Company, manufacturers of men's fine footwear, was founded in 1909. Under the direction of President Erwin C. Greb, this company has made steady advancement.

The Dominion Shirt Company, of which John W. Dreger is President, was founded by Aaron Erb in 1910. It has added to the city's reputation as an industrial centre.

The Huck Glove Company was initiated by President Joseph Huck and an associate in 1913. Mr. Huck is still active and his sons assist him in their progressive enterprise.

The Mansfield Shirt Company is a vigorous company that was founded in 1931. Ex-Mayor C. Mortimer Bezeau is President and his son, H. Mortimer Bezeau, Manager of the company. Their productions are a good advertisement for the city.

In 1916, David Christner, a Kitchener citizen, launched into the coal business, and ever since has been catering to a large section of the city.

In 1923, Harvey J. Graber, who served long as a school trustee and now is a Light Commissioner, founded the Kitchener Coal Company. Mr. Graber has gained the citizens' confidence both as a merchant and a public servant.

About the same year, George Stewart's sons established the Stewart Coal Company. Their venture has met with success through close attention to business and personal popularity.

The father was for many years a traveller for the W. G. & R. Company. Two local associates for the company were Ben Robinson and Robert Wood. Those were the days when W. A. Greene, now of Chatham, N.J., was the firm's manufacturer, and trained up his successor, Frank Hodgins. George DeKleinhans too was on the manufacturing staff, but now is with the John Forsyth Shirt Company. What an interesting story Mr. DeKleinhans could tell of the shirt and collar industry.

McDowell & Lincoln Limited

In April, 1915, H. N. Lincoln and H. O. McDowell organized the International Supply Company. This organization make and distribute machinery for the manufacture of shoes, harness, leather goods, sporting goods, gloxes, textile and hosiery, and distribute these products throughout Canada.

The founders of this company chose Kitchener as a location for the reason that it had so many advantages to offer them. In 1916, a warehouse was opened in Montreal and in 1920 another warehouse started in Quebec City. This company are distributors for large machinery and supply houses in Canada, the United States, Great Britain and Europe. In 1923, it was incorporated under a Dominion charter and the name changed to McDowell & Lincoln Limited. Mr. Harry Lincoln is President of the organization.

Among the long list of Kitchener manufactures are golf balls. The Canadian Goodrich Tire Company makes them.

Realtors

A Kitchener-Waterloo Real Estate Board was formed in June 1937. The officers are: Hon. President, A. C. Bender; President, A. K. Cressman; Vice-President, George Whitney; Secretary-Treasurer, W. F. Hessenaur. Directors: E. R. Reiner, A. L. Wilson, M. B. Shantz, J. Schmalz, Alfred Bender, and A. Kimmel.

SOCIETIES AND SERVICE CLUBS

The Horticultural Society — 1937 Officers

Charles H. Janzen, President; J. W. McDonald, 1st Vice-President; Arthur Shantz, 2nd Vice-President; J. A. Good, Secretary-Treasurer.

Directors: H. W. Brown, M. J. Smith, Ben Warren, A. Hanenberg, A. Schaefer, J. L. Colombo, Earl Becker, W. Dankwardt, W. Sixtus, C. Garth.

Associate Directors: Louis C. Janzen, B. R. Stuebing, Wm. Miller, W. H. Trussler, N. Miller, Floyd Bechtel, C. P. Walker, A. Bindernagel, Judson Dunke, W. Krueger, Neat Potje, C. H. Deckert, J. A. Smith, M. F. Green, C. Seibert, and F. Honderich.

Kitchener Young Men's Club

The Kitchener Young Men's Club originated in 1919 and was the city's first Service Club. Its objects are to stimulate and maintain a keen interest in all matters of civic welfare, to foster and promote all institutions, activities and interests designed to develop and improve the City of Kitchener and make it a better place in which to work and live.

The membership is limited to 100 men. The Chairman of the Executive is elected annually. Harper J. Schofield filled this position in 1937. The Secretary, C. Mac Lester, has been in office since 1927, and Treasurer, Carl J. Heimrich, since 1923.

One of the Club's annual activities is a "Community Christmas Tree." By that means a hamper is sent to every needy family, and a bulging stocking to the kiddies.

Kitchener-Waterloo Rotary Club

The Kitchener-Waterloo Rotary Club was granted its charter in June, 1922, and regular meetings began in September, 1922, with twenty-five charter members.

The first officers were: A. J. Cundick, President; T. A. Witzel, Vice-President; P. V. Wilson, Treasurer; H. M. Cook, Secretary; W. M. O. Lochead, Sgt.-at-Arms.

In their initial year, the Club decided to adopt Crippled Children's Work as a major community service. Rotarian Alex Martin was the father of the movement here, and the K.-W. Rotary Club a pioneer in Crippled Children's Work in Ontario. With the exception of 1924, when the Club had as many cases as it could handle, annual clinics have been held every year since 1923. Upwards of 1600 cases have passed through the clinics, and hundreds have been cured or benefitted. In addition to those free services, the Club has spent approximately $35,000 in hospital fees, appliances, etc., since the work began. In their annual Rotary Year Book, the Rotarians mention two committee chairman, J. A. Martin, 1922 to 1929, and H. M. Cook, who has so ably carried on since then, for their outstanding services, and commend Homer Heard and his predecessors, who have, through the medium of the annual Rotary Carnival, kept the Crippled Children's Committee supplied with funds to carry on the work.

The Crippled Children's Committee has recently donated $1500 to the Kitchener-Waterloo Hospital's new wing. That in recognition of the facilities placed at the Club's disposal each year in connection with the annual Crippled Children's Clinics.

The Rotary Club has now one hundred members. Besides, their ladies have organized the Rotary Anns, who assist at the care of children and parents at the Crippled Children's Clinics at the hospital. Generally, the ladies perform auxiliary services for the Club in which warm-hearted women shine. The officers elected for 1937-8 were: Hon. Presidents: Mrs. H. J. Sims and Mrs. E. J. Hearn; Past President, Mrs. J. D. C. Forsyth; President, Mrs. D. A. Bean; 1st Vice-President, Mrs. E. N. Coutts; 2nd Vice-President, Mrs. J. M. Laing; Secretary, Mrs. H. H. Gould; Treasurer, Mrs. J. F. Scully. Committee: Mrs. W. S. Gurton, Mrs. W. M. Euler, Mrs. F. M. Hearn,

Mrs. C. K. Mader, Mrs. R. H. Henderson, Mrs. F. B. Clausen, Mrs. F. W. Wiley, and Mrs. W. L. Bitzer.

While Dean of Waterloo College, Dr. Alexander O. Potter joined the organization and later on was appointed secretary. His capable services attracted the attention of the International Headquarters in Chicago, and he was for a time stationed there. Afterward he was appointed Secretary of Rotary International at Zurich, Switzerland. His duties called on him to spread Rotary principles in a score of foreign countries, including Europe, North Africa, and Asia Minor. In 1936, the Yugoslavian Government bestowed the Grand Order of St. Sava upon him for his excellent work. That honor is rarely awarded to a foreigner. This year, Dr. Potter was appointed Assistant to the President of Rotary International, a Frenchman, and is now directing Rotary activities from Paris.

The Officers of K.-W. Rotary Club for 1937-8 are: Past President, Wm. Henderson; President, W. R. Bottom; Vice-President, Dr. R. O. Winn; Secretary, F. M. Hearn; Treasurer, W. L. Bitzer; Sgt.-at-Arms, V. M. Wood; Asst. Sgt.-at-Arms, Dr. C. K. Mader; Archivist, H. M. Cook. Directors: W. R. Bottom, Dr. F. B. Clausen, W. P. Clement, K.C., H. H. Gould, W. C. Duffus, W. M. Euler, Wm. Henderson, J. H. Schmidt, A. T. Thom, Dr. R. O. Winn. ,

The Kiwanis Club

The Kitchener-Waterloo Kiwanis Club, a branch of an International Organization, was the third Service Club formed in the Twin City. The objects of Kiwanis International are: To give primacy to the human and spiritual rather than to the material values of life; to encourage daily living of the Golden Rule in all human relationships; to promote the adoption and the application of higher social, business and professional standards; to develop, by precept and example, a more intelligent, aggressive and serviceable citizenship; to provide through Kiwanis Clubs a practical means to form enduring friendships, to render altruistic service and to build better communities; to co-operate in creating and maintaining that sound public opinion and high idealism which makes possible the increase of righteousness, justice, patriotism, and good will.

The motto of the Kiwanis Club is, "We Build." The members take, especially, a deep interest in the problems of youth. Through them and the Kiwaniqueens, the welfare of the boys and girls of the Twin City are promoted in a number of directions, including a Summer Camp at Paradise Lake.

The officers in 1937 were: Immediate Past President, Alfred Haller; President, Harry Schondelmayer; Vice-President, Leo Wallis; Secretary, Cliffe Dier; Treasurer, Reuben Alles.

The officers when the Kiwanis Club was organized in 1921 were: President, Fred H. Boehmer; Secretary, Amos B. Musselman; Treasurer, H. W. Shoemaker.

The present directors are: George Harper, Jacob Howard, Dr. A. T. Turner, Dr. Ty. Gordon, Rev. Louis Buckley, and Oscar Thal.

The Gyro International

The fourth Service Club here is the International Gyro. This Club does work similar to the Lions International. At present, H. J. McKinney, of the Equitable Life, is President.

The Lions International

In the present year, a fifth Service Club had its rise—the Lions International. This organization makes also provision for lady memberships in the Lionesses. Both branches concern themselves with community questions and public welfare. The first officers of the local Lions are:

President, Irvin Edwin Erb; 1st Vice-President, George W. Gordon; 2nd Vice-President, Walter V. Siegner; 3rd Vice-President, William Knell; Secretary, R. C. Cowle; Treasurer, E. B. Pepper; Lion Tamer, A. W. Boos; Tail Twister, J. E. Leinweber; Directors: J. H. MacDonald, Alexander Watt, George R. MacIntosh, and John Penner.

One purpose of the Lions Club is to help the deaf, the dumb, the blind, and the near blind. It is also the hope that recognition will be obtained in the different centres on the continent, in the way of free clinics, for the plaster Cancer Cure that the late Rev. M. Erb was many years so successful with.

WALTER P. ZELLER

Walter P. Zeller, prominent Canadian business man, whose birthplace is Waterloo County—the family residing on a farm about one mile south of Breslau, received his early education at River

Bank School and later at the Public and High Schools of Kitchener. His parents, Mr. and Mrs. Phillip Zeller, still reside in Water Street South, where the family home has been for the past thirty-five years.

The Canadian ancestry of the Zeller family dates back to 1831, in which year the first Canadian Zeller settled in St. Catherines, Ont.

Mr. Walter P. Zeller, whose home is in Westmount, Que., is President and founder of Zeller's Limited, a group of twenty-two retail stores which operate from St. John, N.B., to Winnipeg, Man. He is also Chairman of the Board of Directors of New Universal Stores of Great Britain. He has had a very wide experience in the retail variety store field both in Canada and the United States.

In addition to his wide business interests and activities, Mr. Zeller is active in communal work and is President of the Montreal Kiwanis Club.

BRIEF REFERENCES

Among the longer established dealers in motor-cars are Archie Lockhart, I. G. Neuber, Hall & McKie, Kleinschmidt Ltd., Dobbins, and Nelson Shantz.

Dealers in automobile parts: Canada Auto Top Co., H. F. Dettmer, N. E. Hett, and Don Eby. Supplies: Musselman Tire and Battery Service; and Weber Tire and Battery Service.

Electrical Contractors: The R. W. Bierwagen Electric Co., the Central Electric Shop, Cook & Schneider, the Doerr Electric Co., The Kress Electric Co., the Mattell & Bierwagen Electric Co., Gascho Motors, A. C. Halwig Motors, the Schweitzer Electric Ltd., and Sutherland-Schultz Electric Co., Ltd. Electric Equipment: Ellis & Howard. Electricians: Canada Armature & Electric Co., H. Hanneburg, Smith Electric, and Frank Weiler.

Radio and Refrigeration: A. G. Euler, John A. Colombo, Carl A. Heintzman, Wentworth Radio, Reist Radio Service.

Engineers: the Grant Engineering Co., and J. C. Klaehn.

Fox Breeding: O. W. Thompson, Ltd.

Furnaces: W. D. Battler.

Furniture Dealers: The Acker Furniture Co., Dick the Upholsterer, McGillivray & Braun, Reinhart Furniture Co., Reinhart & Dedels, and Twin City Furniture Co.

The E. L. Hearn Roofing Company.

Osteopathy: H. E. Illing, M. H. Good, Edgar D. Heist, Mary L. Heist, Allan A. MacKenzie, Dr. Olive Matthews.

Plumbers: G. Ruppel & Co., W. D. Battler, C. Hollinger, Walter Mertz, Miller Bros., W. H. Peacock, A. J. Reinhart, John Shiry, H. Youngblut. Supplies: J. B. Allen & Co.

Accountants & Auditors: T. H. R. Brock, Chas. Kissner, C. L. Rason, Wm. Robertson, Scully & Scully, Thorne, Mulholland, Howson & McPherson.

COMMENT

In the last sixty years, civilization has made more progress than in all the centuries that preceded them. That is particularly true of science and invention. While among inventions the telephone, wireless telegraphy, the automobile, and the airplane stand out, yet they are only a few among all. Of possibly more importance are the machines to be found in industries—automatic and semi-automatic. In hard times men are apt to blame the machine for creating unemployment, but it is not the machine in itself, but during such times, a surplus of them. Our fathers worked twelve hours a day for $1.25 per diem; many of their sons worked ten hours for a quarter more. Robert E. Ritz maintains that the North Ward was built up on a $1.50 wage. Today we have the eight-hour day, with skilled men earning say $1200 a year. This should be credited to the machine.

Nor are we at the end of inventions. Radio is still in its infancy. Refrigeration and air-conditioning are in their youth. Television peers above his gown; engineers dream of the wireless transmission of power and aircraft to fly in the stratosphere at 500 miles an hour. Soon Kitchener may be seeking for an airplane factory.

While industries have been and are the chiefest factor in the city's expansion, the home-owners have played an important role. Nowadays the trend is to apartments in large communities, and you can order a custom-made trailer at the George J. Lippert Table Co.'s plant. Notwithstanding, today, 72.83 percent of the citizenry own their own home.

While Kitchener is a large community, it is the general opinion that it will be bigger still. Observant men believe that its only limit is the water supply. However, since the Grand River Valley is in a fair way to procure river control, the Waldemar Dam may open the path to a greater extension of its confines. At a river conference, a speaker predicted that Kitchener and Waterloo will within a generation have 100,000 inhabitants.

Over the years, much of the city's advancement has been owed to the old families, whose sons and grandsons are now in charge.

The End

Thanks—

The writer wishes to thank every citizen who ordered a copy, or copies, of this history before it was printed.

Also those who supplied him with information, photographs or cuts. Included in this number were numerous citizens, manufacturers and organizations. In particular should he mention Mr. R. S. Bean of the Chronicle Press, Mr. W. M. Euler of the Merchants Printing Co., Mr. H. W. Brown, Mr. Allan A. Eby, Mr. J. M. Snyder, and the Historical Society. City officials were also indeed helpful, while without the assistance of the Historical Society in permitting him the run of their Museum it could not well have been written. Mr. Wm. H. Breithaupt, Miss B. Mabel Dunham, Mr. W. J. Motz and other officers were friends in need.

Thank you! —W.V.U.

ERRATA

Page 184—Father Beninger is now Superior of the Canadian Province of the Congregation.

Page 184—Father Dehler was appointed Superior of a new Scholasticate in Washington, D.C.

Page 184—In the second to last paragraph and second to last line read "thus" instead of "also".

Page 412—Read in re Architects of City Hall, "and Mr. B. A. Jones".

INDEX

NOTE

Parentheses ( ) around a page number indicate uncertainty whether the person named on that page is identical with the person of the same name on the other pages cited under the entry.

A page number in italics indicates that a photograph of the subject is found on that page.

The letter "n" before a page refers to a bibliographical entry on that page.

The letter "m" in an entry means "married" (to the person there named).

INDEX

A

Ahrens, Dr. A. E.: 85
Ahrens, Carl H.: 72, 83, 85, 86
Ahrens, Charles, A.: 60, 152, 157,
   163, 206, *209, 216,* 312, 339,
   356
Ahrens, Herman: 85, 86, (317)
Albert, Rev. J.: 94
Aldous, John: 99, 187
Andres, Rev.: 46, 49
Andrews, Rev. J. W. J.: 138
Anthes, John S.: *furniture-maker,*
   51, 88, 159, 160, 193, 206,
   242, 244, 253, 272, 295, *303,*
   305, 307, 310, 339
Argon, Rev. J.: 94
Armstrong, John: 57
Armstrong, T.: 187
Arnott, Dr. W. J.: 368
Asmussen, N.: *263, 392*
Atkinson, Rev. Robert: 120
Austermuehl, Rev.: 94

B

Baedecker, Henry: 219
Baetz, Jacob, Sr.: *mason,* 160, 283,
   348
Bain, W. G.: 222, 234
Baldwin, Rev. (later Bishop): 138
Ball, F. G.: *396*
Ball, H. J.: *396*
Balzer, Harry: *merchant-tailor,* 317
Bands: Berlin Band and Musical
   Society, 70, 99, *264,* 267, 268;
   Berlin Bugle Band, 271; Berlin
   City Band, 271; Berlin Music
   Band (1859), 99; Industrial
   Bands, 271; Kitchener Boys'
   Band, 268, *269;* Kitchener

Ladies' Band, 268, *269;* Scots
   Fusiliers Band, *270;* United
   Band (1867), 172·
Banks: Canadian Bank of Commerce, 324; Clearing House,
   326; Commercial, 104, 323;
   Dominion, 325; Hamilton,
   324; Imperial Bank of Canada,
   326; Merchants/Manufacturers,
   323; Molsons, 323, 324; Mont-
   real, 323, 324; Nova Scotia,
   324, 325; Royal Bank of Cana-
   da, 325, 326; Savings Banks,
   326; Upper Canada, 87, 88,
   323; Waterloo Trust and Sav-
   ings Co., 101, 156, 311, 326
Barraclough, Rev. W. H.: 59
Barthel, Rev. George: *54,* 55
Bauers, C.: 94
Bean (Biehn), John: 9
Beasley, Richard: 8, 9, 10, 13, 18,
   29
Beattie, James: n.30
Beatty, John: *schoolteacher,* 22
Beaumont, Rev.: 138
Bechtel, Jacob: 9
Bechtel, John: 9
Beck, Sir Adam: 69, *334,* 342, 371,
   372, 373, 409, 421
Beninger, W. A.: 180, 184, 243.
Benninger, Joseph: 14
Benton, William: 60, 97
Berberich, Mr.: 144
Berlin: Sandhills/Ebytown, 7, 34,
   98; Berlin Village, 37, 38, 40,
   41, 66, 69, 70, 71, 72, 73, 77,
   78, 79, 80, 85, 86, 87, 88, 89,
   90; incorporated village
   (1853), 94, 97, 98, 99, 100,
   101, 102, 103, 104, 110, 119,

ity United Church, 60; United Male Singing Society, 90; Zion Evangelical Church, *53*
Chrysler, Edgar: 57, 58
Churches: Alma Street Church of the United Brethren in Christ, 116, 139, 140, 143, 144; Benton Street Baptist, *91*, 93, 94, 95, 96, 97; The Bethany Mennonite, 198, *199*, 201; The Carmel (Swedenborgian), *62*, 65; Evangelical Lutheran St. Paul's 42, *43*, *44*, 45, 46, 49, 66; The First Church of Christ, Scientist, 296, *298*, 299; The First English Lutheran, 400, *401*, 403, 404; The First Mennonite, 13, 16, 21, 24, *25*, *26*, 27, 28, 29; The Church of the Good Shepherd, 60, *61*, *62*, 63, 64, 65, 66; King Street Baptist, *298*, 299, 300; Knox United, 60; Pentecostal Tabernacle, 369, 370; The Polish Church of the Sacred Heart (Catholic), *112*, 113; St. Andrew's Presbyterian, *116* 117, 118, 119, 120; St. John's (Catholic), 114; St. John The Evangelist (Anglican), *136*, 137, 138, 139, *141*; St. Joseph's (Catholic), 114; St. Mary's (Catholic), *105*, 107, 108, 109, 110, *111* 113, 114, 116; St. Matthew's Lutheran, 348, *349*, 351, 352, 353, 354; St. Peter's Lutheran Evangelical, *161*, *162*, 163, 164, *165*, 166, 167, 168; Salvation Army, 246; Stirling Avenue Mennonite, *407*; Trinity United, *54* 56, 57, 58, 59, 60; The

Water Street (Swedenborgian), 65, 66; Zion Evangelical, *47*, 49, 50, 51, 52, 53, 55, 56
Cleghorn, W. G.: *232*, 242, *345*, 347
Clemens, David: 30
Clemens, George: 30
Clemens, Isaac: 121
Clemens, Jacob: 74, (156)
Clement, E. P.: *lawyer*, 58, *232*, 277, 278
Clement, Judge E. W.: *75*, 84, 392
Clement, W. P.: 84, 242
Clotilde, Mother: 144
Coffman, Rev. S. F.: 28
Colquhoun, James: 138, 219
Connor, James W.: 122, 124, 126, *127*
Convent, Sacred Heart: 113
Cook, Jonathan: 137, 138
Cookman, Rev. C.: 58
Correll, Mr.: 69
Cossey, J.: 101
Cowan, Miss Alice: 230, 234
Cowan, James: 30, 79
Cree, Muriel, R.: 385, 386
Cressman (Gressman), John: 24
Cressman, M. C.: *315*
Cressman, Rev. Silas: 198
Cressman, V.: 60
Crews, Rev. H. W.: 59

D

Damascene, Mother: 149
Daniels, Rev. E. D.: 65
Dankert, Lydia: 96
Danberger, Joseph: 104
Davey, Fred C.P.: *postmaster*, 73
David, Rev. L. W. T.: 65
Davidson, George: 72, 80, 84, 86, 88, 117, 118, 119, 120, 237

Halliwell, W. H.: 74
Hallman, Rev. E. E.: 55
Hallmann, Rev. E. S.: 28, 278
Hallman, Jacob: 14
Halter, Rev. Joseph: 113, 179
Hammacher, family: 14
Harbin, Rev. John: 63
Harrison, George: *merchant tailor*, 317
Hauch, Rev. J. P.: *48*, 51, 52, 55, n.56, 60, 281
Hauch, Rev. S. M.: 52, 117
Hawke, Gabriel: 83
Hawke, John: 83
Heist, E. D.: 60, 278
Helfer, Rev. Wm.: 45
Heller, Casper: 73, 171, 189, 238
Heller, Johan: 89
Henderson, Rev. W. C.: 59
Henderson, Mayor William: 276
Hendrick, Mr.: 93
Hendry, Charles: 63, 125
Hendry, William: 63, 302
Herschey, Benjamin: 10
Herschey, Jacob: 10
Hertfelder, W.: 222
Hespeler, Jacob: 83
Hess, George: 99
Hett, Casper: 100
Hett, Henry: 89, 152
Hett, Dr. J. E.: 63, 222, 266, 408
Hett, John B.: 89, 124, 164, 187, 237
Hibner, Daniel: 51, 213, *217*, 283, 284, 285, 287
Hiestand, Henry: 49, 50
Hilborn, G. V.: *75*, 84
Hilliard, Thomas: 57, 60
Hinds, Rev. E. G.: *298*, 300
Hines, Peter: 155
Hinsberger, Rev. M.: 150
Hirschman, Rev. C. A.: *47*, 55

Hodgson, Police Chief William J.: 266
Hoffman, Rev. E.: 348
Hoffman, Isaac: 88, 159, 187
Hoffman, Jacob: 66, 88
Hoffman, John: *furniture manufacturer*, 14, 40, 49, 50, 63, 66, *67*, 69, 88, 168, 189, 206
Hoffman, John S.: 238, 283, 284
Honsberger, Dr. J. F.: 222, *254*, 257, 281, 282, 339, 368, 405, 406
Hopkins, Alfred: *schoolteacher*, 38
Hospitals: Berlin/Kitchener-Waterloo General Hospital, 272, *273*, *274*, 275, 276, 277; Freeport Sanatorium, 13, *376*, 404, 405, 406; St. Mary's, 110, *112*, 113, *115*
Hotels and Taverns: The American Hotel, 177; The Black Horse Inn, 89, 171; The Brunswick/Windsor Hotel, 257; The Commercial House (formerly the Western Hotel), 171, *255*, 257; The Delmonica Hotel, 260; The Franklin Tavern, 171; Frederick Gaukel's Wirtshaus, 37, 38, 41, 69, 80, 88; The Grand Central Hotel, 294; Market Hotel, 73, 238; The North American, 171; Queen's Arms, 77, 172; The Railroad Hotel, 163, 171; Rebscher's Hotel, W., 77; The Red Lion Inn, 171; Restaurants, 171; The Royal Exchange, 171; H. R. Steppler's Hotel, *263*; Varnum Tavern, 17, 18, 37, 257; The Walper (formerly The Commercial House), 171, 237, 258; Weaver's Hotel, 99, 171;

turer, 252
Litt, Rev. J. G.: 51, 52
Livergood, family: 9
Logan, Rev. Clarke: *54*, 60
Logan, Robert: 107
Lutz, Daniel: 30
Lyons, Edward: 74

M

Mackie, John A., J.P.: *general merchant*, 154, 157, 185, 187, 219, 295
Manz, Pastor: 166
Marshall, Rev. J. T.: 300
Marshall, Rev. S. E.: 59
Martin, Rev. J. B.: 28
Martinson, J. F.: 227
Matheson, Miss Edith: 220
Mathieson, Robert: 121
Maurer, Rev. J.: *402*, 403, 404
Mc: *See under heading* **Mc**
Meinke, August: 74, 104
Merner, Senator Samuel: 193, 259, 260
Merritt, R. N.: *schoolteacher, 128*, 130, *131, 132*
Metcalfe, J. F.: 57
Metcalfe, Miss Janet: 227
Metcalfe, Wm.: 159
Meyer, family: 9
Meyer, Rev. C. B.: *105*, 150
Meyer, John: 83
Miehm, Rev. A. P.: 95, 96
Milhausen, John: 101
Millar, Alexander, K. C.: 34, 152, (171), 197, 242, 243
Millar, David: 34
Millar, Frederick: 34
Millar, William: 34
Millar, Wm. Henry: 34
Mills, Rev. J. N. H.: *136, 138*

Mills, William: 57
Moodie, W.: 118
Moody, A. D.: 101
Moore, W. K.: 97
Motz, Mayor John: 107, 125, *182*, 187, 243, 260
Motz, W. J.: 107, 126, 390, 410
Moxley, Samuel: 70, 88
Moyer, C. E.: *hardware*, 158, 159
Moyer, P. E. W.: 27, 58, 122, 194, 195, 242, 302
Moyer, William: 14, 22, 27, 58
Mueller, Adolph: 119, 120, 124, 125, 219, 220, 243, 244, 268, 272
Mueller, Charles: 159, (241), (243), 244
Munro, Rev. George Taylor: 120
Murray, Rev. Dr.: 138
Mylius, Dr. R.: 73, 152, 197, 220, 246, 368

Mc

McAllister, Rev. R. E.: 370
McBain, Rev. J. H.: 59
McBrine, Louis,: *luggage manufacturer, 232*, 241, 242, *248*, 249, 339
McCaig, Donald: 219
MacCullough, Andrew: 189
MacDonald, D.: *writer*, n.42
MacDonald, Rev. Ian: 96
McDougall, Dougall: 107, 122
McEwan, Rev. P. A.: 299, 300
Macfarlane, Bros.: *clothing manufacturers*, 159
McGeorge, Charles: 83
McIntyre,Rev. C. L.: 59
McKay, John: 16
McKay, John F.: 57
Mackenzie, William Lyon: 42